ALSO BY

VICTORIA

GLENDINNING

↓

ELIZABETH

BOWEN

1 9 7 8

A SUPPRESSED

CRY

1 9 6 9

EDITH

SITWELL

↓

A

UNICORN

AMONG

LIONS

VICTORIA
GLENDINNING

ALFRED A. KNOPF

1 9   NEW YORK   8 1

Edith Sitwell

A Unicorn Among Lions

Grateful acknowledgment is made to the following
for permission to reprint excerpts from previously published material:
Harcourt Brace Jovanovich, Inc.: Excerpts from THE DIARY OF VIRGINIA WOOLF,
edited by Anne Olivier Bell, from THE LETTERS OF VIRGINIA WOOLF,
edited by Nigel Nicolson, and from DAYS OF MARS: A MEMOIR by Bryher,
© 1972 by Norman Holmes Pearson. Reprinted by permission
of the publisher, Harcourt Brace Jovanovich, Inc.
David Higham Associates Limited: Excerpts from DRAWN FROM LIFE
by Stella Bowen, originally published by Collins Publishers;
from JOURNALS by Denton Welch, originally published by Hamish Hamilton;
and from MEMOIRS OF AN ESTHETE by Harold Acton.
originally published by Eyre Methuen.
Murray Pollinger: Excerpts from MEETINGS WITH POETS by Jack Lindsay.
Elizbeth Salter: Excerpts from THE LAST YEAR OF A REBEL by Elizabeth Salter.
Originally published by Hutchinson Publishing Group Limited.
George Weidenfeld & Nicolson Ltd.: Excerpts from THE DIARIES AND LETTERS
OF HAROLD NICOLSON: THE LATER YEARS 1945–1962,
from THE DIARIES OF EVELYN WAUGH and THE LETTERS OF EVELYN WAUGH,
and from THE DIVINE COMEDY OF PAVEL TCHELITCHEW
by Parker Tyler.

Library of Congress Cataloging in Publication Data
Glendinning, Victoria.   Edith Sitwell, a unicorn among lions.
Includes index.
1.   Sitwell, Edith, Dame, 1887–1964—Biography.
2.   Poets, English—20th century—Biography.   I.   Title.
PR 6037.18z59   1981   821'.912   80–2721
ISBN 0-394-50439-9
Manufactured in the United States
First Edition

FOR

T. de V. W.

Contents

Acknowledgments

My first thanks are to Francis Sitwell, Dame Edith's literary executor; also to Sir Sacheverell and the late Lady Sitwell; and Reresby Sitwell, for their generosity and patience. I am particularly grateful to Sir Sacheverell for permission to quote from his own poetry and prose, to Frank Magro for permission to quote from the works of Osbert Sitwell, and to Francis Sitwell for the extensive quotations from the poetry, prose, and correspondence of Edith Sitwell herself; also to the publishers of the Sitwells' works. The bibliographical details in the text are drawn chiefly from Richard Fifoot's *A Bibliography of Edith, Osbert and Sacheverell Sitwell* (second edition), published by Rupert Hart-Davis (1971) in the Soho Bibliographies series, to which I am greatly indebted.

I am also very grateful to Elizabeth Salter and to John Pearson, author of *Façades*, who have been uncommonly generous; also to Judith Jones of Knopf, who gave me valuable editorial help and guidance, and to John Curtis, Alex MacCormick, and Lynda Poley of Weidenfeld & Nicolson.

I would like to thank the following universities and institutions and their librarians: in the United States, first and foremost the Humanities Research Center of the University of Texas at Austin; also the Berg Collection, New York Public Library; the University of Iowa; the Mugar Memorial Library, Boston University; the Poetry Collection of the Lockwood Memorial Library, State University of New York at Buffalo; in England, the University of Durham; the University of Sussex; King's College Library, Cambridge; Westfield College, University of London; and in Canada, the Scott Library, York University, Ontario.

I also want to say thank you to the many people who have helped by allowing me to use copyrighted material, etc., and in countless other ways; especially Her Majesty Queen Elizabeth the Queen Mother, Sir Harold Acton, Arthur P. Bean, the late Sir Cecil Beaton, Alan Bell, Fr. Philip

Acknowledgments

Caraman S.J., Lord Clark, Norman Collins, Gillian Diamond, John Downing, Rochelle Holt Dubois, Lady Gladwyn, Nigel Glendinning, Olive Glendinning, Paul Glendinning, Livia Gollancz and Victor Gollancz Ltd., Geoffrey Gorer, Geoffrey Grigson, John Gross, Sir Rupert Hart-Davis, Lord Horder, John Kelly, John Lehmann, Rosamond Lehmann, Sean Day-Lewis, Jack Lindsay, Robert Liddell Lowe, C.W. McCann, Frank Magro, Blake Morrison, Hubert Nicholson, Gertrude Nopper, Professor and Mrs. Elder Olson, John Piper, Anthony Powell and Lady Violet Powell, Felix Pryor, Michael Rhodes, Michael Rubinstein, Peter du Sautoy, Lady Snow and the late Lord Snow, Diana Sparkes, John Sparrow, Michael Stapleton, Allanah Harper Statlender, Quentin Stevenson, Donald Sutherland, Denys Sutton, Allen Tanner, Virgil Thomson, Hugo Vickers, Alison Waley, Laurence Whistler — and, above all, Terence de Vere White.

EDITH

SITWELL

↓

A

UNICORN

AMONG

LIONS

Foreword

Just after I began working on this book I was at a party in London where, in answer to a question, I said I was going to write about Edith Sitwell. "I hope," said the man who had asked the question, "that you are going to say what a dreadful poet she was." "Oh no!" said someone else. "I was reading 'Gold Coast Customs' last night, and it was wonderful." The first speaker was a professor of English and a professional literary critic, born in the very early 1930s; the second man too was an academic, though not a specialist in English literature, and nearly twenty years younger.

This conversational exchange exactly represents one of the difficulties in assessing the poetry of Edith Sitwell. The history of her reputation is very largely the history of what *kind* of poetry seemed the real right thing at a particular time or in a particular group. It would be easy to marshal a sufficiently impressive body of published evidence for the importance of Edith Sitwell as a poet—from W. B. Yeats, Maurice Bowra, Cyril Connolly, Stephen Spender, Horace Gregory, for a start. It would be equally easy to muster evidence for a negative view—from Geoffrey Grigson, Julian Symons, A. Alvarez, and F. R. Leavis (who was a fellow of Downing College, Cambridge, when the first speaker of my story was an undergraduate there), to name but a few. But an informed reader would not be impressed by a reliance on the judgment of either group. A critic's value judgment tells you, chiefly, about that critic's values. Criticism of modern poetry in particular is inescapably "political." As John Press wrote in *A Map of Modern English Verse* (1971 edition):

Few if any judgments about literature are purely literary; the divergences over Edith Sitwell are inseparable from the personal, cultural, social and educational principles and prejudices which have inspired them. Given

the background from which a critic has emerged, and the circles in which
he moves, one can make a pretty fair guess at his attitude to Edith Sitwell.

The "kind" of poetry that Edith Sitwell wrote, and how she came to do so, is
part of the story in this book. She is a poet of dream and vision, a musical
wordmonger. Her dream, as Yeats wrote in his introduction to *The Oxford
Book of Modern Verse* (1936), is double: "In its first half, through separated
metaphor, through mythology, she creates, amid crowds and scenery that
suggest the Russian Ballet and Aubrey Beardsley's final phase, a perpetual
metamorphosis that seems an elegant artificial childhood; in the other half . . . a
nightmare vision, like that of Webster, of the emblems of mortality."

It was the nightmare vision and the emblems of mortality that prevailed
in her later years, and her belief, drawn from despair about the world, in the
Christian redemption. Those hostile to her poetry found and find her in this
mode merely "the arch-nurse of empty phrases," as Julian Symons wrote in the
London Magazine of November 1964. Accusations of emptiness have also been
made against her first and most experimental period, the wordplay of the
"elegant, artificial childhood," when she was first pitting her wits and talent
against the prevailing Georgianism, and leaning most heavily on her reading
of the French symbolists. She was among those who provoked T. S. Eliot to
write in the first issue of *The Tyro*, in 1921, that "the poets who consider
themselves most opposed to Georgianism, and who know a little French, are
mostly such as could imagine the Last Judgment only as a lavish display of
Bengal lights, Roman candles, catherine-wheels, and inflammable fire-balloons."

The best poetry transcends the politics of poetry, given time. And literary
critics and journalists, mercifully, are not the only poetry readers. The poetry
to which one privately has recourse is a very personal matter indeed. For me,
the poetry that Edith Sitwell was writing in the mid-1920s — *The Sleeping
Beauty*, "Colonel Fantock," and the *Troy Park* poems — stands up with the best
and greatest. Because, to quote John Press, of the "personal, cultural, social and
educational principles and prejudices" of which I am composed, this high
praise has to be a matter of opinion, not fact, though of course it seems like a
matter of fact to me. I also think that she published much too much of what
she wrote, especially as her obsessional emblems made her increasingly repetitive; I believe that if the world of literary criticism knew nothing but, say, her
twelve finest poems, she would have an unquestioned, uncategorized place on
anyone's Parnassus.

Now that she is no longer a "contemporary" poet, and the personal rows are over, I hope she will be allowed to take a more dignified place in the history of modern English poetry. About her place in the hearts and minds of individual nonacademic readers I am less concerned, because so long as her work is available she will have it. On December 10, 1945, William Plomer wrote to her: "... but I should like to say that your poems become part of oneself and of one's view of life." Stephen Spender was making much the same point in his obituary of her in the *Observer* (December 13, 1964): "In the long run poems survive because people fall in love with them. They live because phrases, imagery, music, echoes, the idea of all the poems coalescing into a world single with the poet, hang about our hearts, become part of our lives."

Edith Sitwell the woman has been very difficult to write about, because her experience was not that of the ordinary woman. On the one hand she lived without the linchpins of most women's history—a home of her own, husband or lovers, children. Nevertheless, her life was intensely emotional. On the other hand, she had a personal fame and a public persona and appearance that she enjoyed and exploited, but which drove the private woman further and further into the shadows.

In the Sitwell mythology, the rows—which were half fun, half deadly earnest—the revenges, the sharp verbal ripostes to the "impertinent," are remembered and well documented. Less well documented have been her talent for gaiety, her childlike lovingness, and great generosity. After she died, Elizabeth Jennings—who was part of a movement in poetry with which Edith conducted a running battle—wrote in the *Spectator*, "What struck me most forcibly—and I suppose most surprisingly—was her gentleness and kindness."

I have ended up with a great respect for her, and a very protective feeling, because of the loneliness and fear that were her almost constant companions. She was always best at describing herself when projecting what she felt onto someone else. In the following passage from her *Alexander Pope*, substitute *Edith* for *Pope*:

The naïveté and fundamental simplicity of Pope, his craving for romance, his warm heart, his genuine response to and understanding of the affections of others; these qualities are seen, side by side with a good deal of genuine silliness, a certain amount of artifice, and an intent and strained gaze fixed upon the verdict of posterity.

V. G.
1980

1

Little E

In a Bayswater boardinghouse, a girl is writing a letter. The year is 1913. "Darling Father . . . We will see if we can find someone else like Miss Fussell, but if not, a flat is undoubtedly cheaper than rooms." The year at Miss Fussell's had cost her father £120, she reminds him, "plus extra food which we had to get in." In May 1914 she is writing again: "If you will very kindly lend me some money towards the furnishing, I will pay you back directly I have sold my diamond pendent, as we want to get into the flat, and can't till we have got some furniture in." She wrote to her mother at the same time: "If you could get him to send me a cheque by return it would be a blessing. You see I want to get some stuff for curtains which Helen is going to make so as to save expense. . . . You were a darling to write me such a nice letter. I will be careful as you say."

The penniless young person attempting to set up house in London is Edith Sitwell. She is twenty-six years old; she is only now making a bid to break out of what amounted to a protracted and painful childhood. Her father, always eccentric, has developed a mania about his children's so-called extravagance. Her mother, in November of the year in which these letters were written, is to appear in the first of a series of criminal actions which will end in her spending three months in prison. Her brother Osbert is a soldier; her other brother, Sacheverell, is still at Eton.

Edith has a confederate in her companion and former governess, Helen Rootham, who, as she tells her father, will be able to pay "exactly half of the entire expenditure . . . to the exclusion of the servant, and I don't think you will find it a heavy drain." She has Helen, and £100 a year, and little else. Even getting hold of what she imagined to be her own property—the diamond pendant—presented difficulties. In the same month she heard from the family jewellers in Scarborough:

Messrs. Bright and Sons believe the diamond pendant Miss Sitwell refers to was brought by Sir George and placed among the other family diamonds which were in accordance with Sir George's instructions sent to Messrs. Coutts & Co. [bankers] some time ago. They are however forwarding Miss Sitwell's letter to Sir George, and no doubt she will hear from him direct with regard to the pendant.

Edith drafted her letter to her father down the right-hand half of a page of her notebook. The left-hand half was already filled with the draft of a poem—not a very good poem, as it stands, but an early version of "Serenade," one of the first she ever had published, in the *Daily Mirror*, in November 1913. Thus the rhyming ends of the longer lines—"sleeping flowers" and "silver showers"— find themselves jostled above and below by her anxieties about Miss Fussell's, and her father's probable attitude, and money. All her life Edith, and her poetry, suffered from cramping preoccupations about where and how to live, about her family, and about money.

Edith was an unwanted child. Her father, Sir George Sitwell of Renishaw Hall in Derbyshire, was in his mid-twenties—the lonely, scholarly son of a dominant widowed mother—when he married Lady Ida Denison in 1886. Lady Ida was only seventeen at the time; she was pretty, silly, and uneducated. After a few days of marriage she ran away home to her parents, who sent her back to her husband at once; these were the circumstances under which her first child was conceived. "No wonder that my mother hated me throughout my childhood and youth," wrote Edith.

Edith was born in Scarborough, at Wood End, a house belonging to old Lady Sitwell, her paternal grandmother. Her birth was precipitated by a flaming row between her other grandparents, Lord and Lady Londesborough, which took place in Lady Ida's bedroom. The quarrel was over Lord Londesborough's latest indiscretion, which was signalled by a lavish gift of emeralds to his wronged wife. Lady Londesborough, divining that guilt was the motive for his generosity, made a terrific scene—but kept the emeralds. (Edith acknowledged in later life that she had inherited this grandmother's violent temper.) Two days later Lady Ida's labour pains began, during a luncheon party given by her father, Lord Londesborough, for the Scarborough cricket festival, of which he was president. Edith Louisa Sitwell was born on September 7, 1887.

"I was unpopular with my parents from the moment of my birth," wrote Edith in old age. She said and wrote the same thing, in different ways, over and over again. She called herself a "changeling"; she said her parents were "strangers to her," and that "they understood nothing of what, from my childhood, was living in my head." Both of them would have preferred a son as their first child; Lady Ida, at eighteen, was ill equipped for maternity. And Edith was not an easy child. " 'You were an exceedingly violent child,' said my mother, without any animus." Just how much animus there was in reality towards the little girl it is impossible to know. Her parents were not happy or united, and Edith did nothing to cement the relationship. But Edith was ever a fantasist, and all one can know with certainty is that she felt herself to be entirely rejected.

It would have been better if she had been pretty, which she was not: "I was rather a fat little girl: my moon-round face, which was surrounded by green-gold curls" had the eyes of someone "who had witnessed and foretold all the tragedy of the world." This self-portrait, presumably drawn from an extant photograph of herself at three, has a romantic theatricality about it which diminishes the truth it may contain. It is a little embarrassing. But then, as she said, "I was an embarrassing child," giving as evidence a much-quoted incident that took place when she was four years old: Her nurse Davis brought her downstairs to see an old friend of Lady Ida's, who said kindly to the child, "What are you going to be when you are grown up, little E?" "A genius," answered Edith, and was rapidly whisked off upstairs again.

"Poor little E," as she was frequently called, was already formidable, which did not further endear her to her parents, nor them to her; it frightens a child to realise that adults are afraid of him. To her father's mother, however, she was "dear little E." Old Lady Sitwell had a second house in Scarborough, Hay Brow; she lived there surrounded by flowers in an odour of piety, tended by ancient and devoted servants. Edith, as a tiny child, warmed to her affection, and from Lady Sitwell's diary rises the image of a lively, responsive little creature. When Edith was just over two years old, for instance: "George's little daughter paid me an early visit, and was wildly excited when I offered her a bit of garden, exclaiming 'E dig and plant flowers. E go to sleep, and wake up and flowers all grown.' "[1] And in July 1891, when Edith was not yet four, her Aunt Florence, Lady Sitwell's unmarried daughter, wrote in her journal: "Baby is just like a child in a story book in appearance, with fat cheeks, sometimes like pink campions, blue eyes and fair curls, a dear little person, touchingly devoted to her dog, Dido [a griffon]."[2] Three weeks later she was seeing the young family off to Scotland, and Edith said at the station, "No little 'gell' has had so many night journeys as I've had—but, oh, how I've had to sing and repeat things to amuse the grown-up people!" (Little E was all too ready to burst into unsolicited song for the solace of grown-ups with headaches.)

The month before Edith's brother Osbert was born, her Aunt Florence wrote: "She is now five years old, a most interesting and dear little person. . . . I have been giving her tiny lessons after tea. Last Sunday, I began the life of Our Lord with her." And when this visit was over, her aunt described how little E had helped her arrange the flowers on her last day: "I think she did four vases with her dear little hands, taking great pains to make them pretty, and making quaint remarks, such as 'We must make the best of things,' 'We mustn't carol [quarrel] with what we've got.'" Little E complained to her grandmother about Martha, her nurserymaid, who she said "does nothing to amuse, and everything to displease me." She was an unusually articulate small child, of the sort sometimes called "old-fashioned," and unusually retentive and intelligent. Her aunt concludes:

> It is wonderful the way in which the child is getting on with her reading —really teaching herself—, asking the meaning of unknown words, and remembering them. Fairy tales have been her especial delight. She is very reflective and at the same time full of fun and mischief, delighting in a joke. . . . Once she got one of her frightened fits, and clung to me.

These unexplained attacks of terror are the only sign that anything is wrong at all for this "dear little person." She was not an unloved or unloving child—not, at any rate, in her grandmother Sitwell's house. "Dear little E has grown round one's heart, and it was sad parting with her."

Osbert was born in London, in December 1892. He was a success with his parents straightaway. He was the looked-for son and heir. A few months after Osbert's birth little E attempted to run away from home. She did not get far, being impeded by her bootlaces, which she had not yet learnt to tie herself. She was brought home a few hours later by a young policeman, to face the wrath of her parents and nurse. Writing about this escapade herself, she does not attribute it to jealousy over the new baby. But as a child and a grown woman her loyalty and devotion to Osbert were unswerving; she would neither be able to remember nor tempted to reconstruct any feelings of rejection specifically connected with his arrival. She described her feelings at this time in grim general terms: "When I was a child I was ineffably cold and lonely." Osbert, although he of course was in no position to do anything except theorise *post hoc*, wrote squarely that his birth "caused Edith to be relegated to a second place in the nursery, a position which her very nature forbade her to occupy anywhere"; and because of this she ran away, hurt by her "first experience of the cruelty and fickleness of men and women."[3]

If this is true, it was not quite her first experience of fickleness, which in her own account is more picturesque. At four years old, she said, she was in love with the peacock at Renishaw; he came to her call; she walked around the gardens with her arms round his neck. He abandoned her for a lady peacock. "I do not think it was the injury to my pride at being jilted by a peacock that I minded. It was my first experience of faithlessness." Faithlessness, the treachery of trusted friends, was to be one of the demons of Edith's cosmology.

There were five years between Edith and Osbert, and another five between Osbert and Sacheverell, who was born in Scarborough in November 1897. From the moment that Sachie was old enough to be companionable, he and Osbert were very close. "I suppose that when Sachie was a very small child I understood him better than anyone else." He was Osbert's "chief friend"; he was a charming, attractive child, beloved of his parents. His childhood was happy.

For this reason Sacheverell was always sceptical about Edith's accounts of ill treatment as a child, ascribing them to her tendency towards fantasy and romance. But by the time he was old enough to have any memory of her she was already about thirteen, divided from her small brother by her regime of schoolroom and governess and by her own reserve. She lived increasingly in her imagination; at about twelve years old, she said, her inner life was "untouched by the brutish outer life." As he grew older, it was this inner life of stories and words and music that she shared with little Sachie, and not the unhappiness. "This is my master from whom I learned," Sacheverell wrote of her, "and there can never be her like again."[4]

Even in the most ordinary and united families, perceptions differ, both of events and relationships. Each family has its external history; and each member has his own private version, the perspectives of role, temperament, and position in the family making each one's story seem distorted to the others. But generally affection, pride, pity, and the strength of the family myth see to it that the private perspectives go unpublicised. The Sitwells were not an ordinary family; moreover, they all wrote down and published accounts of their shared childhood. Edith's experience, and Edith's picture of their mother in particular, were totally different from her brothers'. What the three genuinely had in common was place.

Renishaw Hall in Derbyshire was, and is, the family home of the Sitwells. It is enormous, set in great gardens and woods. The central part of the house, gabled and battlemented, was built by George Sitwell in the 1660s. This ancestor owned an ironworks; and the combination of practical acumen and aesthetic aspiration has served the family well. Throughout the eighteenth century the Sitwells married heiresses, farmed their land, collected books and pictures, and had a respect for scholarship.

In 1777 a nephew, Francis Hurt, succeeded to the fortune and to the estate, taking on the name Sitwell. With this new blood a wild streak was introduced; the ironworks were sold, and the next three generations of Sitwells spent vast sums of money on entertaining, and on enlarging and beautifying the house and gardens. Francis Hurt Sitwell's son, Sitwell Sitwell, added the red dining room and the classical stable block. Later he built the drawing room and finally, in 1808, the ballroom, where the Prince Regent attended a ball; afterwards the Prince made his host a baronet.

Sir Sitwell Sitwell's son, George, met disaster. After the French wars, farm rents fell; a solicitor robbed him of one fortune, and in 1848 the Sheffield Bank failed, the day after he had deposited another fortune realised by a sale of land. Much of the remaining land and the furniture had to be sold up; but the pictures, tapestries, beds, and the original oak furniture of the hall were preserved. The family went abroad. The great house stood abandoned and cold. Sir George never returned. His son, Sir Reresby, died young, discouraged by the hopelessness of the family fortunes.

His widow, with a son and a daughter to bring up, pulled the finances of Renishaw together by her shrewdness and good management. This remarkable lady—née Hely Hutchinson, of Anglo-Irish stock—was the Lady Sitwell who, in her old age, saw so much grace and promise in "dear little E." Renishaw was still shut up in her reign for months at a time (since the crash, no Sitwells have lived there twelve months in a year, or furnished and occupied all the rooms), and so it escaped Victorian "improvements"; it retained within its walls—one façade smiling, the other severe—most of its Stuart and Regency past.

At Renishaw, the past was never eradicated. One of the blankets on Osbert's bed when he was a child had the date 1801 stitched on it. Outside the nursery in the passage stood the same rocking horse—minus an ear—on which a former generation of Sitwell children had been painted in watercolours in 1826 by Octavius Oakley. On their night-nursery window was a cryptic inscription cut with a diamond long ago in the house's palmy days, celebrating a handsome Sitwell girl: "*Charme des yeux* at Renishaw 1825."

The family shared the house with the family's ghosts; the children heard the stories from Davis the nurse and Martha the nurserymaid. Lady Ida believed in them as well. Sir Sitwell Sitwell could be heard from time to time calling to his wife as he lay dying; and he was seen looking in at the windows from outside, a pale face behind dark glass. And a little boy of fourteen, Henry Sacheverell, whose portrait hung in the dining room and who had died by drowning, came back—as he still does—to give cold kisses to sleepers at Renishaw. The great house, in Edith's childhood, was lit at night by candles.

Now, the family spent only the summers at Renishaw. But as Osbert wrote, "Renishaw was home." The gardens, the lake, the bluebells in the woods in May, the carefully sited statues, the long vistas, the wilderness, the quietly coloured flowers and trees—all planned and replanned by their father, Sir George—these were the stuff of their childhood, the raw material of Edith's inner life. Osbert in his autobiography describes long summer afternoons on the lake, rowed by Davis the nurse; "if Edith and I leant over the thick blue wall of the boat, we could watch the fish flickering in their chequered mail through trailing avenues of weeds." Or he and their father would make a "swift darting journey" in the canoe, while

> Edith and Davis would be watching us from the boat, now moored by the island under the light shadow of a grove of young trees. At four-thirty a footman would come down with a hamper. . . . Presently my mother and her friends would join us, and their grown-up laughter—laughter at things hidden and beyond our sight—would sound among the tea-cups.[5]

After Sachie was born, it was Martha the nurserymaid who rowed the elder two on the lake, the blue boat drifting listlessly through the water lilies, while Davis nursed their brother on the bank by the boat house. Sometimes, after tea was brought, the little party waited in vain for Mother to join them; and, trailing back to the house, "as we topped the steep path and neared the gardens, we could hear voices and laughter, and the sound of mallets and croquet balls. . . . They had forgotten all about us."[6]

Osbert called Renishaw a "masculine" house, because of the relative bareness of its interior, free from nineteenth-century decoration and fuss. Other places, equally familiar to the children, had very different atmospheres. Lady Ida's father was the first Earl of Londesborough and her mother a daughter of the seventh Duke of Beaufort. ("I am better born than you," she said to Edith, her daughter. A baronetcy, to the Londesboroughs, did not cut much ice.) At Londesborough, the footmen were not allowed to look at one another in Her Ladyship's presence, let alone speak. Staying with her, in a household given over to what Osbert called "pomps and vanities," he and Edith would be summoned to an audience with their formidable grandmother, before escaping into the gardens with Davis.

Their grandfather Londesborough was more approachable, and devoted to children. He took them out in his buckboard—an equipage precariously balanced on two wheels drawn by "a permanently bolting horse." He was, in the term of the times, a swell. The Londesboroughs, like old Lady Sitwell, also had a house in Scarborough, Londesborough Lodge in the Crescent, where they entertained extravagantly: Their establishments and their way of life were centred on an elaborate concept of "fun." This fun, from the children's point of view, had a baroque comedy of its own. Edith used to be taken for drives with her great-grandmother, the Dowager Duchess of Beaufort. The old lady instructed the coachman to take them for a new drive each day; "she never discovered," wrote Edith, "nodding into a sleep that would soon be eternal, that we drove on the same route every afternoon." Nor that her beloved parrot, brought along for the drive, had been long ago stuffed so that she would not be upset by its demise.

Edith wrote that her bewigged grandmother Londesborough was, as she first remembered her, "a fantastic, wave-like Chinoiserie, a Laideronette, Princesse de Pagodes. Beaked like a harpy, she had queer-roofed, Byzantine eyes, and these characteristics I have inherited from her. . . ." This grandmother had married "a vastly rich man and lived in luxury like a gilded and irascible wasp in a fine ripe nectarine."[7]

After the "vastly rich man" died, the Sitwell children spent their Christmases with their uncle, his heir, and vast numbers of relations, in the opulent and to them dismal grandeur of Blankney, in cold, flat Lincolnshire. In Osbert's account, Blankney at Christmas sounds more like a grand madhouse than a home. Hungarian bands, packs of barking dogs, hordes of tall, loud, tweed-clad male relatives joyfully slaughtering hundreds of furred and feathered creatures daily; quarter-witted and geriatric female aunts and cousins, grubby and bedizened; hectic troupes of French and German governesses, companions, and assorted hangers-on; practical jokes, amateur theatricals, endless bolted meals; scores of children, spoilt, bewildered, quarrelsome, neglected, wretched. "The Golden Horde," the "fun brigade," was what the Sitwell children called these enjoyers of a traditional family Christmas. The women, in those pre–First World War winters, dressed extravagantly, especially for dinner in the evening, watched in their silken descent of the great staircase by "knots and clumps" of housemaids, "phantoms who, in the next generation, were to inherit the earth," Osbert wrote. (He and Edith both dreaded these Christmases, but it was worse for Edith, even though she had at least one friend, her cousin Veronica Codrington.)

> Among the children, I am sure that the child who felt least happy, an alien among her nearest grown-up relations, was my sister. Acutely sensitive, and with her imagination perhaps almost unduly developed by the neg-lect and sadness of her childhood since she was five, she could find no comfort under these tents. . . . And, if anything, my father's inclination to nag at her on the one hand, my mother's, to fall into ungovernable, singularly terrifying rages with her, on the other, because of her non-conformity, seemed stronger when there were people, as here, to feed the fires of their discontent, and other children to set a standard by which to measure her attainments. "Dearest, you *ought* to *make* her like killing rabbits," one could hear the fun brigade urging on my mother.[8]

One result of her unhappiness was the way in which Edith came to identify herself with the sad, the lonely, the scared, the outsider, the mistreated, whether human or animal. She hated the mindless snobbery that underlay the philistine luxury of her Londesborough relations. The governesses and com-panions especially had her sympathy, particularly when they became old and unwanted: "these poor and unloved creatures whose existences have been passed on the surface of other people's lives."[9] For a child, she had an unusual perception of the loneliness of aging, single women. She remembered forever the landlady of a boardinghouse in Lancaster Gate where she, her governess, and Osbert stayed in 1901. She took in the "superannuated spinsters" who were Madame Baker's clientele; most of all she took in Madame Baker herself, fat and painted, who had "swaddled her whole being, in order to protect herself against the cruel mockery that pursues the defenseless, the poverty, the hopelessness of those whose only crumbling defence against the world was the façade of youth." She saw the lady when she was about eleven; she wrote out a fantasy on the theme in one of her notebooks and, near her own end, put it all in her autobiography. With Edith, nothing was wasted or forgotten.

Osbert said that no two backgrounds could be more different than their father's and mother's. Their Sitwell grandmother, little E's champion, was, Edith wrote, "warmer and more claybound" than the Londesboroughs. Lady Sitwell's Scarborough house Hay Brow was three miles out of the town. It was unimpressive as a house; it was the garden, and the atmosphere of peacefulness and innocence, which set the tone. Here, and in her country house at Gosden in Surrey, Lady Sitwell was tended by ancient servants; Leckly, her lady's maid, had already been in her service for sixty years when Edith first knew her.

Lady Sitwell's mother-in-law, wife of the first Sir George, was a sister of Archbishop Tait of Canterbury; his daughter had married Randall Davidson, who also became Archbishop. A familial Anglican piety pervaded the house-hold. Theatres and circuses were taboo. Lady Sitwell and her daughter Florence were cruelly called "Lambeth Palace lounge-lizards" by Edith, who resented the curates swarming in the house; Lady Sitwell welcomed any man in holy orders, and, in Edith's opinion, these were a "particularly smooth and particularly uncultured lot." In a gentler mood, Edith acknowledged that as a child she "liked the hot smell" of her grandmother's furs, "the warm, South of France feeling about her, and her faded hair that was like dry, powdery mimosa. I drove with her sometimes in an open victoria, always on some errand of mercy; and on those days the sea was always thick and homely like her 1880 home-made blue china. . . ."[10]

Old Lady Sitwell's favourite errand of mercy was to Fallen Women. She ran a home in Scarborough where the uniformed unfortunates, rounded up off the streets, "earned their living by tearing our laundry to shreds every week." There were other plans, too, for the tightening-up of female looseness. An entry in Aunt Florence's diary: "We are making plans (Mother's idea) for inviting Bar-maids for quiet Sunday afternoons in this garden, where we could read to them, with perhaps a little sacred singing, and get to know them and help them if we can." (Alas, only two "nice-looking Bar-maids" turned up.)

Vignettes of Edith's two grandmothers and of the styles in which the two sides of her family lived are but appetisers for those interested in genealogy and genetic inheritance. They will find the long and spreading pedigrees clearly and elegantly described in *Left Hand, Right Hand!*, the first volume of Osbert's autobiography.

Although Edith and her brothers were often in Scarborough in the summer visiting their relations, it was in winter that it became "home"—first at Belvoir Lodge and then at Wood End. Scarborough, on the east coast of Yorkshire, set on the top of high cliffs, was a thriving and fashionable resort in the summer months; in the late nineteenth century invalids came in droves to drink the spa waters. The life of the seaside—barrel organs, hurdy-gurdies, Pierrots, side-shows, Punch and Judy—was part of the Sitwell children's world. But to a child of Edith's sensibility and overactive imagination, there was horror as well as laughter in these spectacles: "Even as a small child I was made unhappy and terrified by the unconscious cruelty of these puppets' fate . . . pulled backwards and forwards to love, to annihilation, to murder, by the mechanical actions of that ragged hunger, the showman."

The terror and blackness underlying the sunlit scene was reflected in Scarborough's winters, when wild storms of snow and wind and rain blasted the steep-streeted town. Susan Hill, another writer brought up in Scarborough —though half a century later—remembered these fierce winters:

> There are no "trippers" then—only north-east winds cutting you in half, and scudding grey skies, and enormous seas with waves a hundred feet high roaring over the rocks and rearing up high into the air, to crash, white and seething, on the foreshore road, and the Marine Drive. There is very often snow from December until the end of March. There are always one or two dramatic lifeboat rescues.[11]

The best picture of the Scarborough of Edith's childhood is given in Osbert's first novel, *Before the Bombardment*.

There were contrasts of an equally disturbing kind at Renishaw. The great house in its deep woods and gardens lies close to the mean and blackened villages of Renishaw and Eckington; the great steel-manufacturing city of Sheffield is only seven miles away. This is a coal-mining district; coal was mined deep under the lake in the park of Renishaw Hall. Chimneys rose above the morning mist, flares from the foundries at nearby Staveley lit up the night, and democratic soot settled on even Sir George Sitwell's trees.

The Sitwell children, on their walks, would meet the gangs of blackened miners going home. They lived in an enchanted castle, in a world of planned grace and beauty, but beyond the gates lay that other world of stunted poverty and industrial ugliness. Edith and Osbert found it hard to get on even with children of their own kind (they hated children's parties). How much further were they removed from the children of the miners in the grim, dim pit villages. Sacheverell recalls a blackberrying expedition on Edith's birthday in September, on a misty day. Across the woods and fields the three of them walked, through the long wet grass, to where the blackberries were. There they met a group of local children,

> of a very flaxen, long-headed, Danish type, and their hands and faces were of an indescribable blackness which accentuated the pallor of their skin.... Their speech was slurred and clipped to a degree that made it hard to understand.... The three of us, my brother, sister and myself, were luckily tall enough to get at berries which were out of their reach, for by this time they had left nothing but red, unripe ones near to hand. While the taller children still continued picking the berries, those of them who were too small—hardly big enough to walk, in fact—tottered uneasily round to where we could be watched in stupefied silence.[12]

To the village children, the three tall Sitwells must have seemed as rare as giraffes.

This alienation from other people, whether relations or strangers, was doubly painful for Edith; for while the boys were secure in their mother's love, Edith felt an outsider at home as well. She shared with the boys the physical texture of her days; but her perception of her parents, of her mother especially, was of a totally different colour. Osbert appreciated Lady Ida's "unusual beauty and strange temperament, her kindness, indulgence," even if he also suffered on occasion from her "furious, sudden rages." "I was in the happy position as a small child of being my mother's favourite. I played on her bed, and upset everything with impunity. I adored her."[13] He was a privileged person. He played with her jewels, her hairbrushes, her scent bottles. He was powerfully affected by the clothes she wore, by the scented flowers she pinned to her dress. For Osbert, Lady Ida was romance and beauty and affection.

She was if anything even more precious to Sacheverell. His earliest memory was of riding the old rocking horse out in the garden, with his mother standing by. "It is a memory of nothing in particular. Nothing, indeed, at all. But of the awakening of affection. Of the first warmth of love. Of the safety and comfort of that emotion."[14] Later, going back to boarding school was made worse by the certainty that she missed him as painfully as he missed her. Her character in his early childhood he remembered as "compound of natural high spirits and a sort of palace-bred or aristocratic helplessness."

Yet to Edith, the child bride's unwanted daughter, the "changeling," her mother was a stranger. Edith appreciated Lady Ida's "Michelangelo" beauty, but rejected everything else in return for being herself rejected. Lady Ida was compulsively sociable; and at Renishaw, when there were no visitors, time was for her, wrote Edith in her sad old age, "but an empty round between the night and night. . . . Her rages were the only reality in her life." Lady Ida spent her mornings in bed, on which a blissful small Osbert "played with impunity." Edith did not. She observed only that her mother stayed in bed "because there was nothing to do if she got up." She noted that her mother read novels all day, but remembered nothing at all of what she had read; she noted that if her mother's feet hurt it was because she always bought her shoes a size too small. She wrote of the "nullity" of her mother's days, "the blank stretch between hour and hour." Worse than her mother's idleness was her mother's sociableness; friends and hangers-on would be invited in crowds, gay and superficial, or rather, in Edith's opinion, "semi-animate persons like an unpleasant form of vegetation, or like dolls confected out of cheap satin, with, here and there, buttons fastened on their faces in imitation of eyes."

Perhaps the most striking illustration of the differently coloured lenses through which Edith and the boys saw their mother is Osbert's story of the dancing class to which he and Edith were taken in Scarborough twice a week for several years. It was an ordeal for both of them. Sometimes the mothers of the children taking part would come in before the end and sit on chairs round the edge of the room. Whenever Osbert realised that his mother had come in—usually, before he saw her, he smelt the gardenias or tuberoses she wore—he was delighted. He was proud of her looks, and of how well and easily she got on with the other mothers. She seemed to "act as a link" between his awk-ward, lonely self and the others. More importantly, "her presence afforded me a warm feeling of support in the ordeal. . . . " He presumed Edith shared this warm feeling; and so "it was a shock to me to find out that my sister, whom I loved dearly, did not share this sense of comfort and, indeed, dreaded my mother's appearance in the room, for my mother was always cruelly finding fault with her in front of other people, and behaving to her in a way in which she would never have acted to a son."[15]

The most vindictive things Edith published about her mother were in her autobiography, *Taken Care Of*, written right at the end of her life; she died before it was in print. Containing much material already available elsewhere, it is a bitter, scrappy book; some of the people who loved her thought it should not have been published. Yet there is evidence that what she felt anew as an old, sick woman she had felt as a girl; though there had been rapprochement at different times and an uneasy, intermittent mellowing. The remarks above about her mother's useless life are from *Taken Care Of*; but the relevant passages had been written word for word long ago, as the first chapter of a novel that was never completed and never published.

In this fragment Lady Ida is called Mrs. Londesfield, and Edith/Lily is her granddaughter (but only by adoption—here Edith disowns her blood and confirms her changeling status). Not all the descriptions of her mother in the draft novel-chapter were taken over for the autobiography; one more is worth preserving, even if only to show the cool accuracy of the young Edith's observation:

> But she [Lady Ida/Mrs. Londesfield], who lived for littleness, would at times invent the existence of small affections, less in herself than in others, believing, or pretending to believe, that ennobled by the contemplation of her remarkable goodness, persons not usually addicted to the softer emotions, such as busy harassed hotel managers and head waiters, matrons of hospitals and young ladies enshrined behind desks, were fired by a devotion towards her. And under the spell of this belief she would comment on their nice smiles, a phenomenon on which she would dwell for hours at a time, heedless of the apathy of her listeners, chronicling, too, their slightest remarks and sending them small presents that they did not want, in order that they might be forced to put aside their work and write to her.

Ironically, Edith herself could have been found guilty of this sort of behaviour—by an enemy—in later life. Who could not? Where does generosity and concern end, and egotism and emotional bribery begin? It is easy to feel sorry for Edith, at the mercy of her inadequate and unloving mother. It is also possible to feel pity for Lady Ida, in her mistaken attempts to cope with her watchful, critical, nonconforming, and clever daughter. Compassion is born of affection, and they could give each other neither the one nor the other. Osbert, with hindsight, saw it this way:

> I doubt whether any child was ever more mismanaged by her parents; they failed entirely to comprehend the sort of being who was in process

of flowering before their eyes, they mistook nervous sensibility for awkwardness, imagination for falsehood, and a capacity for throwing the cloak of drama over everyday events—often the sign of an artist—for "being affected."[16]

Instead of allowing her to find "her own range," in the way that she had taught herself to read, they persisted in trying to make her conform to their own idea of what a girl should be like.

Her very appearance was a source of conflict. Her father had always hoped she would have a straight, Grecian nose like her mother; but already by the age of nine or ten it was aquiline. The baby plumpness disappeared early; by the time Osbert was old enough to remember her, when she was seven or eight, "the butterfly had already emerged from the chrysalis, and she was thin, tall for her age, with the budding profile of a gothic effigy or a portrait by a Sienese master."[17]

It was, however, a portrait by the American master John Singer Sargent that gave Sir George the opportunity to brood most damagingly on Edith's unorthodox "budding profile." Edith was twelve when his long-maturing plan for a family group came to fruition. Sargent came to Renishaw to see the portrait of four Sitwell children done by another American, John Singleton Copley, in 1785, for which the new picture was to be a companion piece. He made sketches of the family at Renishaw, but would paint the picture only in his Tite Street studio. So in the spring of 1900 the Sitwell family moved to London and sat for Sargent every second day for five weeks. They took 25 Chesham Place, a house belonging to a sister of Lady Randolph Churchill, done up throughout in the then fashionable colour—mauve. The room in which the children did their lessons was entirely lined with photographs of their landlady's nephew, the young Winston Churchill. They found it impossible to work under his aggressive gaze, and Edith did her best to cover the photos up with newspapers and exercise books.

In the Tite Street studio, Sir George interfered continually with the artist's procedure, taking the role of patron to a point on the far side of bullying. Sargent was very patient. The picture was to be done "as if" at Renishaw, and for this purpose one of the Louis XIV tapestries from the ballroom, the one depicting the Triumph of Justice, was brought to London, along with the huge ornate piece of Chippendale, the most famous of the family pieces, and other impressive and emblematic props for the background of the "conversation piece." Osbert was to devote a whole chapter of his autobiography to the painting of the Sargent portrait, using the episode to show the unpleasantly unreasonable and ludicrous side of his father's personality.

The cruellest moment was when Sir George drew Sargent's attention to the crookedness of Edith's nose, saying that he hoped the artist would emphasise this flaw. But Sargent was a kind man. He resented Sir George's remarks for the awkward girl's sake, and in the picture he gave Sir George a crooked nose and Edith a straight one, which he would not subsequently alter. Sargent was nice to all the children—it was hard to keep Sachie, aged two, amused and immobile for very long—but especially to Edith. The completed picture is curious rather than anything else. Lady Ida and the two little boys take up the foreground, while in the middle ground stand (in Osbert's description)

> my father, with a certain air of distinguished isolation, and "with one hand on Edith's shoulder," rather in the manner of a stage magician producing a rabbit out of a hat, Edith in her scarlet dress, with her lank, golden-green hair frizzed out unbecomingly for the occasion (for my father said that "all hair should be inclined to curl and so soften the lines of the face"), and her pale face very intent, as though waiting.

As for pale Edith, posing day after day and subjected to the humiliating attention to the shape of her nose, "I was white with fury and contempt, and indignant that my father held me in what he thought was a tender paternal embrace."[18]

For all that, Edith suffered more from her mother than from her father. Osbert became obsessed by his father—by his eccentricities, his mannerisms, his irrationality, his despotism—and Osbert's autobiography is a monument to that obsession. He made of Sir George a memorably complex comic figure. All the children dined out on anecdotes about their father ("Ginger") all their lives, even though for Sacheverell the jokes were tempered by an appreciation of Sir George's genuine if egregious good qualities.

It is rare for both parents to have the knack of upsetting the same child so as to cause lasting pain; and for Edith, in spite of her father's gross mishandling of her, it was her mother who had this power. Her mother's indifference, her mother's rages, her mother's weary scorn, her mother's hurtful words in public—these went too deep for the wounds to heal. About Sir George she was more detached; she detested the regimes he prescribed for her, his desire that she should be "semi-adept" at a few accomplishments—never the ones in which she took an interest or showed any talent, on principle; she joked about him, avoided him, and mistrusted him. But he could not hurt her as much as her mother could. She always said that she took after her mother's family, as indeed she did; but she was also very like her father, both physically and in other ways. Perhaps this enabled her to get his measure, and lessened the threat, whereas her mother belonged to the race of good-looking, well-dressed, easy-talking philistines among whom she was always a foreigner.

2
Splendours and Miseries

When Edith grew old, the bitterness about her mother, which in her middle years was overlaid by life's realities, surfaced again; and there is no way of knowing how much fantasy, and the need to find a scapegoat for the sorrows and dissatisfactions of life, contributed to her picture of childhood. She wrote to John Lehmann in 1951: "I can't tell the truth about my sainted mother. If I had been a slum child, I should have been taken away from her. But I wasn't a slum child, and motherhood is a *very* beautiful thing! I often wonder what my poetry would be like if I had had a normal childhood." Writing to Stephen Spender in 1945, about Osbert's first volume of autobiography, she said: "Of my mother I can only say that her physical beauty was far greater than that of the Richmond portrait in the book. But my life as a child and a girl were [*sic*] a squalid *hell*: it was no question of misunderstanding or anything of that kind. There was something very seriously wrong, and I bore the whole brunt."[1] Some of the stories that she told about her mother in her later life are almost certainly untrue, fantastic glosses on a genuinely appalling situation—for example, that she was sent out to pawn her mother's false teeth in order to buy whisky.

Recalling her earliest memories of her father, she described him as "good-looking in an insipid way, the insipidity being largely the result of his blinking, with pink eyelids." In later life, she said, he "became very handsome and noble-looking; with his strange, pale, lonely-looking eyes, and his red beard, he resembled a portrait of one of the Borgias, or some other early Italian tyrant." Whatever he was, he was "early"—"born out of his century," as she wrote in one of her notebooks.

Osbert, however, is the man to read for detailed descriptions and anec-dotes of Sir George. Briefly, the facts are that having inherited an economi-cally restored Renishaw, the scholarly tastes of his remoter ancestors, and the mania for building and garden planning of more recent ones, he spent his life accordingly. He devoted his time to medieval history, genealogy, heraldry, architecture, and gardening. "His life ranged from the date eleven hundred to the end of the life of Queen Anne, and therefore he was never dull, as there were several centuries in which he could browse," wrote Edith. He did not like real life, because it disrupted his inner reverie of the past; so he avoided it, by illness, oddness, and self-imposed isolation. For example, he took luncheon alone, at noon; Lady Ida's chattering guests were unendurable to him.

Edith portrayed him in her only published novel, *I Live Under a Black Sun*, in the guise of Sir Henry Rotherham. She described how he paced up and down in front of the house, or along the passages, slowly, sometimes pausing at a doorway to listen to voices, not because he was interested in what was going on but because "he was enabled in this way to touch, for a moment, the world in which others moved, thought, acted, without being obliged to become a part of it, and thus made him feel real to himself, real in his isolation. . . . " She wrote "my father" over a passage in her novel-fragment which describes "Mr. Londesfield":

> He spoke, always, as if his mouth was full of dust; and this he did in order that he might accuse others, when they were unable to hear him, of being inattentive, and because, too, he was aware that the fact of his mumbling had a strange effect on those whom he engaged in conversation. It produced in them the half-unconscious impression that he must be deaf as well as dumb, and they would, insensibly, speak above their usual tones, which gave Mr. Londesfield the opportunity to drop the mumbling and say sharply, "Don't shout." And coming from his lips the sudden burst of sound had a disconcerting effect, as though a hidden door had been opened and an unexpected scene had revealed itself.

There is irony in these knife-sharp notations of his alienation, but there is also understanding, however dispassionate; it is as if Edith included her father among those who are "a little outside life," like herself.

The boys were sent to preparatory school and then to Eton. But after the portrait episode, Edith withdrew, in Osbert's words, "still further to one side and into the background," receiving "the peculiar education reserved for young girls of her time and class."[2] She stayed at home. She enjoyed playing the piano; but her parents decided she should learn to charm with the cello.

She was encouraged to recite, to develop her small talk, to paint in watercolours (she was sent, briefly and unprofitably, to the local art school). Her father made her do gymnastics, in the interesting belief that there was "nothin' a young man likes so much as a girl who's good at the parallel bars."

Edith grew fast at puberty—she reached six feet in the end, which is tall for a girl even now, but three-quarters of a century ago was freakishly tall, like Alice after eating the cake labelled "Eat Me." She was also very thin; she stooped a little, and her ankles were weak. There are few miseries in this world to be compared to that of the adolescent girl who does not have a conforming kind of looks or easy ways with strangers. To say that such a girl feels awkward is an understatement. She knows agony. Edith had felt "different" always; what she wrote in her life of Pope about the childhood of a poet is a piece of autobiography:

> Even if they try to speak to him kindly, their language is one that is unknown to him. He must suffer within his heart the mad tempests of love for the world of sight, sense, and sound, and the mad tempests of rage against the cruelty and blindness that there is in the world. But he must suffer these dumbly, for among the tall strangers there is nothing but noise and buffeting. The children are terrifying to him; their eyes are on a level with his own, but they are like the blind and beautiful eyes of statues—they see nothing. He loves them and longs to be loved in return, but he knows that they, too, see him as a statue throwing some long strange shadow, or as a little foreigner dressed in mourning for someone they have never known, or playing an unknown game he has learned in far-off gardens.

She had, apart from her brothers, a few friends who were children. There was her cousin Veronica Codrington, and Mollie and Gladys Hume, the daughters of "a Colonel Hume, a tall stork-like personage who resembled a character in *Struwwelpeter*"; he was the original of "Old Sir Faulk" in her poem "Fox Trot." But when she grew as tall as "the tall strangers," making contact with them became no easier. The foregoing passage is very heightened writing; it is poetic truth. How much, in Edith's case, poetic truth diverged from historic truth she would not have known herself.

In this matter of truth, the "Bastille" is a case in point. Because of her weak spine and ankles, and her crooked nose, she was taken to a children's surgeon in London—she calls him "Mr. Stout," Osbert calls him "Dr. Grabbe," in their respective autobiographies—who designed orthopaedic devices. Edith's account of the contraptions she was forced to wear is horrifying. "Mr. Stout," whom she describes as looking like "a statuette made of margarine," prescribed for her "a sort of Bastille of steel":

> The imprisonment began under my arms, preventing me from resting them on my sides. My legs were also imprisoned down to my ankles, and at night-time these, and the soles of my feet, were locked up in an excruciating contraption. Even my nose did not escape this gentleman's efficiency, and a band of elastic surrounded my forehead, from which two pieces of steel (regulated by a lock and key system) descended on each side of the organ in question, with thick upholstered pads at the nostrils, turning my nose very firmly to the opposite way which Nature had intended, and blocking one nostril, so that breathing was difficult.

Once, at Wood End, there was a plague of bluebottles. In bed at night, locked up in her Bastille by her governess, "I was alone excepting for these fat, dirty, helpless creatures which buzzed about me, sometimes touching my face. When I exhibited my terror, a match-box was put in my hand, my wrist firmly held, and I was made to kill the bluebottles." "When this is over," they told her, "you will be a different child."[3]

Sacheverell, the gentle and generous, never believed that she had been subjected to such discomfort and humiliation. But he would have been a very tiny child, in the care of the nurse, when these things happened. And to give her parents their due, such contraptions were not arbitrarily inflicted on Edith alone in all the world; Osbert said the orthopaedic virtuoso was let loose on their cousins as well. These methods, in the first years of the twentieth century, had a certain standing and orthodoxy. Edith's torturer, to guess from the aliases "Stout" and "Grabbe," may very well have been the Mr. Heather Bigg, FRCS, of University College Hospital, who published in 1905 an *Essay on the General Principles of the Treatment of Spinal Curvature*: Here he explained his belief in the application of "spring-force" and "rack-force" (a rack is a lever made to move by a screw). As Mr. Bigg conceded,

> the two words "rack" and "screw" are so associated with certain instruments of torture (which can be seen by anyone for sixpence at the Tower) that they are naturally repellant; indeed, a certain unfair advantage was

invariably taken of this unpleasant connection by those who, for their own ends, opposed the theory of mechanical treatment.

This nasty treatise is illustrated by photographs and sketches, by the author, mostly of the naked rear views of young girls demonstrating the contraptions on their persons. (Mr. Bigg, *en passant*, was also the author of a work of fiction called *Nell: A Tale of the Thames*.)

Edith alleged that the metal rack designed for her nose had to be worn while she did her lessons, and that one particularly unpleasant friend of her mother's, Pilkington by name, used to "intrude into my schoolroom, in order to feast herself on the humiliation I suffered in my Bastille of steel," and bring others with her. Whether or not the Bastille period was quite as lurid as Edith painted it, it did great damage to her; and such "punishment," for so it seemed, to an already insecure young person, had a lasting effect. She was never at ease with her physical self, even after she found, in adult life, ways of exploiting its peculiarities to her advantage. Yet this strange, misunderstood girl, who could not get on with her parents or with most other children, could say of herself at about the Bastille time that her inner life was "untouched by the brutish outer life," that when not being bullied she was "ineffably happy," that "glory was everywhere."

Edith had no physical life as a child, she wrote later, excepting that of two of the senses—hearing and seeing:

> Ever since my earliest childhood, seeing the immense design of the world, one image of wonder mirrored by another image of wonder—the pattern of fur and feather by the frost on the windowpane, the six rays of the snowflake mirrored in the rock-crystal's six-rayed eternity—seeing the pattern of the scaly legs of birds mirrored in the pattern of knot-grass, I asked myself, were these shapes moulded by blindness?

("I had a wild beast's senses, a painter's eyesight," she wrote in her notebook, among autobiographical jottings, in the 1930s.) In the natural world, known in an ordered perfection in the gardens and in the wildness of the woods and fields, "glory was everywhere"; its patterns, "consciously or unconsciously," were what she made her early poems from.

The great house itself did not mean as much to her as it did to her brothers:

> You, my sister, would be bored with architects;
> Buildings mean little or nothing to you,
> You do not even look at them . . . .[4]

But things within the house added to her store of images: the five Louis XIV Brussels tapestries, for example, bought by the lavish Sir Sitwell Sitwell, which were saved from the financial ruin of his son, and one of which figures in the Sargent picture; two hung in the drawing room and three in the ballroom, and, wrote Sacheverell, they exerted "an extraordinary fascination on us as children."[5] He wrote of their "Indian suavity and opulence," and Osbert of their "plumy exoticism." Edith's imagination hoarded the tapestries — the pagodas, the clouds, the black boys, the orange trees, the fountains, the kings and queens; they were mixed in her mind with the reality of the raddled grandeur of Lady Londesborough and of the exotic flowers raised by Grandmother Sitwell's gardener, and they were all used later in her poetry.

Edith, though a great reader, did not consume all and any poetry as a child; she was kept in regularly on Saturday afternoons at one time because of her refusal to learn by heart Mrs. Hemans's "Casabianca" ("The boy stood on the burning deck. . . ."). The reason for her recalcitrance was that "as everybody had left the Burning Deck, and he was doing no conceivable good by remaining there, why in heck didn't he get off it!" At about the same time, however, she knew by heart the whole of Pope's *The Rape of the Lock*. She had come across it at Wood End, and learnt it secretly at night when her governess was at dinner. At the time Sachie was nine or ten she was reading poems aloud to him — "a young girl / vowed to poetry":

> You could read a poem, and inspire one to poetry
> By the inflection of your voice. . . .[6]

The "brutish outer life" could not intrude into this private happiness.

One or two human beings also had something to do with it. At the beginning, the one wholly reliable and affectionate adult in Edith's home life had been the nurse, Davis, whose "real name was comfort." Davis's father was a cobbler in a Berkshire village; she herself had been nurserymaid to Lady Ida. Osbert wrote that placidity and a comforting belief in the beneficence of God and man were her chief characteristics. She taught the children the names of wild flowers. She wheeled Sachie in an ancient pram, and put Butler & Crisp's Pomade Divine on Osbert's bruises. When Edith was especially demanding, her catch-phrase was: "Even slaves have an hour for their dinner." She was naively morbid, and during the winters in Scarborough took Edith and Osbert every Sunday for a walk to the municipal cemetery, to admire the mildewed angels and the "damp-clotted, mouldering chrysanthemums." Sir George, a sceptic in religious matters, would not have been pleased if he had known.

Davis stayed at Renishaw till Edith, "her most prized and cherished charge," was fifteen; but before that Edith had been handed over to a governess, Miss King-Hall, with whom Davis carried on a perpetual feud. Davis left after a violent quarrel with Sir George, during which she gave in her notice, probably not meaning it to be accepted. But tearful demonstrations from the children did not make their parents retract its acceptance.

Henry Moat, Sir George's valet and later the butler at Renishaw, who came in 1893 and stayed, off and on, for over forty years, was another ally of the children's. Edith described him as "an enormous purple man like a benevolent hippopotamus," who had "a voice like some foghorn endowed with splendour." The "off" times in his forty years' service were when he left, for periods varying between months and years, out of sheer exasperation with Sir George. But he always came back. He was the special friend and supporter of Osbert and Sachie; and though Edith came under his blanket protection, especially when Lady Ida was on the warpath, it was Davis who gave her what every child needs.

> I see a group [wrote Osbert], Davis and Edith and myself, beneath a tree bearing golden fruit. . . . Davis is in her grey alpaca dress and straw hat, and has her usual expression of kind and puzzled patience, while Edith is dressed in blue, pale blue, and under a hat like a mushroom, her curved eyelids, lank golden hair and sweet, musing expression, all give her an air of dreamy determination.[7]

The governess Miss King-Hall was also a friend to Edith and Osbert. She took them sightseeing in London, and for long walks in the country. She read Rider Haggard aloud to them in the schoolroom; she was kindly and reliable. She held the stopwatch when Edith and Osbert played the pianola at Gosden, a jealous quarter of an hour at a time, while Sachie, too young to compete, listened with respect.

The children were very often at Gosden with their grandmother Sitwell in the months after the painting of the portrait, and less with their parents. For Sir George began to withdraw from the world in a spectacular fashion. He lost money in litigation with the lessees of the coal mines which ran under his land; poverty, or the threat of poverty, began to obsess him. He must have been haunted by the knowledge of his grandfather's financial ruin and its consequences. The children from now on were to be given only "useful" presents; they got soap and hairbrushes for Christmas.

He abandoned his political interests (he was Conservative M.P. for Scarborough from 1885 to 1886, and from 1892 to 1895), and retreated into invalidism. He called in a retired military man called Brockwell, whom Osbert in his autobiography called Major Viburne, and Edith and Sacheverell in their writings called Colonel Fantock, to help administer Renishaw and keep an eye on the household bills. Colonel Fantock coached small boys and organized an amateur theatrical group in Scarborough; he was a bumbling, uncertain, aging man, "a miniature Blimp, stranded before his time,"[8] said Osbert. He was no good at all at what he was hired for, but the children liked him and listened to his long stories. Sachie drew pictures on his bald scalp with indelible pencil.

Sir George broke down entirely in 1902. His mother let him have Wood End, and he flitted between there, Londesborough Lodge, and, later, Italy for long spells twice a year, attended by shifts of nurses and doctors. The children saw little of him.

Meanwhile Lady Ida, freed from his inhibiting presence, went on spending. She gave bigger and more frequent lunch parties. Her friends, delighted by the absence of killjoy Sir George, led her on, to their own advantage, for she was generous with her jewels and clothes to the point of idiocy. It was a bad time for Edith when she was present, for her mother's friends had no time for the nervous, odd-looking adolescent girl, and with them Lady Ida was encouraged, as Osbert put it, to "find fault with my sister in public and mortify her."

The next year she lost one of her few allies; Miss King-Hall left to marry one of Osbert's old tutors. Sir George was making some sort of recovery, and took Lady Ida and Edith abroad—where she had to submit to more intensive nagging and bullying than ever before.

But back at Gosden her grandmother Sitwell had been charged with interviewing possible new governesses for Edith. Playfully she asked the eleven-year-old Osbert to help her choose. The young woman they picked was Helen Rootham, daughter of Samuel Rootham of Clifton, near Bristol, in whom Edith was to find a champion and a friend.

Helen was dark and intense and vehement, with a developed sense of truth and justice, and a love of the arts, especially music. She was also censorious and hypersensitive; these qualities were to cause Edith problems in the years to come, but to Edith at sixteen she was a lifeline. She had what Osbert described as "an *artist's* respect for the arts," and was a remarkably good pianist; from the moment she arrived, "the music of Chopin and Schumann, Brahms and Debussy, flowered as a constant background to our hours of leisure, and became associated at Renishaw with every expanse of water, every vista seen through green trees."9

There had always been music at Renishaw; ensembles playing in Sheffield were invited to the house, and Sacheverell in *All Summer in a Day* recalled one particularly elegiac afternoon of his childhood when three Poles came over from a nearby village and were given tea by the coal fire in the ballroom, and afterwards played Chopin in the twilight. Edith played well, and reacted strongly to different kinds of music; she claimed that hearing Sousa's "The Washington Post" in the Albert Hall made her "publicly sick." Music came before poetry at first, and Stravinsky was a strong influence when she first began to write poetry herself (as was *Struwwelpeter*, she said in the same breath—not such a strange pair of godfathers as it might at first seem).

Helen coached Edith, who had talent, at the piano; she brought her new music. When Edith first heard Debussy, it upset her. "It was like having a squint. Then after a while I got used to it and I began to listen to him all the time."10 Helen read with her; she talked to her; she gave Edith confidence. She brought Edith new poetry too—the French symbolists, Verlaine, Rimbaud, Baudelaire—to enlarge her own rapt readings of Swinburne, William Morris, Shakespeare, Keats, Shelley, Yeats. The *Fleurs du mal* darkened this paradise garden; "it is poetry of the blood's decline. And her own images began to form. Metaphors of a bony personality. . . . "11

Meanwhile family life picked up again and took on a routine. At Renishaw Sir George immersed himself anew in changes to the house and garden. In spring and autumn, through what remained of the Indian summer of Edwardian England, the family went to Italy. At the end of Helen's first year she and Edith went alone to Paris for a few months for Edith to improve her French; they went on to San Remo to join the rest of the family. The schoolboy Osbert, who had not seen her for six months, was astonished at the change in his sister.

She was now seventeen; and even though her fashionable puffed hairstyle and conventional "young girl's" clothes were "most inappropriate to her gothic appearance," he noticed "an alteration in her way of looking at things, for her absence from home—and, as a result, the discontinuance of the perpetual nagging to which for years she had been obliged to submit—had lifted the whole range of her spirits." She was happier, and therefore more amenable, because she had hope. She had been away from home, and criticism, and scenes, and she had revelled in going to concerts and galleries with Helen—and she could do it again.

> All her interests had blossomed in the short interval that had elapsed, and music and poetry burned in her blood like fire. She had become the most exhilarating and inspiring as well as understanding of companions. And, in spite of her disfiguring, though expensive, clothes, the brown plumage, physically as well as mentally, of the cygnet had gone, and the swan's green-white feathers had come to replace it.[12]

This new Edith was the one perceived by Constance Chetwynd-Talbot, who in 1912 was to marry a Sitwell cousin. She came for a summer visit to Renishaw when she and Edith were in their late teens. On the first evening she, Edith, and Osbert went out into the garden. "Edith at that time described a great many things in terms of music and musicians; she played a lot of Brahms then, and this, she said, was a 'Brahms garden.'"[13] During that visit Constance watched from her bedroom window Sir George "pacing up and down the lawn by himself, with an air of complete abstraction from the rest of the party, and wearing a white suit and pale Panama hat." And she felt awkward visiting Lady Ida's boudoir, with its mixed smell of cigarettes and tuberoses:

> It was full of novels, magazines, and large photographs of women in Edwardian evening dress . . . which stood about on little tables in silver frames, as was the fashion then. A bridge table was set out ready for players, and one always felt boredom was just round the corner with her; the day had to be filled up as best it could with bridge, talking, meals and jokes which were repeated many times in her lazy, rather random fashion.[14]

Later, in the garden with the boys, "the sound of the piano came out to us as we walked about in the sun; Edith was playing Chopin in the ballroom; later on she came out too, and we all sat on the rim of the fountain on the lawn, while she talked to us about Yeats, who was not well known then, and Swinburne."

Edith had paid tribute to both these poets. In 1964, the year of her death, she described her youthful escapade to visit Swinburne's grave in a letter to Judge and Mrs. H. C. Leon (the judge was the author "Henry Cecil"); she called it "the most romantic episode of my youth":

> I was staying in my grandmother Sitwell's house in Bournemouth, and at 6 o'clock in the morning, I ran away to visit Swinburne's grave in the Isle of Wight, taking with me a bunch of red roses, a laurel wreath, and a jug of milk; also my extremely disagreeable lady's maid. . . .
>
> When I returned to my grandmother's house there was, of course, a terrible fuss, and I found that (in my absence) a man called Losey and his wife had induced her to burn my volume of the 1st Swinburne *Poems and Ballads*, because these would corrupt my mind! (I hadn't the slightest idea of anything wrong in them.)[15]

Meanwhile Edith had poured her libation of milk onto the grave, much to the fury of the sexton, and left her roses. A little later, she also left roses on the doorstep of W. B. Yeats's house in London. At seventeen, she was a very romantic girl.

Edith met a real artist, a painter, that year. On her first grown-up visit to London, her cousin Mrs. George Swinton took her to tea with Walter Sickert. She was so shy "that my hands were glued to my sides." She told him she liked a picture of his, *La Vecchia*, which had been the cause of some controversy. Sickert said she must be either very clever, or mad—which was it? Mad, said Edith, mad. A few days later Sickert came to tea with Mrs. Swinton. He brought a drawing with him—for Edith. It was a drawing of four or five hatted women sitting in the back seats of a music hall. "Aunt Floss is such a fool about it," Edith wrote to Osbert. "She doesn't think it 'pretty'. . . . Church of England Saints are the only really suitable subjects for art. She says one ought not to have any character or individuality. It is the devil trying to get hold of one."[16] She brought the precious drawing back to Renishaw with her, where she and the schoolboy Osbert pored over it together.

A woman has two images. There is the magical person seen or remembered by those who love her, her finest qualities of flesh and spirit illuminated. She herself knows this ideal self; she projects it, if she is confident; or she daydreams her ideal self; or she recognizes it with gratitude in the admiring eyes of others. There is at the same time a second image: the woman as seen by those who dislike or fear her. This cruel picture has an all-too-powerful mirror in her own negative idea of herself. She sees with fear her own damaging impulses and, most painful of all, a graceless, freakish, unlovable physical self. This was the mirror her parents held before Edith. Her brothers saw her with love. She herself knew both images. Her life, and her poetry, constituted a flight from the second one.

There is a fanciful description Edith wrote late in life of herself as a girl—she is recalling, in imagination, herself and her Aunt Florence standing hesitantly outside a bookshop in Bath (where her grandmother Sitwell had a house in Royal Crescent):

> The younger maiden lady, then aged about eighteen, had the remote elegance and distinction of a very tall bird. Indeed, her gown had the feathery quality of a bird's raiment, and one would not have been sur-prised, at any moment, if she had preened her quills. She stood there, in the delicate leafless cold with her long thin legs poised upon the wet pavement, as some great bird stands in a pool. She had not the look of one who has many acquaintances—not more, perhaps, than a few leafless flowering boughs and blackthorn boughs, and the early and remote flakes of the snow. Her only neighbour was the silence, and her voice had more the sound of a wood-wind instrument than a human voice. She was plain and knew it.

Very romantic—until the six final abrasive monosyllables break the spell.

And there is in her unpublished novel-fragment a description of the "adopted" seventeen-year-old Lily which may also be taken as a dream image of Edith herself. She is describing a night of wind and tempest:

> Those tides ran in her blood, her nature was tempestuous as these, and changeable as water. In her black dress, with her slim body and her sudden silences, she might, indeed, have seemed one of the dark and mournful shadows that haunted the house, one of its presages of doom, had she not possessed this wild and living quality of ever-changing water,

with her light and glittering fleece of hair, her slanting eyes that were green and filled with light like the fountains in the caverns, her movements that were those of the proud and invincible waves. The tempests were there, but they were hidden under the summer peacefulness.

It was summer peacefulness that Sachie, ten years younger, saw in his tall sister. And with the peacefulness, the magic of words and music that she shared with him; and with the memory of the magic, later, came sadness, for life will fail to measure up to the promise of an August garden of childhood, where Edith is forever

a tall thin young woman in a pelisse of green sheepskin and a wide-brimmed hat, who walks between the hedges upon the smoother grass. She has long, thin hands and jet black rings and bracelets. She has sloping shoulders, and picks her way among the falling twigs. And from her shadow the wood leads on into poetry. For her love is poetry, she lives within a phrase. Look at her once more for there will never be her like again amongst women![17]

Before the adult world claimed Edith, and before she broke away from a home life that would have stifled her, she and her two younger brothers had formed an alliance of the imagination from which Edith and Sacheverell, at least, never departed: "We wrote in communion with one another and mine will always be the freedom of her world." Osbert, more prosaically, called the three of them "a closed corporation."

In 1924, ten years after she had left the enchanted garden—and her parents' troubles—by going to London, Edith published a poem in the *Spectator* which she dedicated to Osbert and Sacheverell. It is one of her most directly personal poems; it remembers their lost Eden:

But Dagobert and Peregrine and I
Were children then; we walked like shy gazelles
Among the music of the thin flower-bells.
And life still held some promise,—never ask
Of what,—but life seemed less a stranger, then,
Than ever after in this cold existence.
I always was a little outside life—
And so the things we touch could comfort me;

I loved the shy dreams we could hear and see—
For I was like one dead, like a small ghost,
A little cold air wandering and lost. . . .

The poem is called "Colonel Fantock"; the "old military ghost with mayfly whiskers" carries death with him. "Boasting of unseen unreal victories," he is Edith's companion in the garden:

All day within the sweet and ancient gardens
He had my childish self for audience—
Whose body flat and strange, whose pale straight hair
Made me appear as though I had been drowned—
(We all have the remote air of a legend). . . .

But no girl of marriageable age could be allowed to remain "outside life" forever. Edith was forced into society. She made a bad impression. At seventeen, dining with the Londesboroughs, she wore her first evening dress, made of white tulle: "With my face remorselessly 'softened' by my hair being frizzed and then pulled down over my nose, I resembled a caricature of the Fairy Queen in a pantomime."[18] Placed next to Lord Chaplin, she committed an enormous piece of bad form by enquiring whether he preferred Bach or Mozart. She went home in disgrace.

Even Helen's company involved her in social disasters. Helen, besides playing the piano, had ambitions as a singer. She was in request to sing at the houses of her friends, who, said Edith acidly, "became grander and grander." Edith used to go along as her accompanist, and at one country house she was introduced by Helen as "Miss Sitwell, who is to play for me":

The butler, obviously primed for this contingency, swept the star of the proceedings off to the drawing-room, while "Miss Sitwell" was asked to accompany him to a small room reserved for staff. Here her tea was served in solitary splendour, and she emerged only when called upon to take her place at the piano.

A more secure girl might have found nothing but mild humour in this reversal of social roles. But Edith, proud and nervous, took her revenge. After the performance, the hostess began to boast about an invitation she was hoping to receive from Lady Londesborough to a charity ball. "I shall see that my aunt invites you," Edith said graciously as she left. However much she despised the narrow snobbery of her mother's circle, she too, when at bay, could take refuge in being "grand."

Her father decided she should have a formal twenty-first birthday party. Her birthday in 1908 coincided roughly with the Doncaster Races in September; the two events were to be celebrated together. Preparations for the house party began eighteen months beforehand. The principal rooms in the house were redecorated. All curtains and stair carpets were taken up and cleaned. A second bathroom was installed. By the month before the party, the household was being driven frantic by Sir George. Osbert described the preparations:

> Chefs arrived. Enormous parcels were delivered every day from London. New linen was bought. All the silver plate, some of it unused for several years, was got out of the bank. Extra footmen appeared, and Major Viburne was called in to manage the whole thing as if it were an officer's mess. The running of special trains to Doncaster and back was arranged. . . . Motors were hired. A Blue Hungarian Band was engaged for ten days. . . . [19]

The party was allegedly for Edith. But of all the thirty or so people invited to stay in the house, only Veronica Codrington and an American boy brought along by someone else were of her generation. The other guests were elderly and ill-assorted; no one knew anyone else.

The Blue Hungarian Band came up every day from the Sitwell Arms in Renishaw village and played old-fashioned waltzes during every meal except breakfast. This continuous noise concealed conversational inadequacies. The visitors were ferried to and from the races as arranged. Edith, the birthday girl, loathed racing and expressed her loathing by keeping her back turned to the horses. Sir George disliked the races too; but Lady Ida enjoyed the "restless stir and activity," and of course the betting. Osbert and Sacheverell were kept in the background; they did not eat with the horde in the dining room but "feasted on scraps in our attic."

"*Très difficile*" was Sir George's verdict on his officially grown-up daughter. He regretted her lack of keenness at tennis. Lady Ida regretted her addiction to books. In an atmosphere of mingled triumph over the party and regret over their daughter, her parents took up their separate existences once more.

The years between eighteen and twenty-five, which are for most women the most vivid and varied of their lives, were for Edith cloistered and uneventful. Marriage, for most girls, was the only way out. But Edith did not marry. Almost no one in the neighbourhood of her home shared her musical and literary interests. Her father was a scholar, and little as she would like to admit it Edith had inherited much of his liking for strange information and the habit of books. But she was close only to her brothers and to Helen Rootham, who was no longer her governess but still came to stay. She lived in a protracted, indecisive adolescence, in a household made tense by her parents' incompatibility with each other and with her. She travelled with them, and sometimes with Helen; she played the piano; and she began to experiment with writing. Perhaps she fell in love; some thought that the first poem that she ever had published, "Drowned Suns," was a reflection of an abortive attachment:

The moon forever seeks in woodland streams
To deck her cool, faint beauty. Thus in dreams
Belov'd, I seek lost suns within your eyes,
And find but wrecks of love's lost argosies.

She had been "writing" in a sense for years; she would copy out into notebooks the poems she liked and the poems she was reading with Helen. When she was about twenty, she began to add her own poems to the notebooks. The notebook habit became the keystone of her working life. When she went to live in London she started using (and continued using to her last day, as did her brothers) large, stiff-covered folio notebooks, for drafts of letters, her poems, articles, prose writing, scraps of other people's writing that she wished to preserve. By the end of her life she had filled several hundred identical notebooks.

Her habit of painstaking copying out as a young girl also had its effect on her method of writing poetry. In the act of writing out, she composed her poems. Again and again and again she transcribed the same lines, with variations, changes of key or of direction, as if by the ritual of writing and repetition she would find the impetus to get a little further in the incantation. In those uneventful years before desperation, and Helen, forced her to leave home, she laid down her lifelong work patterns. But they were in a sense lost years; socially and emotionally she was, when she came to London, a good seven years younger than her chronological age—shy, innocent, totally inexperienced.

3

To Bayswater
1914–1918

Any 27, 127, 27A or 27C bus would put you out at the Royal Oak, Westbourne Grove; and halfway up Queen's Road, on the right hand side, you will find Moscow Road. This is *not* the rich Jewish red-brick block of flats, but the untidy, dingy, badly lighted block of flats just past the garage clock; and my name is on the board in the hall.

These were Edith's directions to Joe Ackerley about how to find her London home. The letter, inviting him to a party, was written in May 1926, some twelve years after she had moved in; but nothing much had changed about 22 Pembridge Mansions, or the Bayswater area of London, in that time.

The flat that Edith and Helen Rootham moved into in summer 1914, when Europe went to war, was on the fifth floor; there was no lift. They had very little money for interior decoration. The diamond locket Edith had been relying on to set them up did not materialize, though Sir George did let her have a diamond star, later in period and not entailed like most of the family diamonds. In any case, she preferred to rely on her own resources. "There were two sitting-rooms, and Osbert, poor as he was, gave us, whenever he came on leave from the front, beautiful hangings to enliven these. Helen's sitting-room was hung with green and silver, mine with red and gold." There was no room for a piano, a circumstance that put an end to Edith's hopes of becoming a professional pianist.

Her mother, in a semi-demented state at this time, made scenes about Edith moving to London, but subsequently wrote a "nice letter" and connived with Edith over getting some money out of Sir George. "You are a saint . . . you were a darling," Edith wrote to her mother—words which were heartfelt then as never before or after. (It is worth noting that she never seems to have shown her mother her hostile feelings; she hoped always perhaps for some miracle, that they might, after all, be a normal, affectionate mother and daughter.)

Sir George had not opposed his daughter's departure. Her mother's childlike extravagance had landed the family in public disgrace, which was about to fill the nation's headlines. According to Edith, her father wanted her out of the way "for fear that the scoundrels who had succeeded in enmeshing my mother might entrap me into telling a truth which would enable them to blackmail him." Be that as it may, it was the saving of Edith that she managed to escape from the now hysterical unhappiness at Renishaw and Wood End.

The trouble had been building up for some years. In 1909 Sir George had bought, in Osbert's name, an immense old castle in Italy, deep in the Tuscan countryside between Florence and Siena, its oldest part dating back to the eleventh century. Nearly three hundred people were living in it at the time, as if it were a village—peasant families pursuing their trades. The cleaning up, restoration, and beautification of Montegufoni henceforth absorbed some of Sir George's unchannelled energies. It was a never-ending project, since the place was, at the beginning, virtually uninhabitable as far as the Sitwells were concerned, and Osbert did not even see "his" new property for another three years.

Around the time of the purchase Sir George was bullying Edith in only a desultory way, considering just that in her he had drawn "a booby prize, an aquiline nose and a body inhabited by an alien and fiery spirit."[1] He did try to persuade her to go and work in a photographer's shop, whose bankrupt business he had taken over in cancellation of a bad debt. She declined. But it was Osbert who suffered most from their father's nagging and harrying in the years leading up to the Great War, and he was very unhappy. The atmosphere of impending doom both in the world and at home lay heavily on them all.

The detailed story of Lady Ida's financial catastrophe has been told elsewhere.[2] Briefly, she confided to Osbert in 1911 that she was more than £2,000 in debt. "Money had no meaning for her," he wrote later. "Further, she had reached an age when reason is apt to lose its sway." He must have meant the menopause—Lady Ida was in her mid-forties. Through an army friend of Osbert's, Lady Ida was put in touch with Julian Osgood Field, who involved her in complicated schemes of borrowing, covered by life insurance. Field, unknown to Lady Ida, was an undischarged bankrupt. He added the role of blackmailer to that of moneylender when Lady Ida was unable to repay the middlemen, plus interest, and Field's own large "expenses": He threatened to tell Sir George. Lady Ida borrowed more and more. Only a fraction of the amount borrowed ever actually reached her own purse. By July 1912 she was liable for debts approaching £12,000. Osbert, who had in his anxiety for her involved two of his brother officers in the plots and counterplots, was near breaking point.

Sir George had probably known what was going on at least from autumn 1912. He settled the debts owed to Osbert's friends, in any case; but he refused, when the truth was out, to pay off £6,000 that was owed to a man named Owles, for he knew that in this particular transaction Field could be proved to have acted illegally. Sir George retained Sir George Lewis to represent him in the impending court actions.

At Renishaw, Lady Ida lived in a state of collapse. She attended to nothing in the house. She lay in bed all day, and drank too much, and railed at her husband and children. Osbert went back to his regiment. Sacheverell, when on holiday from Eton, was shattered by what he found at home. The perpetual duality of the Sitwells' family life—the contrast between the graceful appearances and the black terror that lay beneath, which had characterized Edith's childhood—was now accentuated and made real. The nightmares were all true. Edith was at home more than the boys; she bore the brunt, not of her mother's confidences, but of her mother's loss of control and her parents' violent quarrels.

She hardened her heart. The alternative was, for her also, despair and collapse. Helen encouraged her in the growing knowledge that she must not sacrifice her life and sanity—she was nearly twenty-five already when Lady Ida's first lawsuit was heard in spring 1913—to her impossible, unhappy parents. She disassociated herself as best she could, even while she was still with them. Osbert recalled an afternoon during the worst of the troubles when an air of determined normality reigned. "Helen was playing Debussy in the ballroom; Edith was in her bedroom copying into her notebook a passage from Baudelaire and trying in general to avoid the trivialities of the day."[3]

Edith, in self-protection, was to feel no sympathy for her parents. The series of lawsuits and their culmination became mixed in her mind with the horrors of the war which broke out the summer she went to London. The "sordid" family tragedy seemed "a dwarfish imitation of the universe of mud and flies" to which Osbert, in the Grenadier Guards, was condemned. On the day before he left for the front, Osbert had tea with Edith at Pembridge Mansions. Their mother, with a misplaced access of affection, rushed in, having just got off the train, carrying a heavy piece of shell from the bombardment of Scarborough the previous night. She told her son she had brought it for him to take to France. "I'm sure it'll bring you luck."

Edith thought her parents did not really know what suffering was:

My mother . . . knew fear, otherwise she and my father knew nothing, felt nothing excepting their wish to escape from the results of that which she had, out of sheer stupidity, done. Their lives were completely atrophied. All *she* wanted was to return to her silly daily life of bridge and watching the golfers on the golf-course. All he wanted was to study the habits of the dwellers in Nottingham in the fourteenth century, and spend a great deal more money on building houses on unliveable spots, which would cause him, in the future, as he told me, to be known as "the great Sir George."

In November 1914, at a one-day hearing, judgment had been passed against Field. But Owles's heirs (he had died) and others were still agitating to be paid. Sir George Sitwell considered that Field, now proved criminal, and not the Sitwells, was liable. The final hearing was at the Old Bailey in March 1915. It was all over the papers—in the *Daily Mirror* and the *News of the World*. Edith's revulsion was complete when she understood—rightly or wrongly— that Lady Ida, in desperation, pleaded that all her troubles were the result of her wish to pay off her son Osbert's debts. Because of the involvement of his fellow subalterns, Osbert had to be in court and sit through it all.

Lady Ida, unthinkably, was sentenced to three months in prison. "I can only say," said the judge, "that if it were not for the state of your health it would be a more severe sentence." She was taken to Holloway. The three children—Sacheverell came home from Eton—went back with their father to Renishaw. Sir George could have prevented this disaster for his wife and family, by paying off the debt; whether from principle or for some other reason, he did not do so. He did not talk about what had happened. His children could not talk about it either, at least not to him. From now on, they trusted only each other. The pseudo-normality of Renishaw in the spring of 1915, with the mother absent and the unspoken lying heavily on the air, can only be imagined. Edith has not described it, though she described how, rather later, she was placed next to the famous Mr. Justice Darling at a dinner party: "I suppose they had forgotten, or didn't know," she said, "that he was the judge whom my mother had appeared before."

Her mother's disgrace and imprisonment released Edith psychologically.

These events coincided not only with her setting up her own establishment, but with the first publication of her poetry. The very first poem in print, "Drowned Suns," appeared in the *Daily Mirror* in March 1913, around the time of Lady Ida's first lawsuit. The *Daily Mirror* was not then such an extraordinary place for a serious young poet to appear in as it might seem today; not only did it have a particularly lively literary editor, Richard Jennings, but, as Peter Quennell has written, "Poetry then [he is referring to a few years later] was still 'news'; and that it existed, and might occasionally be worth discussing, was a fact reluctantly acknowledged by the toughest Fleet Street editors."[4] Jennings took five poems from Edith during 1913; one of them, "Serenade," is the first poem of her *Collected Poems* of 1957. He took two more in January 1914 and four in 1915, three of which appeared during the months that Lady Ida was in Holloway. Edith did not include many of these early successes in her final *Collected Poems*. Nor did she include much from *The Mother*, her very first book, a twenty-five-page volume which Blackwell's of Oxford published, at the author's expense, in October 1915; five hundred copies were printed, to be sold at 6d. each. It was well reviewed in the *Times* and the *Daily Mail*. The "mother" of the title poem was, those close to her understood, the ideal mother she would have liked and did not have. (As she grew older, the loving, earthy, self-immolating mother who loses her child became a key figure in her imagination and in her writing.) But "The Mother" is also a highly melodramatic poem of matricide: Her son kills her for her money, which he needs for the woman he lusts after—*eros* drives out *agape*. The mother's ghost takes all the blame on herself:

> He did no sin. But cold blind earth
> The body was that gave him birth.
> All mine, all mine, the sin: the love
> I bore him was not deep enough.

The failure of love and fantasies about murder, usually of older women, preoccupied Edith from girlhood onwards. The first she put into her poetry; but murder became, after her first writing years, a fantasy that surfaced in times of anger, depression, or boredom, expressed sometimes in nightmare terms and sometimes humorously. It is not hard to see how the fantasy arose.

In June 1916 Edith sent Jennings a copy of *Twentieth Century Harlequinade*, twenty-eight pages of poems by herself and Osbert that had been published for them by Blackwell in an edition of five hundred. She went on to ask Jennings to come to a poetry reading at Pembridge Mansions: "Sachie is coming up from Eton: and we have got a young poet of great promise coming; he is only nineteen, but the reviews of his poems (published while he was still at Eton) were really splendid." This was Victor Perowne; precocious young men were already becoming a source of interest and pleasure to Edith. The programme for the evening was five poems, to be read without giving the authors' names; "then we guess who wrote them." Edith added, airily and in conformity with her current preoccupations, "If you could slip in one on the filial affections, or parricide, it would be most welcome."

In one more year she had emerged from vanity publishing to the real thing. She had sent a group of poems to Jennings in late 1916, which he had offered to ask Elkin Matthews to publish. He would do so—if she paid for it. She was able to write to Matthews in January 1917, "I do not want to pay for my book"; she asked him to return the manuscripts. "I have found a publisher for them." Triumphantly she told Jennings that she had "scored off the gentleman, leaving him breathless with surprise." Blackwell published her *Clowns' Houses* the following year. And by that time she was already working on the third number of *Wheels*, a literary anthology of which she was editor, and which had received a great deal of notice.

"There is poetry, and there is the 'poetry scene,'" Donald Davie has written:

> Poetry is highly respectable; the poetry scene isn't. Poets bitching at other poets, rivalries and jealousies, intrigues and connivings, competition in the popularity stakes, the how and why of some reputations being advanced as others are diminished by malice or calculated indifference—this is the poetry scene, and a very squalid scene it is, and no wonder that fastidious readers of poetry shudder at it, and pretend it doesn't exist. It does, though; and because every poet that ever was wants to be known and loved by his fellow mortals in his own lifetime, the poetry scene is where the poet lives for most of the time when he isn't writing poems. A poet's admirers may ignore the poetry scene; the poet himself can't afford to.[5]

Davie was writing in 1978; but his remarks are even truer in regard to sixty years earlier, because the literary world was smaller and tighter. Edith had all the temperament and talent necessary to become an active participant in the "poetry scene"; but her rapid rise was phenomenal. When she came to Pembridge Mansions she was unknown; within a very few years she was a well-known and controversial figure.

Edith's inexperience stood her in good stead. In her abnormal mental isolation at home, Shakespeare, Keats, Shelley, the great figures of literature, were her companions. She had no experience or even knowledge of the seedy, envious undergrowth of the London literary world, where aspiring writers circled nervously seeking a foothold. A complete outsider, such as Edith was, can very often cut through the undergrowth without perceiving it and find himself somewhere near the centre of interest and attention. She was simultaneously extremely unworldly and extremely ambitious, as only those who have led lonely, pent-up lives can be.

She also had a very clear idea of the sort of poetry she wanted to write, and here, in her middle twenties and coming from far outside the world of the mood-making and mode-making intelligentsia, Edith was completely in tune with the decade that was coming—the 1920s. The time and the place and the person coincided. Although she complained all her life about her treatment from British critics, her work was reviewed widely from the very beginning. After years of isolation and loneliness, she was in her element. She soon learnt the rules of the game.

The "poetry scene," when Edith came to London, was dominated by the short-lived empire of the Georgian poets. In 1911, when Edward Marsh edited and published his first anthology of *Georgian Poetry*—thus giving a name to the genre—his new poets seemed to many like a breath of fresh air. T. S. Eliot wrote in 1954 that "the situation in poetry in 1909 or 1910 was stagnant to a degree difficult for any poet of today to conceive."[6] The great Victorians—Tennyson, Swinburne, Meredith, Kipling—were dead, dying, or doting. Yeats published a *Collected Poems* in 1909, but he was born in the same year as Kipling. Eliot was working on "The Love Song of J. Alfred Prufrock" and getting to know Ezra Pound and Wyndham Lewis. But in the years that followed, it was Marsh's Georgian poets who were bought and read.

There were five volumes of *Georgian Poetry* between 1911 and 1922; the first sold 15,000 copies, the second 19,000, the third 16,000—only Rupert Brooke and John Masefield sold more. After the third issue, the decline began.[7]

Georgian Poetry is a portmanteau term which embraces poets who would hardly be considered together had they not all met between the hard covers of Marsh's anthologies. They included, at various times, Walter de la Mare, Rupert Brooke, Edmund Blunden, W. H. Davies, John Drinkwater, James Elroy Flecker, Robert Graves, Ralph Hodgson, Richard Hughes, D. H. Lawrence, John Masefield, Peter Quennell, Isaac Rosenberg, Siegfried Sassoon, Vita Sackville-West, Edward Shanks, J. C. Squire, James Stephens, Francis Brett Young, John Freeman, Maurice Baring, Lascelles Abercrombie, Harold Monro. Not every one of these was a good poet. But no "movement" that could contain such names can possibly be considered futile. Some of the best poets' best poems first appeared in *Georgian Poetry*.

The point is that the good poetry published in *Georgian Poetry* was very much more interesting than the poetic ideals of Edward Marsh and J. C. Squire, the two most powerful patrons of the group. Marsh believed in conventional metrics and total intelligibility; he and Squire favoured "realism," an optimistic Englishness, rural subjects, everyday speech patterns. Georgian poetry, as Alan Pryce-Jones has written, was in the English watercolour tradition. Both Marsh and Squire were anti-"highbrow," and were beguiled by homely thoughts in verse about dogs, moonlight, country walks, games, and, of course, romantic love. Squire, who edited the *London Mercury* from 1919, could not be bothered with something like Eliot's "The Waste Land," which he "could not make head or tail of." Squire aimed in the *Mercury* to distinguish between "the sincere and the pretentious, the intelligent and the stupid, the healthy and the vicious, the promising and the sterile." Cricket-loving and idle, he was very nearly as philistine as a man of letters can be. He was also the most generous of men, and a humourist.

The Georgian ideal claimed to have no truck with (as Harold Monro put it, in a statement of aims of his Poetry Bookshop in Devonshire Street, off Theobald's Road) "formalism, pose, affectation, inflation, and all kinds of false tradition." Edith's riposte to this, in *Aspects of Modern Poetry* (1934), was: "To these men rhetoric and formalism were abhorrent, partly, no doubt, because to manage either quality in verse, the writer must have a certain gift for poetry." The Georgian breath of fresh air was, to their detractors, nothing but a nineteenth-century hangover. Rebecca West, writing in the *New Freewoman* of August 15, 1913, said that "from the beautiful stark bride of Blake [poetry] has become the idle hussy hung with the ornaments kept by Lord Tennyson . . . now supported at Devonshire Street by the Georgian School."

Edith and her brothers were equally scornful. They were personally very friendly with a great many of the contributors to *Georgian Poetry*, and did not underestimate the stature of the individual poets; there was even a question of Edith herself being included in the fourth number. Marsh wanted a woman poet in, and Edward Shanks and Siegfried Sassoon put up her name; but she was rejected, and Fredegond Shove became the statutory woman contributor for the volume. Marsh knew who his enemies were.

It was the "Squirearchy" at the *London Mercury* to which Edith came to raise her strongest objections. Her most reasoned argument against Georgian poetry, and for modernist poetry, is in her Hogarth Essay of 1925, *Poetry and Criticism*: The modernists, among whom she included herself, were "leaving the tradition that leads from Wordsworth. . . . Most of the poets labelled Georgian are still writing in the manner and from the point of view which has prevailed since Wordsworth." Wordsworth, she said, had "brought the language of ordinary speech, the actions of common life, into poetry. . . ." But the process had gone too far. "It is therefore time that we returned to an earlier tradition in poetry, and left the peasant and words suitable to the peasant." If one examined the "new," anti-Georgian poetry, one found in it "much of the great tradition leading from the Elizabethans." Elsewhere and later, she was much ruder about the Georgians. In *Aspects of Modern Poetry*, for example: "Birds became a cult. Any mention of the nest of a singing bird threw the community into a frenzy. Dreary plaster-faced sheep with Alexandra fringes and eyes like the eyes of minor German royalties, limpid, wondering, disapproving, uncomprehending, these were admired, as were bulldogs weeping tears of blood."

Osbert had a little to do with Edith's success, at least as far as social contacts were concerned. He too was blooming in London, away from his father. Many of his literary friendships were made through Robert Ross, Oscar Wilde's old friend, by now and until his death in 1918 a great patron of the charming and talented young, whom he entertained at his rooms in Half Moon Street. Through Ross, Osbert met the snobbish, erudite Sir Edmund Gosse, the most influential man of letters of the time, over lunch at the Reform Club. Osbert, whether his own Wildean inclinations were already apparent or not, was a favourite of these aging literati. Gosse became particularly fond of Edith as well, though she said that dining at the Gosses' at Hanover Terrace was "pleasure not unmixed with terror, for one could never foresee exactly what Sir Edmund was going to do to one conversationally." Edith was poorly equipped for social small talk; once when she was struggling with a silent Swedish poet, Gosse said: "Don't stand there looking so dull and awkward, Edie. You make me feel quite cross and naughty."

Edith, about four years old.

Renishaw Hall

Edith, aged eleven, with Osbert, baby Sacheverell,
and their nurse, Davis.

Design for *Wheels* by Severini, 1920.

Edith (center, with dog) at her art class in Scarborough.

Edith photographed by Cecil Beaton against one of the Renishaw tapestries.

Portrait of Edith by C.R.W. Nevinson, early 1920s.

The Sitwells in Carlyle Square by Cecil Beaton.

Studio portrait of Edith in the early 1920s.

One of Cecil Beaton's early experiments with the Sitwells, c. 1926.

Wyndham Lewis with his portrait of T.S. Eliot, 1938.

Edith at 22 Pembridge Mansions, 1928. Note the ragged upholstery, missing doorknob, etc.

Tchelitchew, Edith, and Allen Tanner at Guermantes, 1929.

Pavel Tchelitchew at work.

Edith at 22 Pembridge Mansions, c. 1930, with pictures by Tchelitchew on the wall.

Montegufoni, the Sitwells' *castello* in Italy.

Edith at Guermantes, 1932.

The Sitwells at Renishaw, c. 1930, by Cecil Beaton: Sacheverell, Sir George, Georgia, Reresby, Lady Ida, Edith, Osbert.

Edith and Sir Osbert in New York, 1948.

Sacheverell Sitwell in the early 1930s.

Front left: William Rose Benet; behind h
Richard Eberhart, Gore Vidal, José Garcia V
Randall Jar

The Gotham Book Mart party, New York, 1948.

...phen Spender; behind him: Mr. and Mrs. Horace Gregory; behind Osbert and Edith (left to right): Tennessee Williams,
...the steps: W.H. Auden; standing in front of him: Elizabeth Bishop; seated in front of her: Marianne Moore; extreme right:
...ront of him: Delmore Schwartz; crosslegged in the center: Charles Henri Ford.

Edith as Lady Macbeth, New York, 1950.

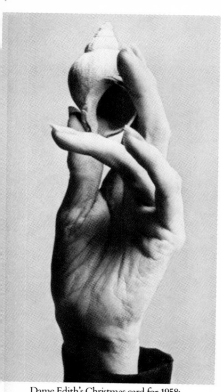

Dame Edith's Christmas card for 1958: her left hand.

Sir Osbert at Renishaw in the late 1950s.

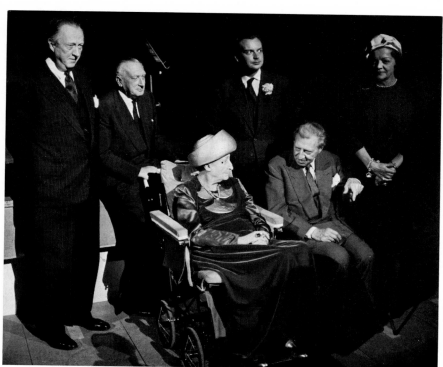

Dame Edith rehearsing for her Memorial Concert at the Royal Festival Hall in 1962: with her are (left to right) Sacheverell Sitwell, Sir William Walton, Francis Sitwell, Sir Osbert, Georgia Sitwell.

"Of course one wants the people one cares for to see one—not humiliated, but beautiful and noble, which is what one really is."

Parker the parlour maid ruled the ménage, in tandem with the gentle and accommodating Lady Gosse; and guests who displeased Parker—such as Wyndham Lewis and Ezra Pound—tended to be rejected by Gosse. Parker made a great impression on Edith's behalf one evening during the war. Edith and Osbert were both bidden to dinner, and Edith was late. Osbert and his hosts sat and waited, while falling bombs and wailing maroons filled the night air outside. Finally Parker appeared and delivered a message from Edith: "Miss Sitwell has telephoned. She sends her compliments, but says she refuses to be an Aunt Sally for the Germans, and she is not coming to dinner."[8]

Gosse appreciated rather than resented this sort of treatment. It was after a Sunday luncheon at Hanover Terrace that he saw all three Sitwells to the front door, "calling after us into the blue dusk, 'Goodbye, you delightful but deleterious trio!,' and waved after us a dapper hand." Of Edith, Gosse wrote to Siegfried Sassoon: "I feel that she is a sort of chrysalis, in a silken web of imperfection, with great talents to display, if only she can break out into a clear music of her own. There is no one I watch with more interest, and her personal beauty and dignity, which are even pathetic, attract me very much."[9]

Osbert, the cultivated guardsman, was as popular with society hostesses as he was with bachelor hosts—attentive, entertaining, and reliable as a guest, something of a "tame cat" even as a very young man. Where he went, his sister and brother were very soon added to the guest list. Edith did not take the same pleasure in the life of society that Osbert did. She was happier in her own, less formal circle. But partly because she did not fit in, and was so unlike other women of her age and class, she attracted attention wherever she went.

Edith enjoyed the literary evenings of Lady Colvin at Palace Gardens Terrace. She was the wife of Sir Sidney Colvin, keeper of prints and drawings at the British Museum; she had been a Miss Sitwell, and a close friend of Robert Louis Stevenson. Edith also went to Sir Herbert and Lady Tree's house in All Souls Place, and to Mrs. Keppel's in Grosvenor Street. Mrs. Keppel, King Edward VII's erstwhile mistress, when consulted once by Edith's parents about what should be done with the graceless girl, had replied: "George and Ida, always remember that you never know what a young girl may become." "She has always been so kind to me," Edith wrote in 1931, "for no reason, just out of sheer niceness."

There was also the family, increasingly avoided. Christmas and the month of August were regularly spent at Renishaw by all three young Sitwells; but when her parents came to London, Edith was frequently found to be "away." Edith's mother, who had behaved in an even more hostile and unloving manner towards her daughter than ever in the fearful months before her imprisonment, was afterwards pathetically conciliatory. She wanted Edith with her all the time. Edith was not prepared to give in totally; but if she did not meet her mother halfway, at least she took a few steps towards her. Lady Ida became "touchingly reconciled to me," Edith wrote. "Suddenly she forgave me for my existence." And one night after the horror of Holloway was over, at Renishaw, when they were both in bed in their adjoining rooms, her mother called out:

> "Edith, have you ever been happy?"
> "Yes, Mother," I answered. "Haven't you?"
> "Never *bird*-happy," she replied. "Still, I have three very nice children."
> Then, sighing, she went to sleep again.

This exchange in the dark makes it possible to see Lady Ida as her loving sons saw her.

There were gloomy evenings for her "three very nice children" with their relation the Archbishop of Canterbury at Lambeth Palace, and a variety of elderly aunts and cousins in London requesting duty visits. Chief among these was Great-Aunt Blanche Sitwell, who lived in Egerton Terrace off the Brompton Road. She specialized in bringing all the disparate members of the scattered family together (even though she was not on speaking terms with her nephew Sir George). Her reunions were effective. Writing in 1920, Constance Chetwynd-Talbot, who had become the second wife of William Henry Sitwell of Barmoor Castle in Northumberland, called at Pembridge Mansions to see Edith, "who annoyed me slightly. There seemed to be a rather silly self-conscious atmosphere in her flat." A few days later Constance met Edith again, at Aunt Blanche's, "and felt for her as of old." Edith was talking on this occasion about Jacob Epstein, "and said how dirty his house was when she went to see him, with the food and clothes all mixed up together on the bed. She thought his wife was rather messy, too."[10]

Edith did not always cooperate by "being nice" to the relations to be met at Great-Aunt Blanche's. Osbert recorded one afternoon there when an old lady was announced whom Edith could not face. Osbert and Sacheverell seized a luckily very loose slipcover off a chair, put their sister inside it, and carried their angular bundle downstairs. They passed the incoming visitor on the stairs, and explained that "one leg of the chair was unsteady," and that their aunt had asked them to remove it. Edith, slipcovered, was safely deposited at the front door.

When Sacheverell left Eton, he, like Osbert, briefly joined the Grenadier Guards. They shared a house, first in Swan Walk, then in Carlyle Square in Chelsea—number 2, on the corner of the King's Road. All the young Sitwells entertained, but in very different styles. For Edith and Helen in Pembridge Mansions it was a simple matter of regular Saturday tea parties in their two small sitting rooms, with strong black Indian tea in a kitchen teapot and buns "to which a heavy coating of white-of-egg had given the lustre of antique glazed pottery," according to Peter Quennell. Osbert described the "extraordinary mixture" of people at these Saturday teas: "relatives, old friends of my mother's, scared but tittering, who had never hitherto heard even the name of a poet, famous poets, school-teachers, the most advanced musicians and painters, hunting men, doctors, philosophers, zoologists, economists, and one or two persons who seemed to exist for no other reason than that my sister was sorry for them." He loyally claimed that her halfpenny buns seemed to have retained "the taste and luscious quality of the buns one ate as a child."[11] But when Osbert and Sacheverell came to the Saturday teas, they did not stay very long. "How are *you*?" they would enquire, and "How are *you*?," "circling rapidly round the room, and as rapidly shaking hands," as Peter Quennell observed. "Bayswater was not their natural habitat."[12] Then they embraced their sister and hurried off down the stairs.

Edith and Helen could only afford a woman to clean the flat; Osbert and Sacheverell had a devoted housekeeper who was also a fine cook. Osbert gave dinner parties, and Edith came to many of them; it was in the dining room at Carlyle Square that W. H. Davies looked at her and pronounced in his Welsh voice that "Edith is always as fine as a queen." Osbert, still in his very early twenties, had great style. The dining room in Carlyle Square was dark, and so, he said, he had tried to accentuate its subterranean air. "With its rich blue and silver tapestry wall-coverings, its shells, and its shell and dolphin furniture, the room resembled a grotto under the sea." The top of the marble dining table came from a monumental mason's yard. "Taking at random the names of friends who have sat round its soft gold and peach-coloured surface, it would murmur, Arnold Bennett, W. H. Davies, Maurice Ravel, Maynard Keynes, Lydia Lopokova, Walter Sickert, Clive Bell, Roger Fry, Virginia Woolf, Leonide Massine, George Gershwin, Harold Acton, Arthur Waley, T. S. Eliot . . . ," Osbert wrote in his old age, gracefully letting the table do his name dropping for him.[13]

Bloomsbury became aware of the Sitwells in 1918, with the ending of the war, when Diaghilev's Ballets Russes were in London; before the war Osbert and Sacheverell had been wildly enthusiastic about what they had seen (which included Cocteau's *Parade*). On the return tour Osbert invited Diaghilev and two of his principal dancers, Massine and Lydia Lopokova, to Swan Walk (the move to Carlyle Square took place the following year). The night of the party happened to coincide with the Armistice celebrations. Virginia Woolf had that very day had a piece on recent poetry published (anonymously) in *The Times Literary Supplement* which included Edith's *Clowns' Houses*; she had also just been introduced to Edith's brothers, who had asked her to come to their party to meet the Russians.

She came, bringing with her Roger Fry, her sister Vanessa, and Maynard Keynes. This constellation of coincidences had consequences for Keynes who, meeting Lopokova for the first time with the Sitwells, fell in love with her, and later married her. And the Sitwells, in their happy position as hosts to the stars, took on Bloomsbury from a position of strength. "It's strange how whole groups of people suddenly swim complete into one's life," Virginia Woolf wrote in her diary after the party. It was an emotional evening, ending up with them all at the Adelphi at an Armistice party given by Montague Shearman; Lytton Strachey was there, dancing, and Lady Ottoline Morrell, and the D. H. Lawrences. The end of the war: "It has made one's nerve go all to pieces, this sudden relief from the intolerable pain," Edith wrote to Robert Nichols. "I cried and cried and cried."

Virginia Woolf also wrote in her diary her first impressions of Edith on that evening: "Edith Sitwell is a very tall young woman, wearing a perpetually startled expression, & curiously finished off with a high green silk headdress, concealing her hair, so that it is not known whether she has any."[14] She said to Edith at the dinner party, "Why do you live where you do?" "Because I have not much money." "How much money a year do you have?" Edith told her. "Oh well, I think we can do better for you than that," said Mrs. Woolf. But nothing came of that project, said Edith, who recorded this interchange, "and I remained in Bayswater." Edith admired Mrs. Woolf's "moonlit transparent beauty," and liked her company, but knew that she was not destined to become part of Bloomsbury. "I was not an unfriendly young woman, but I was shy, and yet, at unexpected moments, not silent—and silence was much prized, sometimes to the embarrassment of persons outside the inner circle of Bloomsbury." She only entered Bloomsbury "on sufferance," she thought.

Virginia Woolf thought Edith's appearance was singular enough to be worth comment; and indeed it was, deliberately. "I suppose I was always rather odd to look at, from a conventional point of view." The fashions for women before the Great War, with their plump and curvaceous outlines, were difficult for her tall, thin frame to adapt to; postwar, as skirts grew shorter and silhouettes both flatter and more revealing, and Edith moved into her thirties, she clung to her long skirts. She ignored the fashion, and evolved a style that was unique to herself.

The appearance she devised was a realization of her dream-self; it was also the reverse of what her parents thought a nice "gell" ought to look like. It was an act of defiance against her upbringing and an act of faith in herself. "If one is a greyhound, why try to look like a Pekingese?" was her opinion. "I am as stylized as it is possible to be—as stylized as the music of Debussy or Ravel."

She claimed to be the first person to paint her nails silver or mother-of-pearl; she wore huge bracelets, necklaces, and rings of jet and ivory. In the evening she wore sweeping dresses in velvet or brocade, and in the daytime "woollen dresses with the narrow bodice, long, flowing skirts, and wide sleeves reminiscent of the gown of an abbess."[15] She accentuated her own uncontemporary looks, and presented herself in her own image.

Necessarily her appearance caused comment. Nearly all the people who recorded their visits to Pembridge Mansions mention what their hostess was wearing. The sometimes disapproving Constance Sitwell found Edith one teatime in 1920 "dressed in black with a chintz pinafore, and wearing a red turban." Headgear was an important part of Edith's costume whether by day or night: Her hair was greenish-pale, thin, and straight. When she first came to London she wore it in a big loose bun, with the sides cut short, curving wispily round her face. In the early 1920s she had it bobbed. Hats dealt with the hair problem and suited her strong, bony face.

It was Osbert, who had provided the "hangings" in rich colours for Edith's flat, who had shrewdly advised his sister to create her own appearance with the same sort of material: no "frills round the neck" for someone with Edith's stark Plantagenet looks. Osbert said that by 1919 they were all three sufficiently well known for people to turn round and look at them in the street. Edith's appearance, as well as her fame, attracted attention. Sitting for her portrait for Roger Fry in 1918, "I wore a green evening dress, the colour of the leaves of lilies, and my appearance in this, in the full glare of the midsummer light of midday, in Fitzroy Square, together with the appearance of Mr. Fry, his bushy, long grey hair floating from under an enormous black sombrero, caused great joy to the children of the district . . . ." Edith was painted a great many times, by a great many artists—witnesses to the power and fascination of her appearance and personality, for the two were indivisible.

4
Wheels Within Wheels
1916–1922

One of the pleasures of Edith's lonely girlhood had been the initiation of her younger brothers into the world of the imagination—fairy stories, music, and poetry. Sacheverell's testimony to her influence needs no further underlining. Osbert was nearer her in age, and a not unforceful personality. Yet he too, in his late teens, as a young officer in the Brigade of Guards, still took Edith as his mentor. She was "my chief adviser on what to read, and poetry was . . . her most cherished form of literature." Osbert began to write poetry seriously—and satirically—as a young soldier in the war in France; but at fifteen he had written a "lurid oriental fantasy." "My sister listened with patience to the reams of blank verse—blanker than the author knew—and praised it with moderation, and after discreetly allowing a certain time to pass, for poet's pride to cool in, tactfully pointed out a fault or two, and finally after a month had elapsed, hinted I might like to burn it." This she did "gently and with such grace" that the boy was not offended.

As each brother reached his twenties he became Edith's ally rather than her pupil; her concern took the form of championing their work—especially Sacheverell's, since he had less inclination to do the job himself—both in private and public. There was a strong streak of the old-fashioned "patron of the arts" in all the Sitwells. After Osbert saw the Ballets Russes' *L'Oiseau de feu* in 1912 he decided, young as he was, "Now I knew where I stood. I would be, for so long as I lived, on the side of the arts. . . . I would support the artist in every controversy, on every occasion."[1]

The first major practical results of this resolution were the exhibition of modern art that he and Sacheverell helped to organize at Heal's in 1919, and the "adoption" of William Walton. (In the same year Osbert, at the age of twenty-five, made a bid for public life—he stood as the Liberal candidate for Scarborough. "He did not 'get in,' " Edith wrote to Robert Nichols. "I suppose they found out he is a poet.") Some of the Sitwells' critics—notably Geoffrey Grigson—have been of the opinion that it was as patrons that they shone, and they should have remained in that role—which is one way of denigrating their writing.

However, this liking for patronage of promising young artists was strong in Edith; she took pleasure in encouraging young (male) poets and fostering young (male) talent. Perhaps she was recapturing the happiness she had had with Sachie, reading poetry to him on summer afternoons at Renishaw. There was something generous and openhearted in her encouragement, and something possessive. Because it came from some strong need in her own personality, it could sometimes seem disingenuous and exaggerated; but Edith, who had had no deep relationship with any man, was in these ways completely ingenuous. She was maternal, and in the years after she first came to London, she was at the age when most women are teaching their children to talk and to read. And then, the company of intelligent young men is so very pleasant.

All her life Edith was to give young people encouragement, criticism, and confidence—sometimes too much confidence—in their own powers. Sometimes her encouragement was misplaced. Some of the talents she uncovered failed to catch fire; some burnt briefly with a false brilliance; some would have made it with or without her help. Her partisan championship of poets and artists—certain poets and certain artists—reinforced her tendency to divide the world into friends and enemies.

One of the first young men she took up was the soldier-poet Robert Nichols, who was shell-shocked after only a few weeks' service in the front line and invalided out in 1916. She met him in December 1917, on the same occasion that she and her brothers first met T. S. Eliot. This was a charity poetry reading at the South Kensington house of Lady Colefax, and Sir Edmund Gosse (who admired the young, voluble, romantic-looking Robert Nichols even more than he admired Osbert) was in the chair. The readers were Nichols, Aldous Huxley, Viola Tree, the three Sitwells, Irene Rutherford McLeod (who read poems by Siegfried Sassoon), and T. S. Eliot.

Eliot arrived late and in checked trousers, and was publicly rebuked by Gosse. Eliot could not help it; he had been kept late at Lloyds Bank in Queen Victoria Street, where he was employed to write abstracts of foreign-language newspapers. The poem he read, finally, was his "Hippopotamus." Huxley wrote a spirited account of the evening to his brother Julian once he got back to Eton, where he was teaching:

Gosse in the chair—the bloodiest little old man I have ever seen—dear Robbie Ross stage-managing, Bob Nichols thrusting himself to the fore as the leader of us young bards—(*bards* was the sort of thing Gosse called us)—then myself, Viola Tree, a girl called McLeod and troops of Shufflebottoms, alias Sitwells bringing up the rear: last and best, Eliot. But oh— what a performance: Eliot and I were the only people who had any dignity: Bob Nichols raved and screamed and hooted and moaned his filthy war poems like a Lyceum villain who hasn't learnt how to act: Viola Tree declaimed in a voice so syrupy and fruity and rich, that one felt quite cloyed and sick by two lines: the Shufflebottoms were respectable but terribly nervous. . . . The best part of the affair was dinner at the Sitwells' afterwards, when . . . we all got tight to just the right extent. . . .[2]

The Sitwells were not too nervous to follow up the evening in their characteristic ways. Lady Colefax was soon dining with Osbert; and Edith got to know the handsome Robert Nichols. He did not really need her support; he was already, however temporarily, "in." But Edith, by now involved in the periodical anthology *Wheels*, had something other than purely moral support to offer her literary protégés.

Wheels was connected in the public mind entirely with Edith, as its editor, but Nancy Cunard was equally involved at the beginning. Indeed Nina Hamnett, artist and mistress of artists, believed that Nancy had started it, and that "three young poets called Sitwell" wrote for it.[3] Nina Hamnett, who described herself at a Sitwell party as a "dissipated Bacchante," and whom Edith thought "one of the most generous people I know," met all the Sitwells during the war. These friendships were made in 1916–1917; Nina Hamnett lived in Fitzroy Street, and so did Edith's old friend Walter Sickert; she took Osbert to tea with him, and the painter became a regular guest at Carlyle Square. And Osbert took Edith to see W. H. Davies, who lived in one room in Great Russell Street. Wooden leg notwithstanding, Davies would walk all the way from Great Russell Street to Bayswater for Edith's parties. They all met and grew fond of Arthur Waley, poet and scholar, "alert under an aloof and impassive manner," as Osbert described him, whose translations *170 Chinese Poems* were published in 1918.

Edith did not like all her brothers' friends—not, for example, Christabel McLaren (Lady Aberconway from 1934, when her husband Henry McLaren succeded to the title). Not for nothing was Christabel the daughter of a former chief of Scotland Yard—she was a gossip, a tale bearer, and a troublemaker. Since Christabel McLaren was Osbert's friend and ally, she was hard for Edith and Sacheverell to avoid. She "recurs like onions," wrote Edith many years later.

Christabel McLaren, as well as Nina Hamnett and that other "dissipated Bacchante," Nancy Cunard—sexy, vital, unpredictable, with great aquamarine eyes—were a new sort of friend for Edith, who was inexperienced and naive in areas in which they were wise. Nina painted Edith in a rainbow jacket; the picture was exhibited at the National Portrait Society's exhibition at the Grosvenor Gallery, and the *Tatler* commented on the "kaleidoscopic breasts." Edith was having notoriety thrust upon her. She did not mind at all.

But it was the other, nunlike Edith who visited Robert Graves and his first wife near Oxford: "It was a surprise, after reading her poems, to find her gentle, domesticated, and even devout. When she came to stay with us, she spent her time sitting on the sofa and hemming handkerchiefs."[4] In 1926, when his first marriage broke up, this friendship languished and came to an end— through no wish of Graves's.

Before the break, Edith had talked a lot with Graves and learnt from him, though she shied away from the Freudian interpretations he insisted on making of her poetry. The idea of "texture" in verse, which comes up again and again in her writings about poetry, was taken from Graves, as Edith acknowledged in her Hogarth Press pamphlet of 1925, *Poetry and Criticism*. Quoting his words from *Contemporary Techniques of Poetry*, texture "covers the relations of a poem's vowels and consonants, other than rhyme, considered as mere sound."

Later, when she no longer saw Graves, her visitors at Pembridge Mansions kept Edith up-to-date on his doings. Yeats used to tell her "of the latest developments in the Robert Graves household,—a source of never-ending interest and wonder, both to himself and to his hearer." Yeats also wrote Edith a letter with "a wonderful description of Robert Graves, hearing that Mr. Yeats was about to go to Majorca," where Graves had gone to live. "'He writes,' said Mr. Yeats, 'that I must not call.'!!"

Wheels, the periodical with which Edith made her mark as editor and poet, owed its title to the poem by Nancy Cunard which was the first item in the first issue, or "cycle," as it was called, in 1916:

I sometimes think that all our thoughts are wheels
Rolling forever through the painted world,
Moved by the cunning of a thousand clowns
Dressed paper-wise with blatant rounded masks.

Rather creaky action, perhaps; but as John Press has written, these lines from the relatively unexplosive first number conjure up the atmosphere of the whole series: "the world of the opulent Edwardian nursery into which have been smuggled the ballet designs of Bakst and the drawings of Aubrey Beardsley."[5] *Wheels* tended to be cynical, "clever," brittle in tone, but the first cycle was not characteristic; Edith included in it her melodramatic "The Mother" and the equally murderous "The Drunkard."

Years later Osbert found in a secondhand book shop a copy of this first *Wheels* with a letter from their friend Lady Colvin still in it, in which she explained the book and its editor to a friend:

> She is a daughter of Sir George, the Bart, and the young school of poetry look on her as their high priestess. . . . They are in Poetry what the Post-Impressionists and Cubists are in painting — very hard to make head or tail of what they write — it is really to make the Bourgeoisie sit up, and with the Sitwells there is a vein of humour wanting to see how far they can gull the public. It is the latest and newest school, but nothing will come of it. . . . They are quite nice and amusing young people if only they would not write poetry. We are so very sorry about the dear bird and do hope she is better.[6]

Osbert was middle-aged when he came across this letter. Whether in fact all "the young school of poetry" looked on Edith as their high priestess is a moot point. Her name did not, in 1916, ring many bells for most people. The wary doubted, like Lady Colvin, whether anything would come of it. Aldous Huxley, for example, hedged his bets with flippancy and condescension. He had met Edith in June 1917, before the Colefax reading, and reported to Lady Ottoline Morrell that Edith was "passionately anxious for me to contribute to her horrible production. These Wheelites take themselves seriously: I never believed it possible!"[7]

Edith and the twenty-three-year-old Huxley lunched together; their accounts of the occasion differ sadly. He told Lady Ottoline merely that he sat "naively

drinking in the flattery of the ridiculous Sitwell." Edith—years later, admittedly
—recalled something more lyrical:

> He invited me to lunch at the Isola Bella . . . in a dreamlike golden day in
> June. The air was like white wine, spangled with great stars of dew and
> sun motes, haunted by sounds like echoes of memories. In a moment, as I
> came out of the light into the cool restaurant, the day seemed quenched
> by the sudden pleasant darkness and by the silence of my host. . . . His
> silences seemed to stretch for miles, extinguishing life, when they occurred,
> as a snuffer extinguishes a candle. On the other hand he was (when
> uninterrupted) one of the most accomplished talkers I have ever known.[8]

(Apropos the quality of people's silences: Ford Madox Ford in *Return to
Yesterday* said of Wyndham Lewis, "I have never known anyone else whose
silence was a positive rather than a negative quality.")

Aldous Huxley did contribute to *Wheels*, the "well-known Society Anthology," as he explained defensively to his brother Julian a couple of months after
the Isola Bella lunch:

> The folk who run it are a family called Sitwell, alias Shufflebottom, one
> sister and two brothers, Edith, Osbert and Sacheverell—isn't that superb—
> each of them larger and whiter than the other. I like Edith, but Ozzy and
> Sachy are still rather too large to swallow. Their great object is to REBEL,
> which sounds quite charming: only one finds that the steps they are
> prepared to take, the lengths they will go are so small as to be hardly
> perceptible to the naked eye. But they are so earnest and humble . . . these
> dear solid people who have suddenly discovered intellect and begun to
> get drunk on it . . . it is a charming type.[9]

In spite of his condescension, Huxley stopped deprecating his involvement
with *Wheels*. He liked "its toreador attitude towards the bloody-bloodies of
this world." He accepted, in his ironical way, the Sitwells as part of the London
scene; they were no longer the "Shufflebottoms": in May 1918 he reported to
Lady Ottoline that at the Gaudier-Brzeska exhibition "I saw almost everybody
—the glorious company of Sitwells, the noble army of poets, including Graves
and Eliot. . . ."[10] When he and his wife, Maria, were first married, in 1921–1922,
and living in Westbourne Terrace, just round the corner from Pembridge
Mansions, there used to be regular weekly dinners of the three Sitwells, the

Huxleys, and Naomi Royde-Smith. Afterwards they would all go to the cinema. Edith was very fond of Aldous Huxley.

Wheels, of which there were six cycles between 1916 and 1921, always received mixed notices; but its great triumph was that it was acknowledged, unequivocally, as a challenge and an alternative to the established and establishment *Georgian Poetry*. "*Georgian Poetry* is like the Coalition Government; *Wheels* is like the Radical Opposition," pronounced Middleton Murry in the *Athenaeum*. "None of them *sing*," grumbled *The Times Literary Supplement* about the Cyclists on December 27, 1917; "most of them are far too much inclined to stand outside the scene of life, grumble and make faces, and roll big words in their mouths." T. S. Eliot, reviewing the same volume of *Wheels* in the *Egoist* on March 18, 1918, said that the Cyclists "have a little the air of smattering. . . . Instead of rainbows, cuckoos, daffodils and timid hares, they give us garden gods, guitars, and mandolins. . . . " Yet he called it a "more serious book" than the latest *Georgian Poetry*. It was the anthology system itself that was beginning to annoy critics; it was almost as fashionable as drawing-room poetry readings, society's response to the poetry boom. Murry complained in the *Athenaeum* of May 16, 1919, that "ladies with independent incomes and advanced drawing-rooms have competed for the condescensions of poets not averse to reciting their own compositions. The poetical tea has run the *thé dansant* close in social estimation."

A contributor to the early cycles of *Wheels*, and the artist who designed the endpapers for the first cycle, was Alvaro Guevara. Edith was very drawn to Aldous Huxley; but she was in love with Guevara. He was seven years younger than she was, a Chilean who had come to England as a boy and attended Bradford Technical College and the Slade School of Fine Art in London. He liked Edith's poetry and was deeply impressed by her. In 1916 he painted a portrait of her — *The Editor of Wheels* — which has become famous and now hangs in the National Portrait Gallery in London. Their friendship was at its height around the time he was painting her, but in 1920 she was still his beloved Edith; they were together at a party given by Lady Ottoline Morrell early that year. Ten years later Edith confided to Allanah Harper that she had loved "Chile," as he was called, and that she would have married him if it had not been whispered to her by some mischief maker that Chile suffered from a disqualifying disease. . . .

The truth was harder. Chile was promiscuous — with both sexes. He was extrovert, physical, unstable, and very Latin; he was everything Edith was not. It was an attraction of opposites. But what actually disqualified him was that he was not in love with her. His feeling for Edith was romantic and, according to his biographer, spiritual: "It was obvious to everyone that Chile worshipped Edith, their visits to the ballet and concerts, her tea parties and poetry readings, her love, her wit and sympathy, all proved a solace, but Nancy obsessed him."[11] The spoke in Edith's wheel was Nancy Cunard. In 1919 it was Nancy whom Chile was painting. She obsessed him for years (though he married Meraud Guinness in 1929).

Chile was out of England—in Chile—between 1922 and 1925; during that time, though they wrote to each other, Edith got over it and regained self-confidence. When he came back to London, the Sitwells supported an exhibition of his paintings. Edith was the loyalest of rejected lovers. In 1927, when Chile was planning to move to Paris, she wrote to Gertrude Stein asking her to look after "one of my oldest friends": "He is a painter, and also a writer, of real genius—not one of those dear little intellectuals. . . . It would be an awful thing if a man with a mind like his had to have it fretted away by the vulgar little clothes-moths that sit drinking and pretending to be geniuses in the cafés." Like her erstwhile colleague Nancy Cunard, presumably. Robert Nichols fell in love with Nancy, too; and Aldous Huxley, who had met her in 1917 during his *Wheels* involvement, was desperately enamoured of her a few years later. Osbert loved her, too, and was as much "in love" with her as he could be with any woman.

Recurring names in the early cycles of *Wheels* are Iris Tree (like Viola, a daughter of Sir Herbert), Sherard Vines, and Arnold James, as well as Guevara, Nancy Cunard, Huxley, Helen Rootham (with her translations from Rimbaud), and all three Sitwells. The fourth cycle—November 1919—was dedicated to the memory of Wilfrid Owen (unfortunately spelt "Wilfid" on the title page) and contains seven of his poems. This was both an act of piety and a scoop on Edith's part. Owen was an intimate friend of Siegfried Sassoon, who wrote from France in 1918 asking Osbert to look out for his young friend. That summer, when Osbert, Sassoon, and Owen were all in London, the three passed an afternoon together with music and raspberries and cream; Owen went back to the front and was killed a week before the war ended.

Edith never met Owen at all. But she acquired through Osbert some of his poems in manuscript, and had the acumen to write and ask Owen's mother if she might publish some of them—including "Strange Meeting"—in *Wheels*. When the fourth cycle came out, Owen's quality was recognized by Middleton Murry—and dismissed by J. C. Squire in the *Mercury*. Murry pontificated in the *Athenaeum* of December 5, 1919:

> We have our opinion; we know that there is a good deal of good poetry in the Georgian book, a little in *Wheels*. We know that there is much bad poetry in the Georgian book, and less in *Wheels*. We know that there is one poem in *Wheels* beside the intense and sombre imagination of which even the good poetry of the Georgian book pales for a moment.

He was referring to "Strange Meeting"—and making again the now statutory comparison between the latest *Wheels* and the latest *Georgian Poetry*. This is even more striking when one looks at the figures, which for *Georgian Poetry* were impressive. The Owen issue of *Wheels* was printed in an edition of only one thousand; most of the other cycles were printed in even smaller numbers.

Edith now wanted to edit a book of Owen's war poems, but was thwarted. She explained to Owen's mother that Sassoon came to see her "and told me it was your son's wish that he [Captain Sassoon] should see to the publication of the poems, because they were such friends. In those circumstances I could do nothing but offer to hand them over to him. . . ." She asked Mrs. Owen to send the poems by her son still in her possession "to *me*." In the event she almost got her way, for in January 1920 Sassoon went off to America, "leaving all your son's manuscripts with me to get ready for the printers by February 1st. Captain Sassoon has done nothing in the way of preparing them."[12] Edith was very interested in Captain Sassoon, but her relationship with him was uneasy, and she was always finding fault with his behaviour.

In June 1920 Blackwell published a collection of Edith's poems under the title *The Wooden Pegasus*. One of the new friends the book brought her was the young William Plomer, who was to be a friend for life. He was South African and sent for the book from Johannesburg; and, as he wrote in his autobiography, "when the book arrived, in its bright magenta cover, it confirmed that she had obeyed the summons of the ninety-eighth psalm, a summons which only a poet is able to obey: 'O sing unto the Lord a new song: for he hath done marvellous things.'" Soon after, the aspiring writer came to London, where he saw Edith for the first time at a reading at the Swedenborg Hall; she had a manner, he wrote, "without the least taint of affectation or pomposity": "There was a dignity that seemed as if it might sharpen into asperity; an underlying compassion in the voice and in the shape of the eyelids; an easily accessible sense of the ridiculous, the impertinent, and the commonplace." The second time he saw her, reading with Osbert and Sacheverell at a full-dress evening gathering in a private house in Mayfair, he sensed that she had a "slight lack of *rapport* with the audience," as if there were "a gulf unbridgeable." He was quite right. Drawing rooms in Mayfair were not to be Edith's milieu.

In the last cycle of *Wheels*, which came out in November 1921, Edith published a poem called "Barouches Noirs" by a sixteen-year-old boy, Brian Howard, who was still at Eton. He was a most precocious child. Edith took him up as if he were a reincarnation of her brother Sachie. He had already appeared in print the previous year, in a pastiche called "The New New" in the *New Age*. It was a modish performance, a knowing, satirical guided tour round current art and journalism, ending with a fashionable dig at the *London Mercury* and a reference to *Wheels*:

> Then there's the new *Wheels . . . remplissage, remplissage.* It's the fourth (bi)cycle *réchauffée,* and I wonder if Edith Sitwell has dreadful dreams . . . re, Scarabombazons. The worst of it *is*—this passion for houseling.
>
> What is the future going to be? And not only that, but even that's getting so previous!

In early 1921 Brian Howard wrote in his diary, "Polished off some Dadaïste poems and sent them to Edith Sitwell"; and then, "Received a *wonderful* letter from Edith Sitwell." It *was* a wonderful letter, written from Pembridge Mansions on February 14:

> I am going to do a thing I have never done before,—I am going to give you detailed criticism and advice about your poems. I get a great many manuscripts sent to me, and I invariably return them with a short note of regret. But in your case it is different. You have quite obviously very real gifts, and I hope to publish some work of yours in *Wheels*—perhaps this year, perhaps next. It depends on you.
>
> You may be angry at first at what I am going to say; but your promise is far too real for me to risk your future by publishing these poems of yours *in their present state. . . .*

The delighted youth sent eight more poems to Edith by return of post, and on the eighteenth she wrote to him again at even greater length. "There can be not the slightest doubt that your gifts and promise are exceedingly remarkable":

> "Born writers" are subject to one great danger—they are apt to grow careless, and to be too easily satisfied; but I do not think this is a temptation to you. . . . In any case, you will have me on your track pretty quick if I see any trace of it. I will tell you something; I see more remarkable talent and promise in your work than in that of any other poet under twenty I have seen, excepting that of my brother Sacheverell. . . .

So Edith attached his promise and his future to herself, and flattered and encouraged him. It did his writing no good. It "rather turned my head," he wrote, "and my poems became increasingly affected, cerebral, self-confident and poor."

Towards the end of her second letter, she had written: "Do you live in London, when you are not at Eton? Or, if you do not live in London, do you ever pass through? If so, come and spend the afternoon with me. We would work at your poems before tea, and after tea we would talk about books, pictures and music." "Send me everything you write," she concluded. "I will do everything in my power to help you."

His "Barouches Noirs" duly went into *Wheels*, sixth cycle; it is a vision of

> Old, broken-down barouches that followed
>   their soundless horses soundlessly,
> And contained loads of young dead people,
>   propped up in outrageous positions.

Edith said it was "his best." She had wanted to put more of his poems in, but *Wheels* was in trouble. "Owing," she said, "to the persistent attacks made on us by various people," Blackwell's had refused to go on publishing it. C. W. Daniel, after a good deal of trouble, had agreed to publish a much-reduced issue (64 pages at 3s. 6d., as opposed to 128 pages at 6s., plus endpapers by Severini, in the fifth cycle). *Wheels* turned no more, but Edith was on to something else. She wrote to Brian in the month that his poem appeared, "Will you by any chance be in London on the evening of December 15th? If so, will you come with me to a meeting of the Anglo-French Poetry Society,—I am one of the Committee—and hear William Davies read his poems, Mrs. Arnold Bennett recite, and meet them both?"

Arnold Bennett had recently done Osbert a good turn: Through him, Osbert had the joint literary editorship, with Herbert Read, of *Art and Letters.* By 1919 Edith too had become friendly with both Bennett and his wife. Marguerite Bennett was French, and a *diseuse*—that is, a reciter of poetry in drawing rooms. Edith was very impressed by her. "I always thought I loved French poetry and could understand it; but your interpretations have told me a hundred things." She dedicated the 1920 cycle of *Wheels* to "Mrs. Arnold Bennett, Poetry's greatest interpretive artist," and wrote to her, "I needn't tell you the pride we felt at being allowed to dedicate *Wheels* to such an artist. The book is honoured greatly by the dedication."

In 1920, Mrs. Bennett, Edith, and Helen Rootham instituted the Anglo-French Poetry Society, largely as a platform for Mrs. Bennett's recitations. Arnold Bennett agreed to be president. As *Wheels* declined, Edith felt the need to create a regular power base—something much more grand than the musical evenings and teas she and Helen were holding at Pembridge Mansions. Her attempts to include Robert Nichols and hopes of involving Osbert and Sachie in her scheme were ultimately futile. But in her alliance with Mrs. Bennett, for whom a regular platform was an obvious professional advantage, Edith was rather more successful, even though her desire to teach "workers to care for the arts in an intelligent manner" went to the wall. The first meeting of the Anglo-French Poetry Society was held in June 1920 at the Bennetts' house. The French dimension initially appealed to Helen rather than to Edith; but afterwards, Edith wrote in a rapture of happiness to Mrs. Bennett (they were not yet on Christian-name terms):

> I think your art must have been an absolute revelation to nearly the whole of the audience on Wednesday—certainly to all those people who had never heard you before. Never have I heard you recite more beautifully, and never have I heard your voice in better form. It was a triumph. I assure you the audience was overwhelmed. I know, because I was sitting where I could realize their attitude. It was the greatest privilege to hear you; and I want to thank you once again.

The honeymoon was sweet. Edith invited the Bennetts to Renishaw (they did not come) and to musical evenings at Pembridge Mansions, where Helen in full voice was the star performer. When Mrs. Bennett went on a tour of Scotland reciting Baudelaire (an undertaking which "requires nerve," as her husband remarked in his journal), Edith and Helen sent good-luck telegrams ahead to greet her. Every time Edith heard her recite, she wrote a letter of warm, affectionate admiration. They soon became "Edith" and "Marguerite" to one another.

There were private sessions with Marguerite as well as the organised ones. A young war widow, Olive Valentine, of whom both the Bennetts were very fond, was present at a private performance with only herself, Edith, and Robert Nichols as audience. First they were given a cup of tea, and then guests and hostess took up their positions for the recitation. Olive Valentine described it:

> I was sitting with my back to the window giving me a very vivid picture of the scene taking place in a small extension of the very large drawing-room in their London flat in Maddox Street. Edith Sitwell was sitting nearest to me and Nichols in an armchair just beyond her. Marguerite was sitting about ten feet in front of them to my right. Behind her as if observing the scene was the marvellous Modigliani painting *The Woman in Grey* and to Marguerite's right also looking on with curiosity was the excellent almost Picassoesque painting by Edward Woolf. . . . Marguerite with eyes closed began with her deepest possible tone of voice with a *terrifically* long-drawn-out "SILENCE," twice raising her hands from her lap in front of her to about shoulder height. Edith's eyes were also closed but she sat perfectly still, apparently listening very intently: in a few minutes of the "recital's" monotonous poem—very good—Robert Nichols was gripping the arms of his chair swaying with emotion.[13]

Olive Valentine, the only member of the party with her eyes wide open, had difficulty in not bursting out laughing. "It all seemed unreal and rather ridiculous, though the words were probably well worth listening to, poetry by Baudelaire on that occasion. But I was unable to listen—I was too preoccupied with looking at the whole set-up."

"Unreal and rather ridiculous" as it was, it made Edith happy for a time. In August 1921, at Renishaw, she was anticipating in her letters to Marguerite Bennett an autumn "full of interest, hard work and success" for the Anglo-French Poetry Society.

But life was not so promising for Mrs. Bennett. Her marriage was going very wrong. Bennett himself was kind about the Society, even when things were at their worst between him and Marguerite, for he liked Edith and Helen; after a party at Pembridge Mansions in December 1920 he had written in his journal: "Two small rooms full of smoke and people. But not dull. I have never been bored there."[14] He delayed breaking the news to Marguerite that he had seen his lawyer about a separation until the October 1921 meeting of the Society, in Lady Swaythling's drawing room, was safely over. Then he told her.

At about the same time Edith was becoming less adoring and more dictatorial. Playing second fiddle did not suit her, as Osbert had observed about her in childhood. "What heaps of programmes you have composed," she wrote to "My dear Marguerite":

> Do you agree that it will be a good thing to sandwich a modern programme between each classic programme? By modern, I mean from Baudelaire and Swinburne onwards? Because I think if we have too many "old" programmes together, the audiences may think we are too educational. Don't you agree? — Also, it would seem so reactionary.

Possibly a whiff of negative reaction from the audience had been reaching even Edith's nostrils. Though distinguished poets — W. H. Davies and T. S. Eliot among them — were willing to involve themselves in the Society for friendship's sake, it is probable that not a few people shared Olive Valentine's amused view, and Lytton Strachey's malicious one, of the proceedings. Strachey described a meeting of the Society — "an incredibly fearful function" — held at the Bennetts' in June 1921, in a letter to Carrington:

> *He* was not there, but *she* was — oh my eye what a woman! It was apparently some sort of poetry society. There was an address (very poor) on Rimbaud etc by an imbecile Frog; then Edith Sitwell appeared, her nose longer than an ant-eater's, and read some of her absurd stuff; then Eliot — very sad and seedy — it made one weep; finally Mrs. Arnold Bennett recited, with waving arms and chanting voice, Baudelaire and Verlaine till everyone was ready to vomit. As a study in half-witted horror the whole thing was most interesting.[15]

A full-scale row blew up between Edith and Mrs. Bennett in late 1921 over one of the latter's protégées, a Mlle Gabain, who was invited to recite. Not only was Edith not pleased over her choice of poems, but Mlle Gabain criticized the merits of the Rimbaud poems that Edith wanted. Here Helen's particular expertise was called into question, and she too entered the fray, in writing. Edith justified her friend's intervention to Mrs. Bennett: "It so happens that Helen is extremely well known in the literary world both in France and England as the finest translator of Rimbaud there has yet been. Therefore the patronising letter Mlle Gabain complains about was called down by her own impertinence and presumption."

Loyalty to friends is a fine thing. But it is easy to see the looming, fuming shadow of Helen over Edith's shoulder and to hear her breathe as Edith wrote out her outrage to Mrs. Bennett. Helen was intense, ambitious, and no longer young. Only a few months after this episode, in July 1922, Brian Howard described her to Harold Acton as "one of those terrifying forceful women. . . . She proffered me a picture by Kandinsky—an incoherent smudge of colour and murmured with great vim into my ear, 'Isn't that *pure* beauty?' I replied in the affirmative. I always do when I meet muscle." However much vim she had, in a little while, as she must have known, Helen would be outstripped entirely by her former pupil.

The fracas with Mrs. Bennett ("I, as the poet on the Committee, had the casting vote," Edith had written to her) was the first of innumerable occasions when Edith would stand on her dignity as an expert and a professional, in a grand and crushing way that poets do not generally find necessary. She must have been encouraged in this by the combative Helen, who was for so long her only confidante and supporter against the philistines, and with whom she associated everything that had been genuinely liberating and reassuring in her girlhood. A good genius, given enough time, will become a succubus.

But there was fruitful ground in Edith's own personality, too, for aggression and cries of "impertinence." Edith's insecurity led her into extremes in her relations with people. She had never been loved steadily and unconditionally, except by her brothers, and they had other fish to fry. She tended to leap into friendships headlong, expecting from them more than they could sometimes carry, though with perhaps half a dozen people in her life her sympathy and need met an answering sympathy and need. And she countered criticism or imagined criticism with an exaggerated and unconcealed defensiveness. She hit back at once. Her emotional processes were the same as everyone else's up to a point, with the difference that most people conceal a good deal of what they feel; Edith did not dissimulate. She was not an actress at all, even though she learnt so well to project her public persona. Her reactions were as immediate and as violent as a child's.

By now Mrs. Bennett had had more than enough of Helen, and she let Edith know it. And that, for Edith, was the end of Mrs. Bennett.

I don't know why you thought you dared write such a letter about Helen to me. Your spiteful impertinence merely throws a most unpleasant light upon yourself.

Conceit about any form of art is really the last thing that Helen can be accused of! As for her art,—I do not choose to discuss Helen's art with you.

Edith's attitude toward "Helen's art" was unfailingly generous. If the world did not appreciate Helen, it was not because Edith tried to keep her ex-governess in the shade. She tried to help on one occasion by pushing Helen's suitability as a lecturer:

Might I suggest your asking Miss Helen Rootham, the former musical critic of the *New Age*, who has lectured a great deal in various centres, to give her extraordinarily illuminating lecture on Modern Consciousness as expressed in Music, Poetry, and Dancing. I have heard this lecture, and it is of quite an extraordinary quality. She is a great friend of mine (indeed, she shares a flat with me, and is therefore very much in touch with all the modernist artists and their ideas)—and I know she would do this lecture for the terms you mentioned.

Helen's lecture on Modern Consciousness sounds like hell. But relations between her and Edith were maintained at a high level only so long as Helen could feel herself equally in demand and equally gifted. Edith did her best to keep the balance. From the breakup of her *entente cordiale* with Marguerite Bennett, however, she was able to salvage her friendship with Marguerite's husband, and was asking him in November 1922 whether she might dedicate a book of poems to him (new ones, she told him, plus the whole of *Façade* and the poems from *Wheels*, 1920 and 1921); this was *Bucolic Comedies*, which came out in the spring of 1923. "Helen and I both send our love," she ended her letter to Bennett.

Edith had been very touched by Bennett's mention of her in an article on James Joyce's *Ulysses* in *Outlook* earlier that year (April 29, 1922). He had written: "Valéry Larbaud . . . once amazed and delighted me by stating, quite on his own, that the most accomplished of all the younger British poets was Edith Sitwell; a true saying, though I had said it before him." Edith wrote to thank him, saying how his words "had compensated me for all the neglect and rudeness I get from people who don't count. . . . I wish I could tell you how much praise from you has helped me to go on with my work, at moments when I have been discouraged." Bennett went on giving her this sort of encouragement all through the 1920s, bringing her name frequently into his *Evening Standard* review articles, and always in an amiable and respectful way; he called her "a real poet."

He was one of the few people who showed perfect common sense about the Sitwell phenomenon: He enjoyed them, encouraged them, but was neither dazzled nor defensive about them. Nor was he afraid of telling them when they went too far, even Edith. "She had been saying," wrote Osbert, "how low she rated the writings of an author whom I had lately named Muddleton Moral" (who was of course Middleton Murry), and Bennett interrupted her: "Spiritual Pride is a . . . terrible thing, Edith! Remember whatever I may think of your work, or you of mine, or both of us of Moral's, on the Judgment Day it will appear to the Almighty as pretty-much-the-same-thing."[16]

But this was in private. In public he was generous. When Osbert's *Out of the Flame* came out in 1923 Bennett wrote:

> The Sitwells can all write. . . . Further, the Sitwells are all personages. Further, they all afflict the public—I mean the poetic public—which is a grand thing to do. . . . They exult in a scrap. Battle is in the curve of their nostrils. They issue forth from their bright pavilions and demand trouble. And few spectacles are more touching than their gentle, quiet, surprised, ruthless demeanour when they get it, as they generally do.[17]

This is affectionate, but not blindly so. That *ruthless* tells that he understood them.

Osbert's book of 1923 was published by Grant Richards; but Edith's *Bucolic Comedies*, which appeared in the same year with its grateful dedication to Bennett, was the first of many Sitwell books to be published by Duckworth.

5

Façade
1921–1923

In January 1919 Sacheverell had gone up to Oxford—briefly. It proved too narrow a world for a twenty-two-year-old whose brother and sister were already deeply involved in London life and letters—a young man who, rather more importantly, had himself already had poems published (in *Wheels* and in the *Egoist*, which was also the first periodical after the *Daily Mirror* to publish a poem of Edith's—"Minstrels"). He even had a book of poems out already, *The People's Palace*, published by Blackwell. The important thing, from Edith's point of view, about Sachie's sojourn at Balliol, was his meeting with William Walton, only sixteen years old, an undergraduate at Christ Church with what seemed to Sachie a musical talent that amounted to genius. Osbert, on a visit to Oxford to see his brother and Siegfried Sassoon, was introduced to Walton. The two Sitwell brothers took the young composer over; by the end of the year Walton was installed in their London house to work on his music in his own way and with every aid and encouragement from his hosts. He became, in his shy and unassertive way, one of the family, "an adopted, or elected, brother" to Edith, Osbert, and Sacheverell. He even looked a little like them.

The idea that Edith's poetry should be recited to music specially written by William Walton was, she said in her autobiography, her brothers'. For the poems themselves, of course, no one else except herself was "in the least to blame." Osbert said they got the idea as a result of the technical experiments Edith was making—experiments in obtaining dance measures like waltzes and fox-trots through the use of words alone. But "it is difficult to say which of us thought of the various parts of the production, for we were all four continually in one another's company." Osbert and Sacheverell were keener on it, initially, than Walton himself: "I remember thinking it was not a very good idea, but when I said so they simply told me they'd get Constant [Lambert] to do it, if I wouldn't—and of course I couldn't let that occur."[1] They got down to it, Edith and William, she speaking her words over and over again while he marked and accented them "to show where the precise stress and emphasis fell, the exact inflection or deflection." But is that how it really was? Edith, as an old woman, told her secretary that the music came first and that "Willie gave me certain rhythms and said, 'There you are Edith, see what you can do with that.' So I went away and did it. I wanted to prove that I could."[2]

It seems right that there should be confusion over so faultless a collaboration. When Sacheverell was eighty years old, he wrote a poem—which is not so much a poem as a letter to his sister, who was no longer of this world—called "The Octogenarian," an extended gloss on Edith's own poem of the same name, which was one of the original *Façade* poems (though not later included). He conjured up in the poem the atmosphere of that happy, hot summer of 1921:

> There seemed to be a new poem of yours
>   to read to us,
> Almost every time we came to see you,
> And climbed the four double-flights of stone stairs
>   up to your flat:—
> Poems in a rich vein of fantasy
>   invented for yourself,
> And all your own,
>   like nothing before or since. . . .

She wrote the poems in bed in the early mornings, in her bedroom looking out at the back, from which, wrote Sachie, "I even remember the dismal view." When she read them what she had written since last time, they heard "her happy laughter in the poems."

No one who has habitually heard the words and music of *Façade* together can disentangle them in the mind's ear, even though Edith's poems are not a libretto nor is Walton's music only an accompaniment; both have always had independent lives. The *Façade* music is witty and elegant, full of pastiche and reference. Charles Osborne wrote of it: "These pieces, some of them gay parodies of popular music, others wry comments on past Edwardian splendour, are as funny as anything in music can be. But, like the poems they accompany, they carry under their light, mocking tone, their own nostalgia for days gone by."[3] Sachie wrote of Walton, not yet twenty years old when he worked with Edith on *Façade*:

> No lover of poetry in particular,
> But he worked instinctively I remember,
>   as if blindfolded or under a spell,
> And as though led or guided:—
> The poems themselves,
>   that is the wonder of his partnership with my sister,
> Being, as has been said, like nothing else before or since. . . .4

Osbert and Sacheverell were impresario and stage manager. The idea of uttering the poems through a mask in a curtain was Osbert's; he was being sculpted by Frank Dobson at the time, and when Dobson heard of the project he offered to design and paint the curtain. Sacheverell got the megaphone—called a Sengerphone—from a singer called Senger up in Hampstead. It was large and made of papier-mâché, and fitted over the speaker's face. They started rehearsing in the upstairs drawing room at Carlyle Square in November 1921. "The cold outside was terrible and, in spite of two large coal fires, the players had to be brought to by copious draughts of sloe gin." These consisted of six "rather angry" instrumentalists: flute, clarinet, saxophone, trumpet, cello, and percussion. They rehearsed all through the winter, Walton conducting his baffled troupe, "holding his baton with something of the air of an elegant and handsome snipe."

The very first performance took place, again in the Carlyle Square drawing room, at 9:30 p.m. on January 24, 1922, before an invited audience. "The front part of the room was so densely packed with thin gold chairs, it was scarcely possible to move. Across the narrow opening where had been the conventional double doors, now stretched the Dobson curtain." The assembled guests—mainly painters, musicians, and poets—made enthusiastic noises. But in the relatively small drawing room the volume of sound was so overpowering that the more orthodox among the audience were at a loss for words. "We had fortunately arranged for an ample supply downstairs of hot rum punch, an unusual but efficacious restorative."

Among the guests that night was Mrs. Robert Mathias, patron of the Ballets Russes, and she invited her hosts to repeat their performance in her house in Montague Square. This took place a couple of weeks later, on February 7. Diaghilev was there; "the audience was stunned", Edith wrote to Brian Howard.

Edith had not yet actually met Brian Howard; that happened a few months later, in July 1922. Meanwhile Howard and his Eton friend Harold Acton had between them edited the first and only number of *The Eton Candle*, which carried contributions from old Etonians, including the Sitwell brothers, and an article on "The New Poetry" by Howard himself. "She is a genius," he wrote of Edith in this essay, "and the greatest poet of the *grotesquerie de cauchemar* that has ever existed." (Brian Howard never used an English phrase when a French one would do.)

When he went to see the "genius" during his summer holidays, he was disappointed. Howard was an ambitious, precious young creature, indulged by an adoring mother, intoxicated by his own cleverness, which was to come to very little; his adult life was not happy. Edith, in her middle thirties and her unassuming surroundings, had nothing to offer except support and friendship, and it was not enough. Brian Howard wrote to Harold Acton:

> I arrived at Moscow Road — an uninviting Bayswater slum — and toiled up flights and flights of bare Victorian stairs. From outside Pembridge Mansions looked like an inexpensive and dirty hospital. I arrived at a nasty green door, which was opened by Edie herself. She has a very long thin expressive face with a pale but good complexion. She looks rather like a refined Dutch medieval madonna. She had on an enlarged *poilu* hat of grey fur, an apple green sheep's wool jacket, and an uninteresting "old gold" brocade dress. Her hair is thin, but of a pleasant pale gold colour, bobbed at the sides and bunned at the hind. I do not care for the people she usually has around her. . . . They are common little nobodies. Also I don't like her teas — *as teas* at all. Tell William I got *one penny bun and three-quarters of a cup of rancid tea in a dirty cottage mug*. Also I don't like her apartment, or, rather, room. It is small, dark, and I suspect, dirty. The only interesting things in the room are an etching by [Augustus] John, and her library, which is most entertaining. The remainder seems to consist of one lustre ball and a quantity of bad draperies. Miss Helen Rootham, whom she lives with, is one of those terrifying forceful women. . . .

Over tea, Edith told him that she liked *The Eton Candle* but disagreed with some of his article, "especially about Sachie (of course) and curiously enough about Aldous — whom she admires most reservedly." She tried to enlist Brian in the lost cause of *Wheels*, in a last effort to keep it going. "She has made me virtual business editor of *Wheels*. A most damnably unpleasant position. There will be no 1922 *Wheels* unless I can get advertisements for it. . . ." Brian was much more concerned with getting advertisements for a second edition of his *Candle*. And of course, there was no 1922 *Wheels*.

In the autumn Edith went down to Eton at Brian's invitation to give a lecture: "It is going to be 'somewhat of an ordeal' for me," he told Acton. "Especially if she comes in her fur cap and green wool coat! It will be amusing, though." "Edie" (as he insisted on calling her) came down, he wrote afterwards, "looking like one of her own poems," and lectured for an hour to a "tiny audience":

> She whispered her speech into a table, and as a result it was horribly difficult to hear anything at all. Ostensibly lecturing on Modern Poetry, she went on for hours about Stravinsky. What people *could* hear of her speech astounded them so much that they sat there smiling, with their mouths open, and tittered every once and a while—genteely [*sic*], of course.[6]

She must however have spoken well, for even Howard conceded that it was "an excellent lecture ('Squire's poems exude the odour of wet mackintoshes') and quite a success." At the end, when he had thanked the speaker, the "beastly old Vice-Provost" got up and "advised Edie to *speak louder in future*! Eton is a queer place, isn't it? I nearly smacked his face." He concluded his letter with a compliment to a poem Acton had written, "Orangerie." "Excellent, my dear, EXCELLENT. . . . That poem is *subtler* than Edith."

His correspondent, Harold Acton, himself paid a visit to Pembridge Mansions a few months later, in December of 1922. Acton's account of that first visit was written many years afterwards, and with a lifetime's sustained friendship with Edith colouring his first impressions; but he too, aesthete that he was and remained, found himself depressed by her surroundings. Yet for him Edith herself was not a disappointment. She was dressed that day in emerald brocade and seemed to him

> a rare jewel, a hieratic figure in Limoges enamel . . . clamped in some tin biscuit box, but rarer, more hieratic against this background. . . . The pale oval face with its almond eyes and long thin nose, had often been carved in ivory by true believers. Her entire figure possessed a distinction seldom

to be seen outside the glass cases of certain museums. Physically, she was an extraordinary survival from the Age of Chivalry.[7]

She told him ludicrous stories of the bores and boors who inflicted themselves on her attention, and of the would-be poets who bothered her with their worthless effusions. Her chief difficulty, she told him, was "to procure a calm in which to write above a hurly-burly of interruptions." Young Acton began to worry whether he himself was not in fact one of these interruptions. "Suddenly I felt ill at ease, my conscience smote me. . . . Thanking her for her encouragment of our efforts in *The Eton Candle*, I took my leave."

Soon afterwards, having left Eton and gone up to Oxford, Acton invited Edith down to address the Ordinary Society. It became evident in the discussion that followed that few of the critical voices in the room had actually read her poems. "Edith's retorts were swift and sensible, but the arguments grew so involved that she nearly missed her train."[8] She praised on this occasion the poetry of Peter Quennell, who had just come up to Balliol. ("I had thought Brian Howard precocious," wrote Acton, "until I met Peter Quennell.") Richard Hughes, the compiler of the anthology *Public School Verse*, in which Quennell had figured, introduced him to Edith, taking him along to Bayswater one summer afternoon:

> And there upon the threshold stood the famous poetess, tall, attenuated and elegant as one of those sculptured saints and martyrs who keep guard around the portals of Chartres. Sheathed in a garment of gold brocade, wearing a toque of gilded feathers and a large jewelled cross which, I afterwards learned, had originally belonged to Cagliostro, Miss Sitwell raised a finger to her lips—on her long pale distinguished hand were several impressive rings set with big fragments of semi-precious stone—and murmured warmingly, before we advanced, that there was a madman in the room beyond. Again, I was not to be disappointed.[9]

The madman was the poet they called the Icelander; and sitting on the sofa, in some alarm, was Oscar Wilde's friend Ada Leverson, the Sphinx. "At last," thought young Quennell, "I had entered the literary world, in which beauty, lunacy and genius were woven together into the pattern of everyday life."

All three children continued to spend their Augusts at Renishaw. Their relationship with their parents did not mature. One summer day in the early twenties their inconsequential father stroked his red beard (he had grown it at the beginning of the First World War; it made him look like the Kaiser and gave rise to the nickname "Ginger"), saying: "It's a pity that you three children haven't got a little of this sort of thing." Later, at luncheon, wrote Osbert:

> the younger members of the family—my brother, my sister and myself—were wearing beards, designed by my sister, and made out of the hideous, lightly tasselled fringe of an orange-coloured rug; they fastened over the ears with two loops of tape, and had small bells attached to them, which, with the movement of the jaws when eating, gave out a melodious alpine tinkle.[10]

This sort of practical-joke mockery of their father was not new. When Edith was twenty-four Sir George brought out a small volume of family history called *The Pilgrim*. Edith picked up a copy that was lying on a table in the ballroom and with a pen made an omission mark in the middle of the recurrent name Walter de Boys (otherwise del Bosco, or del Wode, and father to Simon Cytewel, first of their line), writing above it, "né Hopkins." "A simple joke," said Osbert, "but one received by the author of the book with particular displeasure."[11] Which of course was the point of doing it, and also the point of the jape with the beards and bells—by which time Edith was well into her thirties. There was an awful lot of the un-used-up schoolgirl in Edith. She'd never been to school, never even been taught in a group of other children, never had the usual childish gang, the feuds and alliances and giggling conspiracies that most girls have—another explanation of her lasting combativeness and her readiness to take sides and indulge in public quarrels. Sir George ably countered the beards-and-bells joke by refusing, throughout the meal, to acknowledge that anything unusual was taking place.

Façade, even before its first public performance, had begun to be a talking point. Virginia Woolf, writing to her sister Vanessa on February 20, 1922, a fortnight after the recital at Mrs. Mathias's house, reported that she had heard from Violet Dickinson that "the Sitwells have been reciting what seems to her sheer nonsense through megaphones."[12]

The "sheer nonsense" (Edith might not have balked at the description; "The audience is meant to laugh," she said) was given its first public performance on June 12, 1923, at the Aeolian Hall in Bond Street at 3:15 in the afternoon. A large audience had already assembled when Osbert and Sacheverell, after lunching together, arrived at the hall to join their sister. Osbert described how "I proceeded on to the platform first, walking in front of the curtain to make a speech describing the novel elements in the performance and attempting to explain its aims." He said, for example, that the purpose of reciting from behind the curtain was to stop the reader's personality from invading the poems. "After acknowledging the applause, I went behind the curtain to announce the various items of the entertainment through the mouth of the mask. . . . Then the fanfare which heralds *Façade* sounded, and the fun began."

Accounts differ as to the nature of the fun. The Sitwells took pride, afterwards, in stressing the outrage and hostility of the philistines in the audience. Edith wrote that "the attitude of certain of the audience was so threatening that I was warned to stay on the platform, hidden by the curtain, until they got tired of waiting for me and went home."[13] And "for several weeks subsequently," wrote Osbert, "we were obliged to go about London feeling as if we had committed a murder. When we entered a room, there would fall a sudden unpleasing hush. Even friends avoided catching one's eye. . . ."

If they did, it was probably through ordinary embarrassment. William Walton has acknowledged that this performance was a "shambles." Edith occasionally lost the beat of the music, and her incantation broke down into girlish giggles from behind the curtain. For a family who considered themselves "professional" artists, it was all pretty amateur. The reaction was not passionately hostile, not passionately sympathetic. "The hall wasn't very full, and the whole thing fell distinctly flat."[14] Virginia Woolf was there herself this time, and reported to a French friend: "Though I paid 3/6 to hear Edith vociferate her poems accompanied by a small and nimble orchestra, through a megaphone, I understood so little that I could not judge."[15] Young Harold Acton's reaction was more positive. He told Brian Howard at the time that "it was beautifully done," and later in life he described Edith as reading "very distinctly, stressing the rhythms in a dispassionate voice." Some people in the audience "tittered and made inopportune remarks," but "the poems moved so buoyantly that it did not matter."

There was a party that night at 2 Carlyle Square, which Harold Acton now entered for the first time: that "shrine of eighteenth-century shell furniture, sailing ships of spun glass, humming birds under globes, petit-point screens, porcelain spaniels . . . so many and so varied that at moments one felt one was in an aquarium (the walls had a subaqueous iridescence), at others in an aviary." Evelyn Waugh was there, Lytton Strachey and Clive Bell, Eugene Goossens, and Ada Leverson (who adored Osbert). Edith was looking like a Flemish madonna (thought Acton) in emerald brocade. "The reading had exhausted her, and I could see her turning slowly into alabaster."[16] And yet, years later, he remembered this evening as one of the very few occasions when he had seen her happy. Around her, the party played charades.

In the morning, there were the reviews of *Façade* in the papers. The *Daily Graphic*'s critic Hannen Swaffer, as "Mr. London," under the heading "Drivel They Paid to Hear," reported that

> a friend of mine who was there tells me that, when he laughed, as Edith Sitwell recited drivel through a megaphone, a woman turned round and said, "How can I study a new art if you laugh?" That sums up the whole performance. If three had laughed, the Sitwells wouldn't dare to do it again. . . . Surely it is time this sort of thing were stopped. . . . Grant Richards wore a white carnation specially for the occasion; his son wore another carnation. But otherwise it was all dreary and hopeless.

The *Evening Standard* attempted a parody:

> In the afternoon at the Aeolian Hall,
> Through a megaphone we heard Edith bawl. . . .

And so on, with the *Daily Telegraph*, the *Morning Post*, the *Times*, and the *Daily Express*.

Five days later there were the Sunday papers. In the *Observer* Percy Scholes referred to "Miss Ethel Sitwell," and said of the music, "In itself it is harmless." The *Sunday Express* on the same day was effectively laconic: "Miss Edith Sitwell monotones her own lines with musical accompaniment. Foghorn effect. Usual audience. Long-haired men, short-haired women. Megaphone in great form. . . . Very depressing, but raises the status of the megaphone."

This was all depressing reading, not so much because of the critics' hostility, but because of their dismissiveness. It was less humiliating for the Sitwells to elevate the opposition into a thoroughgoing persecution, which is what they did. It was nevertheless dismissiveness on a scale, in terms of coverage and publicity, that not many avant-garde artists attain, when one thinks of the vast number of semi-amateur experimental recitals, performances, and happenings of all kinds going on in hired halls all over London in any one week. The Sitwells' defence was attack. Osbert in his autobiography, written long after the event, when one might have expected a balanced view, said that Swaffer's facetious line in the *Daily Graphic* ("Surely it is time this sort of thing were stopped") "appears equally to have summed up the Fascist and Nazi approach to the modern developments of music, painting and literature." This seems Sitwellism at its silliest and most inflated. It is the kind of thing that gave ammunition to their enemies, seeming to justify modern opinion of the Sitwells "forever taking offense at imaginary or invented slights and detecting envy and malice in others when *they* were the culprits," and artistically "splashing around in the shallow end of a very small pool."[17] Nevertheless it is important to remember that modernism, abstraction, surrealism, and experimentation, in all the arts including poetry, were brought into the arena of morality and of politics. The Sitwells caught an authentic whiff of the poison gas that was in the air between the two world wars, and shrilled the alarm.

It was not the Sitwells, however, who would go to the gas chambers, and it is the discrepancy between their protests and the triviality of the persecution that they suffered that irritated and irritates their critics. Osbert and Edith were immoderate people. Persecution would have suited their temperaments; they were capable of rising nobly to an occasion. What they got was more insulting. They got mockery and parody, which they dignified with the name of persecution, and it diminished them.

The Sitwells were easy to parody. *Wheels* was parodied in 1921 in a publication called *Cranks*, by "Osbert, Sebert, and Ethelberta Standstill"; it included an "Idyll" by "Ethelberta":

Walnut larks in the cotton-wool air
Choke the ear. On the hill-sides bare
Wooden sheep with hearthrug backs
Follow clay shepherds with creaking sacks.

Noel Coward earned the enmity of Edith for forty years by daring to write a sketch sending up *Façade*, which he had been to see at the suggestion of Osbert himself. His revue *London Calling* opened at the Duke of York's Theatre in early September 1923. His sketch, as published, is very short, and those who saw it say variously that it was "quite funny" and "quite unfunny." "Really not unfunny" was William Walton's verdict. The "Swiss Family

Sargent's group portrait: Sir George Sitwell and Lady Ida with Edith, Osbert, and Sacheverell.

Portrait of Edith by Roger Fry, 1918.

The Editor of Wheels by Alvaro Guevara, 1916: portrait of Edith at 22 Pembridge Mansions.

The "interrupted" portrait of Edith by Wyndham Lewis, begun in 1923.

Portrait by Felix Topolski, 1959. Edith did not like it.

Portrait of Edith by Tchelitchew, 1935—his finest.

The "Sibyl" portrait of Edith by Tchelitchew, 1936.

Whittlebot" consists of Hernia Whittlebot and her brothers Gob and Sago. Maisie Gay played Hernia. The stage directions, which the audience could not enjoy, are the funniest part. For example:

> Miss HERNIA WHITTLEBOT *should be effectively and charmingly dressed in undraped dyed sacking, a cross between blue and green, with a necklet of uncut amber beads in unconventional shapes. She must wear a gold band rather high up on her forehead from which hang a little clump of Bacchanalian fruit below each ear. Her face is white and weary, with a long chin and nose, and bags under the eyes.*

Hernia delivers a prose prologue: "To me life is essentially a curve, and Art an oblong within that curve.... My brothers and I have been brought up on rhythm as other children are brought up on Glaxo." She then recites poems, "accompanied in fitful gusts by Gob and Sago." Her final piece, announced as "very long and intensely primitive," ends:

> Oxford and Cambridge count for naught
> Life is ephemeral before the majesty
> Of Local Apophlegmaticism
> Melody semi-spheroidal
> In all its innate rotundity
> Rhubarb for purposes unknown. . . .

> *The* STAGE MANAGER, *having despaired of making her hear, has signed to the Orchestra to strike up the next number. Unmoved by this* MISS WHITTLEBOT *produces a megaphone—at last in desperation the* STAGE MANAGER *begins to set the next scene and the* WHITTLEBOT FAMILY *are eventually pushed off the stage still playing and reciting.*[18]

London Calling was a hit. For the Sitwells, the mockers mocked, it was infuriating. Edith never even went to see it, and in her imagination the Whittlebot sketch was much more humiliating and damaging than the reality. Worst of all, she understood—wrongly—from what someone told her that she had been portrayed obscenely and as a lesbian. Always touchy and insecure about herself, she could not bear the public mockery. She became ill. She put off a performance of *Façade* at Oxford because Osbert advised her that "probably little Coward's supporters (being far in excess of intelligent people in number) would flock to the performance to insult me," as she told Harold

Acton. She was quite unable to do what Beverley Nichols thought she should do—"rise above it." Coward, elated by success, had a small volume of *Poems by Hernia Whittlebot* privately printed.

Osbert, in defence of his unhappy sister, and because he enjoyed a row, and perhaps because he felt a little responsible, wrote furious letters to Noel Coward. The row was not quickly over. Three years later Noel Coward was writing to his mother from New Jersey, on November 25, 1926:

> Oh dear I've made it up with Osbert Sitwell and it's all very funny—I wrote him a note saying that as we were both in a foreign country we ought to put an end to The Feud then he came round and suggested quite pleasantly that I should apologise to Edith publicly in all the papers! I gave him an old-fashioned look and explained gently that he was very silly indeed which he seemed to understand perfectly and we parted very amicably. It really was becoming a bore because he wasn't being asked anywhere poor dear owing to my popularity being the greater so that's that.[19]

Of course he didn't make a public apology to Edith, but a personal one by letter a few days later, and she replied from Pembridge Mansions on December 6: "Dear Mr. Coward, I accept your apology. Yours sincerely, Edith Sitwell." But that still wasn't that, even if Osbert had ceded a little ground in America for tactical reasons. Noel Coward had become one of the enemy. The painter C. R. W. Nevinson was at dinner at Osbert's house when another guest said that he wished someone would exterminate "the little *pastiche*"—Coward. "I wish you would," said Osbert. "Edith would be so obliged."[20] It was all a pity, because, as Lord Clark has said, Edith and Noel Coward "were really 'made for each other, my dear.'"

Edith and Wyndham Lewis were made for each other, too. He was a contributor to *Art and Letters*, on which Osbert worked, and became a friend of all three Sitwells. He was at the private performance of *Façade* at Carlyle Square, and also at the Aeolian Hall (afterwards he wrote to Osbert with modified approval that it was "an improvement on the first performance"). He came to Edith's tea parties in Pembridge Mansions, where the young Peter Quennell once spotted him "stationed moody and pallid beside the window," aloof from "a numerous assemblage of country cousins and lame dogs." He was by no means one of her protégés: Osbert rightly referred to him as a "veteran." He was five years older than Edith herself; his Vorticist period, the editorship of *Blast*, and service in the war already lay behind him. He had exhibited with the Camden Town group in 1911, and had had his first one-man show in London shortly after the war ended, in 1919; it had been after all this that Edith met him.

Lewis's personality, she said, changed from hour to hour:

> When he grinned, one felt as if one were looking at a lantern-slide . . . a click, a fade-out, and another slide, totally unconnected with it, and equally unreal, had taken its place. He was no longer the simple-minded artist, but a rather sinister, piratic, formidable Dago. For this remarkable man had a habit of appearing in various roles, partly as a disguise . . . and partly in order to defy his own loneliness.[21]

One of his favourite roles was the Spanish one, in which, she said, with irony, "he would assume a gay, if sinister, manner, very masculine and gallant, and deeply impressive to a feminine observer." Yet she was stimulated by him. As others of his admirers have done, she compared him with Swift, albeit unfavourably; and she diagnosed sentimentality and a longing to be liked behind the charades and the brusqueness.

Edith published two very similar accounts of Wyndham Lewis: one in her autobiography and another in her novel *I Live Under a Black Sun*, where he appears in the guise of Henry Debingham. They are both toned-down versions of a provocative essay she wrote in Paris in 1931, which survives (in Cornell University) but which was never published. In it she tells how Lewis "spent a very large part of his time with my brothers and me in the years 1921, 1922 and 1923, indeed, during this time he rarely absented himself from us for more than a few days." He wore a black patch, which he changed from eye to eye according to the person who was sitting next to him. When both eyes were uncovered, "they wore a blinking look of yearning and reproachful affection, extremely disconcerting to the object of the gaze." This look varied "from that of the canine friend of the well-known pictorial advertisement of His Master's Voice records, to that of a returning Wanderer seeing, from afar, the old Homestead." (Hemingway, who met him in Paris in the twenties, said he had the eyes of an "unsuccessful rapist.") And when the "look" did not bring results, Lewis would invoke the "aid and admiration" of "noisy frothing little Mr. Roy Campbell (that typhoon in a beer bottle), and little, imperceptible Mr. Cyril Connolly." (Edith was later to revise her 1931 estimates of these two.)

Lewis always pretended, she said, that he was being watched or noticed, behaving so oddly that he "attracted immediately that attention which might not, otherwise, have been forthcoming." She described his conversational manner in a paragraph that reveals a graphic and dramatic talent equal to his own. One afternoon she arrived for a sitting to find him shaving:

"D'you mind waiting whilst I shave?" "Not at all." Mr. Lewis heaved a sigh. "And *after* I've shaved, I mean" (very impressively) "to *wash my hands.*" Mr. Lewis sighed again. "I suppose you do everything one after another, don't you?" And he built an edifice in the air. "I mean you" (pause) "probably have a bath in the morning?" I assented. "And after that," (looking studious) "you probably" (pause) "brush your hair?" I agreed. Mr. Lewis at this moment remembered something and retraced his steps with an appearance of great despondency. "But *before* that you—brush your teeth?" "Yes." Mr. Lewis gave a sigh that was deep even for him. "It's that damned *Time!*" he assured me. "I seem to have so little Time for anything. Now sometimes I'll" (pause) "wash my hands in the morning—" (pause—another edifice) "and shave in the afternoon. At other times I'll . . ." he reflected. "Well, I suppose I'd better get on with what I'm doing."

This sort of dialogue is pure Lewis Carroll, and Edith, like Alice in Wonderland, enjoyed it all until it began to go wrong.

She was in great form, as Constance Sitwell, on a trip south from her home in Northumberland, found out. Constance had grown a little shy of Edith; one never knew what to expect, these days. She always wrote about her three cousins-by-marriage in her diary as though they were as unpredictable as the weather—except perhaps Osbert, who was always charming to her.

I went to tea with Edith feeling some excitement. . . . She had on wonderful clothes, as usual. She wasn't alone, which I was a little sorry for. But as the visitor was Cedric Morris,* I didn't regret it really since he was so nice. We all sat and talked very happily about poetry and the spirit of the English people and of artists. Edith read "The Kingfisher" of W. H. Davies beautifully. It really was lovely. Also talked of visions and E.S.P. Edith was very pleasant and natural.[22]

---

*Born 1889. Painter and horticulturist; member of the London Group.

And when all three Sitwells turned up to have tea with her the next day, "I loved having them; they were all so fresh and modern. Edith, as usual, in marvellously coloured clothes; she had been sitting for Wyndham Lewis." Edith sat for Wyndham Lewis for many drawings (as did her brothers) and for one major portrait. The sittings ended abruptly after ten months. ("Every day but Sundays," she said—she must have enjoyed his company to give up so much time to him.) The portrait, though worked on later, was never properly finished; Edith, in the picture, has no hands, and her hands were the feature of which she was most proud.

Wyndham Lewis had taken liberties with Edith, who in her old age put it this way: "He was, unfortunately, seized with a kind of *schwärmerei* for me. I did not respond. It did not get very far, but was a nuisance as he *would* follow me about, staring in a most trying manner and telling our acquaintances about the *schwärmerei*. So, eventually, I stopped sitting to him...."[23] This is the only occasion on record when any man is alleged to have shown direct sexual interest in Edith.

Wyndham Lewis became from then on indeed The Enemy. The year after the portrait episode, in February 1924, Lewis published part of his novel *The Apes of God* in the *Criterion*, which was edited by T. S. Eliot; but it was not until the full version appeared in book form in 1930 that the full force of his irony at the expense of Edith and her brothers was to break on their heads. The extended feud, however, gave some satisfaction to all parties; and in *Blasting and Bombardiering* (1937) Lewis wrote cosily that Edith "is one of my most hoary, tried, and reliable enemies. We are two good old enemies, Edith and I, *inseparables*, in fact. I do not think I should be exaggerating if I described myself as Miss Edith Sitwell's *favourite enemy*." In the year that appeared, Edith's only novel, *I Live Under a Black Sun*, was published, containing the caricature of Wyndham Lewis in the character of Henry Debingham. It is a very mild caricature compared with his treatment of her in *Apes of God*. The practical jokes she and Osbert played on Wyndham Lewis after *The Apes of God* came out were crueller. For example:

And when I feel cross, which is often, I tease Wyndham Lewis. Osbert and I tease him without stopping.... We also send him raving mad telegrams. I got one sent to him from Calais to his address in Percy Street, which ran thus [the German is a reference to his book on Hitler]:

Percy Wyndham Lewis, 21 Percy Street etc. *Achtung. Nicht hinauslehnen.* Uniformed commissar man due. Stop. Better wireless help

> Last night too late. Love. *Ein Freund.* Signed. Lewis Wyndham, 21 Percy Street.

> And two days ago he got a telegram saying "*Achtung. Nicht hinauslehnen. The Bear dances.*"[24]

Rows and teases of all sorts had become a way of life. It was impossible for an acquaintance to keep up-to-date with them all. There were as many quarrels with fellow writers and poets as there were with the philistines. Osbert was every bit as combative as Edith, and Sacheverell was dragged along in their wake. The situation in March 1924 was summed up by an amused Arnold Bennett in his journal:

> Edith Sitwell last night told me of the feuds in the verse world. Osbert is always planning some literary practical joke against someone. Siegfried Sassoon won't speak to Osbert now because (he says) Osbert will never leave him alone. He won't speak to Edith, because Edith will not stop Osbert doing his tricks. "But what can I do," said Edith. In revenge, Sacheverell Sitwell swears he will never speak to Siegfried again. It appears also that either Siegfried won't speak to Robert Graves or vice versa.[25]

One would imagine that it would be hard to work well in such a climate, amid so many tensions and time-wasting petty jealousies. But the very reverse was the case. Edith was writing some of the best poetry of her life in 1923 and 1924. In May 1923 she took part in a discussion on poetry with Alfred Noyes at the London School of Economics. Her poetry readings, both private and public, were numerous. That year saw the Aeolian Hall *Façade* and the publication of *Bucolic Comedies*; in January 1924 she had a short story in *The Golden Hind*, and that March, Duckworth published *The Sleeping Beauty*, her major work from this period, and for some people, notably Cyril Connolly, "one of the loveliest poems I'd ever read." That spring "Colonel Fantock" and "Mademoiselle Richarde" were published in the *Spectator*, and later included in *Troy Park*. Edith was drawing deeply on her childhood memories for this poetry, using up the deposit of early impressions and early experience which can only be used once to significant effect.

6
Entr'acte: Early Poetry

In her *A Poet's Notebook* (1943), Edith quoted Goethe: "To know how cherries and strawberries taste, ask children and birds." This young, sharp knowledge, she said, was also in folk songs and in "many of the sweet and exquisite nursery rhymes. In these respects, I, for one, am both bird and child."

In her early verse, of the period of *Wheels* and for a few years after, nursery-rhyme language is mixed with the sort of evocative nonsense poetry peculiar to England, laced with a set of mannered images that recall the English 1890s as well as the French symbolists. Traditional tales and rhymes, Edward Lear, Lewis Carroll, J. M. Barrie, the drawings of Aubrey Beardsley, the ballet designs of Bakst, the monkeys, negroes, and emperors of the Renishaw tapestries. . . . "It is at once very sophisticated and very simple," wrote Stephen Spender.

In one of Edith's early poems, "Portrait of a Barmaid," first published in the *Cambridge Magazine* in April 1919, there is an adult consciousness showing, and an indication of the way in which she might have developed had she turned her eyes on the outside world:

Metallic waves of people jar
Through crackling green toward the bar

Where on the tables, chattering white,
The sharp drinks quarrel with the light.

. . . .

Outside the bar, where jangling heat
Seems out of tune and off the beat,

A concertina's glycerine
Exudes and mirrors in the green

Your soul, pure glucose edged with hints
Of tentative and half-soiled tints.

It is poetry of fantasy and artifice, with an undertow of the macabre, which is always present even in the "strange secluded world," well described by Kenneth Clark, in which most of her poetry seems to be written:

> We picture her imprisoned in an enormous kitchen garden where, to her childish eyes, the flowers, leaves and fruits are all of giant size. At one end of the garden is a summer house in the Chinese taste, faded and ramshackle, a few bells still tinkling from its eaves. . . . No human beings enter this garden, except a governess and an ancient, wrinkled gardener, who remains for long the most important figure in her imagination. . . . [1]

"We are in pagoda country," wrote L. P. Hartley of her early poetry, "superimposed on an English landscape."[2]

Sometimes, as in "The King of China's Daughter," she simply adapts an existing nursery rhyme. Other childish pieces are very much in the idiom of Walter de la Mare's "Peacock Pie"; he is one of the poets whose lines she used to copy into her earliest notebooks. "Three poor witches," for example:

Whirring, walking
On the tree-top,
Three poor witches
Mow and mop.
Three poor witches
Fly on switches
Of a broom,
From their cottage room.
Like goat's-beard rivers,
Black and lean,
Are Moll and Meg,
And Myrrhaline.

"Gardener Janus Catches a Naiad" is typical of Edith's early manner (it is from *Bucolic Comedies*). Love or lust is known only glancingly, in the flight of silly pretty girls and the stylized, inconclusive pursuit of the gardener-satyr:

> Ma'am, I've heard your laughter flare
> Through your waspish-gilded hair:
> > Feathered masks,
> > Pots of peas,
> > Janus asks
> > Naught of these.
> > Creaking water
> > Brightly stripèd,
> > Now, I've caught her—
> > Shrieking biped.
> > Flute sounds jump
> > And turn together,
> > Changing clumps
> > Of glassy feather.
> > In among the
> > Pots of peas—
> > Naiad changes—
> > Quick as these.

It is cool, self-concealing stuff, an end in itself. Aldous Huxley perceived this, and wrote about it in the *Chapbook* of March 1920, when there was still very little of her published verse on which to form a judgment:

> By thinking about it hard enough, you can make the sunshine dance and sing, you can cause the whole landscape to crepitate and twitch galvanically as it does in the poetry of Miss Sitwell. Brilliantly accomplished and exquisite as the poetry of this talented writer often is, one is always conscious of its limitations. It is difficult to see how it can advance. Obviously, you cannot carry the process of dissociation beyond a certain point. Great poetry is surely created by the opposite method . . . by a passing outwards from the immediacies of consciousness towards the universal.

With the *Façade* poems of 1921–1922 came greater concentration and control. Edith liked to quote Jean Cocteau's remark about his *Parade*, which was a direct antecedent of *Façade*: It was "the poetry of childhood taken over by a technician." Meaning, always elusive in Edith's early poetry, became a very minor consideration. "The poems in *Façade* consist of enquiries into the effect on rhythm and speed of the use of rhymes, assonances, and dissonances. . . ." Another variable was "texture," "the subtle thickness and thinness brought about by changing one consonant or labial."[3]

Like all interiorized technique, it is mercifully not apparent. What is apparent is an originality and a rhythmic vitality that still seem provocative and extraordinary sixty years after. The *Façade* poems were written very quickly, in almost daily consultation with her brothers and William Walton; the concentration and unlaboured fluency of the poems are part of their comic charm. The rhythm is sometimes aggressive:

SOMETHING lies beyond the scene, the encre de chine, marine, obscene

Horizon

    In
       Hell

Black as a bison
See the tall black Aga on the sofa in the alga mope, his
Bell-rope
Moustache (clear as a great bell!)
Waves in eighteen-eighty
Bustles
Come
Late with tambourines of
Rustling
Foam. . . .

Or the rhythm is silky and swooping, as in "Popular Song":

Lily O'Grady,
Silly and shady,
Longing to be
A lazy lady,

Walked by the cupolas, gables in the
Lake's Georgian stables. . . .

Or as in "Waltz":

So Daisy and Lily,
Lazy and silly,
Walk by the shore of the wan grassy sea,
Talking once more 'neath a swan-bosomed tree.
Rose castles,
Tourelles,
Those bustles!
Mourelles
Of the shade in their train follow. . . .

It is very hard to separate the rhythms and melodies when one is accustomed
to hearing them read as they were designed to be, to Walton's music. Sometimes the words are the purest nonsense, as in "The Wind's Bastinado":

Said Il Magnifico
Pulling a fico —
With a stoccado
And a gambado,
Making a wry
Face: "This corraceous
Round orchidaceous
Laceous porraceous
Fruit is a lie!"

"Some of the poems have a violent exhilaration; others have a veiled melancholy," as Edith herself wrote. "Their apparent gaiety caused them to be
suspect. They were useless. They were butterflies. They were spivs."[4] The
nearest contemporary English-language comparison with Edith's abstract-
sound experiments comes from Wallace Stevens, on the other side of the
Atlantic, eight years her senior. Edith included his "Bantams in Pinewoods" in
her anthology *The Atlantic Book of British and American Poetry*:

Chieftain Iffucan of Azcan in caftan
Of tan with henna heckles, halt!

> Damned universal cock, as if the sun
> Was blackamoor to bear your blazing tail. . . .

But however glittering and staccato her language, the enchanted garden is never far away in Edith's poetry, with its "Emily-coloured primulas" and "Martha-coloured scabious," the orange and lemon trees, the flitting kitchen maids and, in "Early Spring" (from the last cycle of *Wheels*), the French governess who, as the child knows,

> If she could think me distant, she
> In the snow's goat-locks certainly
>
> Would try to milk those teats, the buds,
> Of their warm sticky milk—the cuds
>
> Of strange long-past fruit-hairy springs—
> The beginnings of first earthy things.

As in Christina Rossetti's "Goblin Market," sensuality in Edith Sitwell's poetry is expressed in vegetable terms.

Edith was, however, in no sense a "nature poet," as the term is generally understood. "The world I see is a country world, a universe of growing things, where magic and growth are one," she wrote.[5] Her poems are made of leaves, flowers, fruit, beasts, trees, furs, and feather. But they are not the actual, ordinary garden varieties. In her fugue into being "both bird and child," she thought magically, as a child thinks before it has learnt to conceptualize. She took into this primitive perceptual dimension the ideas of the French symbolists.

She said that she used to study the repetitions of patterns in nature: the patterns of fern and feather reflected by the patterns of frost on a windowpane; the scales of a bird's legs repeated in certain grasses. These formal echoes were one manifestation, for her, of the "correspondences" of Swedenborg and Mallarmé. Her flowers and fruit are in a notional, "corresponding," Platonic dimension, at one remove from the real things grown by her grandmothers' gardeners.

Real flowers were only spurs to imagination. Edith did not need them very much; she did not fill her rooms in Pembridge Mansions with bowls of flowers. She could not afford to; but in any case, as her cousin Veronica

(Codrington) Gilliat said (not unkindly, for they were devoted to one another), Edith "didn't care much for flowers unless she could make a phrase of them." She said herself that she "killed flowers, nourished jewels"—and her flowers have often the enameled glitter of metal.

This unreality irritated her critics. "It is this inability to see and hear what is around her that is Edith Sitwell's limitation as a poet,"[6] wrote Julian Symons, apropos of her "artificial" imagery. He was right in that she did not fully see the real world; Sacheverell, who knew intimately her inner world, was astonished by the way it was created, not so much from observation as from the opposite. A glance, a glimpse, a colour, a botanical name, was enough to set her alight. Exterior nature was a source for fantasy, sound, and symbol. One would say for this reason that she was a supremely literary writer, were it not for the fact that her imagination operated on a childlike, preliterary system.

Harold Acton summed up the position in relation to her contemporaries and to the "literary scene" as she found it: "Had Rimbaud been known in England, we should have been spared Georgian poetry."[7] Helen Rootham had soaked Edith in the French symbolists. Already intoxicated by the heady rhythms and ambiguities of Swinburne, the abstract music of the symbolists, the "*sanglots longs des violons*" of Verlaine, his harlequins and clowns and Scaramouches, lightened and syncopated her own melody. Rimbaud, like Edith, had been deprived of maternal affection. Her feeling of being "a little outside life" echoed his "*Je ne suis pas au monde.*" Rimbaud had an influential teacher, Izambard. Edith had Helen Rootham, herself a *dévote* of the Rimbaud myth and of Rimbaud's gift.

"*Il s'agit d'arriver à l'inconnu par le dérèglement de tous les sens*," Rimbaud wrote to his teacher. Edith said much the same thing: "My senses are like those of primitive peoples . . . and they are interchangeable."[8] (There's one crucial difference: Rimbaud's "primitive" sensualism was also explored physically. Edith sidestepped that dimension. She stuck to music and literature for her sense experiments.)

Edith's analysis of her own prosody is generally dreary to read, as in "Some Notes on My Own Poetry," since it mainly consists of detailed explanations of the sound patterns. For example, on a passage from "Waltz":

In the lines

> Shades on heroic
> Lonely grass,

> Where the moonlight's echoes die and pass.
> Near the rustic boorish,
> Fustian Moorish
> Castle wall of the ultimate Shade,

the long "o"s of "heroic" and "lonely," cast at opposite ends of two succeeding lines ("lonely" being slightly longer than "heroic"), the still deeper "oo" of "moonlight," the hollow sound of "echoes"—these throw long, and opposed, shadows. . . . The "oo"s in "boorish" and "Moorish" are still darker, and the shadows seem at once blown forward by the "r"s, as by a gust of wind . . . .

And so on—Edith's answer to Practical Criticism, written in 1934. Of more interest is the importance she put on explaining her imagery, feeling that it ought to be capable of rational interpretation—which cannot always be done, and should not always need to be done. Of "Aubade," for example: "The reason I said 'The morning light creaks' is this: after rain, the early light seems as if it does not run quite smoothly. Also, it has a quality of great hardness and seems to present a physical obstacle to the shadows. . . ."[9] Maybe. But this is defensive. The *dérèglement de tous les sens* needs no literal justification if the senses are to remain properly *déréglés*, still less a prosaic schoolroom discipline. But there was no canon for the symbolist tradition in England when Edith began her experiments, and no one, unless the undergraduate Dadaistes of the 1920s are admitted, picked up her torch. She felt aggressively on her own. It was not until twenty years later that her experiments could be seen historically, as for example by Jack Lindsay: "If you look carefully you can find the English equivalent of Symbolism beginning in poets like Beddoes or even Darley (with the unknown giant Blake behind it, and many roots in Keats and Shelley). But the Tennysonian betrayal killed it off. The English form reappeared in Edith Sitwell, at a white-hot intensity."[10]

"Aubade," first published in the *Saturday Westminster Gazette* on October 2, 1920, is an ideal poem for seeing Edith's mixed-sense imagery in action:

> Jane, Jane,
> Tall as a crane,
> The morning light creaks down again;
>
> Comb your cockscomb-ragged hair,
> Jane, Jane, come down the stair.

Each dull blunt wooden stalactite
Of rain creaks, hardened by the light,

Sounding like an overtone
From some lonely world unknown.

But the creaking empty light
Will never harden into sight,

Will never penetrate your brain
With overtones like the blunt rain.

The light would show (if it could harden)
Eternities of kitchen garden,

Cockscomb flowers that none will pluck,
And wooden flowers that 'gin to cluck.

In the kitchen you must light
Flames as staring, red and white,

As carrots or as turnips, shining
Where the cold dawn light lies whining.

Cockscomb hair on the cold wind
Hangs limp, turns the milk's weak mind. . . .
    Jane, Jane,
    Tall as a crane,
    The morning light creaks down again!

"The poem was written like this," Edith wrote of "Aubade" to R. G. Howarth in 1937; "it was about a year after I had emerged from a longish period of poverty in London—(I am the poor member of a rich family) . . . the whole experience was mine *and* the servant's, but seen through my mind."[11]

In the same way, in "Mademoiselle Richarde," she saw "through her mind" the life of one of the many governesses who lived out their half-lives in the great houses of her childhood:

There are sad ghosts whose living was not life
But a small complaining, dying without strife,

A little reading by sad candlelight
Of some unowned, un-cared for book, a slight
Rustling then, a settling down to sleep.

. . . .

Yet there are those who do not feel the cold;
And Mademoiselle Richarde was thus, —both old
And sharp, content to be the cold wind's butt;
A tiny spider in a gilded nut
She lived and rattled in the emptiness
Of other people's splendours. . . .

This is a quite different kind of poetry. It is from *Troy Park* (1925). After *Façade*, her experimental pyrotechnics over, Edith rejoined the English romantics from a new starting point, and wrote in leisured lyric measures of what she remembered. The three collections of the mid-1920s—*The Sleeping Beauty* (1924), *Troy Park*, and *Rustic Elegies* (1927)—contain the most realized poetry that she ever wrote. She had not only the desire to write, always strong in her, but she had struck a vein, unique to herself, of material to write about—her vision of an idealized childhood and of the past. Content dominated form, and feeling dominated striving for effect:

Those magical bright movements of a dream
Flashing between the lustrous leaves evoke
One memory of childhood, still undimmed.

("The Child Who Saw Midas")

"Colonel Fantock" is in *Troy Park* ("But Dagobert and Peregrine and I / Were children then. . . . "); and the nursery world of her brothers, in the years before they were old enough to walk with her in the gardens, are recollected in earlier poems, in *Bucolic Comedies* (1923). In "Evening,"

Prince Absalom and Sir Rotherham Redde
Rode on a rocking-horse home to bed.

Troy Park itself is Londesborough, not Renishaw. Edith's great-grandmother Londesborough is in "Colonel Fantock," and her grandmother Londesborough in *The Sleeping Beauty*, in a grotesque role as the Wicked Fairy, "Laideronette, Princess of the Pagodas," whose black slaves

> Unwigged her for the night, while her apes beg
> That she will leave uncurtained that Roc's egg
>
> Her head, a mount of diamonds bald and big
> In the ostrich feathers that compose her wig.

And her great-grandmother again, as the Dowager Queen, who reads her Latin missal:

> And this is now her only pleasure—
> This and her parrot long ago
> Dead—but none dared tell her so
>
> And therefore the bird was stuffed and restored
> To lifeless immortality; bored
> It seemed, but yet it remained her own;
> And she never knew the bird's soul had flown.

The Princess herself, the Sleeping Beauty, is *intacta* and untouchable:

> She seems, as she glimmers round the room,
> Like a lovely milk-white unicorn
> In a forestial thicket of thorn.

Because the poetry of her later years is different in mood and manner from her early work, a distinction has to be made when evaluating "the poetry of Edith Sitwell." It is in her early work—in the vitality and inventiveness of the *Façade* poems, and in the personal fantasy of *The Sleeping Beauty*, "Colonel Fantock," "Mademoiselle Richarde," and the *Troy Park* poems—that Edith best inhabited her peculiar talent. It is in these poems that she is a "first-rate" poet, in Hazlitt's definition: "It is easy to describe second rate talents, because they fall into a class, and enlist under a standard; but first rate powers defy calculation or comparison, and can only be defined by themselves. They are *sui generis*, and make the class to which they belong."[12]

Once Edith had written out her childhood themes and dreams, she had nowhere else to go. The dark side of the moon began to take over altogether. The shadow of Eliot, and the English metaphysical poets, whom she read closely, reinforced this tendency. In spite of her absorption in the French symbolists she had not, until now, taken into her own repertoire their charnel imagery, their squalors of the big city, the "*spleen*" of Baudelaire. When Edith turned her thoughts away from her mythologized childhood, she found only disillusion. "When we were young, how beautiful life seemed!" she wrote in *The Sleeping Beauty*:

> But age has brought a little subtle change
> Like the withdrawal caused by the slow dropping
> Of cold sad water on some vast stone image:
> A slow withdrawal, a sad, gradual change. . . .

It is as if for her there was nothing between childhood and old age; or as if the prelapsarian summer garden of childhood had been just a veneer over the awful truth of life, as the park at Renishaw covered the coal mine.

It begins in "The Hambone and the Heart," a reworking of her early matricide poem "The Mother," and included in *Rustic Elegies*:

> Could we foretell the worm within the heart
> That holds the households and the parks of heaven,
> Could we foretell that land was only earth,
> Would it be worth the pain of death and birth,
> Would it be worth the soul from body riven?
>
> . . . .
>
> O crumbling Heart, I too, I too have known
> The terrible Gehenna of the bone
> Deserted by the flesh. . . .

In a poem of which the first, and longer, version was written in 1929, "Metamorphosis," the themes and symbols of all her poetry of the 1940s and 1950s are already present: Lazarus, the bone, the grave, the worm, the stone, the fire, the ape. It ends on a note of resurrection:

> Then my immortal Sun rose, Heavenly Love,
> To rouse my carrion. . . .

But it was to be many years before she was to find the fulfilment of that metaphysical sunrise; and even then, the reassurance of Heavenly Love did not always work for her. In the same year as "Metamorphosis" she wrote the black, drum-beating commination "Gold Coast Customs." And then almost nothing for ten years.

When she began to write again in the 1940s, childhood and death, little by little, became part of the same thought. The easy measures of her *Troy* poetry turned sometimes to hectic rhetoric; her imagery and vocabulary, always repetitive (she was an instrument of a few clear notes, and should have been more economical), became oppressively so. She found new material in the "second Fall of Man": war and the atomic bomb. This new poetry found an audience and made her famous again. It is a cruel irony, however, that when she adopted Aldous Huxley's recipe for the creation of great poetry, that of "working outwards from the immediacies of consciousness towards the universal," her gift became blurred.

It was not, as Julian Symons said, her "inability to see and hear what was around her" that defined her limitations as a poet. The reverse is true. Her gift was the transcription of what she saw with her inner eye and heard with her inner ear. Her experience of adult life was so circumscribed that it gave her little new life-material; only death-material. All she could do was to make Janus-turns between childhood and the grave. Sometimes she achieved a synthesis, as in "The Wind of Early Spring," a poem of the early 1950s:

> The past and present are as one —
> Accordant and discordant, youth and age,
> And death and birth. For out of one came all —
> From all comes one.

It was the difficulty of her passage between the two that limited Edith Sitwell's poetry after the 1920s. As the Duke said to Claudio in *Measure for Measure*:

> Thou hast nor youth nor age;
> But, as it were, an after-dinner's sleep,
> Dreaming on both.[13]

7

A Unicorn Among Lions
1924-1926

So profound was Edith's involvement in her own work in the first years of the 1920s that it was not until early 1924 that she read T. S. Eliot's "The Waste Land," which by then had already been out for two years. She wrote to a new friend, John Freeman, asking him what he thought of it. Freeman was a "Georgian" poet who worked for the Liverpool Victoria Friendly Society for a living; Edith wrote to him, "Robert Graves must meet you. He *must*. . . . The meeting must be arranged, though at the moment the Graves family is invisible, as there is a new small son. They are both most charming people." About "The Waste Land," Edith seemed uncertain and amateur: "Some of the lines are really wonderful, I think. Do tell me your opinion, if you have read it." When Freeman criticized "The Waste Land" for lacking form, she disagreed with him, but wrote that she did not know how to argue her points—as, it became apparent when she tried to do so, was indeed the case. But Eliot's poem, which she came to tentatively and late, was to affect what she herself was to be writing in the next five years—though she denied Eliot's influence. She was careful not to miss anything else he wrote, for she was writing to the bookseller Bumpus in November 1925, "Will you please send me Mr. T. S. Eliot's 'Poems' as soon as they appear?" (This would have been *The Hollow Men*.)

In late 1924, exhausted by overwork, severe back trouble, and other people, her next volume of poems, *Troy Park*, already completed, Edith fled to Paris, to stay for a few months with Evelyn Wiel, Helen Rootham's sister, who had a small flat at 129 rue Saint-Dominique, in the seventh arrondissement. This sister had married a Norwegian, Truels Wiel, who had been Norway's vice-consul in Paris. He deserted Evelyn for another woman in 1921, and finally left France; Evelyn stayed on in Paris, keeping herself—just—by an office job. In 1927 she obtained a divorce. Seven years older than Edith, she shared her sister's devotion to her, and, like Helen, was to become the most loyal of lame dogs.

However, in 1924, Edith was writing happily to Harold Acton from the rue Saint-Dominique that "I am in hiding, doing my writing. But Valéry Larbaud has been to tea with me,—last week,—and I shall be seeing him again in a day or two. He is dedicating a prose poem to me. . . . And this afternoon, I am going to tea with Gertrude Stein."

Amid these distractions she could not forget the home battlefield. She wrote to Mr. Wilson of Bumpus's book shop shortly after her arrival in the rue Saint-Dominique, asking him to send a copy of W. J. Turner's *Smaragda's Lover* to Osbert at the Hotel Bristol in Rapallo. Turner had written a "dramatic phantasmagoria" which was seemingly a skit on the Sitwells. Edith wrote to John Freeman asking if he had read it too:

> It is all about my family,—about us—and he has been cad enough to make out that I write verses which are disgustingly dirty, and common; and, besides this, that we have a debauching influence on people. I don't mind a bit if he says I can't write, because that is within the proper scope of literary criticism, but *this* is simply one mass of lies.

This is disingenuous. Edith found some satisfaction in picking her scabs. She could never let a hurt heal of its own accord, still less in silence.

Yet in truth there was more to it than that. In the September 1922 issue of Harold Monro's *Chapbook* there had been a satire entitled "The Jolly Old Squire or Way-Down in Georgia," the subject of which needs no explanation. In it "T*urner" figures as a ludicrous weekend rustic poet who lives in London. The author of the piece was Osbert Sitwell. Turner was doing no more than getting his own back.

In 1925, when Edith was thirty-eight, the closed corporation of the three Sitwells began to fall apart. They were together in Spain at Easter; Osbert had paid Edith's fare out so that she could recuperate from the operation she had had for her back trouble. *Troy Park* had come out from Duckworth in March, and from Knopf in the United States a little later. "I was very gloomy about *Troy Park*, I don't know why exactly," Edith wrote to John Freeman from Granada. "Perhaps because one always hopes to do so much better." She had seen two notices, one "imbecile" and the other "impertinent." "Her need is for stringent self-criticism," said *The Times Literary Supplement*'s reviewer on May 28; but he gave her a long review.

Cyril Connolly, then an undergraduate at Balliol, encountered the three Sitwells at the Washington Irving Hotel in Granada. "All of them were wearing black capes and black Andalusian hats and looked magnificent"—but alarming. Connolly was "totally bowled over by them." He had been enchanted by Edith's *The Sleeping Beauty*, and also told her how much he admired "The Waste Land." "I'll tell Mr. Eliot next time I see him. He'll be delighted," said Edith.[1]

Connolly wavered in his feelings about the Sitwells; he did not go to the tea parties at Pembridge Mansions to which Edith invited him when they were all back in England. And in November 1926 he was writing to Noel Blakiston:

> I don't hold with the Sitwells you know. I think they are very tiresome but they were very nice to me in Spain and have been nice since. As a matter of fact I haven't read anything they have written in the last year or so. Edith is tedious, humourless and combative, Osbert advertises, Sashie is the most remote but none are really our style.[2]

That summer of 1925 Sir George, now sixty-five and hypochondriacal, and Lady Ida removed themselves from Renishaw and Scarborough to make Montegufoni their principal home. They virtually emigrated; Sir George took his capital with him, entailed Renishaw, and left Osbert in charge, though the latter had no intention of giving up his London life. Renishaw became for the moment a place for retrenchment and short holidays for Sir George and for all his children.

For a year Sacheverell, "the most remote," as Connolly said, tall and slim and shy like a Donatello youth, had been making plans of his own. Osbert had met a Canadian girl called Georgia Doble at a party at Arnold Bennett's house in the spring of 1924; he invited her to come to Carlyle Square to tea. There she and Sacheverell fell in love.

Georgia was one of two beautiful sisters—her elder sister, Frances, was an actress on the London stage—the daughters of a Montreal banker of Cornish extraction, Arthur Doble. Georgia was fascinated by the Sitwellian scene; but Edith and Osbert were taken aback by the idea of Sachie—or of any of them—marrying anyone at all. (Edith's old love Chile Guevara was back in London that year after a four-year absence; they met as friends.) The Sitwells felt that Georgia's background was too unlike their own; Edith felt her younger brother should put his work before everything. But it was Osbert, with whom Sachie shared the Carlyle Square house, and for whom Sachie was the ideal and familiar companion, who was hardest hit.

The young couple stuck to their guns, and were married in St. George's Church in Paris in October 1925. Edith nearly missed the wedding; she could not afford the trip to France, she told Sachie. She and Helen were both overdrawn at the bank. Possibly Osbert paid her fare; for both he and she were at the wedding, and Georgia's parents and sister. Sir George and Lady Ida remained at Montegufoni.

It was a happy marriage. Besides being attractive and intelligent, Georgia had toughness to complement Sacheverell's pliancy, and was the most loyal and supportive of wives. The Sitwells, of whom Georgia was now one, continued to present a united face to the world.

The reality was necessarily a little more complicated. Osbert dedicated a book to Georgia even before the marriage took place, but they were never close to each other. In his loneliness after Sachie's apparent defection Osbert made new attachments, and came out of the closet sufficiently to make them, though never far enough to endanger his reputation. He became obsessed by his friendship for Adrian Stokes, and in the new year broke new ground by going for the first time to the United States.

Edith, in her unconditional love for Sacheverell, embraced Georgia as well. When she was living in France in the 1930s Edith sketched out parts of an autobiography, which she headed *Family Portrait*, sections of which were used thirty years later in her published autobiography, *Taken Care Of*. This draft includes material about her feelings for Georgia that was not later used. She listed as one of the best things in her life "having a sister-in-law who is as much and as strongly part of my life (and I of hers) as if we had been born of the same parents." Edith praised Georgia's beauty, and her character: "wise, just, sane and sweet; and her friendship for me has been one of the greatest beauties of my life." (She described herself in the same draft as "too violent in my passions, too trustful, and too shortsighted.") The friendship between the two did not always live up to this ideal. But Georgia helped Edith a great deal, just because she was more worldly, less hypersensitive, socially easier.

Edith's close friendships with women in the 1920s were not numerous. She always made things difficult by pouring scorn on women in the same line of business as herself. She was not at ease in large social groups, as Virginia Woolf, herself in a withdrawn phase, recognized: She described in a letter to Vita Sackville-West being at a Bloomsbury party in January 1926, "sitting outside, with glass between me and everybody, hearing them laugh; and seeing, as through a telescope (she looked so remote and washed up on a rock) poor Edith Sitwell, in her brocade dress, sitting silent."[3] Two mute Andromedas they seem, on two widely separated rocks, with the party swirling between them—both of them "not waving but drowning."

Most women with pretension to culture and sensibility filled Edith with horror. Back in 1919, she had written to Robert Nichols: "As for the kind of women you mention—they should have been allowed to remain an organism with as much life as a sea-anemone. The trouble is, that these creatures realise that it is fashionable to be smeared with brain and in consequence they lose their one usefulness." In the same letter she told Nichols about a "depressing evening" where all the guests were female poets. She had been invited to meet Charlotte Mew:

> What a grey tragic woman—about sixty in point of age, and sucked dry of blood (though not of spirit) by an arachnoid mother. I tried to get her to come and see me; but she is a hermit, inhabited by a terrible bitterness, and though she was very nice to me, she wouldn't come. Besides her, I met an appalling woman called Madeline Caron Rock, extremely fat and exuding a glutinous hysteria from every pore. I sat beside her on the sofa, and became (much against both our wills) embedded in her exuberance like a very sharp battle-axe. Whenever anyone mentioned living, dying, eating, sleeping, or any other of the occurrences that beset us, Miss Rock would allow a gelatinous cube-like tear, still warm from her humanity, to fall upon my person, and would then leave the room in a marked manner.[4]

Somewhat surprisingly, Edith ended this anecdote with "She is rather a good poet, all the same."

Edith, in the 1920s or at any other time, did not care for professional competition from her own sex. She did not want to believe that there was any worth speaking of. Yet she did need female friendship. What she needed was a jagger.

Jagger is a word coined in the 1920s by Evelyn Waugh and the Lygon sisters from the surname of a woman they knew who embodied the concept. A jagger is a supportive, uncritical, generous-hearted friend who is always pleasant and helpful while remaining wonderfully undemanding on his or her own account. It is tacitly understood that it is the jaggered one, and not the jagger, whose thoughts, words, deeds, and needs are uppermost in both their minds. It is such a useful notion that it is capable of being taken further than Waugh took it. A jagger is not a "groupie," even though most famous men are well jaggered—usually by wives, secretaries, or agents. A jagger should be of similar social and intellectual standing to the jaggered one, so that the latter's qualities may be properly perceived and appreciated. Dr. Watson was Sherlock Holmes's jagger, and Lord Byron had five or six, most of whom recorded their conversations with him. A jagger can pursue a career of his own—indeed if he is wise he will, for he will not be wanted all the time, and his role is not to be dependent, but to be dependable. He must discharge the duties of a patron with the demeanour of a client.

Edith already had a jagger, it might be thought, in Helen Rootham. But Helen could not stimulate Edith anymore. As the 1920s progressed she moved imperceptibly from her role of adviser and fellow conspirator and deeper into the role of dependent. She was aging, ailing, and frustrated. Her ambitions to be a singer had not come to very much. Through A. R. Orage, editor of the *New Age*, she had come into contact with Dmitri Mitrinovic, a Serb who peddled cabalistic religion, and Ouspensky, the follower of Gurdjieff. She was passionately interested in these people. Edith inherited £3,000 from a great-aunt, and gave £1,000 of it to Helen, and £100 to Helen's sister Evelyn. When Edith's Aunt Florence heard this—and moreover that Helen had handed her share to a "bad painter" with whom she was taken up—she cut Edith out of her will. But Edith, for whom loyalty was the first and last virtue, was never to let Helen down. Their lives were too deeply intertwined, and she owed Helen so much. As, in the late 1920s, they went increasingly often to Paris, Helen's sister Evelyn Wiel also became part of Edith's life—and, as time went on, another of her responsibilities.

But Edith met the perfect dependable friend in Allanah Harper, a tall, fair English girl with a great enthusiasm for modern art and literature, who spent a lot of her time and money in France. She was the daughter of a successful engineer who had been one of the two British consultants on the first Aswan Dam project, and Allanah had spent much of her childhood abroad. Allanah first saw and heard Edith in early 1925, reciting her poems in Lady Mond's house. Edith seemed to Allanah then

> a legendary figure who seemed to have moved out of the tapestry of *La Dame et le Licorne*. Here was the beauty of a Piero della Francesca. Her flat fair hair was like that of a naiad, her hands as white as alabaster. On her long gothic fingers she wore huge rings, lumps of topaz and turquoise, on her wrists were coral and jet bracelets. She began to recite and a window opened on an enchanted world. Never had I heard a more beautifully modulated voice.[5]

Allanah left without saying good-bye, repeating the lines she had heard—

> When green as the river was the barley
> Green as the river the rye. . . .

The two met, and Allanah was asked to tea at Pembridge Mansions, a little astounded to find the "legendary figure" opening the door herself with a kitchen teapot in her hand. The first time she went to tea she met Eliot; the second gathering included Virginia Woolf, Edmund Blunden, William Walton, Arthur Waley, and Humbert Wolfe. Edith and Virginia Woolf, Allanah thought, were like "two praying mantis putting out delicate antennae towards one another." The conversations turned to Vita Sackville-West's long poem *The Land*, which had just won the Hawthornden Prize. "It is not poetry," said Edith. "It would be entirely suitable for the use of farmers to help them to count the ticks on their sheep." (This was the first but not the last time she made this particular joke.) Mrs. Woolf, who loved Vita Sackville-West, said: "Edith, must one always tell the truth?"[6]

Virginia Woolf was constantly adjusting her estimate of Edith. She had dined with all three Sitwells at Carlyle Square in May 1925, and afterwards wrote in her journal:

> Edith is an old maid. I had never conceived this. I thought she was severe, implacable & tremendous; rigid in her own conception. Not a bit of it. She is, I guess, a little fussy, very kind, beautifully mannered. . . . She is elderly too, almost my age, & timid, & admiring and easy and poor, & I liked her more than admired or was frightened of her. Nevertheless, I do admire her work, & thats [*sic*] what I say of hardly anyone: she has an ear, and not a carpet broom; a satiric vein; & some beauty in her.[7]

Edith was humble, she wrote, with nothing of the protester or pamphleteer or pioneer about her, "rather the well born Victorian spinster. So I must read her afresh." She liked Edith's brothers as well that evening, and the "goodnatured generalities" of the after-dinner talk. "But why are they thought daring and clever? Why are they the laughing stocks of the music halls & the penny a liners?" The following month the Woolfs invited Edith to dinner; Vita Sackville-West, Morgan (E. M.) Forster, and George Rylands were there too. On this occasion Edith was "like a Roman Empress, so definite clear cut, magisterial & yet with something of the humour of a fishwife—a little too commanding about her own poetry & ready to dictate—tremulously pleased by Morgan's compliments (& he never praised Vita, who sat hurt, modest, silent, like a snubbed schoolboy)."

Allanah Harper took Edith and her work very seriously. After hearing her recite, Allanah had bought Edith's most recent book, *Troy Park*. And later in the year she wrote an article on the work of the Sitwells for a Belgian review, *Le Flambeau*, and sent from Paris a copy of what she had written to Edith. Edith's response was enthusiastic, and she wrote from Pembridge Mansions on the last day of 1925:

> I am absolutely delighted with the article dealing with the three Sitwells. It is quite evident to me that you get every single implication in our work, and I'm more pleased with it than I can say.
>
> I don't think there's anything to question at all. You have presented the whole thing so clearly. How nice it is to have people understand one's work like this.

She did have one reservation—a knockout blow for an old rival: "If I may say so, I regret that you are mentioning Nancy Cunard, because I think she can hardly be regarded as a serious poet. Her work at it's [*sic*] best is a bad parody of Mr. Eliot, and at it's [*sic*] worst is without shape and without meaning." Edith never let up over Nancy Cunard. A few years later Allanah was starting up her own literary magazine, and Nancy—as well as Edith—favoured her with some editorial advice about whose work Allanah should and should not print. "I have never heard anything so outrageous as the Cunard's behaviour," wrote Edith when she heard of this. "I suppose she was drunk, as usual. Mind you print Norman Douglas' work, and if you take my advice, you *will print the Cunard's letter*, if it is so insulting as really to show her up. And if the handwriting is *drunken*, I should *photograph* the letter, and print the photograph."

Allanah and Edith were to be friends for life, and the friendship was based not only on Allanah's enthusiastic appreciation of Edith's poetry but on an everyday sharing of unpoetic problems. In a letter to Allanah quite soon after they became friends, for example, Edith thanked Allanah, as she did frequently and wholeheartedly, for her "wonderful missionary work": "It is such a comfort to find someone writing about poetry who really has a sensitive and understanding love of it." She asked Allanah, who was in Paris, to do one or two things for her: "If you should be going to the Amis des Livres in the Rue de l'Odéon, if you would find out for me if Valéry Larbaud has reviewed my

Troy Park anywhere. . . . Mademoiselle Monnier, who is in charge of the book shop, is certain to know." And she had another request of a more "homely order": "I *cannot* get the manicure stuffs I use over here. I would be too grateful for words if you would import for me 12 little boxes of 'Rubis Pompadour' and 12 little boxes of 'Ruba,' made by Houbigant, the latter, I don't know who makes the former. . . . I don't know how much they cost, so will pay you back when I see you, if you don't mind." Edith liked cosmetics; she wrote with only half-humour to her cousin Veronica Gilliat seven years after this about "the greatest discovery ever for the Female Face":

> My dear, there is an old lady who is an illegitimate Hesse, and a clairvoyant, who determined suddenly to discover the stuff which Ninon de Lenclos used on her face. All I can say is, that though it looks more repellent when put on the face than anything you can conceive, — it is made partly of the blood of the lamb, and one looks like a cannibal — one comes out looking *at least* fifteen years younger.[8]

In the year that they met, Edith took Allanah with her to Oxford, where she was to lecture not to Harold Acton's Ordinaries this time but to the young women of Lady Margaret Hall and Somerville College. They lunched at L.M.H., the "rather plain looking" undergraduates staring a good deal at Edith. "She seemed a peacock among peahens," thought Allanah. The principal of the college was Pernel Strachey, Lytton's sister, who organized a meeting after lunch, over coffee, with some of the dons and undergraduates. One of these enquired of Edith why she liked Swinburne. "Because he is a pure poet whose verbal beauty is perhaps the most wonderful in our language," replied Edith. "But he has no ideas," objected the girl. "Thank God," said Edith. "You had better return to your Browning."

It was not more congenial at Somerville, where they dined after the lecture. Here the principal was Margery Fry, sister of Roger whom Edith liked. But the atmosphere after dinner in Miss Fry's study was strained. "Both eminent ladies seemed to be on the defensive and retreated into protective silence, broken only once by Miss Fry who asked Edith if she believed in God. Edith was not going to be involved in a discussion of that nature. She replied: 'I do not wish to say.' General disappointment and long silence."[9] The fourth person present, an English don, quoted from E. M. Forster: "Perhaps life is a mystery and not a muddle." "Yes, but don't destroy the mystery by pulling off the wings in order to dissect the butterfly," replied Edith sharply. At the end of the evening: "Well," said Edith to Allanah, "Well, well." The earnest, grey-cardigan world of female academe was not for her, nor was the world of rational analysis. She was not going to pretend, or even try. She wanted to be with the peacocks and the butterflies.

And yet, when a quarter of a century later she became an honorary Litt. D. of Oxford University, she told the then vice-chancellor, Maurice Bowra, how much this honour meant to her: It was "the arrival at my destination."

In 1926 there were two more public performances of *Façade*, on April 27 and June 29 at the Chenil Galleries in Chelsea. William Walton said, "This time we finally seemed to have got it right." There was less embarrassment, less amateurish bungling, and *Façade* was now officially a success. The accolade came from Ernest Newman, music critic of the *Sunday Times*. Past and future met, unknowingly, at the Chenil *Façade*. The Sitwells' bohemian friend Nina Hamnett brought along Jack Lindsay, who was to be a close friend of Edith's many years later; Allanah Harper brought the aspiring photographer Cecil Beaton, twenty-two years old, who described the occasion the next day in his diary: "The Chenil Gallery was crowded for the Sitwell recital: not a seat to be had. Allanah and I stood, along with masses of other thrilled and expectant people." Half the audience seemed "nicely arty," he wrote, "and the other half merely revoltingly arty."

After the performance the Sitwells and half the audience went off to the Eiffel Tower for dinner. "There was a lot of trafficking between tables." Tallulah Bankhead came in, and a "somewhat playful" Augustus John, "making grabs at some silly little idiots dressed up as Sapphists. . . . We stayed on until very late. Stulik, the fat old proprietor, waddled about sleepily begging people to go."[10]

A few months later, in December 1926, Allanah took Edith to lunch with Beaton and his mother. Edith looked to Cecil Beaton like "a tall, graceful scarecrow with the hands of a mediaeval saint." He did not read poetry—not even Edith's, though from now on she lovingly sent him copies of her books—and had expected her to be "ethereal and beyond worldly concepts." So he was delighted and relieved when she "embarked upon a pungent assessment of people and events." During dessert she recited a bit of Gertrude Stein's "Portrait of Tom Eliot": "Silk and wool, silken wool, woollen silk." ("She could make any rubbish sound like poetry," thought Beaton.)

After lunch they went up to Beaton's sister's bedroom—he didn't even have a studio yet—for a photographic session. And a miracle happened. He unlocked in her a talent that complemented his own and led to years of collaboration profitable to them both:

> She posed instinctively. . . . Surely this was a unique opportunity. I must perpetuate the image in front of me, of a young faun-like creature sitting against my leaping-faun design, looking surprisingly Victorian in her crudely cut Pre-Raphaelite dress, with her matador's jet hat, and necklace, her long mediaeval fingers covered with enormous rings. When the hat was discarded, she became a Brontë heroine, and her pale silken hair fell in rats' tails about her face, while the big teapot handle bun made the nape of her neck appear even more impossibly slender.[11]

As the afternoon wore on, Beaton suggested "more exotic poses. . . . I even persuaded her to asphyxiate under a glass dome. She became quite hysterical kneeling on the floor, her knees and joints popping and cracking. A Chinese torture she called it, but loved it all the same."

At last Edith said she had to "finish a poem," and took her leave. "I caught an approving twinkle in her eye as she left. It meant that we were going to be friends."

Beaton was trying to make a name for himself, and so he was naturally delighted to secure Edith as a sitter, and anxious to please her. And it is a measure of the Sitwells' success and news value at the time that a friend of Beaton's should have told him not to worry too much about what "to become in life," but to "become a friend of the Sitwells, and wait and see what happens." One of the things that happened was that within a few months Edith was inviting him to the very best of her Pembridge Mansions parties: "What day will you and your sister come and have tea with me? Should it be next Saturday, you would find Yeats, the Eliots perhaps, E. M. Forster perhaps. Anyway I am asking them, and Yeats says he is coming. Oh bother, he wants me to be a Rosicrucian. Such a strain, and so bad for the clothes, as it seems to lead to sandals and blue veils."[12] When Yeats came to Pembridge Mansions he used to "stay . . . and stay." "One day he arrived at four o'clock and did not leave till seven. I lost stones. But I was flattered because he really is the most wonderful poet." Geoffrey Gorer told Tom Driberg about one of Edith's parties at which Yeats performed "a magical ceremony supposed to evoke the scent of roses. The company waited tensely; the mumbo-jumbo went on; but nothing happened, there wasn't the ghost of a rose."[14]

Self-interest apart, it was a great tribute to such a young and inexperienced person that Cecil Beaton was able to release Edith—stiff, insecure, unused to expressing herself physically, and nearly forty—from her carapace, so that she was in front of his camera "a young, faun-like creature," and to enable her to be beautiful and uninhibited. "What an extraordinary gift you have," she wrote to him after he sent her the photographs. "Really it is quite unbelievable." No wonder that she, who never knew him in her youth, wrote to him when she was old that "every time I see you, I feel young again."

He made her feel and look the very opposite of the stiff, stranded figure Virginia Woolf had perceived at the Bloomsbury party. The atmosphere of Bloomsbury chilled Edith. She summed up her feelings about that world at this time in a letter to Allanah Harper:

> I've been having a lot of trouble with silly little Bloomsburys, lately. They think that it matters to me if they, and people like Desmond MacCarthy, like my poetry. It doesn't. I don't expect them to. They've civilised all their instincts away. They don't any longer know the difference between one object and another,—or one emotion and another. They've civilised their senses away, too. People who are purely "intellectual" are an awful pest to artists. Gertrude Stein was telling me about Picasso, when he was a boy, nearly screaming with rage when the French version of the Bloomsburys were "superior" to him. "Yes, yes," he said, "your taste and intellect are so wonderful. *But who does the work?*"

Meanwhile Virginia Woolf was now frankly fascinated by Edith. She wrote to her sister Vanessa on March 20, 1927: "Society here has become intolerable—save for Edith Sitwell who was fascinating the other day—very beautiful—and full of astonishing stories about her mother's frauds: how she was made to catch bluebottles as a child and so on. . . . " And to Vita Sackville-West, three days later:

> I had a visit from Edith Sitwell whom I like. I like her appearance—in red cotton, many flounced, though it was blowing a gale. She has hands that shut up in one's own hands like fans—far more beautiful than mine. She is like a clean hare's bone that one finds on a moor with emeralds stuck about it. She is infinitely tapering, and distinguished and old maidish and hysterical and sensitive. . . . I like talking to her about her poetry—she flutters about like a sea bird, crying so dismally.[15]

This inspired pen-portrait of Edith was stimulated by a desire to make Vita jealous; the letter ends, "But honey can one make a new friend? Can one begin new intimate relations? Don't mistake me. No precipice in this case. . . . "

She was increasingly provocative a year later, writing to Vita on July 25, 1928: "But Edith Sitwell is waving her hand—the loveliest in London—at me: says I'm the only person she wants to know. Now how do you read 'know': it has 2 senses."[16] Edith would have been infuriated by the arch innuendo.

She did like Virginia Woolf, and indeed told her, "You are one of the only people whom I *really* enjoy talking to."[17] They were alike in many ways—both of them profoundly shy, uncertain, and vulnerable; both hypersensitive about their literary standing; both capable of deep, loyal attachments and malicious-humorous vendettas; both veering between social isolation and social "performance"; both very ready for laughs, yet formidable to outsiders; both with access to unmapped regions of fantasy and imagination; both possessed of odd bony beauty and exquisite hands.

Edith and Vita Sackville-West were not destined to be friends, and not only because Virginia Woolf used Edith to tease Vita with. "I don't think you probably realise," wrote Mrs. Woolf to Vita on July 24, 1927, "how hard it is for the natural innovator as [Edith] is, to be fair to the natural traditionalist as you are. Its [*sic*] much easier for you to see her good points than for her to see yours."[18] Edith did not like Vita's poetry, and she did not want to spend too much time with Virginia Woolf either—not only on account of her strictures on Bloomsbury, as expressed to Allanah Harper. Whether or not she sensed the precise nature of the "precipice" to which Virginia would or would not lead her, she most probably had an instinct to avoid the black side of Virginia's temperament—her own was quite enough to grapple with, and she avoided exploring it. (She would analyse the technical aspects of her own poetry ad nauseam, but not its psychological sources.) She disliked intimacy, and did not want, or was unable, to get too close to people, as Allanah Harper discovered. The virginal, hampered side of Edith's personality bred a healthy craving for its opposite—glitter and sensation and nonhighbrow direct involvement in art and in the world. This she could not altogether achieve—she could confront some kinds of realities but not others—but it was what she was drawn to. Cecil Beaton and Allanah Harper, in their very different ways, helped her to find the self that she wanted to be. Beaton's pictures even helped Edith to be, momentarily, the Edith her mother wanted her to be: Over one batch of prints "we are all, including Mother, half off our heads with excitement. . . . Mother is quite mad about the one playing the harp. . . ." This meant more to Edith than she could have admitted.

Others drew attention to the self she did not want to be, and aroused her fury. In June 1927 she was sent a "caricature" of herself by Pearl Binder, probably intended as a frontispiece for Jane and Ann Taylor's *Meddlesome Matty and Other Poems for Infant Minds*, for which Edith had written an introduction. "It is gross and offensive," she wrote to the publishers, John Lane, "and it is inexplicable that such an outrageous insult should be offered to any decent woman. . . . The fact that I am a distinguished poet only makes things worse." She was assured that the drawing would not be used; nevertheless she showed the "filthy drawing" to her solicitor, who also sent a letter of protest to John Lane. Edith's final thrust was, "I shall *not* return the drawing, and I enclose one farthing which I request you to hand to Miss Binder. It is one farthing more than the drawing is worth."[19]

Edith was fluent in outrage. The most annihilating of her letters conveyed her outrage in the third person ("Miss Sitwell asks me to say . . . ") and were signed "G. Richards (Secretary)." Whether G. Richards (Secretary) had corporeal reality is a moot point.

In general, however, the mid-1920s saw Edith and her brothers riding on the crest of the wave. In 1926 Sacheverell published his *All Summer in a Day*, which Rebecca West reviewed for the New York *Herald Tribune*. It was, she wrote,

> in many respects a delightful book and one that should shine in the public eye, since neither the importance of the Sitwells as a group nor of Mr. Sacheverell Sitwell as an individual can well be exaggerated. . . . The three Sitwells, Edith, Osbert and Sacheverell, are among the few illuminants England possesses which are strong enough to light up post-war England. They are legatees of perhaps the most glorious group that English life has ever produced, the Whig aristocracy of the eighteenth century . . . . They have indeed by merely moving through society very excitingly, being themselves, done as much for culture in London as anybody since Mr. Ford Madox Ford severed his connection with the *English Review*.[20]

Edith Sitwell, wrote Rebecca West, "writes poetry as gay as a flower garden; its confused joyousness half heard through jazz music, as it is in the performance she and her brothers give called *Façade*, is to me a deal pleasanter than much of the confused passionateness one hears at the opera through the music of Wagner or Strauss, and surely just as legitimate."[21]

Diaghilev had been at the Chenil Galleries performance of *Façade*, and the Sitwells reinforced their connection with him. In 1920 Edith had written *Children's Tales from the Russian Ballet*, and since she was a Sitwell, it was generally assumed that ballet was one of her great enthusiasms and a source of inspiration. In fact, she was moved hardly at all by ballet. For Osbert and Sacheverell, however, it was much more central; and Sacheverell now wrote the story for a new "English" ballet for Diaghilev's company, with music by Gerald Berners. It was called *The Triumph of Neptune*, and at its first night in December 1926 at the Lyceum Theatre, Edith's escort was Alvaro Guevara.

In January 1927 she was in Paris, staying with Evelyn Wiel, to attend the ballet's French premiere. "During both entr'actes, I noticed a tall, desperately thin, desperately anxious-looking young man circling round me, staring at me as if he had seen a ghost."[22] Three days later, in Gertrude Stein's house at 27 rue de Fleurus, Edith was introduced to him. His name was Pavel Tchelitchew.

He was to be the most important man in her life. She was forty, and he twenty-nine, when they met. She loved him until his death thirty years later. Loving him brought her some happiness and a great deal of unhappiness. Given her temperament, and his, it could not have been otherwise.

8

Gertrude Stein and the Boyar
1926–1927

In general, Gertrude Stein conversed only with her male visitors at the rue de Fleurus, while Alice Toklas coped with their wives. Edith was neither a male nor a wife and "I was, I am glad to say, always put next to Gertrude," she said proudly. (Stein thought Edith had "the mind of a man.") Gertrude Stein had already been interested in Edith at the time of their first meeting in 1924. Edith had given Stein's *Geography and Plays* an ambivalent review in the *Athenaeum and Nation* (the two periodicals merged in 1921) in July 1923; later she revised her opinion of this book, writing to John Collier in 1931: "By the way, do you know Gertrude's *Geography and Plays*? It is a most remarkable book. . . . It is her best work, and free from her recent fidgettiness [*sic*]. Sometimes her work is awful. But when she is good, she is perfectly outstanding, as much so in her own way, as Joyce in his."[1] Edith wrote about Stein again in *Vogue* in October 1924, comparing her favourably with Dorothy Richardson and Katherine Mansfield, and a year later, also in *Vogue*, she wrote a considered piece, "The Work of Gertrude Stein." It was the then editor of British *Vogue*, Dorothy Todd, who effected the introduction between the two.

Alice B. Toklas wrote of this first meeting that "Miss Sitwell was a great surprise to us for she looked like nobody under the sun, very tall, rather the height of a grenadier, with marked features and the most beautiful nose any woman had. She was a gendarme, she wore double-breasted coats with large buttons."[2] (Edith's clothes attracted as much attention in Paris as at home. She must have been wearing a gendarme overcoat the day of Tchelitchew's show at the Galerie Vignon, when Allanah Harper saw her being pursued up the street by little boys calling out "*Soldat anglais, soldat anglais!*" Edith turned and routed them with the words, "*Sans les soldats anglais vous n'auriez pas gagné la guerre!*" In another and more pungent version of the same story, perhaps informed with *esprit d'escalier*, her riposte was, "*Souvenez-vous de Waterloo!*")

The first visit to the rue de Fleurus was "the beginning of a long friendship," as Alice Toklas wrote. Edith, since she became an admirer of Gertrude Stein's writing, had been enthusiastically championing her in England. In the autumn of 1925 the Woolfs had published Edith's thirty-two-page *Poetry and Criticism* in their Hogarth Essays series, with a dust jacket designed by Vanessa Bell; in it Edith described the way Gertrude Stein "is bringing back life to our language by what appears, at first, to be an anarchic process," by breaking down familiar groups of words and rebuilding them "into new and vital shapes." Edith found it "miserably disappointing," as she wrote to Gertrude Stein, that Virginia and Leonard Woolf were not interested in publishing a British edition of Stein's *The Making of Americans*.

Edith's aim was to get Gertrude Stein to cross the Channel. Stein had already turned down an invitation to lecture at Cambridge, but "I do feel your actual presence in England would help the cause," Edith wrote in late 1925. "It is quite undoubted that a personality does help to convince half-intelligent people."[3] No one knew this better than Edith. She was working "very hard at propaganda," and was successful the following spring. Harold Acton, who not only was an ally of Edith's but had met Gertrude Stein in Italy with his father, invited her to speak at the Ordinary Society at Oxford in early June, and Stein accepted; a lecture at Jesus College, Cambridge, was set up for the same trip.

It is at this point that one can come to grips with the famous judgment of F. R. Leavis in *New Bearings in English Poetry* that "the Sitwells belong to the history of publicity, rather than that of poetry"—at least where Edith is concerned. Sacheverell is only guilty by association, and it was Osbert, not Edith, who kept his press cuttings in a bowl on his table. As for Edith—when she believed, rightly or wrongly, in what someone was doing, whether it was herself, or a fellow poet, or a painter, or in this case the prose writer Gertrude Stein, she believed wholeheartedly. The gospel must be spread, by all and any means at her disposal—parties, preachings, persecutions, the press. A good example of her use of this last was the occasion when she was being pursued by the *Daily Express*, which had discovered that a murder victim called Messiter was a distant connection of the Sitwells: "*My fourth cousin* (whom I have seen twice in my life) married as his second wife a woman who is sister to the murdered man's wife, from whom he had been separated for twenty years!!!!" as Edith put it to Allanah Harper. "Reporters were on my doorstep all day, from the *Daily Express* (which has had orders *never* to mention us as artists, because of course we are not artists, we only write poetry to gain publicity!)." (This happened in 1929. Leavis's dictum about publicity was not published in book form until 1932, by which time it was evidently part of the conventional unwisdom.) Edith went on: "I gave the reporters absolute hell."

> Then I said, "You have come to ask me about something ugly, but I will show you something beautiful" (and I showed them Pavlik Tchelitchew's pictures). . . . "You have dragged me into this ugly scandal; in return you shall please me by photographing these beautiful pictures and speaking respectfully of the great artist who painted them, in your paper!" And they have sent a photographer, so I am hoping they will do what I ask.[4]

Edith's single-minded devotion to the art and the artists she believed in was like that of a mother to her child or a religious fanatic to a deity. It was the kind of devotion that can quite well lead to crime, but more often to silliness. When directed to one's own work as well as to that of others, it is like an act of faith, a plank bridge over the pit of uncertainty and self-doubt. Leavis's remark rests on a false dichotomy; Edith (whatever about Osbert) does not belong to the history of publicity rather than that of poetry, but to the history of poetry *and* the history of publicity.

Her propaganda on behalf of Gertrude Stein was successful. She involved both her brothers in the organization of the visit, and Stein was under the Sitwells' wing throughout; her first public appearance in England was on the platform at a poetry reading given by the three Sitwells. On June 1, 1926, Edith gave a party for her at Pembridge Mansions; Gertrude Stein looked, thought Tom Driberg, "massively commonsensical like a reliable *hausfrau* in brown boots and black woollen stockings"[5]—a great contrast to her hostess. Virginia Woolf was there too, and sent a report of the evening to Vanessa: "We were at a party of Edith Sitwell's last night. Jews swarmed. It was in honour of Miss Gertrude Stein who was throned on a broken settee (all Edith's furniture is derelict, to make up for which she is stuck about with jewels like a drowned mermaiden)."[6] Morgan Forster was there, and Siegfried Sassoon, and Miss Todd of *Vogue*. In her journal Virginia wrote that Edith was "distraught," and that there were "cherries in handfulls, & barley water."[7]

Gertrude Stein was exceedingly nervous about lecturing. After the Cambridge evening (where the men in the audience asked her a great many questions, and the women asked nothing at all), Osbert drove her to Oxford and was soothing and supportive. At Oxford the Sitwells and their guest lunched with Harold Acton and afterwards led her into the packed lecture room—standing room only. Gertrude Stein forgot her nervousness. "A squat

Aztec figure in obsidian," she seemed to Harold Acton, "growing more monumental as soon as she sat down. With her tall bodyguard of Sitwells and the gypsy acolyte [Alice Toklas] she made a memorable entry."[8]

Gertrude Stein gave a "placid reading" of her own work in her flat, matter-of-fact American voice, including her word portrait of Edith, "Sitwell Edith Sitwell," who was sitting so near that the portrait could be compared with the original:

> ... Supposing she had had a key supposing she had answered, supposing she had had to have a ball supposing she had it fall and she had answered. Supposing she had it and in please, please never see so. . . .
> Absently faces by and by we agree. . . .
> Apparently faces by and by we agree.

While she was reading, Harold Acton was looking at Edith. "No, I could not see any likeness, nor, apparently, could Edith, for she was trying not to look as embarrassed as she felt. Sachie looked as if he were swallowing a plum and Osbert shifted in his insufficient chair with a vague nervousness in his eyes."[9]

The large audience listened attentively, and some took notes. After the reading there was a vigorous and at times indignant questions session, and Edith was delighted with the way Stein managed the hecklers. She dealt with them in "reassuringly motherly tones, patting and soothing the obstreperous with gusty sallies, and everyone joined in her laughter," wrote Acton. But Gertrude Stein would not be persuaded to prolong her visit to England; the following day she was off back to Paris with Alice Toklas.

Edith kept up her efforts on behalf of her new friends. In April 1926 she had praised *The Making of Americans*—"the product of one of the richest, and at the same time most subtle, minds of our time"—in the *Criterion*. And on her next and crucial visit to Paris in the new year of 1927, Edith was writing to Cecil Beaton from Evelyn Wiel's flat in the rue Saint-Dominique asking him to send Gertrude Stein "one of the photographs of myself lying in my tomb (*the one with the best hands*, as I am fussy on that point)." He was to send Siegfried Sassoon one too as he was about it, "*and send the lovely account to me.*"

In the same letter she told Beaton that she had just met Picasso at Gertrude Stein's house, "and as she is about his greatest friend the evening was a charming one":

> He is a delightful kindly friendly simple little man, and one would know him for a great man anywhere. At the moment, he was extremely excited

and overjoyed because his mother-in-law had just died. Also he was looking forward to the funeral, because, according to Gertrude, all Spaniards prefer funerals to circuses any day. Gertrude is in fine form at the moment, she told me that the Bloomsburys are like the Young Men's Christian Association. "Oh but anti-Christian, surely," I said to her, "and anti-moral." "That's just it," she replied. "In America the Young Men's Christian Association is *always up to something!*"

Gertrude Stein not only introduced Edith to Picasso; she also, finally, introduced her to the "desperately anxious-looking" young man she had noticed at the ballet.

Pavel Fyodorovitch Tchelitchew[10]—his friends called him Pavlik—had come into Gertrude Stein's life through Jane Heap, the Paris editor of *The Little Review*. Stein had seen his painting *Basket of Strawberries* in the Autumn Salon of 1925, and his work interested her—for a while, that is, until his painting "went bad," as she put it, and then all the pictures of his that this arch-collector had acquired were relegated to the "*salon des refusés*," a small, nonpublic room at 27 rue de Fleurus. Through Pavlik, Gertrude Stein also knew the blond, blue-eyed surrealist poet René Crevel (Alice Toklas's pet). She became the focal point for the so-called neo-romantic group of young painters who exhibited with Tchelitchew at the Galerie Druet in February 1926: Eugene and Leonid Berman (Russians, like himself), Kristians Tonny, who was Dutch, and Christian "Bébé" Bérard, for whom Tchelitchew nurtured a passionate and rivalrous enmity. In the years 1925–1930 Gertrude Stein orchestrated and fomented the quarrels and alliances of her group of young men, backing one against the other, until she dropped the lot of them; Tchelitchew himself was the first to get the chop, in 1928.

But when he met Edith, he and his paintings were still in favour at the rue de Fleurus, and the welcome there included his constant companion, an aspiring American pianist, Allen Tanner (Tchelitchew, obsessive worshipper of a female muse, was homosexual): They were "*les enfants de la maison.*"

Tchelitchew was born on his father's estate, Doubrovka, near Moscow, in 1898. His family belonged to the old nobility of Russia—of boyar descent (Edith used to call him "the Boyar"). There were four elder half-sisters from a previous marriage of his father's; Pavlik was the eldest son of the second marriage. The important one among his full siblings was his sister, Choura, five years younger than he, who was to live with him in Europe. Choura was delicate and tubercular. For her, as a child, Pavlik was "the Czar and God." He was a handsome, favoured child, adored by mother and nurse, and a disappointment to his father, who mistrusted Pavlik's unorthodox interest in what his sisters wore and in the ballet.

The family were forced to leave Doubrovka—a large house in a wooded setting, as magical and resonant for Pavlik as Renishaw was for Edith—in 1918. By this time Pavlik had submitted his first stage designs, based on scenes of Doubrovka, to the Bolshoi Ballet; he was also taking lessons in dance. Members of the revolutionary soviet of Doubrovka village delivered an order of expulsion, and the family, like many other landowners, had to leave with only forty-eight hours' notice. The large family moved to the Kiev area, where Pavlik continued his studies at the Academy. The family began to fragment; sisters died or married and moved away, his brother Mischa was killed in the civil war. Pavel got out. Via Turkey he reached Berlin, where the gifted, aristocratic young exile soon found work designing for the Russian ballet and theatre; he designed in his "new" Rabelaisian manner Rimsky-Korsakov's opera *Le Coq d'Or* at the Staatsoper.

It was in Berlin that he met Allen Tanner, a young man from Chicago studying the piano on a scholarship: "a gilded willowy youth with a shock of black hair, a soft, half-hidden, languishing glance, a handsome face and the primmest lips and largest romantic ideas in the world."[11] Pavlik lost his excitement about Tanner quite soon, but he was devoted to Tanner's devotion, and Tanner became for Pavlik the perfect jagger.

Pavlik's ailing sister, Choura, who had been working as an army nurse, had already escaped to Paris when he and Tanner arrived on their first visit in July 1923, in time to catch the end of Diaghilev's season. Pavlik felt at home at once in Paris, and arranged to come back to stay; Choura remarked that he looked a Parisian from the first day.

Their first base was the Hotel Jacob, where by a stroke of luck Jane Heap was also staying; Tanner knew her already, and Pavlik's network of contacts began to form. Through Jane Heap he met Brancusi and Léger; in the ateliers where he went to draw from life he met the Berman brothers; soon he was exhibiting at the Galerie Henri in Paris and the Redfern Gallery in London.

Tanner and Jane Heap ran into Gertrude Stein in the street in autumn 1925, soon after her first sight of Pavlik's *Basket of Strawberries*. They made an appointment to meet again at 150 Boulevard Montparnasse, where Tchelitchew, Tanner, and Choura were living in a pokey little studio. But when Stein turned up only Tanner was at home, so she saw the paintings but not the artist. She liked what she saw (Tanner had to force the lock of the cupboard in which the paintings were kept with a wrench from her old Ford car), and left an invitation to tea at the rue de Fleurus the following day.

So began the brief patronage of the Boyar by the woman he called "Sitting Bull"—Gertrude Stein. The "Knitting Maniac," as he called Alice Toklas, never liked him; she thought him a "dreadful little arriviste." Sitting Bull hung a Tchelitchew canvas on her dining room wall, and placed Pablo Picasso at the table where he had perforce to look at it. She told the Boyar: "Picasso broke the object. Pavlik, don't break the object." This became his much-repeated gospel. She became his Sibyl, the "Great Mother." But characteristically he was already worrying about how he would get out of what he saw as her clutches.

This is partly why Edith Sitwell's arrival on the scene awoke such a response in him. Their meeting at the rue de Fleurus was not by chance: With Gertrude Stein, very little happened by chance. She had already told Stella Bowen, the Australian painter, who was living in Paris with Ford Madox Ford, that she had found an Englishwoman for Pavlik to paint. And she said to Edith: "If I present Pavlik to you, it's your responsibility because his character is not my affair." By making each seem intriguing to the other, and by suggesting to Edith that she might be able to help the temperamental young genius, and to Pavlik that the patronage of the famous English poet with the extraordinary looks might help his career, she gave the friendship an armature of promising tensions from the start.

She did not perhaps intend the relationship to take flight quite as it did. Jealous disapproval of Edith's new role—she displaced Stein as Pavlik's Sibyl—played some part in her relegation of his work to her small back room the next year.

At the first meeting of Edith and Pavlik in Gertrude Stein's house he explained why he had stared at her so at the ballet: She looked, he said, exactly like Father Amrovsky, his father's confessor, the *staretz* of the monastery Petcherskaya Lavra, to whom he had paid a solemn visit just before he left Russia. Father Amrovsky, he said, was the original of Father Zossima in *The Brothers Karamazov*. He could not believe Edith was not related to him. He could not believe that she was not Russian. (He knew perfectly well who she was, and that she was English.)

The friendship had an exciting but brief first flowering. Edith was back in London by the end of January 1927. Duckworth brought out her *Rustic Elegies* that March (Knopf published it in New York in the summer). This book consisted of just three poems—"Elegy on Dead Fashion," which had been published on its own in book form the previous November; "The Hambone and the Heart," which incorporated sections of "The Mother"; and "Prelude to a Fairy Tale," which included poems from *Façade* in a framework based on the mystical teachings of Rudolf Steiner, in whom Helen Rootham was extremely interested: This sequence is dedicated "For H. R., to whom I owe much of the knowledge contained in this poem." *The Times Literary Supplement,* writing about *Rustic Elegies* as a whole on April 7, 1927, referred to the "silly heaven" her fairy-tale world proposed, and to the "bewildering succession of images." Of "Elegy on Dead Fashion," the same journal had said: "The strangeness and newness of Miss Sitwell's poetic *clichés* tends to blind the reader to the fact that they are *clichés.*" But she had, the reviewer said, "a true ear, a sure command over metre and rhyme."

She had also done some homework; for it was in poems such as "Elegy on Dead Fashion" that Edith developed the technique of using lists of forgotten words for stuffs and unguents and dances, foods, colours, to evoke atmosphere and historical period. Edwin Muir, who gave "Elegy on Dead Fashion" a long, respectful review in the *Nation* for September 18, 1926, referred to her "great powers": "No other poet of our time has written so many lines which delight the imagination and give us a sense of magical freedom."

At the same time as she was receiving this degree of attention Edith was keeping Pembridge Mansions going by journalism of the most cheerful and popular kind: "Who are the Sitwells—and why do they do it?" for the *Weekly Dispatch* on November 14, 1926; "Our Family Ghost," "When Is Poetry a Crime?," "My Awkward Moments," and "How Fame Looks to a Poetess" are sample titles of pieces for various papers during 1927. Edith was very serious about her poetry; but outside that, she wanted fun. Evelyn Waugh, remembering in the *Sunday Times* in 1952 the Sitwells in the 1920s, wrote that they "radiated an aura of high spirits, elegance, impudence, unpredictability, above all sheer enjoyment. . . . They declared war on dullness."

One newspaper mogul who was not keen on Sitwellian contributions was Beaverbrook of the *Daily Express.* On August 17, 1929, the *Express* carried a piece by Edith entitled "Oh, to be in Scarborough, now that August's here." Lord Beaverbrook was away on a cruise; he dictated a letter to his office asking "who engaged Edith Sitwell to write the leader page story": "He [Beaverbrook] says he has stood in the breach for ten years defending the paper against the publicity stunts of the Sitwells. His Lordship is betrayed from time to time, and he would like to know who gave to the Sitwells the key of the gate. . . . This family is less than a band of mediocrities."[12]

Popular journalism gave Edith pleasure and profit and the nonintellectual fairground glitter that she enjoyed. At the other end of the continuum of sensation was Virginia Woolf, responding with sensitivity and delicacy to *Rustic Elegies* a few days after the book came out:

> I'm not going to write to you about your poems—I'm going to talk to you about them. They interest me greatly: I dip in and pick up something that makes me spend 20 minutes staring at the fire, inventing theories about you. Are you changing? Then where are you going? And what sort of loveliness are you reaching down from your strange and very high trees? . . . Of course you are a good poet: but I can't think why. The reason may strike me in Sicily.[13]

Yes, Edith was changing. One result of her new involvement was that she wrote very little poetry during the rest of that year, 1927. Real life had taken over, and when she next came to write a major poem it would something outside her former range.

In May she was writing from London to Allanah, who had also met Pavlik in Paris, full of an excitement that had nothing to do with her own work:

> Pavlik's vernissage is on Tuesday June 2nd, at the Galerie Vignon, and he has asked me to "receive" the people, as Choura is too shy. So I am going over there on Saturday.
>
> He has asked me to absolutely *beg* you to go over there *as soon as possible*, and either to send him lists of people to whom to send cards,—or, better still, to send them yourself. And I do *beg* you to do so, too, as I want the exhibition to be a huge success. . . . I shall need your help, as well as Pavlik, on the day of the vernissage; in fact, if it is possible, I simply must have you there.

For Edith was very nearly as shy and awkward with strangers as Choura was, and her contacts in Paris were distinguished but not numerous; Allanah knew far more people in the art and literary worlds: "I was wondering, too, whether you would feel like giving a joint party with me, in honour of Pavlik, on the night of the vernissage? I feel it might be a great help to him if people knew you were so interested. We would give it together. . . . Let us have a real campaign."

The *tout Paris* came to the private view at the Galerie Vignon. Pavlik was difficult. "Let us leave," he said, "and sit in a café, I hate them all." "Most certainly not," Edith told him. Pavlik must stay till the end, and be nice to people. He kept on trying to escape: "Oh, no you don't, old boy." Suddenly he changed his mind. A "beautiful woman with . . . eyes like purple velvet pansies" came up to him and told him that his paintings were more profound than those of Bérard—music to his ears. "I stay," Pavlik assured Edith and Allanah. "This woman, she interests me." Edith would have preferred another reason for his docility. When the critics arrived, they glanced around rapidly and were about to slip away when Edith captured them, and politely insisted on introducing them to Pavlik, saying, as she was to say so often in the future, "For he is a great painter . . . ."[14]

9
Hunnish Practices and Gold Coast Customs
1927-1929

Before helping to organize Pavlik's show, Edith had been to Italy to join Osbert, who was holidaying on his own. His companion of earlier years, Sacheverell, was now not only a married man but a father, and Osbert's other relationships were temporarily on ice. Together Edith and Osbert went to see D. H. Lawrence and his wife, Frieda, who were living at Sandicci, a few miles outside Florence.

Edith had met Lawrence before, and admired his poems; and Lawrence had been to see their parents at Montegufoni. "A funny little petit-maître of a man," Lady Ida had reported to Osbert. "His wife is a large German. She went round the house with your father and when he showed her anything, would look at him, lean against one of the gilded beds, and breathe heavily." According to Sir George, Frieda had also "jumped on all the beds after luncheon—to see if the mattresses were soft." "Queer couple," was Lawrence's own verdict on his hosts.

Osbert and Edith drove out to see the Lawrences in their Tuscan farm-house one afternoon at the end of May 1927, and stayed for a couple of hours. Lawrence, who was ill, got the tea himself. His account of his visitors, in a letter to the Russian translator S. S. Koteliansky, was not uncharitable: "They were really very nice, not a bit affected or bouncing: only absorbed in themselves and their parents. I never in my life saw such a strong, strange family complex: as if they were marooned on a desert island, and nobody in the world but their lost selves."[1] He and Frieda were "moved" and "disturbed" by their visitors and had to go for a long walk, after they had gone, to recover. Osbert, particularly, caught Lawrence's imagination.

Lawrence, then working on the final draft of what was to be *Lady Chatterley's Lover*, added to his portrait of Sir Clifford Chatterley some final touches which grew from his acute observation of Osbert on that afternoon, and from his knowledge of Osbert's background: Renishaw is only a few miles from Eastwood, where Lawrence grew up. Osbert was not the original model for the impotent, cuckolded Sir Clifford; but woven into the already realised character, it appears, is an impressionistic but thoughtful analysis of Osbert and his family that Edith, for one, recognized and resented. Osbert recognized it too; but he, who was very quick to protest if he or his ideas were used in his acquaintances' fictions, did not complain publicly. Perhaps he was impressed by Lawrence's perspicacity about his character; perhaps it was near the mark, and he did not want to draw anyone's attention to it.[2]

Osbert took a small revenge, however, in a novel published in 1933, *Miracle on Sinai*. Edith read it in manuscript, and wrote to a friend in Paris that it was "absolutely brilliant": "He is perfect on the subject of the D. H. Laurence [*sic*] ménage, — but they really deserve everything they have got, for Laurence's scandalous attack on Osbert." Lawrence's near and dear made a comeback in the same month that Osbert's book was published, as Edith told her Paris correspondent:

> Mrs. D. H. Laurence's [*sic*] daughter has just telegraphed to Osbert asking for permission to photograph this house [Renishaw] for a film which is to be made of *Lady Chatterley's Lover!!!!!!* Words fail me. You realise, don't you, that Osbert was portrayed as the cripple in that filthy novel, — in unprintable words? We have telegraphed back saying that her request is as gross and coarse as it is libellous.

In *Miracle on Sinai* Osbert depicts Lawrence as T. L. Enfalon, a "sickly and ascetic bachelor," with a "thinly bearded head of weak though intellectual order," who "loved to pose as the son of a collier, brought up in a miner's cottage." Enfalon preached a "humorless cult of dark gods and blood-wisdom" and the dominance of the "male principle": "Such, then, was the chief apostle of force, or, as he loved to call it, *guts*, in literature; a weak, weedy, bearded man, stooping and emaciated." It was a small revenge in both senses; for Lawrence had been in his grave three years when this appeared, and the dead cannot take umbrage, or legal action.

As for Edith, she did not let rip until she was old (perhaps Osbert asked her not to) and even then did not make it clear just why she felt so vehemently. She put into her autobiography a belittling account of Lawrence (he "looked like a plaster gnome on a stone toadstool in some suburban garden") and of the innocuous teatime visit to Sandicci. Mr. Lawrence "was determined to impress on us that he was a son of toil"; he "talked to us a great deal about our parents, ascribing to them characteristics that were completely alien to them"; he "had a very bad chip on his shoulder. He hated men who were magnificent to look at. He hated men who were 'gentlemen.'"

And as for *Lady Chatterley's Lover*, it was "to me a very dirty and completely worthless book, and unworthy of the man who could write 'The Snake' and 'The Mountain Lion'—two beautiful and most moving poems." The gamekeeper Mellors was guilty of an "unutterably filthy, cruel and smelly speech" ("It's not for a man in the shape you're in, Sir Clifford, to twit me for having a cod between my legs"). And "my respect for the olfactory sense and that of my readers, prevents me from quoting Mr. Lawrence's enthusiastic descriptions of Mr. Mellors' sexual equipment." The descriptions of sexual intercourse, she wrote, would "freeze any impulse to love between boy and girl." The book was "worthless as a work of art. And I can only apply to it a five-letter word which, until Mr. Lawrence got hold of it, was only allowed by our cricket-loving, golf-loving, tennis-loving compatriots to be used in connection with those games—not in connection with the game that interested Mr. Lawrence."

And so on. *Lady Chatterley's Lover* might not have been the fastidious, virginal Edith's favourite book at the best of times. But without a special impetus and the collected spleen of years, she would not have given a novel she disliked so much house-room in her autobiography. Her animus towards Lawrence produced one of her most-quoted pieces of facetiousness. In a lecture at Liverpool she described him as the head of the "Jaeger school of literature," since he was "hot, soft and woolly." (The reference is to warm winter underwear.) Messrs. Jaeger contacted her to protest that while their products were indeed soft and woolly, they were never hot, "owing to our system of slow conductivity." Edith alleged that she replied, regretting the comparison, since Jaeger's works "are unshrinkable by Time, whereas the works of Mr. Lawrence, in my opinion, are not."[3]

From Italy, where the Chatterley time bomb ticked, Edith went to Paris for Pavlik's exhibition. And back in England, she corresponded with both Pavlik and Allen Tanner. Her inclusion of Tanner in her new friendship was partly from the loyalty that made the loved ones of her loved ones a part, as it were, of the family; it was also an instinctual move to secure a secondary link with the important person. Pavlik might not always answer her letters, but Allen Tanner, moved by the same needs, would.

She urged them to come to England. Allen continually stressed their

—genuine—poverty. He and Pavlik would probably have been surprised to know how little actual money Edith, the daughter of Renishaw and Montegufoni, had to live on. Edith went back to her own work, and to her own problems. Nineteen-twenty-seven ended for her with simultaneous flu and toothache. She had to have an extraction without anaesthetic, because her heart was not strong enough. Physical pain punctuated Edith's life like the dark hiatus she loved to point out in her poetry.

Allanah Harper (who had already dutifully bought a Tchelitchew painting at a gallery price) was in Paris, planning to start a literary review of her own. It was to be done on £500 capital, cheaply printed by a Russian émigré. Edith was enthusiastic and full of ideas as to who the contributors should be and of general advice. "As you ask my ideas about payment, I think if I were you, I would level out the payments to poets and prose writers more. I should give the prose writers £4 for an essay, and the poets £5 *only* if it is a long poem, otherwise the same as the prose writers, at least that is what I should do if I were having a Review."

"I've sent part of my Oxford lecture on 'Sitwellism,'" she wrote to Allanah on January 16, 1928, apropos of the first issue of *Échanges*, and, inevitably, "Helen Rootham is sending a quite *extraordinarily* interesting essay on music. . . . (I am sending her essay with mine)." She told Allanah to ask Gertrude Stein for something ("Tell her you are a friend of mine"); and "another writer who to my mind is going to be terrifically important is Adrian Stokes." She enclosed Stokes's address in Rapallo where Osbert, currently besotted with him, was as well; Edith's loyalty was fiercely at work on his behalf. "Also why not ask Siegfried Sassoon and Arthur Waley to write for you?" Constant Lambert was also recommended.

So far, it was all in the family. But there was one new name: "Thomas Driberg should most certainly be cultivated," and would be sending a poem. "I consider he has *very* great promise as a poet, and if he works, ought really to do something."

Driberg did "do something"—he became a journalist, a Labour M.P., and a peer, but not a poet.

In 1928 he was twenty-three. He had read *Wheels* as a schoolboy at Lancing, and met Edith when he was an undergraduate at Oxford. She encouraged him to write and even, he later claimed, included one of his poems in a lecture as an illustration of texture in verse. After he left Oxford, Driberg wandered into Soho, where he worked in a cheap café; above the café was a brothel specializing in particularly fat prostitutes. He emerged from this ambience on Saturday afternoons to go and have tea with Edith at Pembridge Mansions, where he found that

> the famous tended to get together in close little groups and talk, invariably about money—royalties, and the merits or demerits of their respective agents or publishers. . . . Sometimes, at Edith's bidding, I would get there a bit early and we would talk quietly. I had merely told her that I was doing "a rather humdrum job." One day, when she asked me again, I told her what it was and described it . . . fat women and all (but not my own sleeping arrangements). She was horrified: I must be got out of there. I at once took not hope, but fright. I was habituated to my sordid routine. . . .[4]

Then her other guests arrived. But Edith did not forget; as Driberg said, she was "a woman not only of great compassion, but of great pertinacity." She got Osbert and Sacheverell to use their influence to get Driberg a job on the *Daily Express*; he became "William Hickey," the gossip columnist.

All through the 1920s Edith's parties proliferated, and Driberg was there at their final and established best: Alan Searle brought Somerset Maugham, "Mrs. Patrick Campbell sailed in"—and later sent Edith a dozen silver teaspoons, having being inconvenienced by the fact that these articles were not provided at 22 Pembridge Mansions. She meant it kindly. Mrs. Patrick Campbell was an old friend of Lady Ida's, and used to say to Edith: "You'll never have your mother's beauty—poor child! . . . But never mind! You look at one in such a nice way, it doesn't matter." This became so regular an observation that Edith learnt to get it in first: "How d'you do, Mrs. Campbell? I know I shall never have my mother's beauty, but I look at you in such a nice way, it doesn't matter."[5]

Ada Leverson was still a regular guest, old and deaf and dotty, in an orange-gold wig that Osbert said was permanently fixed to her tulle-swathed black hat; Frank Buchman, founder of Moral Rearmament, once had Edith unwillingly on her knees to pray for the conversion of Geoffrey Gorer, who had been teasing him; John Hayward in his invalid chair; Roy Campbell; and Stephen Spender, "soaring above the smoke and the babel like an innocent pink crane."[6]

In 1948, Tom Driberg M.P. wrote to congratulate Edith on her honorary doctorates. Edith thought of him, when she was old, as "one of the few grateful people alive."

The first issue of Allanah's literary review *Échanges* came out in late 1929. In spite of Edith's recommendation, Driberg's poems were not included. In the first issue, as well as Edith's own work there was a story by Virginia Woolf, a translation by André Gide from *Hamlet,* and some poems by Tristan Tzara. Allanah apologised to Edith for the inclusion of these: "they are not good enough, but he was in the room at the time I was making a list of French writers. . . ."

Edith wrote to congratulate Allanah and subscribe to the review; but *Échanges* only survived for a very few years. This first issue introduced Edith to the poetry of Rainer Maria Rilke, which made a great impression on her: "Do tell me something about him," she asked Allanah. "I once saw a translation of another lovely poem of his in that awful paper *Transition.* Arthur Waley, to my great distress, tells me he is dead. . . ." The first number did Allanah great credit, she said; it "should teach the French a lot about English literature."

In the summer of 1928 the Sitwells were in great form. The following advertisement appeared in the personal column of the *Times* on June 5: "Miss Edith and Mr. Osbert Sitwell have much pleasure in announcing a general amnesty. This does not apply to habitual offenders." In July Pavlik and Allen Tanner came over to London; Edith's energetic jaggering on Pavlik's behalf had resulted in a one-man show at the Claridge Gallery. He had by then completed two portraits of her—both, in their own way, sinister rather than anything else—one in gouache and sand, the other in gouache, sand, and coffee. After he had painted her the first time, Tchelitchew wrote to Edith from Monte Carlo, where he was working on the designs for Diaghilev's ballet *Ode*: "I am very glad and very touched that you like your portrait, I am still rather anxious about it in spite of the fact that Gertrude Stein is pleased that you like it. She thought it a good likeness!"[7] He asked her to get Helen to photograph her in the dark-gold dress he liked, sitting on the sofa. For his London exhibition, Osbert and Sacheverell threw themselves into promoting his interests.

Another Tchelitchewian ally was the writer, future traveller, and anthropologist Geoffrey Gorer, who had come across Pavlik in Paris before Edith did, also at Gertrude Stein's. He had met Edith herself when he was an undergraduate at Cambridge and she came to lecture to the Cambridge Literary Society; after this she invited him and his friends to the Chelsea *Façade*, beckoning round the edge of the curtain to signify they should go round and talk to her. Gorer brought his mother to Pembridge Mansions, and she and Edith became close friends. Gorer, who felt possessive about both Pavlik and Edith, was a stirring-up rather than a reconciling influence in early days, though nowhere near as damaging as Allen Tanner suggested to Edith in 1930: "Geoffrey, I am sure, tried, *not unconsciously*, as you say, but *consciously*, as he has always done, to foment trouble between you and P—that seems to be his mission in life."[8] But Gorer kept the friendship of Edith in the long run, invariably ending his letters to her, "My love and respect always." Fomenting trouble, as it turned out, was more in the hapless Tanner's line.

Gorer's verdict on the 1928 Claridge Gallery show was that it was "not very successful." But more publicity was gained for Tchelitchew in London than Edith and Allanah had so far been able to drum up in Paris. The *Graphic* gave him a big spread on July 28. It would not have escaped Edith's attention, however, that there was a query mark after the heading "Miss Edith Sitwell Presents a Genius?"; and there was an ironic tone in the subheading "Her Eulogistic Comments on a Young Russian Artist"; and even more irony in the caption under the example of Edith's poetry printed in a box alongside.

Edith's interest in the intrigues of the smart set was minimal. The fashionable poetry readings in London at which she was invited to perform, and hear others perform, had lost most of their charm for her as well. Earlier in 1928 she had been writing to E. M. Forster—who had written to her after he had read and admired *The Sleeping Beauty*, and whom she held in some reverence— about an evening when Robert Nichols had read from his verse play *Don Juan* for forty long minutes. "The whole thing made me feel like a bird that has blundered into a room and is thumping its head against the ceiling trying to get out.... At moments one did not know if one was in Church or in a music-hall."[9]

During that summer, at Renishaw, she had completed a poem that "I am very pleased with," she wrote to Cecil Beaton. "I started it in London and finished it here. It is exceedingly grim, and is all about low rich people, negro horrors, and slums, welded into one." Edith had been oppressed by the hypocrisy and unfairness of the world, and though this was something she had always known, she had been experiencing it recently at closer range. She saw the poverty and unemployment in her own country; she saw too how the artists lived in Paris, hand to mouth; she had seen all that was "ugly and horrible and sordid," as Allen Tanner reminded her in a letter, in the flat in the Boulevard Montparnasse. She saw friends she believed to have genius growing older, unrecognized. She was aware of herself, over forty, living in cheap rented apartments.

She responded to unknown correspondents at this time out of raw sympathy. Normally her approach to the eccentrics who wrote to her was robust. But in May 1929 she was writing to Mr. Frederick Willis of Hendon:

> It is indeed terrible to be friendless and poor. I have been aghast, lately, at the cases of unhappy creatures who have fallen in the streets from starvation and cold, and who have died from these, on reaching hospital. One cause of this is, that the feeling has been encouraged deliberately that it is "a disgrace to go to the Workhouse." It is no disgrace whatsoever, in my opinion. It is a fearful disgrace to be lazy and useless, but it is no disgrace whatsoever to fail. . . .[10]

Edith was all too familiar with the "lazy and useless"—her mother, and her mother's friends, the Fun Brigade and the Golden Horde, and the extravagant, insensitive, brutally stupid people she still met in some London drawing rooms.

"Gold Coast Customs" is about the artificiality of human behaviour and the barbarism that lies beneath the surface. It is a poem in which tribal customs of the Ashanti are mixed up with fashionable London life. In a letter to Geoffrey Singleton she spelt out the real sources of the horror:

> Mostly that poem was the result of things I have actually witnessed, or have been told. ("The rat-eaten bones of a god that never lived," I quote from memory, was the result of a frightful thing I was told in youth about an illegal operation;—which shocked me appallingly.) As for the part about the wind beating "on the heart of Sal"—during the time of the hunger-marches, I saw, in a procession *three* times, a ragged creature, with nothing under his outer suit, unspeakably famished looking, and with a face that looked as if it had been ravaged (I imagine from T.B.) beating on an empty food tin with a bone. That is *where* that passage came from."

"Gold Coast Customs" is written in the rhythms of the tom-tom and the rhythms of jazz; her technical expertise is put to horrid effect.

Chasing a rat,
Their soul's ghost fat
Through the Negro swamp,
Slum hovel's cramp,
Of Lady Bamburgher's parties above
With the latest grin, and the latest love,
And the latest game:
To show the shame
Of the rat-fat soul to the grinning day
With even the rat-skin flayed away. . . .

The heart of Sal
That once was a girl
And now is a calico thing to loll
Over the easy steps of the slum
Waiting for something dead to come.

From Rotten Alley and Booble Street,
The beggars crawl to starve near the meat
Of the reeling appalling cannibal mart,
And Lady Bamburgher, smart Plague-cart. . . .

In her later collections, "Gold Coast Customs" has a confident ending, showing a way out of this triple hell:

Yet the time will come
To the heart's dark slum
When the rich man's gold and the rich man's wheat
Will grow in the street, that the starved may eat,—
And the sea of the rich will give up its dead—
And the last blood and fire from my side will be shed.
For the fires of God go marching on.

That is not how she ended it in 1928, when she wrote it, or in 1929, when she
published it. Then, she left it on a note without hope:

But yet if only one soul would whine
Rat-like from the lowest mud, I should know
That somewhere in God's vast love it would shine;
But even the rat-whine has guttered low.

Edith wrote to Anthony Powell, then working for her publisher, Duckworth, about the dust jacket—she wanted the portrait of King Munza in full dress from Schweinfurth's *The Heart of Africa*, and she wanted "a reproduction of my portrait by Pavel Tchelitchew (the one in *my* possession)" as a frontispiece. This she got. Duckworth brought out *Gold Coast Customs*—the title poem, plus some additional short poems—in January 1929. The *Times*'s reviewer wrote on February 29 that it was the "richest of these symphonies of far and near, of legend and precise experience, that Miss Sitwell has given us," while remaining of the opinion that the poem itself "must remain in the esoteric order." *Gold Coast Customs* did not solve the problem of Edith's bank balance, even though Houghton Mifflin brought it out in New York.

But it was a turning point. When Edith turned her back on the Garden of Eden, on the nostalgia for childhood and lost innocence that had enabled her to write *The Sleeping Beauty* and *Bucolic Comedies*, she turned her face the other way and saw ahead emptiness and death. There seemed, for her, nothing in between; she is no poet of midlife preoccupations. There is death in her poems of childhood, and fear beneath the sunlit leaves; there is a child's hope and a child's faith in the poems of her later years. She was always a child and always an old woman. In between, there was only desperation. After *Gold Coast Customs*, Edith wrote virtually no poetry at all for ten years.

10

Preoccupations in Prose
1929–1930

Even before *Gold Coast Customs* came out, Edith had decided to earn some money by writing a prose book. In a letter thanking Allanah Harper at the end of 1928 for the gift of an aquamarine brooch, she said: "I have just started my enormous work on Pope." Her *Alexander Pope*, for Faber and Faber, the publishing house where T. S. Eliot was now a director, was not to be researched without interruptions. That same Christmas, Tanner wrote to her, "We are living in expectation of your next visit to Paris. . . . Best wishes for a happy New Year, we shall be thinking of you on Monday night at 12:00 p.m. and may 1929 be a magical, miraculous, magnanimous one for you."[1]

In November 1929 Allen had entrusted Edith with a valuable book, asking her to take it in to Sotheby's to be sold. He had bought it cheap in Paris, on the quays, he said. "Be brazen," he wrote to her. "Ask a good sum." She asked Sotheby's to put a reserve of £700 on it, which they thought too high, but they nevertheless agreed to include the book in a forthcoming sale. Even if Edith had qualms about the provenance, the advantages of selling the book, for all of them, were clear. Allen had written, "If I get this money I will be able to bring Pavlik and self to London, perhaps at Xmas time—we could live near you and be *free* to have a *real* and happy visit." No prospect could have been more attractive to Edith, who loved Pavlik and whose Christmases in the past few years had been described by her as "quiet."

The book had belonged to Count Louis de Lastéyrie, nicknamed "Lolotte," a descendant of the great Marquis de Lafayette and a confirmed bachelor and amateur of the arts. A close friend of his, Vladimir Semenoff, had accepted the book as part-payment for legal services, paying the Count the nominal sum of 1,800 francs. Semenoff was leaving France, and foresaw problems with the customs over exporting such a valuable book; Allen Tanner there-fore bought it off him, again for 1,800 francs. Unhappily for himself, he did not ask for a receipt. Tanner knew that the real value of the book at public auction would go a long way towards relieving the financial problems of the "triumvirate," as he called Pavlik, himself, and Edith. Semenoff warned him, however, that the Count would be upset and embarrassed if the family heirloom were sold publicly in France. Tanner then enlisted Edith's help.

Sotheby's catalogue for their sale of March 19, 1930, described the book under the heading "Property of a gentleman living in Paris." It was *Notes on the State of Virginia* by Thomas Jefferson, in contemporary mottled calf with a gilt back, printed in Paris in 1782. What made it more valuable still was that it was the copy presented by Jefferson to the Marquis de Lafayette, and carried a long inscription in Jefferson's own hand. It was bought by the New York dealer Rosenbach for £1,030, far more than Tanner had hoped to get. When the Count heard about the sale, as he inevitably did, he claimed the £1,030, and Tanner, unable to establish his legal ownership—Semenoff had left no address —ordered Sotheby's to pay the whole sum over to him.

Edith was mortified and furious at having been involved in a possible deception, and began to talk. ("Don't forget it's a secret," Allen had written when they were arranging the sale, "nobody must know—it's better that way.") She sent a telegram and a letter to Allen Tanner, who replied with a flood of self-justification and reproach:

> All through this business of ours I have repeatedly appealed to your intelligence, your judiciousness *and* your loyalty, to keep all this a strict secret *between us*—asking you not even to tell Helen. The fact that you proceeded to carry out whatever arrangements I asked you to carry out was a promise or at least an aquiescence. The "lie" I am so furiously accused of unwittingly linking your name to was simply meant to be an arrangement, between two friends and another—for safety and good results —and was committed (if "committed" it was) in the greatest innocence possible. . . . I have explained repeatedly to you *why* I wanted it kept secret. . . . However: *when I love—I love* and I am more than willing to forgive, most readily the most serious errors between friends. . . . But I am *exceedingly exasperated* that you cannot keep our secret and above all that you have taken Peter [Gorer, Geoffrey's brother] into our *most intimate situation.*

Edith had accused Tanner of damaging rather than helping Pavlik: Pavlik, she implied, needed to be protected from him. In a second letter hot on the first,

Allen Tanner told her that for "sheer cruelty" her letter "beats anything I have yet witnessed." The unkindest cut of all, from Edith's point of view, was at the end of his first outpouring: "I have long ago—before receiving your telegram even, told Pavlik and explained everything—he understands and is happy and desirous to keep our secret. Is it going to be you, after all, who will fail to—in spite of everything???"

Poor Edith. Loyalty, which Allen questioned in her, was the first virtue. If she kept up the quarrel with Allen, she would most likely lose Pavlik. She capitulated, and so did Allen. Edith paid for the next trip Pavlik and Allen made to London ("Edith, one day soon you must let us reimburse you for our voyage," wrote Allen). She had also to cover her tracks vis-à-vis the people to whom she had talked. She wrote in April 1930, for example, to a new friend, Terence Fytton Armstrong (who wrote under the name John Gawsworth), "to *implore* you, by all that is sacred, *not* to tell *anybody where* that American book which was sold came from, or from *whom*."[2] Edith also wrote to Stella Bowen in Paris, asking her what Pavlik's attitude to the affair was. Stella Bowen replied that she had not seen Pavlik alone, but "he is bound to uphold Allen's innocence, as you say. . . . I think they have both had a good shaking up about it, not to speak of losing the money." She said she wished Edith did not take things so hard, and so, she said, did Pavlik. She broached a subject of some delicacy:

All he *said* was that he wished you were less frightened about everything. He also said that you suggested his going on a visit to London to stay near you and take his meals with you, but that he thought the "mauvaises langues" would comment frightfully on such an arrangement—and I think Edith darling that possibly he is right, if you were more disposed not "to give a damn" you might do as you liked but I'm afraid you *would* be hurt by gossip. . . .[3]

She was right. Those women who did not "give a damn" did what they pleased and got away with it. Edith kept testing the temperature. The following year she wrote to her cousin Veronica Gilliat that she wanted to go to Venice for a week "and stay in a quiet hotel and go sight-seeing with the Boyar—as he screams at me to do by every post and sometimes by airmail":

I shall have to pretend to Helen that I'm staying with people, as she'd kick up the hell of a row otherwise. She can't realise I am over forty (alas).

Tell me honestly, do you think I *dare* (being as aged as I am) stay for three or four days in Milan, on the way home, at one hotel with the Boyar staying at another hotel and go sightseeing with him? Or do you think my "good name" would be gone for evermore?[4]

"Shall I part my hair behind? Do I dare to eat a peach?" Edith heard the mermaids singing; but she was no bohemian. Pavlik, though, was probably much more afraid of compromising himself than of compromising Edith.

Christmas 1929 brought Edith not only the anxiety over Tanner's machinations, and "the most exquisite necklace and bracelet I have ever seen," from Allanah, but the proofs of her life of Pope to be corrected, "*and* which is a thrill for me, Duckworths is going to publish my *Collected Poems* in May." This was recognition. "Of course, any amount will be thrown out. I shall hardly keep any poems from *The Wooden Pegasus*, and very few from *Clowns' Houses.*"

She was sending out copies of *Alexander Pope* with Rex Whistler's wrapper design by February 1930. "I set some store on the chapter on his poetry," she told Allanah, "which I believe says some new things entirely, and throws a new light on various prosodic matters." The most original idea expressed in her Pope book is implied in a statement that the Pastorals "suffer from an over-delicacy and debility which is a result of the poet's physique." She spelt out her theory in the final chapter: "If we were to ask any of the poets of the past, we should without doubt be told that poetry is just as much a matter of physical aptitude as of spiritual." Poetry is a "result" of physical and spiritual sensitivity; but the form it takes "is dependent, very largely, on muscle":

> It is nearly always possible to judge of the poet's physique from his technique. Blanks, for example, would have been impossible to a poet of Pope's tiny and weak body; but the stopped heroic couplet, with its sustaining rhymes, its outward cage . . . this was born to be his measure. And it was because of his physical pain and weak physique that he, so wisely, perfected himself in the use of the couplet. . . . He must, I think, have had strong and sensitive hands, otherwise he would not have attained to his supreme mastery of texture—that texture and understanding of the accumulation of qualities to which his extraordinary variation is due.

This theory of Edith's was not a passing one; it affected or explained her feelings about the differences between women and men, as we shall see, and about mental development in general. In 1944, when Stephen Spender was thirty-five, Edith wrote to him: "Thirty-five is a grand age. One is just beginning to be at the height of one's powers. That is, if one has your kind of physique. Small people's full powers die far earlier, as they come to their height, in some cases, earlier."[5]

Since Edith was a large person with fine and sensitive hands, she should, by her own theory, have been content about her physique from the point of view of poetry. But she was also a woman, not physically energetic or strong; and she did not have the use of her body. Writing about Pope, she projected onto the warped little figure all her doubts about herself: "Though he was deformed, people with beautiful shapes surrounded him, were proud of knowing him—if he did not make love to them. And only too soon he learned not to do that." Her description of the "childhood of a poet"—"a strange weaving together of the ecstasy that the poet knows and the helpless misery that is known by a child who is lost in the unfamiliar street of a slum"—is a description of her own childhood. She describes Pope in relation to Ambrose Philips ("Namby Pamby") rather like herself in relation to the sheep-loving Georgians. And her sympathy for her much-maligned subject leads her to make excuses for all his quirks and dishonesties. Persons of genius, she wrote in her introduction, have always been subjected to attack and calumny. "The quarry is possessed of genius, and is therefore meant to be hunted and half-killed."

Her forte in *Alexander Pope*, as in all her subsequent prose books, is the evocation of period and atmosphere. She exploited and incorporated lists and catalogues: of illnesses ("Colick and Wind, Dropsie and Tympany . . . Falling Sickness, Flux and Smallpox . . ."); of town cries ("A Bed-Matt or a Door-Matt," "Old Shoes for some Brooms," "Maids any Cunny-skins" . . .); dress materials (the "Isabella colour kincock gown flowered with green and gold . . . Sarsnets, Italian mantuas, Spanish and English druggets, Calaman-coes . . ."). Just as Edith always quoted Shakespeare in Second Folio spelling, with an *e* on the end of everything, so she left the spelling of contemporary documents untreated wherever practical.

The essential narrative of Pope's life is there, taken wholesale from respectable secondary sources, though Edith censored some parts of Dennis's *Reflections on Pope's Essay on Criticism* as being "too coarse to be quoted." One or two passages in this lively, partisan, uncomprehensive, nonscholarly, but sympathetic biography are like prose transcriptions of the author's poetry—as in a description of Jonathan Swift and Alexander Pope walking together in the country among the fields, where the dust was so dry that it might have been the dust of all the dead philosophers in the world—where the Martha-coloured scabious waved aimlessly, and, from time to time, from far beyond the cotton-nightcap trees, there came a sound of crazy hen-coop laughter, cackling at the Dean, and raising the black anger that was lying like some dark well in his heart.

Faber printed four thousand copies of *Alexander Pope*; the edition did not sell out, and the remainder were used for a cheap edition five years later. Edith had one very hostile notice, in the *Yorkshire Post*, virtually the local paper for the inhabitants of Renishaw, on March 27: "Miss Sitwell asks for it. By her arrogance, her self-satisfaction, her superiority to mere critics and scholars, she exasperates the critic into forgetting his rules and his politeness and retaliating with her own weapons." It was signed G. G.: Geoffrey Grigson. It would be easy to pillory, he wrote, "her ignorance of psychology, her occasional ineptitude in analysing even the technical qualities of Pope's poetry, her parrot repetitions, her tricks of fine writing which cover absence of original research and shallow-ness of thought."

The period of her first and best fame was all but over. It was 1930 and the mood of poetry was changing, as Edith had noted in her introduction to *Alexander Pope*; "as if there could be fashion in poetry. Such an idea degrades the art to the level of a dressmaker's shop." But she saw it was changing—how, in her terms, "the poet must not be a poet, he must be some sort of moral quack doctor."

Edith's *Collected Poems* came out in June 1930, with a grand limited edition costing £3, signed and with a portrait of her by Tchelitchew, and an ordinary edition of twenty-five hundred copies. The *Times* assessed her devel-opment with perception, and made a prophecy: "The instruments are all tuned and we wait [*sic*] the tune ... clear, complete and controlled." The month the book came out Edith was in demand; she had to give passwords to the more favoured callers at 22 Pembridge Mansions. "Miss Sitwell has a message for me," as she told Terence Fytton Armstrong, was the formula for getting past the maid and into her sitting room. There never was a maid till recently; she or Helen used always to open the door themselves.

Edith had been ill during the first half of 1930, and not only because of the anxiety over Tanner's book. She had poisoned glands, and what seemed like the symptoms of concussion. Osbert explained it to David Horner, saying that she had had a bad fall in March, the injury from which she had concealed from the doctor she consulted, because she didn't want him to know that she had seen another doctor.

The Sitwells were seeing quite a lot of Evelyn Waugh, then aged twenty-seven, that summer. It was about this time that there occurred "the awful moment . . . when Edith Sitwell leant towards me like a benevolent eagle and said: 'Mr. Waugh, you may call me Edith,'" as he told P. G. Wodehouse twenty-five years later. "I did not dare address her for five years."[6] But he went to tea with her that May, noting in his diary, "Stale buns and no chairs. Numerous works by Tchelitchew in wire and wax." Harold Acton was there too, and Diana Guinness (née Mitford, later Lady Mosley) "in a hat of the grossest eccentricity." Edith, Waugh said, "talked only of poetry." He was luckier than he knew; the alternative topic would have been the genius of Pavel Tchelitchew. Waugh met her again at the end of June, at dinner with the Duchess of Marlborough — Consuelo Vanderbilt's successor, the ill-fated American Gladys Deacon. Edith liked her, and used to send her poems: "I do *want* you to like . . . 'Gold Coast Customs,' I set great store by it. And you will understand it. Hardly anyone does."

At the Marlboroughs' dinner, Edith and Evelyn Waugh were put next to one another. "The dining-room was full of ghastly frescoes by G. F. Watts. Edith said she thought they were by Lady Lavery." Nellie Melba, the singer, was there, and Waugh reported this interchange: "I have read your books, Miss Sitwell." "If it comes to that, Dame Melba, I have heard you sing." It must have been a joyless evening. "There were two ambassadors and about forty hard-faced middle-aged peers and peeresses."[7]

Anxiety and ill health caused Edith to put on weight. Virginia Woolf was at a party she gave in July, and wrote in her journal:

> Edith Sitwell has grown very fat, powders herself thickly, gilds her nails with silver paint, wears a turban & looks like an ivory elephant, like the Emperor Heliogabalus. I have never seen such a change. She is mature, majestical. She is monumental. Her fingers are crusted with white coral. She is altogether composed. But though thus composed, her eyes are sidelong and humorous. The old Empress remembers her Scallywag days. We all sat at her feet — cased in slender black slippers, the only remnants of her slipperiness & slenderness. Who was she like? Pope in a nightcap? No; the imperial majesty must be included. We hardly talked together. . . ."[8]

Edith retreated to Renishaw for the rest of the summer. Sir George and Lady Ida were there. The family was not alone. "It rains and pours here the whole time," Edith wrote to Fytton Armstrong, "and my parents have succeeded in amassing about a hundred deaf people, all of whom quack like ducks, saying 'What, what, what.'"[9] Waugh went up with Robert Byron to stay at the end of August and found a house full of people; he was not greatly impressed by Renishaw or its setting. In his diary he wrote:

> Arterial main roads, coal mines, squalid industrial village, then a park, partly laid out as a golf course, and the house; north front, discoloured Derbyshire stone, castellated. Very dark hall. Many other rooms of great beauty, fine tapestry and Italian furniture. Ginger in white tie and tail coat very gentle. Ginger and Lady Ida never allowed to appear together at meals. The house extremely noisy owing to shunting all round it. The lake black with coal dust. [10]

"The household was very full of plots," he wrote. "Almost everything was a secret and most of the conversations deliberately engineered in prosecution of some private joke." Osbert was very shy, he thought. "Sachie liked talking about sex. . . . Edith wholly ignorant."

> The servants very curious. They live on terms of feudal familiarity. E.g. a message brought by footman to assembled family that her ladyship wanted to see Miss Edith upstairs. "I can't go. I've been with her all day. Osbert, you go." "Sachie, you go." "Georgia, you go," etc. Footman: "Well, come on. One of you's got to go."

Anthony Powell too was invited to Renishaw in the summers of the late 1920s, and he recalled how, since Sir George disapproved of alcohol, "a house party of perhaps twenty persons sitting down to dinner would be individually lucky to get more than a glass of white Bordeaux." There was no port or brandy for the men after dinner either, while Sir George held forth on one of his favourite topics, such as "Nottingham in the Middle Ages." But chosen guests were secretly bidden to assemble before dinner in Lady Ida's upstairs sitting room, where the taboo against alcohol was discreetly broken. [11] Osbert has described Edith in the 1920s, sitting on the bed in Lady Ida's room:

> Now a person of the utmost distinction and beauty, with her long slender limbs and long-fingered hands, and the musing but singularly sweet

expression which had always distinguished her, she belonged to an earlier, less hackneyed age, in which the standards of Woolworth mass production did not exist: (in fact, as an American is said to have remarked in front of her portrait in the Tate Gallery, "Lord, she's gothic, gothic enough to hang bells in!").[12]

Their mother, Osbert wrote, who had so "cruelly ill-used" Edith, "had come to love her society, her wit and perception, and it was symptomatic of Edith's fineness of character that she responded. . . ."

It is hardly surprising that under these circumstances all Edith succeeded in completing that summer was two introductions: one to *The Pleasures of Poetry*, first volume, her anthology of poems from Milton to the Augustan age which Duckworth was to bring out in November, and one for the exhibition of Serge Lifar's picture collection at Tooth's Gallery which opened on September 16—but before that date she had escaped again with Helen to Paris, her promised land.

Autumn 1930 was a strategic time for Edith to be out of England, for it was in that year that Wyndham Lewis's novel *The Apes of God*, begun back in the early 1920s, was published, with its long-drawn-out and virulent mockery of the Sitwells. It is a roman à clef, a satirical indictment of contemporary society: Bloomsbury, Mayfair, and Chelsea are all pilloried; James Joyce, Roy Campbell, Aldous Huxley, Stephen Spender, Gertrude Stein, André Gide, and Jean Cocteau are all implicated; but the chief butt is the Sitwell family, trading here under the names of Lord Osmund, Lord Phoebus, and Lady Harriet Finnian Shaw.

Lewis allied his aims with those of Pope's *Dunciad*; and Ezra Pound in the *New Review* (January 1931) said that the novel should be given a purely literary reading—in eighty years' time no one would care "a kuss" about who was meant to be who, and "the colossal masks will remain with the fixed grins of colossi." Fifty of those eighty years have passed, and the main interest of this long (625 pages) and nearly unreadable book is still who's who.

The Finnian Shaws are "God's own Peterpaniest family," permanent adolescents, middle-aged enfants terribles, endlessly retailing the eccentricities of their father, "Cockeye," seeing themselves as just a little naughty and dangerously daring. Harriet (Edith) is desperate for literary fame and, when an editor arrives, "she made no pretence that she could not have wrung his neck here and now for not putting *all* the poems of the Finnian Shaws that they had ever written into his beastly anthology." And as for her own poetry—"All about arab rocking-horses of true Banbury Cross breed. Still making mudpies at forty."

The only comfort for Edith in all this (although in her loyalty she would not take it) was that Phoebus/Sacheverell is treated just as roughly as she herself, and Osbert far worse. For once all the Sitwells lay low under attack. All Edith said to Sacheverell, in a letter written from Evelyn Wiel's flat in the rue Saint-Dominique, was that *The Apes of God* was "an unadulterated bore, and very gross." She had heard "nothing at all" from Osbert since she had come to Paris. (Osbert was in the Balearics with David Horner.) All three Sitwells were away from each other and from the inflammatory centres of gossip; Sacheverell had moved that year with his young family to Weston Hall in Northamptonshire, which was to be home for them forever after.

Nevertheless, it seems at first extraordinary that Edith, who reacted to the mildest criticism, the faintest possibility of insult and libel, with furious letters sent off to all quarters and threats of legal action, should have been so quiet about *The Apes of God*. The malicious jokes and facetious persecution of Wyndham Lewis, through the mails and whenever possible in the press, continued; but she did not bring out the heavy guns.

One explanation, other than the obvious one that she was too deeply involved in her own life to bother, is suggested in a letter to Pavlik's sister, Choura. Edith wrote to Choura as frequently as and even more intimately than she wrote to Allen Tanner; since Choura had no English, Edith corresponded with her in her wildly inaccurate schoolgirl French. She wrote during that dreary month of August at Renishaw:

> Un écrivain et peintre très connu a Londres, (j'ai posée pour lui presque tous les jours pendant un an, il y a sept ans) ayant essayé avoir un succès personel avec moi, en vain, s'est vengé sur moi en ecrivant un livre nommé *Les Singes de Dieu*, entièrement sur moi et ma famille, en lequel il dit que j'ai cinquante ans bien passée!! [he does not] et que je suis une vierge entêtée!! (Ça, oui!) Vraiment! C'est comme la vengeance d'une demi-mondaine dédaignée! C'est curieux qu'il me connait si peu qu'il pense que cela m'irritera! C'est une des choses qui ne m'irrite nullement. (Et je suis complimentée par une des noms!) . . . Et naturellement, comme je suis une lady, je ne peux pas dire (sauf a une amie très intime) la raison de cet haine.

Vraiment, she said, the revenge of people who don't get what they want is "un peu trop."

If Edith could see Lewis's attack as revenge on her for not having succumbed to his advances, she was in a strong position; she could afford to be generous. Wyndham Lewis as a "demi-mondaine dédaignée" was a triumph rather than a defeat. The men who made advances, who attempted a "succès personel" with Edith, could at a generous estimate be calculated on the fingers of a severely mutilated hand. However unwelcome his advances, the incident had a disproportionate significance for her. *The Apes of God*, if seen as a consequence of her rejection of him, proved that the incident was of great significance to him as well. They were worthy adversaries. He was, she told Choura, "un assez grand écrivain."

The Apes of God brought another triumph in its train. At the end of September, Edith was writing to Anthony Powell, still working for her publisher, Duckworth: "I want to ask you to be an archangel and send me *by return of post, and registered*, Wyndham Lewis's new pamphlet, which apparently contains a letter from Yeats, ticking him off about me. I can't get hold of it here, and am mad to see it." The pamphlet was *Satire and Fiction*, in which Lewis combined self-advertisement of his genius and justification of the controversial *Apes of God*. Yeats, canvassed for his support, came out as an admirer. Busy in his own twilight, outside the gossip circle of literary London, he did not recognise the caricatures in the book. "I have heard that you attack individuals," he wrote in the letter to Wyndham Lewis that was printed in *Satire and Fiction*, "but that drove me neither to detraction nor admiration for I knew nothing of it; I recognised nobody—I spend one week in London every year." He ended his letter thus:

> Somebody tells me that you have satirised Edith Sitwell. If that is so, visionary excitement has in part benumbed your senses. When I read her *Gold Coast Customs* a year ago, I felt, as on first reading *The Apes of God*, that something absent from all literature for a generation was back again, and in a form rare in the literature of all generations, passion ennobled by intensity, by endurance, by wisdom. We had it in one man once. He lies in St. Patrick's now under the greatest epitaph in history.

By associating them with Jonathan Swift, the old seer, in his devious innocence, gave first prize to both parties.

11

French Leave

1930–1932

Edith was back in England in 1930 for a lonely, dreary Christmas—an eye infection, influenza, Helen's influenza, and the Depression: "I have seen very few people, because most people are away, and those who are not, are too gloomy to come. . . . I think a lot of rich people are making a terrible fuss about nothing," she wrote to Allen Tanner. On top of all this, there was "a hell of a row" in *The Times Literary Supplement*, in which Edith was unequivocally at fault, and defended herself with a breathtaking defiance, as she explained to Tanner on January 23, 1931:

> I misquoted some Baudelaire in my *Pleasures of Poetry*, —as a matter of fact, as a poet, I'm convinced Baudelaire *would* have written that particular thing *if* he'd got it in his head, because the effect is very subtle and beautiful. I put
>
> > Mon ange, ma soeur
> > Songe à la douceur
>
> instead of
>
> > Mon enfant, ma soeur,
> > Songe à la douceur—
>
> The misquotation is, I still hold, infinitely more beautiful and strange. Anyhow, some suburban spinster caught hold of what happened, and wrote a *furious* letter to *The Times L.S.*

Edith's reaction to her misquotation is typical: it was, she said, "infinitely more beautiful and strange" than what Baudelaire had written. She does not speak of the *meaning*. Sound and suggestion, for Edith, always came before meaning.

T. S. Eliot and John Hayward tried to defend Edith, which can only partly be ascribed to their concern for her reputation and happiness; rather more prosaically, they cannot have welcomed the prospect of having the always oversubscribed letters columns of the *TLS* taken over for weeks by a long and vituperative correspondence about Edith's inaccuracy on the one side and her inspired improvements of Baudelaire on the other.

Edith was resilient. The more she was put down, or shown to have been at fault, as in this case, the harder she fought back. She was in most respects inwardly uncertain, shy, and frightened. Such a person when challenged has only two possible courses to follow: She can fall into despair, all her worst fears about her abilities, reputation, and unloveableness confirmed; or she can rise up in defiance, and behave with what in a child is called "uppishness," denying all fault, ascribing malice to her detractors, and righteousness to her supporters, and end up believing herself to be the victim of unjust persecution. What she absolutely cannot do is take a middle course—accept criticism or correction or disapproval gracefully, while preserving her own sense of purpose and self-esteem. It takes a strong person to behave in that way, and Edith was not a strong person.

There were others weaker even than herself. Letters came to her as she convalesced from influenza ("I still feel as weak as a rat") from Allen and Pavlik about lack of funds, ill health, and the treachery of Gertrude Stein. This all made Edith "horribly sad," she wrote to Allen. She begged him to let her know what they needed. "It is a question of *is* one a real friend, or is one *not*." She was going to be back in Paris early in the new year, and was plotting ways of advancing their careers. "I'll introduce you to Comtesse Anne Jules de Noailles, the daughter-in-law of the old girl who writes bad poetry." And she was inviting Eddie Marsh—Sir Edward Marsh of *Georgian Poetry*—to tea in London to see Pavlik's pictures. For Pavlik's sake she would treat with the enemy, even though Osbert was having a "running fight" with Marsh "because he is a fool about poetry . . . but he *does* buy pictures, and is useful." As for Gertrude Stein: "If she starts any of her games with us, we shall just laugh. I refuse to be rattled in any way at all."

Her commitment to Allen and Pavlik was wholehearted; she was using "us" and "we" as she had not been able to since she and her brothers had been the "deleterious trio" ten years and more ago: "Don't let Pavlik be too wretchedly unhappy, we *shall* pull through, honestly we shall. I *mean* us to. We *will*. Don't despair. Please don't. You will see. Things will change. You know the motto about God helps those who helps themselves. No fool wrote that."

And Pavlik wrote to Edith: "Nobody has ever understood you better, or come closer to you than I have and nobody ever will." Theirs was "a friendship that has neither beginning nor end and which brings me enormous happiness and a limitless feeling of tenderness."[1]

During 1931, the only work Edith managed to do was the editing of the second volume of her *Pleasures of Poetry* anthology; the poem *Epithalamium*, which Duckworth brought out in a small edition for Christmas at one shilling; *Jane Barston*, which was brought out by Faber in the Ariel Poems series; and a mini-edition—only fifteen copies—of her poem *In Spring*, with engravings by Edward Carrick, privately printed by Terence Fytton Armstrong ("John Gawsworth") in May, at a guinea. Fytton Armstrong was losing his place in her good books. "When my maid says I can see no one, it means that I cannot see anyone,"[2] she was telling him in November 1931; no more passwords for him.

Edith's anxieties over her work and her private life were rather more important to her than the fact that *Façade* was being given a new dimension. Frederick Ashton was the choreographer of the very successful ballet *Façade*, first produced by the Camargo Society on April 26, 1931, in London, and then in New York, with Lydia Lopokova, Alicia Markova, and Ashton himself in the leading roles. The ballet was taken into the repertory of the Sadler's Wells—now the Royal—Ballet, and, more recently, into that of the Joffrey Ballet in New York. It was of course William Walton's music, and not Edith's poems, that interested Ashton; and Edith disassociated herself from the project at its inception, since she was not particularly interested in ballet. It was only after it got off the ground and was a success that she wanted her name associated with it; and the official description of the ballet now includes the words "based upon poems by Edith Sitwell."

What was chiefly harassing Edith around the time of the ballet's first production was her own shortage of money—not only for herself and Helen, but for the fulfillment of her fairy-godmother role with Pavlik. Her *Collected Poems* had done well, but there was still, as she told Choura, "la question terrible de l'argent—cela ne fait rien dans la poésie, car on ne gagne rien de la poésie." Her agent wanted her to write her memoirs, for £200; outraged, she changed agents, moving to the firm of Curtis Brown, where the young David Higham began what was to be a lifelong association with her. (He later, at Pearn, Pollinger and Higham, then at David Higham Associates, looked after her brothers' interests as well.)

Edith was working unwillingly throughout most of the second half of 1931 on a prose book about Bath—a city she had frequently visited but where she had never lived. In France that summer she was struggling with it for six hours a day—in Paris she "stayed" with Helen and Evelyn in the rue Saint-Dominique, but slept and did most of her work on *Bath*, surrounded by books sent from the London Library, in a small room at the nearby Hôtel de la Bourdonnais. Many of her Paris contacts were made through Allanah Harper; through her she met the painters Louis Marcoussis and Amy Nimr. Being young, pretty, rich, and the editor of a literary journal, Allanah had the entrée to what literary salons there were. Many of the hostesses expressed a wish to meet Edith; and drawing rooms were the only places where Edith could be met, since she worked long hours and refused to sit around in the cafés where writers gathered.

Allanah took Edith to the salon of the Duchesse de la Rochefoucauld, where she met Sir James Frazer, of *The Golden Bough*, and Paul Valéry, and to the salon of the Comtesse Marthe de Fels, where she met Saint-John Perse. Chez Amy Nimr, Edith happily discussed Lewis Carroll's "Jabberwocky" with Léon Paul Fargue; and Allanah took her to see an old lady who had been "one of Rilke's intimate friends": she had "crimson hair, aquiline nose, small piercing blue eyes . . . in the streets, in her cloak and huge floppy hat, she frightened the children who took her for a witch." Edith was interested in everything and anything about Rilke, but "unfortunately, once this lady started to talk, nothing stopped her."[3]

It was at Edith's request that Allanah had taken her, in spring 1930, to the two famous bookshops opposite each other in the rue de l'Odéon—Adrienne Monnier's La Maison des Amis des Livres and Sylvia Beach's Shakespeare & Company. Adrienne Monnier saw Edith through the shop window, recognized her, and greeted her with "appropriate ceremony." Both bookshops were famous for their "readings"; and on the night of Edith's, a month after this introduction, the room at Shakespeare & Company was packed: "People stood on the doorway and were pressed against the walls. James Joyce, Valéry Larbaud, Henri Michaux, Stuart Gilbert, Jean Prévost, and a good selection of the literary *monde* of Paris," wrote Allanah. This successful evening ended in a discussion, and a select party in Sylvia Beach's flat above the shop.

But a later appearance of Edith's at Shakespeare & Company ended in disaster and embarrassment. Invitations were issued for 9 p.m. to "listen to what Edith Sitwell had to say about Gertrude Stein—and in Miss Stein's expectant presence," according to the literary lesbian Natalie Barney, who was there on the night. Alice Toklas accompanied Gertrude Stein; James Joyce was also in the audience. It was a rare opportunity to hear one outsize personality expound the talent of another; all hoped for "a striking view of the rival summit."[4]

But something was very wrong. Edith, in a dress designed by Pavlik, first recited some Shakespeare and Elizabethan verse. She "sat well and majestically remote above her audience. Her long Elizabethan hands, bearing no papers, met in their virginal loveliness, sufficient unto themselves." She then opened a book and began to read aloud her own poetry. Gertrude Stein sat there, bolt upright, forbidding, seeming to meditate "a more gentlemanly reprisal than immediate exposure." It would have been a relief to the embarrassed audience if Gertrude Stein had walked out; as it was, everyone sat and listened to "this singular monologue, devoted exclusively to Miss Sitwell's self."

Afterwards, upstairs in Sylvia Beach's flat, drinks and sandwiches were passed, and conversation made, but no reference to the curious change of programme. Gertrude Stein had gone straight home. Later, according to Allen Tanner, she sent Edith a note expressing her displeasure in "her own curiously indirect way."

Why had Edith done it? Was it a genuine misunderstanding? Or "Did we not detect," wrote Natalie Barney, "a faint gleam of suppressed mirth filtering down to us through her blond eyelashes?" Tchelitchew's biographer interprets the incident thus: "She knows that Tchelitchew is not seeing Gertrude Stein any more, and has decided . . . not to include her [Stein's] work in the program."[5] Sylvia Beach punished Edith, long after, by not mentioning her at all in her book *Shakespeare and Company*, which contains a roll call of every author of note who graced her shop. Gertrude Stein seems, grandly, to have forgiven.

Pavlik, for his part, was absolutely delighted. Edith had snubbed the old Sibyl who was snubbing him and his art. (At about this time Stein was telling Cecil Beaton that Pavlik had no "aesthetic sense.") His new Sibyl, Edith, enjoyed a "glamorous triumph": "I am as sure of you as I am of myself," Pavlik wrote to her. "The more I know you the more I become attached to you. I am sure you will write some wonderful poems, you who are too great even for your brothers to understand. You have a magnificent soul and a magnificent heart. . . . In fact there is only one Sitwell soul and that is you."[6]

Edith was spending more and more time in France. One of Pavlik's kindest friends was Stella Bowen, who has described those early happy days when Edith was the unequivocal "good angel" of the Tchelitchew ménage. Stella was fond of Edith, divining the "soft, flagrantly human woman behind the façade. . . . The English aristocrat, six feet tall, aquiline, haughty, dressed in long robes and wearing barbaric ornaments was a strange sight in happy-go-lucky Mont-parnasse." There was "a great deal of affection all round," wrote Stella Bowen, and even teasing. But, she added, "No one could have guessed at the vulner-ability concealed behind that mighty shield and buckler. . . . Pavlik in his way was fragile as well. Indeed, they were each of them a packet of nerves. . . ."[7] Stella Bowen painted Edith in her studio in the rue Notre-Dame-des-Champs, sitting on an old inlaid chest used as the coal box. "She was a lovely subject for a painter and gave me all the sittings I wanted. We talked hard all the time and when the picture was finished we knew each other very well indeed."

Stella Bowen and Ford Madox Ford, who were now beginning to part company, had acquired the lease of "an old stone labourer's cottage with four rooms and a small orchard" in Guermantes, then a whitewashed, slate-roofed village with no commuters, an hour by train from Paris. Stella was sorry for the household in the "little black hole of an apartment" in the Boulevard Montparnasse, and handed over the Guermantes cottage to Pavlik, Allen Tanner, and Choura. She thought Pavlik was "a genuinely important painter," and "the most brilliant Russian" that she knew, though she was well aware of the muddled way he lived, "in a perpetual haze of nerves, emotions, far-sightedness, blindness, silliness and wisdom."

There were happy country days for Edith at Guermantes. Allanah drove her there one Sunday when Pavlik was in good form, "always laughing, and how he made us laugh." Edith and Amy Nimr lay in the hammocks strung between the apple trees and laughed too. On the way home in the dark, Allanah ran over a dog. "Amy ran to find a butcher to kill the dog. Edith sat in the car, her face white and still." After the deed was done they went on, and Edith talked hard all the way into Paris, to take poor Allanah's mind off the dog, as she explained to Amy afterwards. Edith's sensitivity and consideration always touched and impressed Allanah, who was much the younger of the two and in enamoured awe of Edith. Edith did not want intimacy with Allanah, nor to get too close to her or to anyone else; but she gave her enthusiastic and affectionate companionship.

In spite of her fastidiousness, Edith had a liking for simple entertainment and would choose to meet Allanah in large, noisy restaurants. Like her brothers, she loved music halls, which she preferred to the straight theatre. She was a fan of Nellie Wallace, a pantomime comedienne who played the Widow Twankey. Once, waiting with Geoffrey Gorer outside the Finsbury Park Empire, she was herself mistaken for Nellie Wallace—which delighted her.

Edith wanted fun. She had been starved of fun as a girl. In those days beer was her usual drink, not wine; and she liked being taken by Geoffrey Gorer to backstreet restaurants in Paris to eat pigs' trotters and *tripes à la mode de Caen*—"most people," as Gorer said, "took one look at her and ordered quails' eggs."

Edith was in France for Christmas 1931. Stella Bowen has described Pavlik's absorption over the decoration of a Christmas tree, "more serious and concentrated than any child, stepping backwards and announcing critically, '*Il faut un peu plus de mystère à gauche.*' He would then proceed to create the *mystère*. . . ."[9] His sister, Choura, was away, taking a cure for her TB, and Edith wrote to her at Christmas reporting on the Paris scene. She said that Pavlik and Gertrude Stein were on better terms, and that she had come to attribute all Gertrude's capriciousness to the change of life—"Une difficile moment de sa vie!!!! Imaginez-vous! J'ai pensée qu'elle avait au moins 55–60 ans, et maintenant, si elle me dit la vérité, elle ne peut pas avoir plus de 48–50 ans! Mais c'est étonnant! Est-ce que c'est possible!" No, it was not possible: Gertrude Stein was fifty-seven in 1931.

Edith wrote home to Georgia that the holiday was doing her "all the good in the world": "I am enjoying myself *fearfully*, rushing about from morning till night, and as I've never, in all my life, been free or able to do what I want, and am now able to do so for the first time, I am just going to do it."[10] Helen called it a "moral dégringolade." "I go a lot to the Duchesse de la Rochefoucauld. . . . Last night, Lifar sent Pavlik and me a box for the Opera, where he is dancing, and afterwards, we went behind and saw him."[11]

In the early summer Pavlik was in England, where he painted a new portrait of Edith, and then went off to Somerset with the Gorers. Meanwhile, Edith was writing an essay on Wyndham Lewis, which, she said, was to be published in the autumn; it was "absolument écrasant, c'est tuant, vraiment," and, she told Choura with cryptic archness, "très feminine en même temps." This was the essay that never was published, though it was cannibalized a few years later for her novel, and again nearly thirty years later for her autobiography. In the last paragraph she wrote:

This is all I can say at the present moment about Mr. Lewis, but one day when he has long been dead (I mean, more dead than usual), and I have passed my prime, I shall write the story of his life for those who may still remember him. And in it I shall show how every little fault and every little mistake made by this fundamentally gentle and affectionate character is the result of the fear that engrosses him, the fear that he is not loved, the crushing impression that those on whom he has set his affections do not return them. . . . [12]

But of course she never did write it. She had a great deal of unacknowledged fellow feeling for Lewis. She credited him, even in this essay, with "definite intellect," but opined that he had never produced "a really satisfactory picture or book." She nevertheless hung his work on her walls; and the portrait of Edith Sitwell by Wyndham Lewis that now hangs in the Tate Gallery in London is part of the legend of both artist and sitter. Edith set more store, however, on the six portraits of her painted by Pavel Tchelitchew.

12

Entr'acte: Maiden Voyage

On a sunny June day in Bath in 1924 Constance Sitwell had chatted with a cousin of the "shoreless sea" of their countless relatives. "And we talked of Edith. I suppose she *does* care more for romantic love than appears."[1]

She did; though she had no access to the simple sort of romantic love that Constance Sitwell meant. Her relationship with Pavlik was hopelessly complex—in part because of their roles as patron and artist. Pavlik knew that Edith and her brothers could help him in his career, and had no qualms about this. She was one of the keys to his social and professional transformation. Yet this aspect of their relationship was only the tip of the iceberg. According to his biographer, Pavlik found in Edith "a beautiful sheltered eroticism, the purely passive female sensibility that lives forever, a glass flower under glass, behind the opaque façade so remarkable in itself."[2] He did not, as real lovers do, try to grasp the creature behind the façade; he helped her to elaborate and perfect her façade, since the one thing he feared was that it would crack, and he would be left face-to-face with a living, bleeding, demanding woman. Pavlik's one terror was that their charade of courtly love would break down. The thought that Edith wanted to lay hands on him appalled him. In 1930 he was in England, staying not with or near Edith but with Geoffrey Gorer and his mother in Highgate. Mrs. Gorer became a secondary Sibyl; he painted her portrait, and said that the Gorers "protect me against Edith's forays." He was hardly ever alone with Edith and betrayed her horribly—and no doubt strategically—to Allen Tanner, who feared rivals of any sex: "What—alone with Sitvouka? Non mon cher! What do you want? *I should be raped!*"[3]

She was to be the eternal virgin queen, his muse and his mental intimate; but because he could not believe in the image he created, she was also the eternal predatory and voracious woman. He was, after all, a homosexual. And like all women who take up a great deal of space in a man's interior world, she had to bear the burden of representing purity and corruption alternately and sometimes simultaneously. In Paris in the autumn of 1930 he was flattering her and playing up to the image of her that he loved and needed, designing strange clothes to bring out her "Plantagenet look"; and she responded with simple pleasure. "I'm awfully excited about my new clothes," she wrote to Fytton Armstrong. "Tchelitchew designed them all, and they look sometimes like a della Francesca, sometimes like a Giotto."[4]

Whatever the flaws in the relationship—and they were fatal—in those precious moments when Edith and Pavlik were living up to their untenable images of one another, when their "souls as man and woman" really were "touched to the quick," Edith was very happy. Allanah was witness to this. Edith was taking her to meet Gertrude Stein; they agreed to meet outside the house in the rue de Fleurus so that they could go in together, as Allanah was shy. Allanah arrived first: "A taxi drew up and out flew Pavlik Tchelitchew, waving his arms in the air, then dancing back to help Edith to alight. Crossing the courtyard of the Pavilion, Pavlik made several leaps in the air, ending in a pirouette. He possessed the gaiety of a child. . . . Edith blushed with pleasure at the sight of him."

After they left Gertrude Stein, Pavlik suggested going back to his studio to look at some new drawings. "We walked back through the Luxembourg. Edith and Pavlik were fascinated by the patterns and texture of the bark on the trees. 'This is like an elephant skin,' Edith would say, and Pavlik, 'That one is like a crocodile.' And Edith again, 'And that one is like the pattern on a snake skin.'"[5] At their best and happiest Edith and Pavlik were magically clever children, she dressed up as a princess with robes trailing on the ground, he cavorting ahead, playing in the garden—the garden at Doubrovka, the garden at Renishaw.

It is in the gardens of Renishaw that the best metaphor for Edith's submerged sexuality is to be found. In 1958, after a visit of Edith's to Weston, Sacheverell wrote a long, sad poem, "Serenade to a Sister."[6] Tchelitchew had died the previous year; Osbert was ill; Edith was growing old. Sacheverell wrote of her:

> I have known no being so imprisoned in poetry,
>   As if besieged, embattled there. . . .

"Your poetry," he says, "is your nunnery." It was she who brought poetry
to him:

> My sister
> And abbess of the nightingales,
> Who wound up the clockwork in my mortal frame.

For Sacheverell, poetry and a normally ardent temperament led on to a wider
world of nature, art, and travel, and also to love and desire; but everything
began with his sister:

> To live as a young man in your flowering shade
> Was wonderful indeed.

But she remained locked in, like a nun in a convent, just as she would not,
when they were children, go into the bluebell wood beyond the garden:

> In your pelisse of green sheepskin
> And wide-brimm'd hat
> Standing by the statues
> Where the walk goes down into the wood,
> But you would not come more than a foot or two into the bluebells;
> I suppose they are in bloom again at this moment,
> In this month of June . . .
> You would not walk, I say, into the bluebell wood. . . .

She never left the safety of the garden, in one respect; and thus cloistered she
carried inside her what Sacheverell called in his poem a "bitter dichotomy"
that "divided and haunted" her. Most of the nervous energy that is part of
sexuality went into her poetry, her loyalties, and her crusades; the undischarged
residue ate into her heart.

No one in all Edith's life took the trouble to lead or coax her more than a
foot or two into the bluebell wood. It was not her brothers' business to do so;
and no other man loved her quite enough. She did not attract men sexually.
Her strange face and long white hands and her gestures were beautiful, but her
body carried no sexual messages. It looked, Rosamond Lehmann said, like a
Henry Moore column. It was hard to imagine her naked. If she had no
confidence in her attractiveness, if she felt even that she was freakish and

deformed, nothing that happened to her ever persuaded her that she was deceived. Nevertheless, Virgil Thomson, among others, thought of her as "sensually aware."

No one except herself can say for certain that any woman is a virgin. It is possible that Edith's friends were mistaken in their assumption that she was, as one of them put it, "a hardened virgin" by the time she fell in love with Tchelitchew. It is possible in the same way that it is possible that Elizabeth I was not a virgin queen. As an old woman, Edith was found weeping one day by her secretary, Elizabeth Salter; when asked what was the matter, she said she wept because she had never known physical love, "and I feel I was made for it." In a way she was; she had a loyal and loving and passionate nature. But she was trapped in her strange physique, and in her music and poetry, she was the abbess of the nightingales. Apocryphal stories of Edith's infantile innocence are, simply, apocryphal—for example: that she was looking with Tchelitchew at one of his erotic paintings, depicting two people making love on a river bank. "But what are they doing?" she asked. "He's giving her artificial respiration." Nevertheless, it is only about Edith that such a story could be told. She herself told Demetrios Capetanakis in 1943 that she thought these lines of Emily Dickinson "remarkable" and "extraordinary":

> I did not want eternity
> I only begged for time:
> In the trim head of chastity
> The bells of madness chime.

The trap was set long before she met Pavlik: Her most beautiful poem, *The Sleeping Beauty*, must be the only version of that well-known story in which the Prince never breaks into the palace to kiss his bride awake. (Significantly, perhaps, the suitors appeal to the queen for her daughter's hand, and the queen, being asleep, does not hear.) The poem ends:

> "And oh, far best," the gardener said,
> "Like fruits to lie in your kind bed,
> To sleep as snug as in the grave
> In your kind bed, and shun the wave,
> Nor ever sigh for a strange land
> And songs no heart can understand."

So Edith remained chaste, from a mixture of circumstance, infantile regression, death wish, pride, habit, and, as in the nursery rhyme, "Nobody asked me, sir, she said." An English gentlewoman of her time had less difficulty in keeping the world of sex away, whether from her own consciousness or in social life. The ear and eye were not then subjected to a continuous barrage of sexual reference. She projected, too, the dignity, the pathos, and the power of chastity, and even the loose-tongued were circumspect in her presence—she relished scandal, but not salaciousness.

She made a virtue of necessity. Poets should not marry, she said. She surrounded herself with homosexual men to a degree that is not sufficiently explained by the observably higher number of homosexuals in the world of the arts than in the population as a whole. They presented no awkward sexual challenge to her, nor she to them. She found young gay men compatible, and whether or not she realised the exact nature of their proclivities is neither here nor there. It is questionable whether she did know, for a very long time, what male homosexuals actually do together. She found nothing odd in men living together—her brothers and Willie Walton had done so, and it was the normal thing for people who were neither rich nor married to share a house with someone of the same sex. She herself shared a flat with Helen. She understood love, even exclusive and possessive love, between friends. She knew how attached Osbert had been to Adrian Stokes, how devoted he was becoming to tall, fair-haired David Horner, who moved into Carlyle Square on a perma-nent basis in May 1930. It is unlikely that her thoughts followed any of these tender friendships past the bedroom door, even though Tanner had tried as nearly as he dared to rub in his special relationship with Pavlik in his letters following the book-sale episode.

Edith was no fool. She had read the great works of English literature, and she knew a lot of history: She knew, and observed, that men loved men. But her imagination, unfed by any sexual experience of her own, went no further at this time. Paradoxically, in her acceptance of her friends' attachments she came nearer to a candid, unprejudiced attitude than many more knowing and worldly people ever could.

As she grew older, the realities of homosexuality, if only because of Osbert's involvement with Horner and its consequences, could not permanently be kept at bay. She referred to homosexual activity, when she needed to, in terms of childish distaste: i.e., "piggy things." Her final word on the matter came in 1958, when she was seventy-one, and had been asked to sign a petition about changing the law. She wrote to her secretary: "I suppose I ought to do something about it (what a nuisance they are). I think of course that the law should be changed, but I do think it's a very nasty, messy subject. I could yell when I think about it."[7] By that time she had good reason to yell. To choose to fall in love with a homosexual was to choose a dead end. It matters little how much she knew or guessed, then, about Pavlik; our hidden selves know more than we do, and prompt us to attach ourselves to people who fill some need of which we are not aware, or to reinforce some pattern we cannot see.

Falling in love with Pavlik at the age of forty neatly ensured that Edith would never know requited love in the ordinary sense, that the Sleeping Beauty would never be kissed or shaken into response. All she could do was to be unhappily in love; and the relationship could only work so long as she remained what he wanted her to be—the Sibyl, the Muse, "a glass flower under glass." Allen Tanner, who was with them together a great deal, said that he "never once saw the faintest indication that she had the slightest romantic or above all erotic delusions" about Pavlik. Her tenderness was manifested rather by a "fondly grim and humorous attitude." But since she was only human, and he was a very vain, touchy, and temperamental man, tension and falsity were built in from the start. Rows and misunderstandings and resentments were in store, heightened by sexual feeling in Edith that she would not and could not acknowledge, let alone express, and that he feared like the plague. But at the beginning, just to be with him, just to talk about his genius to other people, made her happy.

His Monkey Wife, by John Collier, was a fashionable and successful novel that came out in November 1930. It makes fun, in a literate, literary, "modern" way, of men's expectations of women and women's of men. It is very much of its time—rather in the *Lady into Fox* genre—and a little Sitwellian too. All is seen through the eyes of Emily, a sympathetic chimpanzee who is gifted with an understanding of English. She herself represents feminine devotion of the most traditional and servile kind, tender and true, directed to her master, the inadequate Mr. Fatigay. The human females in the book are frigid and capricious; they cannot love Mr. Fatigay, but neither is he in danger of being swallowed up by them. It's a sophisticated and entertaining book, treating a serious subject lightly; and Edith went overboard for it.

She did not read *His Monkey Wife* until it was already in its third impression, in June 1931; and then she wrote to its author in white-hot enthusiasm, at 4:30 in the morning. It was not a work of talent, she told him, but a work of genius: "I don't think I know a work that contains more wisdom and more terrifying destructive and constructive wit. The word 'wit' has been debased from meaning Swift to meaning that wretched buffoon Noel Coward. But *you* have wit as Swift understood it."[8]

The terms in which she wrote to him suggest the way she herself was feeling about men's expectations of women:

> I don't think anything is left to be said now either about men's attitude to women, or about women's inmost thoughts. . . . How on earth do you know so much? . . . The comprehension of women . . . as man's "gentle pet" . . . the complete understanding of the average man's view of his womankind, — (together with all women's day dreams) in the fancy-dress ball scene; man's attitude to his womankind's emotions in "Drag her out by the legs, and throw a bucket of water over her!" . . . Honestly, as exposing the point of view of a man towards an accustomed woman, and of the secret view a woman takes of herself, I don't know anything to touch the fancy-dress ball scene. . . . The Church's attitude towards science. The average man's ideal of womanhood — as wife and mother — I don't think anything is left to be said of these, I don't really, after this book.

She begged him to come to Pembridge Mansions on his own, as well as with Osbert and David Horner, since "I never can talk to anyone in the presence of anyone else." She was sending him "Gold Coast Customs," "because it meant the hell of a lot to me when I wrote it: the critics have all tried to pretend it is about Africa! And everyone excepting Yeats and Osbert and Arthur Waley pretend it is obscure!!"

Writing again a week later, she told him she had read his novel three times more. By now she was reading into it everything she had ever thought or felt on the subject of men and women, and much more than it suggested to most readers. At the end of Collier's novel, Mr. Fatigay succumbs physically, one infers, to the chimp Emily's devotion. "I realise more profoundly," wrote Edith, "the horror of the quotation at the top of the last chapter, when combined with the last sentence of all, about the candle being 'strangled by the grasp of a prehensile foot,' and darkness receiving the last happy sigh; this as a final epitaph for civilisation as seen throughout the whole book."

Whether Collier intended anything so inflated is dubious. But her response to *His Monkey Wife* was all mixed up with her feelings about herself, about the "average man," and about Pavlik. If the price of love response was the hairy beastliness of the bed, she didn't want it anyway. Her passion was adolescent in its anguish, and all in the head; if Pavlik, unthinkably, had made straightforward physical advances to her, she would have been compelled to react with outrage and disillusion. For all that, like Emily the chimp she shared "all women's day dreams" and "the secret view a woman takes of herself." She now recommended Faulkner's *Sanctuary* to Collier—to show she was no prude—and Romanoff's *Three Pairs of Silk Stockings*—which was "terrible, because of the conditions described, but also, to those who know the Russian character well (I am one of the greatest authorities on that in western Europe) exceedingly funny." And she wanted to show him her pictures by "a young Russian of really extraordinary powers. I believe, firmly, that he is going to be one of the three greatest painters in Europe"—the other two being Picasso and Rouault.

It would be wrong to place too much importance on Edith's *Monkey Wife* phase; she was a woman of sudden enthusiasms, and there are a hundred cases in which she wrote warmly, repeatedly, and at length to fellow writers about their work. But most of these cases reveal little but her responsiveness and her generosity; few of them reveal her to this extent.

Edith referred significantly to *His Monkey Wife* in her *The English Eccentrics*, on which she was working at this time, and in which, eccentrically, she displays a good many of her feelings about the relations between the sexes. In her book she described the ambivalence with which Emerson and Carlyle regarded the learned and earnest American woman Margaret Fuller, and developed her theme:

> Scholars . . . are notoriously difficult to please; stupidity and flippancy in women, learning in women, all these offences may, at different times, prove equally unpalatable to them, though the last offence is usually the most unforgivable—largely, I imagine, because it is sometimes a little too readily assumed that heaven deems the charms of the mind to be sufficient of an endowment, and therefore bestows no other. In any case I suspect that the feeling cherished by both Mr. Emerson and Mr. Carlyle towards the learned Miss Fuller was very much as that natural male feeling expressed by Mr. Fatigay, in my friend Mr. John Collier's *His Monkey Wife*, when he learns that his pet monkey has taught herself to spell: "Come, come, Emily, if you are as clever as all that, you must be sold to perform on the Halls."

"There was a time in England, as everywhere else, when women were regarded as a subject race. But that phase is over in England . . . ," Edith wrote in her introduction to *English Women*, written during the Second World War. Edith, with her unorthodox looks and her lack of interest in the conventional girlish pursuits of Edwardian England, had suffered as the daughter of her parents. She was not made to be a member of any "subject race." She fought for her freedom and won it.

A bare account of her life would seem a text for militant feminism: She defied her parents' expectations, she lived independently without the emotional or financial backing of men, apart from her brothers. Both of them loved her, but both had lives and ménages of their own. Sacheverell had no money to spare, and Osbert's financial support was neither regular nor considerable. In any case, Edith hated being dependent on him. She earned her own living, and was devoted to her writing to the exclusion of almost all "feminine" occupations. She was not a homemaker—not for a man, not even for herself. Like a cuckoo, or the Dorothy Richardson heroine, she perched in provisional nests.

But because she was unpoliticized, uninterested in social action and social theory, and a "lady," with a lady's care for the traditions, she remained a closet feminist, even to herself most of the time. Her respect for her own sex was in some ways considerable, and not only for those who were "achievers" in a career sense. In *English Women*, she wrote:

> I would like to have written of those unrecorded women . . . who have never found fame, but whose daily example has helped to civilise our race: the ordinary women in their hundreds of thousands, beings whose warmth of heart and love of country and family, whose unswerving loyalty and gallantry, and gay, not dour, sense of duty, are among the glories of Britain.

Character was what Englishwomen were notable for, she wrote, as opposed to the "peculiar physical energy" of Latin women. This was wartime "propaganda" writing. But Edith did have a great respect and reverence for the "good mother," whom she wrote about in her only novel and whose feelings she imagined and empathised with as, herself childless, she grew older. She was strikingly lacking in the "peculiar physical energy" which she also denied here to the majority of Englishwomen. She was in every sense other than speech and gesture physically unanimated: She liked to work in bed; she hated going for walks, and never did if she could help it. Her physical life was as torpid as her mental life was active. This lack of physical energy is perhaps not unconnected with her inability to strike a strong sexual spark; it is as if in Edith's body the sap never rose.

Edith was always meticulous about including the wives of her literary friends in her invitations to parties—if not always in her conversations. Where she made a genuine friend of both spouses, she corresponded with each separately, never treating the married pair as a conglomerate. She would send Sir Kenneth Clark (later Lord Clark) and his wife, Jane, separate copies of her new book—one each. "We're not going to separate, you know," they said to her. "I know, but I like you each to have your own."

An attempt to make a feminist heroine out of Edith may falter, however, after a consideration of her attitude towards the difference between men and women. She had no doubt that there was a difference, and it was bound up with her theory, elaborated in *Alexander Pope*, about the influence of physique on artistic performance. In 1930 she wrote to Sacheverell about poems that he had sent her in manuscript: "Will you give the last Canto of Donne . . . another overhauling? Being a female, I could not *weigh* the *blanks* properly—(as you know, I never attempt blanks myself, because I am sure they don't lie in a woman's physique). I think the poem needs tautening up, in various places."[9] She was, in practice, a very unphysical person, yet she evolved a physical theory of poetry. And her reaction to most women's poetry was profoundly negative. In her heart, she saw women, and herself, negatively. In March 1946, at a period when she was very successful, she wrote to Stephen Spender:

> I am asking myself whether I ought to go in, now, for a strict "purifying down" [of my poetry]. But on the whole, I don't think so, because a woman's problem in writing poetry is different to a man's. That is why I've been such a hell of a time learning to get out my poetry, there was no one [i.e., no adequate female model] to point the way, and I had to learn everything—learn, among other things, not to be timid, and that was one of the most difficult things of all.[10]

She was disgusted if she was referred to as a "poetess." She was a poet. Except on one occasion: Walter Sickert was present at an exceptionally noisy dinner party at Carlyle Square, and called for quiet: "Poets and Poetesses! Don't all speak at once!" Edith for once allowed the offending term to pass, because, she said, it was as if he had said "Tigers and Tigresses!"[11]

Any sort of mawkishness was anathema to her—in theory, at any rate. "The woman's problem in writing poetry," as Edith saw it, becomes apparent when one reads what she had to say in her late middle age about women poets. She had no time at all for "personal" poetry, for the confessional lyric that does not detach itself from the particular case. To John Lehmann, on July 7, 1943, she wrote: "The young women are the worst. Oh, these Raines and these Ridlers. 'The raine it raineth every day,' (and *how*!!!). I don't know which is the weaker blitherer. Nothing to say, and no technique."[12] And to Maurice Bowra, on January 24, 1944, she put the case more precisely:

> Women's poetry, with the exception of Sappho (I have no Greek and speak with great humility on that subject) and with the exception of "Goblin Market" [by Christina Rossetti] and a few deep and concentrated, but fearfully incompetent poems of Emily Dickinson, is *simply awful*—incompetent, floppy, whining, arch, trivial, self-pitying,—and any woman learning to write, if she is going to be any good at all, would . . . write in as hard and glittering a manner as possible, and with as strange images as possible—strange, but believed in. Anything to avoid that ghastly wallowing.[13]

The violent but unspecific sexuality of "Goblin Market" found a response in Edith, as the poetry of Swinburne had in her adolescence. She was anything but a cold woman. It was the "ghastly wallowing" that she abhorred most, and which led her to tell Lincoln Kirstein, in May 1950, "I disapprove of poets being divided up into poets and *women* poets. If one can't write like a man one has no business to write at all."[14] Like Professor Higgins in *My Fair Lady*, she seems to be saying, "Why can't a woman be more like a man?" rather than arguing, like Virginia Woolf or Rebecca West, for an "androgynous" sensibility.

Women prose writers came in for less animus. She told her secretary Elizabeth Salter that "women novelists at their best have a peculiar insight and sensibility, added to passion, which differentiates them from the male insight and sensibility."[15] This is often true; but in her forthright division of labour she overlooked the fact that men, including several of those she knew well, are by no means exempt from "ghastly wallowing," either in life or letters. It is as if she took her male stereotype as an ideal and her female nature as a handicap to be overcome and controlled, its consequences avoided. "Women are hell" was one of her not infrequent remarks. (There was no trace of lesbianism in her nature.) Thus her feelings about herself meshed disastrously well with Pavlik's fears of women. Her maiden voyage was a lonely one, and it lasted all her life.

13
Good-bye to Bayswater
1932

Helen Rootham and Edith were no longer equal partners, either professionally or in their friendships. Edith ceased to preface her signature to letters with a statutory "Helen sends her love." Helen had been unwell since 1929, with a series of aches, pains, infections, and unspecific malaises. The following year cancer was diagnosed; and in April 1931 she made her will, leaving everything to her sister Evelyn Wiel for her use during her lifetime, "with remainder to Edith Louisa Sitwell." (Helen's whole estate, when the time came, was valued at less than £500.) By September that year Edith was telling Terence Fytton Armstrong that she could no longer have visitors at Pembridge Mansions in the evenings, since "there is a more-or-less invalid in the flat." She probably wanted to put him off: What is new here is the casually anonymous reference to Helen, no longer formidable.

Helen, in her mid-fifties, had invalidated herself not through her illness so much as through the personality changes, or the exacerbation of traits already pronounced, that her illness brought with it. "Suddenly life rotted," Edith wrote in her autobiography:

> Helen, a wonderful friend to me when I was a child and young girl, seemed to become semi-poisoned by the smell of money, and a silly wish to "get into society." She and her sister (when the latter paid a visit to Pembridge Mansions) sprouted into such high super-lineage, that it became obvious to me that they were absentees from the *Almanach de Gotha*.

Helen was desperately trying to keep up with her former charge, now flying miles beyond her grasp. Helen's conversation too was becoming embarrassing. She liked to tell people about her strange dream:

She saw two Beings, lying side by side. Suddenly, out of one Being, issued something that might have been a huge leaf, or might have been a great flame of fire, and this deliberately entered the other Being. What *could* it mean? . . . She would . . . give full details to all the young males of my acquaintance, and enquire, "Do you know what it means?"

They said that they did.[1]

According to Edith, whose testimony of the long and dreary finale to a long and loving friendship is not necessarily reliable, Helen was persuaded by her Serbian friends that she was the reincarnation of a Serbian princess who had routed the Turkish invaders. Her delusion was inconvenient, since everyone she saw became "automatically, the advancing Turkish army. . . . Anybody who spoke to me and did not confine their entire attentions to her, must, necessarily, have criminal instincts, otherwise, for what reason could they possibly wish to speak to me?" Helen seems to have rationalized her jealousy by irrational methods.

Helen decided that she would go permanently to her sister Evelyn in Paris. In 1932 the rent of 22 Pembridge Mansions was being raised; the neighbourhood was becoming less and less salubrious; it was time to leave. Edith would go to Paris as well. She could not afford the higher rent with no one to share expenses.

There was little to hold Edith, homeless and single, in London. At Weston, with Sacheverell and Georgia, she found some security: "We really are a happy family," she wrote to Georgia during the 1920s, after one of her many visits. "Sometimes when I think of it, I can't believe you were born so far away, because it seems to me as if I have always known you." On another occasion she wrote: "In your house, I find the home I never had. (Though Renishaw, if left to itself, would be also my home, though not a safe one.)"[2] But apart from Sacheverell and Georgia and Osbert, who had their own circles, the people—above all the person—that she loved were in Paris.

In London, she saw threats and insults on every side. William Gerhardie, for example, who had been a friend and whose *Futility* she had admired, had published his *Memoirs of a Polyglot*; in that book he had said that Edith "puts me in mind of a Russian colonel who, after dinner in the Mess, sat naked on the roof of his barracks and, like a dog, bayed at the moon." Her poems, he said, were "pure rant":

Edith Sitwell is not without some talent. But she shrinks back when you talk to her, as if your voice were too loud and your presence too actual.

She shrinks from telephones and such things, and is as fragile as if she came from a waxworks. You need have no compunction in writing freely about the Sitwells, for they are capable of standing up for themselves.

Gerhardie's lack of compunction was unjustified. He overlooked the private unhappiness behind the public bluster. Gerhardie got his laughs and Edith her tears.

But Pavlik still seemed to need her. He begged her to write to him: "There is sometimes such hell in my soul that I am afraid to touch it, and you know that there isn't a single person who can understand and console me more than you."[3] If only she would come to Guermantes, and join the family: "We could be together, and read and work and laugh at things." In May 1932 Edith was writing to Allen Tanner: "You don't know how much I am looking forward to the late autumn. I shall be there for much longer than you know. As a matter of fact, I cannot stand this life much longer. I want to be where I can work quietly, and see the few real friends I possess." There is no mention of Helen or of Helen's condition. Helen was not included in the circle around Pavlik. They were not interested in her. Edith knew better than to force the issue.

Edith wrote regularly to Pavlik as well as to Allen, but the vast majority of these letters are not accessible, being locked away in the Beinecke Library at Yale until the year 2000. So apart from the evidence of those few (from Pavlik to Edith principally) that got away, there is little information about the terms in which they wrote to one another. Edith conducted parallel and continuous correspondences with Allen Tanner and with Choura, with Pavlik and the problems of their household always in the forefront of her mind; if there is a gap between these two blocks of communication, the gap is Pavlik-shaped.

Edith's book about Bath, called simply *Bath*, was published by Faber in May 1932, with wrapper and decorations by Rex Whistler showing the author, quill in hand and surrounded by putti, floating over the city on a rose-coloured cloud. She dedicated *Bath* to her parents—perhaps because it was the first of her books that she expected them to make head or tail of. She was deprecatory about the book: It was "the rottenest book on this earth," she told Georgia.

It is composed entirely from secondary sources, with a reliance on extended quotation that, as in most of her prose books, betrays her lack of real enthusiasm for her task. There is little internal evidence of personal study of the town; in fact, she drove over from Lord Berners's house at Faringdon on one occasion with Sacheverell and Georgia when she was working on the book, but was mulishly unwilling really to look at very much.

But her printed sources gave her some very good copy, especially on the subject of the unhygienic and scandalous conditions of the baths before Beau Nash became the master of ceremonies. She was also able to make use of her old researches into Pope and his circle. She linked her patches of recycled material with the impressionistic passages that were to become a hallmark of her historical prose writing. She was cavalier about chronology, seeing the ghosts of the visitors to Bath flitting eternally through the crescents and gardens: "what does it matter in two hundred years, if the clock has struck 1709 or 1739?" This technique conceals weaknesses of organization, but it is also a true reflection of her nonlinear vision of history. Echoes of music and voices are "floating like little cold airs round the deserted room"; echoes of the ladies' skirts sweeping the floors are like the sound of "thin and drifting leaves." These formulae for evoking past animation were repeated in varied form but scarcely varied vocabulary in later prose books, as were her lists of exotic words for fabrics and stuffs, her paragraphs of "ghost-ladies in dresses of russets, shalloons, rateens, and salapeens . . . ." Ladies in pretty dresses are repeatedly compared with birds—"great birds in bright plumage"—as she had described herself, at eighteen, standing with her aunt outside a bookshop in Bath.

She wrote the book in unsettled physical and emotional circumstances, mostly in Paris, and one can sense this from the put-together feel of the finished product. She used the life and career of Beau Nash as her principal structural prop, and after she killed him off—most gracefully, in a fine set piece, an imaginative incursion into the pathos of old age—the book was still not long enough. In the final few chapters she retraced her steps to cover a few more aspects of Bath society—she does not pursue the "foolish laughing crowd . . . over the edge of the century," so the ghosts of Jane Austen and William Beckford are not eligible to fill the gap. These last chapters hang heavily because by now her "foolish laughing crowd" is dangling over the edge not only of the eighteenth century but of Edith's ill-planned book. But *Bath* has charm. It sold well enough; the initial printing was only fifteen hundred copies, but there was a second printing in July, and Harrison Smith brought it out in New York in November.

In the spring that *Bath* was published, Edith lectured at Oxford, gloriously escorted by Pavlik and Geoffrey Gorer. At the lecture Pavlik, watching her, remarked how thin she had got and how the overhead lights "brought out ridges in her face."[4] After Pavlik's departure, life consisted of "lumps of indigestible boredom punctuated with weeping widows and bores," she told Allen. The widow was Alida Monro, relict of Harold Monro of the Poetry Bookshop; she was "perfectly stony with grief" and apparently picked on Edith, who did not know her at all well, as "the only person she wished to see." Added to this, Vivienne Eliot, first wife of the poet, was completely out of her mind and causing distress not only to her husband but to their friends and acquaintances. The situation had been deteriorating since the early 1920s, and in 1926 both Edith and Osbert had been worried and baffled by long, incoherent letters from Vivienne. Now she was wandering about, Edith told Allen, "smelling, first of ether (to such a degree that I nearly became unconscious) and then of a drug which is only given to people when they are in the last stages of violence." The very last time that Edith saw Vivienne, on Oxford Street, Vivienne refused to admit that they knew each other, or that she knew who Edith was.

As if all this disturbance were not enough, Sir George and Lady Ida were in England from May to August: "My mother is more tiresome than ever," Edith told Allen, "and the awful thing is, that not having seen her for eighteen months, and having been through quite a good bit since then, I haven't got the patience I used to have. All this life of gossip, malice, and tiny 'interests' wears me out." As for Sir George, he was "after us like a fox after chickens."

There is one last glimpse of Edith through a stranger's eyes, before she left Pembridge Mansions for good. Hubert Foss had started the music department of the Oxford University Press—he was the first to publish William Walton, whose friend he became. Foss's wife, Dora Stevens, was a singer; and they invited Edith to their house in Rickmansworth to a recital of three of her poems sung to Walton's settings. After the recital the Fosses took Edith to meet Sir Henry Wood and his wife, who lived nearby. Lady Wood had sat behind Walton and Edith at the opera the year before, and had been overwhelmed by their likeness. "She simply can't get over it," Mrs. Foss told her husband. "I told her all the mock-scandal about it and she loved it." The "mock-scandal" was that Willie Walton was the natural son of Sir George Sitwell and Dame Ethel Smyth. Their names had been, as the newspapers say, "romantically linked." In January 1935 Virginia Woolf, writing to Ethel Smyth, told her that she had just seen Osbert and that he had said,

Hows Ethel Smyth? Do ask her when you see her, — did my father propose to her? Because that's the family story. . . . Did he? And was that why he married the woman who went to prison, (hereby breeding O. and Edith and Sashy — not I think to the ultimate glory of the British tongue, fond as I am of parts of them).[5]

In May Mrs. Foss paid a return visit to Edith at Pembridge Mansions, and reported to her husband:

My dear, she lives in a positive SLUM. I call her flat a tenement. It is up five storeys and *stone* steps. I got there — panting: a respectable sort of maid let me in and showed me into the sitting room. Edith mountainously rose at me. She was dressed in some sort of furnishing material unhooked at the back at intervals.

She was extremely nice and I tried my best to be intelligent. The tea consisted of tea and farthing buns. The room is filthily furnished, you never saw such coverings to sofa and armchairs; it reminds me a little of Edwin Evans's abode, although perhaps there was not so much *loose* dirt about. . . . The walls of her room are plastered with paintings and drawings by a Russian who she told me (with a suspicion of girlish coyness) was her greatest friend.[6]

The painting by Edith's "greatest friend" that most impressed Mrs. Foss was the *Green Venus*, of which she drew a very creditable sketch for her husband, explaining it was "of a naked lady in a hammock. . . . You know if you lie in a rather loose hammock your behind feels so heavy and huge — well this picture was like that. The parts that one feels are the heaviest are drawn the largest." Encouraged by her guest's interest, Edith brought out portfolios of Tchelitchew drawings, "ranging from sleeping cats to nude gentlemen. I gathered that some were for sale. . . ."

Hubert Foss replied to his wife that "apart from all eccentricities, you must remember she has no money, and spends it on party dresses of a peculiar kind. And she capitalizes on her poverty as the Sitwells always capitalized every advantage or disadvantage. They are commercial first and nice second."[7]

Foss evidently shared the view of F. R. Leavis, who that very year brought out his *New Bearings in English Poetry*, with its ringing remark that the Sitwells "belonged to the history of publicity, rather than of poetry," thereby making an enemy of Edith for life. May 1932 saw also the first issue of *Scrutiny*, the literary journal in which over the next twenty years Leavis promulgated his moral, cultural, and educational theories of literature. Leavis influenced a whole generation of readers, teachers, and critics, worldwide, and the poetry of Edith Sitwell meant nothing to him. Anyone who criticized Leavis, therefore, gave Edith much innocent pleasure. Geoffrey Gorer published a novel, *Nobody Talks Politics*, in 1936, in which he portrayed Leavis as the high-minded and self-important Dr. Litespring, author of a book called *All Ye Need to Know*: ". . . What could be better, what more important than to propagate a love of the more arid poetry (there was something slightly disreputable about the sensuous poets such as Milton, Keats, Swinburne, Edith Sitwell, something too easily enjoyable; how right Dr. Litespring was to pulverise them! how worthily abstemious!). . . ."

"The poetry scene" was coming up with new names, quite apart from F. R. Leavis. A number of them appeared in Michael Robert's Hogarth Press anthology *New Signatures*,* also in 1932. In 1930, Faber and Faber had published the *Poems* of a young man called W. H. Auden. The title of Gorer's novel, *Nobody Talks Politics*, was as satirical as its content; suddenly, everyone was talking politics.

Edith's only politics were personal politics. She never stopped beating the drum for Pavlik. Before she left for Paris she persuaded Colin Agnew, of the Bond Street gallery, to look Pavlik up there. She worked on Gerald Berners: "Lord Berners will be *most* useful," she explained to Allen, "as he is a rich man who knows *everybody* and is an enormous admirer of Pavlik's." In April she heard that Pavlik had been "seeing Lady FitzHerbert": "I hope she has bought a picture. She has well over £3000 a year and nobody to consider but herself." Rich people had just one justification now in Edith's eyes—as buyers of Tchelitchew masterpieces. Not that she liked him to see too much of women such as Lady FitzHerbert; they were to be converted, but not fraternized with. Edith was jealous, and so, in the cause of his own advancement, was Pavlik. They were both very ready to accuse each other of wasting time with worthless "fashionable" people. Tchelitchew's biographer commented that between "two such titanic snobs" as Edith and Pavlik "the word 'fashionable' necessarily earns a terrific beating."

---

*The "new signatures" are those of W. H. Auden, Julian Bell, C. Day Lewis, Richard Eberhart, William Empson, John Lehmann, William Plomer, Stephen Spender, and A. S. J. Tessimond.

Edith invited the wealthy Sam Courtauld, Christabel McLaren's admirer, to tea. She remembered, in a letter to William Plomer years later (April 29, 1948), "a fearful lunch," where she sat between Sir Edward Marsh and Sam Courtauld (both of whom she was courting on Tchelitchew's behalf): "The first made me feel like a dock policeman with an extra size in boots. The second made me feel unpardonably flippant—just a wisp of chiffon drifting toward the Great Beyond and the Judgment Day."

She cultivated too the rich dilettantes Edward James and Peter Watson (the future co-founder of O2Horizon) on Pavlik's behalf—he painted a portrait of the latter in blue armour. Edith got restive, however, as soon as Pavlik showed himself more than commercially interested in any of the sitters she found for him. "I hear the new name for Pavlik's friend Mr. Watson is 'Trumpet-Lips.' I am afraid he is not *really* appreciated in London," she wrote to Allen (August 1933). She also got restive if any of her friends refused to subscribe to Tchelitchew's genius. Harold Acton, a loyal friend to Edith and a man with a deep knowledge of painting, had no great opinion of Pavlik as a painter; in Acton's opinion, the best things he ever did were the stage designs for *Ode* and *Ondine*. He was honest to Edith about this, and she was cross; she removed the dedication to Harold from her 1920s poem "Poor Young People" (but later she dedicated another one, "La Bella Bona Roba," to him). Acton did submit to being painted by Pavlik, but the portrait was not a success. He was unimpressed also by Pavlik's temperament, his glooms and *cafard*, and retained a memory of him "moping in his little studio, with a stolid Russian sister and a frenchified American friend who sat thumping the piano in his dressing-gown"[8]—an unattractive but, in view of Edith's own view of the persons concerned, a salutary vignette. In her efforts to further Pavlik's career she did not forget the claims of his "frenchified American friend," nurturing his career as a pianist, and she wrote to Allen that she planned in Paris to "weave a net round such people as the Princesse de Polignac, so that you get paying engagements."

Cecil Beaton met Tchelitchew at this time; he thought him intimidating at first—"he could be devastating in his disapproval"—but soon found that Pavlik had "cast an almost hypnotic influence" on him. Pavlik painted a portrait of Beaton, too. And it was Beaton who witnessed the tail end of one of Pavlik and Edith's private psychodramas, enacted when she was in his temporary London studio in South Kensington one "terrible Saturday afternoon." This is her account:

I was sitting to him for one of his portraits of me. Suddenly a storm of particular violence blew up—I do not know—have never known, for what reason. . . . In any case, he took to hurtling the armchair in which I sat across the slippery floor as if it were a perambulator, at the same time uttering shrieks of rage, and at moments, hurling bare canvases past my head, being careful, however, that they did not hurt that organ.

"Yes, yes, I choos [just] *keel* you, you know! I choos keel you." "Very well, old boy," I said, resigned to my fate. "If you must, you must! But kindly respect my amber!" (I was wearing the enormous ornament which figures in his portrait of me at the Tate Gallery.) He had locked the door, and put the key in his pocket. . . .

However, suddenly footsteps were heard ascending the stairs. . . .[9]

It was Cecil Beaton, coming to tea. Pavlik unlocked the door at his request. "We had a nice quiet tea party," concluded Edith, "and no reference was made to the storm." Indeed, Cecil Beaton, who heard this story told many times, had no evidence that anything had happened at all. And had it? And if it had, was it quite as Edith said? Beaton took notes of some of his conversations with Pavlik, who "made even the simplest anecdote a marvel. He whispers and then shouts; he becomes alternately a bull or a child." "He tells how most people (if no one is around) will touch the private parts of statues in the museum; and in consequence these parts have continually to be washed!" In a conversation with Virgil Thomson about music, Pavlik said, "Some sensitive people are frightened by the flutter of a falling piece of paper, the whisper of a breeze through a window."[10] Perhaps he was thinking of Edith, who, he had said, was too "frightened about everything."

Already a serpent was entering the hoped-for Garden of Eden in Paris. Allen, Pavlik's longtime companion, was by now not even a grass snake; he was Pavlik's guardian angel, as far as Edith was concerned. While Allen shared his life, no one else could. But even before she left for Paris, Allen was writing in panic that the worst had happened and he was in despair. "You *can't* leave," Edith wrote to him. "It would break the hearts of everyone concerned." She blamed Pavlik's "fatal habit of endowing the most worthless people with a glamour that they do not possess." But young Charles Henri Ford was there to stay. Allen did not leave—yet.

Edith's hope of a new and happy life in Paris was losing its brightness. She cleared out of 22 Pembridge Mansions, her home for eighteen years, in August: "The hours of turning out everything in the flat, storing most things, and packing others, sorting manuscripts—and the sadness of leaving my home, became too much for me," she told Allen. She made a round of family visits, and was in Paris by the beginning of September.

Pavlik and Allen were not there to greet her; they were at Guermantes. Whatever happened on her first visit to them, Pavlik did nothing to make her feel any happier. She wrote to Allen from Evelyn's flat on September 5 that she was expecting a visit from Cecil Beaton, "and I am glad, because he has always treated me with great chivalry, and does not set false values on things that do not count." She did not intend to go out much—she had "no clothes"; she would just work hard on her next prose book, *The English Eccentrics*. There was nothing to look forward to:

> I am feeling very much like an old cab-horse today, and am dreading my life in Paris. When I first thought of coming, I was so glad to escape from the insults and slanders in London, and looking forward with such happiness to my life here! I thought I should put all the unhappiness of my past life behind me. Now I realise that I shall be more wretched here than I have ever been anywhere, as I just do not "fit in," either with the exterior or interior life of Paris.

By December some balance had been struck: Pavlik took her to see the German film version of *Die Dreigroschenoper*: "It is simply terrific. It is the *only* great film I have ever seen,"[11] she reported to Georgia. On Christmas Day—she told Georgia—she dined with Pavlik and Choura. Perhaps she did. But in her autobiography she wrote simply that her life in Paris was "unmitigated hell."

14
Rats in the Woodwork
1932–1934

She dreaded going into the local post office, because she was stared at. She hated all the business of identity cards and regular reporting to the police, which as a foreign resident in Paris became her lot. Allanah Harper, driving by in her car, caught a glimpse of Edith one day flattened against the wall in a busy Paris street, looking like a great flightless bird, helpless.

In October, a few weeks after their migration, Faber brought out Helen's translations, *Prose Poems from "Les Illuminations" of Arthur Rimbaud*, with an introduction by Edith in which she gave a verbal portrait of the boy poet at eighteen: clumsy, with red hands, bony wrists, chilblains, too-small clothes. Of Rimbaud's excesses, Edith remarked—rather in the tone of an indulgent godmother—"Both [Verlaine] and Rimbaud seem to have been a perfect nuisance at this time, both in their home-life and to their casual aquaintances." "The translations are *admirable*, really fine," Edith wrote to Allen Tanner. "I like my essay, too, better than most of my prose."

Helen was not in a condition to take much pleasure in this fruit of their long partnership, and neither was Edith, whose third anthology volume of *The Pleasures of Poetry*, covering the Victorian period, was published by Duckworth in the same month: "I have been in bed now, on and off, for some days, because losing weight so much too quickly has affected my heart. What a bore!"

"Were there a French equivalent of Moscow Road and Bayswater during the 1930s," John Pearson has written, "it would have been the faded quarter sprawling each side of the rue Saint-Dominique in the seventh arrondissement of Paris." Number 129 was "a tall, anonymous grey building with a coal shop opposite."[1] Evelyn Wiel's flat was on the top floor, so there was a dreary climb, as at Pembridge Mansions. The flat consisted of six small rooms; Helen's was nearest the hall door, so that it was impossible to receive visitors without disturbing the invalid. Edith's own room was tiny, made even smaller by her piles of books and papers and stacks of pictures. A place that had been fun to visit when it had spelled excitement and escape, the flat quickly lost all its charm for her now.

She was working seven hours a day on *The English Eccentrics* after she arrived and into the new year of 1933; it was published by Faber in May 1933, and by Houghton Mifflin in New York in September. Mr. Cox of the London Library faithfully sent her the books that she needed—as he had for *Bath*—though even he almost bilked at the postage on Pink's *History of Clerkenwell*, which weighed four and a half pounds. "My boring book on the Eccentrics," she called it to Allanah. "Oh how glad I shall be when it is finished and I can get back to poetry!"

She dedicated *The English Eccentrics* to her doctor, H. Lydiard Wilson, and his wife. The *Times*'s review, on May 18, 1933, said that the book "bore traces of the formlessness, the diffuseness, the insatiable lust for detail (as of an encyclopaedia spilled out of its bindings) that distinguish the 'anatomies' of the pre-Augustan Age."

Her enthusiasm and stamina for "copying out" were certainly standing her in good stead; for much of the book consists of long extracts from other books, which include Osbert's *Sober Truth* and *Victorians* as well as her own *Bath*. There was plenty of lively material available, to which Edith responded with a cheerful irony, and it is this sustained editorial tone that binds the book together. She is good, for example, on the predilection of eighteenth-century noblemen for hiring Ornamental Hermits to embellish their grottoes. When they needed a new Ornamental Hermit, they placed an advertisement in the paper. "No one, it was felt, could give such delight to the eye," wrote Edith, "as the spectacle of an aged person with a long grey beard, and a goatish rough robe, doddering about amongst the discomforts and pleasures of nature." The salary was not high, but neither were the duties arduous. (When Edith felt particularly low, in Paris, she described herself as an "Un-Ornamental Hermit.")

For the reader interested in that developing English Eccentric, the author herself, the most significant chapter in the book is "Portrait of a Learned Lady." The lady in question was in fact American, not English: the feminist and bluestocking Margaret Fuller. Edith made some jokes at Miss Fuller's expense; but onto the imaginative account of Miss Fuller's love for the unsatisfactory James Nathan she projected her own unsatisfactory relationship with Pavlik, the subject uppermost in her mind during the writing of the book.

Between Miss Fuller and Mr. Nathan, wrote Edith, there developed "one of those innocently incestuous brother-and-sister relationships which are always so grateful and convenient to the gentleman, so shattering to the nerves of the lady." They had, Nathan said, "a *spiritual* affinity": "He proposed that it should be recognised, that their relationship came from *within*, although I imagine that this high spiritual life was interspersed, even then, by interludes of a distressing tenderness." And when Miss Fuller's face began to show the marks of advancing age—"partly owing to overwork, partly to the wrack and worry and wear and tear of this inhibited incest"—Mr. Nathan became moody. "But these signs of mental pain only made the woman who loved him move more closely to him, with a deeper, more foolish, phoenix-like love." Mr. Nathan, however, needed money: "Margaret, he felt, might ask her rich and influential friends. . . . " And so on; it is all there.

No one, having read this chapter from *The English Eccentrics*, could fail to believe that, on one level at any rate, Edith was fully aware of the specifically sexual ambiguity of her friendship with Pavlik, nor that she had a normal woman's feelings. She is heavily ironic about men's expectations of women:

Perhaps she might have broken the bond that held her, but although Mr. Nathan felt himself as free as air, it would have injured his high ideals to see any signs of such a frailty on the part of Woman, whose legendary fidelity is her birthright, bestowed on her by heaven. What an inspiration is this fidelity to Man, supporting as it does his belief in human nature on those many occasions when he is weighed down by the disillusionment brought about by the contemplation of his own lack of fidelity.

No one has ever put that particular point better. And Edith made no more striking a display of self-knowledge in all her writings than in her final summing up of Margaret Fuller: "She lived, indeed, a life full of noble ideals, backfisch nonsense and moonshine, silly cloying over-emotionalised friendships and repressed loves, (friendship being often disguised as love, and love as friendship), extreme mental and moral courage, and magnificent loyalty to her ideals, friends, and loves."

Yet self-knowledge, at one remove, was as far as she could go: she was unable to act on the self-knowledge, and so free herself. Liberation from her own obsessions carried too many threats; above all, the sex threat. In the same chapter of *The English Eccentrics*, Edith makes some remarks about the "Emancipation of Women," a movement in which learned, trousered and vivacious ladies like George Sand made presents of themselves with the same frequency, cheapness and indiscrimination as that with which other ladies present Christmas cards. This caused them to be collected with great eagerness by sex-snobs, who, unlike all other snobs, or collectors, prefer the ubiquitous to the rare.

"I am *longing* for my exile to be over," she told her cousin Veronica Gilliat at Christmas 1932. Rescue was in sight. "Do you think I might propose myself for about the 20th of February? The Boyar is having a show at Tooth's then [on the 23rd] and I had promised to come over and help him."[2]

"I am so glad and happy to be going away for so long," she wrote to Allen; "indeed, I am counting the days." She was in England from the beginning of February 1933 until March, planning Pavlik's publicity campaign, at first from Weston, with Sachie and Georgia. They, she reported to Allen (who wasn't coming over), thought it best *not* to have a party for Pavlik before the exhibition, in order to ensure a crowded gallery on the night of the private view. Also Osbert—who had written the introduction to the catalogue—was away with David Horner, and the Carlyle Square house was closed up; if they gave a party somewhere else "the most frightful lot of night-club habitués and studio hangers-on" would gate-crash and "have a drunken orgy."

The exhibition was a great success. Pavlik sold a lot of pictures. Afterwards Edith wrote ecstatically to Allen and Choura. "Sam Courtauld says Pavlik is absolutely made, and his only danger is, that he may be too much of a fashionable success. . . . For once, one of Pavlik's rich friends has behaved well—Mr. [Edward]James. He is in beautiful contrast to the others. . . . Pavlik seems well, but is of course very tired." Pavlik had been to stay at Weston with Sacheverell and Georgia, which had not been altogether a success. In the room in which he had slept, by the bedside, there was by chance a book about the coronation of the last Czar. Pavlik, for no very clear reason, took this as an insult, or at least as an insensitive touch. Nor was he reassured by the fact that Sachie put on a dinner jacket in the evening. Pavlik had no dinner jacket. No one ever questioned Pavlik's charm and attraction; no one ever questioned the fact that he was very difficult and very unpredictable. He left Weston the next morning.

Helen, who had been having a remission, collapsed again in the summer and had another operation. Edith, racked with pity, was not a natural nurse and was grimly preoccupied with her own work and problems; she did not pretend to a sanctity she did not possess. Evelyn Wiel was aging and ineffectual. It was a wretched situation for all three women. "Just over ten days ago," Edith wrote to Allen on July 24,

> it was discovered that Helen had got this frightful thing back again, and in the same place. . . . The time has not been exactly amusing, — it isn't fun to have someone announce, quite suddenly, the awful name of the disease. . . . Nor is it fun to do all the housework and marketing, and then, at night, have the poor creature's nightmares. Yesterday, I was up at 6, and at 8 helped her down the stairs to go to the nursing home for her dressing.

Edith's escape to England the next month was only half an escape, since she was followed by "terrible" letters from Helen. And at Renishaw, as she told Allen on August 15, "the rows are continual." She was writing "what should be a satisfactory poem"; this was "Romance," which she had been tinkering with for nearly eighteen months. But working on it at Renishaw in that hot August of 1933 she was "interrupted every other minute, and on every trivial pretext." Her parents were back from Montegufoni for the summer. Sam Courtauld was staying too—nice, but "hard to talk to." And her father walked up and down the lawn under the windows, Edith told Allen, dictating to his secretary: "Messrs. Humdinger, Humdinger and Humdinger. As I remarked in my last letter. Wrm [*sic*]. Worm. Worm. Read what you've got."

The rows were between her brothers and her father, about money: He was, she said, trying to tie up his fortune in such a way that if Osbert, Sacheverell, and Sacheverell's little son, Reresby, all predeceased Georgia, she would not get a penny. Also, as Edith told Choura, Sir George accused Osbert of owing him £2,000.

She left this happy family party to stay in comfort and some grandeur at Badminton with her aunt the Dowager Duchess of Beaufort, and thence went on to stay with an old friend of all three Sitwells, the harpsichordist Violet Gordon Woodhouse, near Stroud in the same county, Gloucestershire. Her rounds of visits were not just pleasurable; they were necessary if she was to get away from the dreaded "Gingers"—her parents—at all. Now in her middle forties, Edith still had no home of her own.

This tour was brought to a halt by an onslaught of tooth abcesses which prostrated her; she ended up back at Renishaw after treatment in London, where she had been staying in a hotel with Lady Ida—"I couldn't stand mother's whining any more." The only bright spots of the summer were completing "Romance," a secret decision to write a novel (which she revealed to Choura), and a reunion at Violet Gordon Woodhouse's house with W. H. Davies, her trusted and nonjudgmental friend from the old days. "We sat talking till two in the morning," she told Allen, "and I am afraid our hostess was worn out."

Edith did not confide in Choura her agonies over Pavlik, nor the Pavlik–Allen Tanner–Charles Henri Ford crisis. To Choura she wrote, overwhelmingly, about the nonstop ill health of their little circle, including her own: headaches, toothaches, colds, grippe, and—unique in Edith's correspondence—the trials of menstruation, as in March 1933: "Comme toujours, la méfortune qui est infligée par le ciel sur nous tous [sic] a choisi ce moment pour me visiter!!!!" It was a topic that elicited a great many exclamation marks; Edith, in this rare luxury of feminine confidentiality, wrote like a schoolgirl. Her cycle, it transpired, coincided with Choura's to a remarkable degree. As for Choura and her repertoire of ailments—"Choura's métier is illness," Pavlik is reported to have said.

The Pavlik problem, like the Helen problem, followed Edith to England. Charles Henri Ford, Pavlik's new love, twelve years his junior, was an extremely handsome blue-eyed boy from Mississippi who had arrived in Paris in the spring of 1931 to try to find a publisher for his novel *The Young and Evil*—a "naughty novel," said Parker Tyler, Pavlik's future biographer, who collaborated with Ford on it. Pavlik met Ford at tea with Djuna Barnes, with whom Ford lived for a while. Pavlik was fascinated. He started to paint Ford, and to write to him—"my darling huckleberries finn."[3] Pavlik sent Ford, and his naughty novel, to Edith, who was furious and disgusted—especially as Ford had obviously never read a word she herself had written.

If Edith had declined to look beyond the bedroom door in regard to the alliances of her friends up till now, *The Young and Evil* forced reality of a sort on her unwilling consciousness. There is nothing very innocent or unworldly in what she wrote to Allen about it from Renishaw in that quarrelsome August of 1933:

> I *know* that creature must be most dangerous. In the first place, judging from that foul and unspeakable book, he must know the most appalling underworld. That book . . . is like a dead fish stinking in hell! . . . *You send him to England* if he's tiresome, Allen dear, *with that book*, and I'll see to it that he gets from three to six months board and lodging free, from the

moment he lands!—Do you understand me?—Just one little word from me, and what a reception from the authorities!

In the event, *The Young and Evil* did not get past the immigration officials when it was published in spring 1934. There is a perhaps apocryphal story that Edith and Edward James—that "beautiful contrast" to Pavlik's other rich friends, whose wife, Tilly Losch, was to dance in Balanchine's *Errante*, designed by Pavlik, the following year—solemnly sat together and burnt a copy of the novel in the fireplace.

But not only Helen wrote "terrible letters" to Edith that summer. As she told Allen, in August at Renishaw she had received one from Pavlik that "has hurt me terribly":

> I did not need this extra blow to convince me, to prove to me, that he has lost any affection he once had for me,—if indeed he ever had any. When he had been betrayed by the last of the cheap worthless people by whom he is so dazzled, perhaps he will realise the kind of friendship that mine is, and with what loving care I have watched over him and tried to help him in his worries, and comfort him. But who knows that it will not then be too late.

She had irritated Pavlik with some mock prognostications for his coming birthday, in which she had conveyed her opinion of the company he kept and his plans for the future; for, as she confessed to Allen, "I dreaded either him or you going to America; because it will only mean rats in the woodwork...." But Pavlik, in pursuit of fame, fortune, and Charles Henri Ford, would go to America, and soon.

In her poem "Romance"—first published in *Five Variations on a Theme* in 1933—Edith went on trying to salvage something eternal from the wreckage of love. It begins, "She grew within his heart as the flushed rose / In the green heat of the long summer grows," and moves on to the Worm, and winter, and the sleep of death:

> For the vast eternal Night shall cover
> The earth from Pole to Pole, and like a lover
> Invade your heart that changed into my stone,
> And I your Sisyphus. We two shall lie
> Like those within the grave's eternity....

She continued to urge Allen by letter to stick to Pavlik; Allen "must never believe . . . that he does not love you, for he does, deeply. His trouble is that he gets taken in by cheap flimsy little horrors of people."

This was, though she would have repudiated the idea, part of Edith's problem as well. For too long she had been enmeshed in the neurotic, self-seeking, self-regarding Tchelitchew circus. It was diminishing her; her horizons were contracting. We cannot choose whom we love, and the unworthiness of the beloved does not diminish the quality of the love. But love consumes irretrievable time and Niagaras of energy. For some people, success comes a very poor second in importance to love. But the people around Tchelitchew — the pathological state of jealous emotion in which they lived, the way they manipulated one another, and the misery of the ménage in the rue Saint-Dominique — were all damaging to Edith.

No one could advise her. Osbert and Sacheverell were not in her full confidence. Stella Bowen was not afraid of home-truths, with the result that Edith was writing to Choura in October that she was keeping out of Stella's way: "Je ne veux plus de vérités; j'en ai eu assez." To Georgia she said: "Stella Bowen is being a frightful bore, and very impertinent, and I'm not going to see her."[4] Things were very bad indeed by Christmas 1933, when there was confusion and embarrassment over who would have Christmas dinner with whom, Pavlik clearly trying to avoid Edith, and making Allen miserable by not being able to tear himself away from the one Edith ironically referred to as the "Proust de nos jours." Edith challenged Pavlik about his behaviour. He assured her that his feelings had not changed, towards either Allen or her. She remained unsatisfied and wrote to Allen on December 23: "My word, I wish we were living in the Middle Ages. My charming forebears just used to have people's teeth taken out if they were tiresome, and their skins removed. I'd have a certain skin made into a bath mat!"

It comes as a relief to see her correspondence with someone quite outside the foetid circle — Charlotte Haldane, for example, the German-Jewish wife of the scientist J. B. S. Haldane, to whom she had written a few days earlier, on December 12. She did, indeed, refer to her personal problems ("I've seen people behaving in such a dreadfully ugly way just lately. And I never can get used to it. I mean, in my personal life it has been very bad, oh very bad"), but she links these troubles with outside troubles. She wrote about the lynchings in America, and "the departure last week of the French convict ship for Devil's Island." She wrote also to Mrs. Haldane about "the primal horror of Germany at present" and "the rage and horror that I feel in the cruelty of the Nazis." She wrote about Willie Walton's new symphony, and Arthur Rubinstein's piano technique, and her favourite music: "I love Bach, too. But though I admire Mozart, I love him less, which is my fault—preferring infinitely Gluck, because he is less sweet. Bach is my god. He seems to have created a perfect world, in which there is no sin. And in which sorrow is holy and not ugly." Sorrow was ugly for Edith. In her Christmas letter to Geoffrey Gorer, she wrote:

> Your remarks about "Romance" brought me real happiness in the midst of absolutely unparalleled gloom. Nobody could conceive what my life is like here. I can't go into details in a letter, but what between the misery of seeing poor Helen so desperately weak and ill, and the fact that I'm supposed to be slightly insane (I am treated as though I were) it is a little depressing. I *know* I look wild and odd when I've just been writing; but they'd look wild and odd too if they wrote my poetry. . . .[5]

(She said in her autobiography, "I did not mind, in the least, carrying the 'boîte à l'ordure' downstairs every night. But I *did* mind the open accusations of wickedness, and the threats that I was going mad. 'Have you looked at yourself in the glass?' "[6]) Her letter to Geoffrey Gorer continued: "In addition to this, I am very worried about Pavlik. I hardly ever see him now, though, as he is too occupied with that creature who wrote the immortal book we know."

In January of the new year, 1934, she was in London to be presented by Sir Henry Newbolt with the Royal Society of Literature's medal for poetry—an honour which she owed to the championship of W. B. Yeats. This was a world to which she could claim to belong; and yet, in the context of her Paris life, it seemed the merest postscript: a fact thrown away, as it was, at the end of her letter to Gorer.

Pavlik was doing his best to alienate her, or so it seemed. Allanah Harper recalled visiting with Edith the flat at 2 rue Jacques Mawas, in the fifteenth arrondissement, that the Tchelitchew ménage now used in addition to the Guermantes cottage. Pavlik refused to see them. Edith's humiliation was painful to witness. Parker Tyler wrote that Pavlik deliberately treated Edith to "regular periods of coldness (say about three days) because he doesn't want her to work herself up into, he claims hyperbolically, an amorous state."

The result was that she grew more and more bitter and hurt. She wrote to Allen in April 1934:

I realise now that on the rare occasions when he even attempts to behave with decency, or even ordinary politeness to me, it is that he realises that with your one exception, I am the only person on whom he can rely. Well, I will *never* let him down, and will do my best to see him out of these straits, but he has murdered my love for him.

Pavlik was painting another portrait of her; but she did not intend to turn up for the next sitting—"he can *wait* for me."

Poor Pavlik, he is a terrible fool. . . . A very great artist indeed, as great an artist in a different medium as he is, and someone who loves me (not one of my brothers) said to me when I was in England, "What a fool you are, Edith, to waste yourself on someone who does not know what you are." And he paid me the greatest compliment I think I have ever had. He said: "Any man who was an artist could do great work if you were beside him."

It has been suggested that this compliment was paid by T. S. Eliot. But it does not sound like Eliot. It sounds more like the simple affection of W. H. Davies, "one of the four finest living English poets," as Edith described him to Allen when she told him how Davies and she had sat up talking till two in the morning the previous summer.

In May 1934 Edith, with Helen and the cat, went for a couple of months to the Hotel Excelsior in Levanto, near La Spezia, in Italy, for Helen to get some sun and Edith to work on her next commissions—a life of Queen Victoria for Faber and a book on modern poetry for Duckworth. (Edith's French was for once adequate in her nice description, to Choura, of the sexual status of her cat, who accompanied them: "Il est moine; il a prit ses voeux quand il était un enfant.") They lived very quietly, for the most part "despised and rejected by all the cultured gentlewomen of both sexes in the hotel," as she told Allen. Her parents were not so very far away, at Montegufoni. "Don't let the Gingers know I'm here," she admonished Osbert.

She wrote nothing to Osbert about her nagging misery over Pavlik; her main worry was that she might not see him again before he took off for America, as he planned to do. "Perhaps Pavlik did not realise, when he said goodbye to me, that he will probably not see me again for a year," she wrote to Allen.

From Italy she went back to France, to Bride-les-Bains, where she and Osbert took the cure together at Osbert's expense. "My Darling Old Boy," she had written to him in June, "It will be lovely to be with you again! . . . What fun we will have, and what a sell for Ginger." But Osbert was missing David Horner, and Edith, with her private worries and her reading for the Queen Victoria book, was not lively company. "I hardly ever see her 'cept at meals," Osbert wrote to David. They extracted one joke from the holiday: An "enormous Swiss woman" attached herself to them, asking Edith if she wrote under her own name. "Edith said, no, we were both very shy: so she wrote under the name of T. S. Eliot and I under the name of Clemence Dane. And that . . . she was to be sure to ring us up under those numbers."

In September Edith returned to Paris and the rue Saint-Dominique. She was not too late; Pavlik did not sail until November. Allen went with him. Edith and Choura saw them off at the railway station in Paris—along with Serge Lifar, René Crevel, Kristians Tonny, and a crowd of others. While Edith had been with Osbert, Pavlik had been with Ford in Spain, whence he had returned, Edith wrote to Veronica Gilliat, "looking like a melancholy and fairly repentant gorilla, and remembered my birthday for the first time since I have known him. He painted me the most exquisite fan. . . ."[7] After his departure, Edith wrote to Allen that the station good-bye had been "one of the saddest and gloomiest times I have ever known. . . . And at the moment I have no physical vitality with which to combat sadness."

Pavlik had gone, for six months. The Atlantic lay between them. Calm, of a sort, descended.

15

Brickbats and a Best Seller
1934–1936

Edith had quite expected to be "assassinée, déchirée en morceaux" when her *Aspects of Modern Poetry* came out. "I've half-murdered Leavis, and Grigson, *and* Lewis. Oh! the brickbats that will be flying about this autumn!"[1] she prophecied to Georgia. But she had not expected to be so shaken when the expected happened. The book was published in England on November 15, 1934; it was dedicated to Helen Rootham.

It was not until she was at the Hotel Excelsior in Levanto, where she and Helen had retreated once more soon after Pavlik left, that news of the critics' reactions reached her. She was in poor physical shape; Pavlik's departure coincided with a disturbance of her menstrual cycle that distressed her. "Croyez-vous que je serai comme la femme dans le Bible?" she asked Choura. (She was forty-seven years old.) She was also being provoked from Montegufoni by her mother, "qui est dans une de ses rages." That Christmas, the hotel in Levanto was especially dreary; no one in it under eighty, she reported.

In these circumstances critical attack made her "très nerveuse"; but she put a braver face on it for Allen in America: The book was "evoking an enormous storm; all the whipper-snappers are rushing to each other's rescue, and Lewis is absolutely howling with rage."

The first part of the book, "Pastors and Masters," is written with patent enjoyment (parts of it had already appeared in article form in the *Morning Post*), with Edith at her journalistic best and worst carving up her immediate predecessors, including, inevitably, the Georgian poets. She then took a swipe at F. R. Leavis, "a gentleman who plays in the literary life of Mr. T. S. Eliot, and in a lesser degree that of Mr. Ezra Pound, much the same part as that played by the faithful Doctor Watson in the life of Sherlock Holmes . . . and, as a rule, bringing about much the same results as were obtained by Dr. Watson when he was left to himself." And on to Geoffrey Grigson: "I hope I will not offend the aunts and other admirers of both these gentlemen if I say that the only difference between them lies in Dr. Leavis's gift for wincing. Mr. Grigson has not yet, I believe, taken up this occupation seriously as an indoor sport." And on to Wyndham Lewis, who

> according to himself, is not appreciated, though he even goes so far as to apologise for any little brusqueness that may have been noticed: "I'm sorry if I've been too brutal, girls." Now, Mr. Lewis, not another word. Please. I *beg*! You know you ought not to spoil them. And besides, the pretty dears like your Cave-man stuff. For it is not often that they meet a real He-man. . . .

"I must say," she wrote to Christabel McLaren, now Lady Aberconway, "—(there's nothing like laughing at one's own jokes)—I laughed till I nearly cried as I was writing it."[2]

The jokes over, she wrote serious chapters on Gerard Manley Hopkins, W. B. Yeats, W. H. Davies, T. S. Eliot, Ezra Pound, and her brother Sacheverell. It was these chapters, and her "Envoi," rather than the almost scurrilous first section, that caused the trouble.

G. W. Stonier reviewed the book in the *New Statesman* on November 24, pointing out that in spite of Edith's dismissal of Leavis, there were extraordinary similarities between Leavis's remarks on Yeats (in *New Bearings*) and Edith's: "For example, Miss Sitwell begins by quoting Lang's sonnet 'The Odyssey'; this sonnet was quoted, with the same intention and effect, by Dr. Leavis." He cited other parallel passages and references, ending up by saying that he preferred Leavis's version, since at least his quotations were transcribed accurately. The following week H. Sydney Pickering contributed a further and longer list of Edith's "plagiarisms"; and Geoffrey Grigson entered the field, pointing out the curious parallels between what Herbert Read had written about Hopkins's "Sprung Rhythm" in *Form and Modern Poetry* and Edith's account of Hopkins.

Edith and Osbert both wrote in reply. Edith's letter said that had she known Dr. Leavis was the author of Lang's "Odyssey" sonnet, she would have acknowledged her debt. She concluded: "It is right and natural that Mr. Stonier should prefer Dr. Leavis's criticism to mine. It reminds me of Miss Nellie Wallace's appeal to her slightly denuded feather boa: 'For God's sake, hold together, boys!'"

Osbert's counterattack brought Wyndham Lewis crashing in, in the issue of December 15: "Miss Sitwell has built such a really enormous glass-house for herself in *Aspects of Modern Poetry* that when that big stiff of a brother butted in and discharged a brick at me . . . ," and so on; he harked back to his favourite theme, the Sitwellian youth cult, saying that in his own review of *Aspects* (in *Time and Tide* of November 17) he had

> tried to bring out the truly disarming picture of these incorrigibly "naughty," delicately shell-shocked, wistfully age-complexed, wartime Peter Pans —dragging out of their old kit-bags for the thousandth time their toy "great men". . . ; their Aunt Sallies; their aviary of love-birds, toucans and tomtits; their droned-out nursery melodies, accompanying the plunges of old rocking-horses. A bit sad, a thought dreary, like all circuses that have survived—dominated, this one, by the rusty shriek of the proprietress. . . .

But she rallied to his trumpet call, as she always did. From Levanto she wrote to Christabel Aberconway on January 7, 1935, that Lewis had "taken refuge with the old ladies of *Time and Tide*, and from the shelter of their skirts, and amidst the atmosphere of lavender and old lace, is yelling defiance at me. What has infuriated him especially is my reference to the fact that he was 'formed to be loved,'—to his sentimentality, and to his age! (He is revoltingly sentimental. That is the trouble.)"[3]

The same Tweedledum and Tweedledee battle was fought, with variations, in the columns of *The Times Literary Supplement*. Bonamy Dobrée listed her misquotations in the *Listener* on November 28, 1934. Edith felt compelled to write in March 1935 a cutting and cutting-off letter to John Hayward, Eliot's great friend, on account of a review of *Aspects* he had written in the New York *Sun*. In one way this general rumpus was the best thing that could have happened to Edith. The adrenaline flowed again; Osbert fought at her side; it was like the old days.

There's no doubt that her detractors were justified. The book was riddled with misquotations. She had written it in loneliness and depression. Working in her eyrie in the rue Saint-Dominique, or in the hotel bedroom in Levanto, she was light-years away from other writers and their world. She was in a vacuum, professionally. She was used to cannibalizing her own work— paragraphs from *Pope* reappear in *Bath*, and snatches of *Bath* turn up in *Eccentrics*. If something she read struck her as right and relevant, in it would go: incorporated not slyly but naively. She had no training in or experience of the elementary conventions of scholarship.

Geoffrey Grigson did not lose the opportunity of lambasting her in *New Verse*. It was the first time he had permitted the name of Sitwell to grace its pages, for reasons he explained in the issue of December 1934: "And Miss Sitwell. In dealing with this lady and her brothers, silence has always been the rule in *New Verse*. 'The wisest way' I have held 'is not once to name them, but' (as the Madman advised the Gentleman, who told him he wore a sword to kill his enemies) *'to let them alone and they will die of themselves.'*" He diminished all three Sitwells by lumping them together, as if their products and their persons were indistinguishably undistinguished. This always maddened them. As Edith wrote on July 14, 1949, to Rache Lovat Dickson,

> Osbert, Sachie and I are extremely displeased when we are treated as if our works are a *mass* production. We do not like to be treated as if we were an aggregate Indian god, with three sets of legs and arms, but otherwise indivisible. . . . It vulgarizes and cheapens everything. . . . We are individual artists, and the fact that we are two brothers and a sister is the business of nobody else considering our work.[4]

Grigson's final judgment was the following:

> They have as writers a talent for perching head into the wind, for appropriating, like bower-birds, shining oddments of culture, and for mimicking, like starlings, the product of more harmonious throats. . . . They have written nothing worth a wise man's attention for five minutes, but like eels, or "obscure authors, that wrap themselves in their *own Mud* they are mighty pert and nimble. . . . " Best leave these minimal creatures, these contemptible elvers, wriggling away in their dull habitat.[5]

Since this was "the poetry scene," small wonder that a fastidious spirit such as Virginia Woolf considered it impossible to review poetry. How, she asked Stephen Spender on October 29, 1934, could one write about one's contemporaries? "Isn't it inevitable that one should Grigsonise? (I mean get into a groove, and write out the malice of one's miserable heart.) And how can one know the truth?"[6]

Edith was able to field, in this shouting match, one impressive new ally—John Sparrow, whose *Sense and Poetry*, "essays on the place of meaning in contemporary verse," had come out earlier that year. He and Edith had subsequently corresponded over his comments on her odd imagery, and they had met in London that summer. Sparrow was a barrister, and a fellow (later, in 1952, the warden) of All Souls College, Oxford.

"The way he 'takes on' my enemies is most amusing," Edith told Allen Tanner in January 1935. Sparrow had reviewed *Aspects of Modern Poetry* generously (and anonymously) in *The Times Literary Supplement*; and he defended her in the correspondence columns of the *New Statesman*. He was anti-Leavis; and he noted, as did other reviewers, that *Aspects* was very largely a defence of the author's own view of poetry against Leavis's. "The Doctor thinks of poetry as a sort of moral hygiene, Miss Sitwell sees it rather as a means of creating beauty in language." Edith, before the book was published, had sent John Sparrow a copy and explained its purpose:

> It follows up, though on different lines, *Sense and Poetry* [Sparrow's book]. Someone *has* to tell the truth. As a matter of fact I think I've got the less instructed reviewers up a tree for I definitely admire all their mature gods, Tom Eliot for instance and Mr. Pound, and yet refuse to be rushed by all these young gentlemen whose chief characteristic is their garrulity. What a bore Master Auden is. And as for Master Spender, who doesn't appear in this book, he is just a heightened and refined version of Mr. W. J. Turner. By now I have seen the following geniuses in poetry come and go in this order, J. C. Squire, Edward Shanks, Robert Nichols, W. J. Turner, Humbert Wolfe. Où sont les neiges d'antan.

The sadder truth that emerges, involuntarily, from *Aspects of Modern Poetry* is something rather different. Edith was fighting a rear-guard action. Without her talent having qualitatively changed, she was no longer an innovator. Like Robert Graves and T. S. Eliot, she was one of the older generation of poets. In her "Envoi" to *Aspects* she castigated, with cruelly selective quotation, several young and *New Verse* poets, among them Auden:

> Mr. Auden has an able mind, but, unhappily, he writes uninteresting poetry, or, at least, his poetry nearly always lacks interest. When, therefore, we are told by an admiring reviewer that, since the publication of his first volume, two or three years ago, "it has been generally recognised that he is one of the four or five living poets worth quarrelling about"—and that "Here is something as important as the appearance of Mr. Eliot's poems fifteen years ago"—I can only reply that this is sheer nonsense.

Today's reader may agree or disagree with her, on that precise last point, without too much animus. But in 1934 such certainty marked her as reactionary, out of the current of thought and feeling. The Auden generation had begun to dominate "the poetry scene" while she was immured in the rue Saint-Dominique, pouring out prose to make ends meet, with one poem to show for five years.

The Auden generation of poets—in which may be included Stephen Spender, Louis MacNeice, C. Day Lewis, John Lehmann, and Charles Madge—was one reared on childhood memories of the Great War and on Eliot's "The Waste Land." Its members were highly conscious of history and their own place in it, of modern psychology, social class, social documentary techniques, and Marxism. (The leftwards "politicization" of writers in the 1930s has become a literary historian's cliché.) Most of them aimed to write poetry in the rhythms, and with the vocabulary, of common speech, of science and technology. Image makers turned to engines, carbines, insulators, and turbines—a far cry from Edith Sitwell's incantations, her imagery of artificial flowers, charnel compost heaps, and Marvellous salads. Yet the Auden group—and Auden was intimately connected with *New Verse*—were in their way equally romantic. Their ideals were of peace and progress; myths of heroes, leaders, and martyrs, sometimes of a rather schoolboy sort, were close to many hearts. They were nostalgic and lyrical about the traditional England that ideologically they rejected; and they were amorous.

Not that the Auden group were the only 1930s manifestation in England of new directions in poetry. Most of those whose fields were more specialised, individual, or academic had a commitment to the left politically, even if they joined no party. But this general "politicization" embraced a wide variety of views and stances. As Arnold Rattenbury has written:

> If most intellectuals were left-wing, some communist, then most of the people rediscovering Raleigh, the Silver Poets, the Metaphysicals, Clare, Blake, the Radicals, Hopkins, the First World War poets and, as it happens, nuclear fission, were left-wing, some communist. . . . Of course Helen Gardner was knitting blankets for Spain while editing Crashaw. . . . Communist or not, I will be damned if she ever had much of a brush with Proletkult or heresy, or that anyone tried to brush her with them.[7]

Edith knitted too; sweaters for her family and friends, not blankets for Spain. She was no part of that particular 1930s world. She was so much older; and her poetry of the 1920s seemed, to most of the serious young of the 1930s, passé and irrelevant. The spirit of "Gold Coast Customs" might, as indeed it did later, have made friends for her on the left. But in the early 1930s its "meaning"—always elusive—seemed to many to be lost in rhetoric, sound, and fury.

Pavlik wrote to Edith from America—a little, not enough. The misunderstandings and contrived crises continued. Cecil Beaton was in the doghouse and due to be "écrasé"; Edith had commissioned him to keep an eye on Pavlik in New York, but it transpired that he was now in league with the enemy. He temporarily joined the ranks of the "personnes très inférieures" with whom Pavlik insisted on striking up "de violents amitiés."

Pavlik was back in Paris for Choura's wedding to a compatriot, Alexander Zaoussailoff, in May 1935.

Edith was working all through that year on her book about Queen Victoria. The trauma over the reception of *Aspects*, and the heavy amount of reading she had to do for this new book, made her slow in starting it. But as she wrote to Choura from Levanto at Christmas 1934, she felt confident that she could write "un livre assez bien," by dint of using "beaucoup de décorations très fantastiques." Queen Victoria's diaries depressed her—"le journal bien embêtant de cette femme à même temps si grande et si stupide!" She and Helen stayed in Italy till March; hotel life meant no housekeeping, and it was cheap.

Early in 1935 Edith had solved her problem of how to live when she was in England. She could not permanently impose herself on either of her brothers. Renishaw, when none of the rest of the family was there, was dismal and too far from London. So Edith joined a ladies' club—the Sesame and Imperial Pioneer Club, known as the Sesame, at 49 Grosvenor Street, W. 1 (a very good address)—and it became her London base. Georgia sent the application forms to her in Paris. Hubert Nicholson has described the sort of place the Sesame Club was (it has since been altered and modernised):

> The club has a dark red narrow frontage with black marble pillars, but inside is large, rambling and old-fashioned, with windows that look out on an enclosed court with flowers, a statue and a fountain. Its corridors

seemed haunted by dowdy peculiar ladies with inquisitive eyes, wandering about clutching glasses of sherry.[8]

The inquisitive eyes of the Sesame Club members found plenty to stare at once Miss Sitwell joined their number. No longer a perpetual house guest of her relations, or of the Gorers, she was able to entertain her friends herself on the club premises, almost as in the old days at Pembridge Mansions. She gave "une énorme réunion 'cocktail'" at the club in the summer—the first of hundreds of Sesame parties. She had been to dinner with the Courtaulds, and with Leonard and Virginia Woolf, and had been to a Royal Garden Party. And she had been teasing Tom Eliot, who would not come to her big party—he did not care for parties—but who wanted to see her before he left for America, by sending him confusing and contradictory messages about alternative meetings. (Morale had not been so high for months.)

She gave a second Sesame party in October, to which she invited Leonard and Virginia Woolf and Stephen Spender; it was the day before the private viewing of another Tchelitchew exhibition, at Tooth's, and the artist was to be present. If she had not gained the upper hand where Pavlik was concerned, she was no longer the emotional pensioner of the previous year. He painted his most beautiful portrait of her that autumn, in pastels: a clear, bony, unearthly profile, with a web of blue veins at the temple.

Pavlik went back to the United States, and Edith and Helen went to Spain for the winter, to the Hotel Marina at San Felíu de Guixols on the Catalonian coast. *Victoria of England* was now completed—"larger than the telephone directory and just as dull," Edith deprecatingly said to David Horner in December—and dedicated to Helen and Evelyn Wiel. The book came out from Faber in February 1936 in an optimistically large first printing—eighty-four hundred copies. (Houghton Mifflin brought out a more circumspect edition—thirty-five hundred copies—in America in August.) The hopes of Edith's British publishers were justified. Edith wrote in rapture to Choura from the Sesame Club: "Ma chère, mon livre est devenu ce qu'on appelle un 'best-seller'!!!!" A second printing was in hand after only ten days. It was selling at the rate of one hundred and fifty copies a day. It was her first really popular success.

Wretchedly mindful of the accusations of plagiarism made against *Aspects of Modern Poetry*, Edith had been much more careful this time—not about using secondary sources, which were the only ones open to her, but about acknowledgments. (Like Lytton Strachey in his *Queen Victoria*, she documents one or two points of royal behaviour with the discreet and patrician note "Private information"; hers was probably gleaned from Osbert, who was a great favourite with Queen Mary.) In her foreword she disclaims attempting more than "a portrait of the Queen and of some of her contemporaries, and . . . a record of certain social conditions." For the latter, she made use of Engels's *The Condition of the English Working Class in 1844* in her chapter "March Past," an effectively imagined procession of the starved and sickly victims of the industrial revolution.

But her major debt, as she acknowledges, is to Lytton Strachey; his *Queen Victoria*, by no means the first, but the first nonhagiographic, biography of Victoria, had come out in 1921. Her debt to him is indeed very large; the first section of her book is little more than a paraphrase of Strachey, though in her foreword she tries to forestall criticism:

> If a common stock of information has been drawn upon of necessity, she hopes at least to plead a different treatment of necessarily similar material. Writers on Queen Victoria cannot avoid continual quotation from her *Letters* and *Journal* . . . and it is only natural that some passages, being the cream of her correspondence, must be quoted in every book that deals with her life.

God knows that is true. Nevertheless her *Victoria* is well paced, sprinkled with pleasant irony, and full of "the exuberance that carries the reader along," as Roger Fulford wrote to her on February 25, 1936—his *The Royal Dukes* had been one of her sources. She had other post-Strachey sources—notably E. F. Benson's biography of the Queen, and Hector Bolitho's of Albert. It is chiefly over Albert that Edith diverges from, and falls short of, Strachey. She was not so fascinated by the Consort as Strachey was, and therefore not so suggestive. (She is also less beguiled by Lord Melbourne.) Strachey, however, dealt rather summarily with Victoria after the death of Albert, and Edith gives the latter half of her reign, and her relations with her children and grandchildren, much fuller treatment. The *Observer*'s reviewer, remarking on the Strachey connection, commended Edith's version as "warmer and broader."

She used her now customary catalogue technique for evoking atmosphere —this time it is of nineteenth-century cosmetics, a pageful of "Essence Etherée Balsamique, the Bouquet de Fürstenberg, the Baume de Judée, Ruban de Bruges, Papier de Vienne, Bois d'Aloès, Gomme d'Olivier . . . ." Her descriptive imagery is the garden imagery of her poetry, transposed; and her bridging passages are characteristic scatterings and summonings of sun-motes, little drifts of dust, shadows, little cold ghosts, and drifting leaves, as in her previous prose books. But it is only with her *Victoria of England,* and the necessary comparison with Strachey's *Queen Victoria,* that the reader will realise quite how much she owed, in all her historical narratives, to Strachey who wrote, in the style that had become Edith's, of the dying Stockmar "exploring the shadow and the dust." Her impressionistic scene shifting too is his:

> Lord Palmerston's laugh—a queer metallic "Ha! ha! ha!" with reverbera-tions in it from the days of Pitt and the Congress of Vienna—was heard no more in Piccadilly; Lord John Russell dwindled into senility; Lord Derby tottered from the stage. A new scene opened; and new protagonists —Mr. Gladstone and Mr. Disraeli—struggled together in the limelight.

That is Strachey, not Edith. And in Strachey's famous ending to *Queen Victoria,* the dying matriarch's "secret chambers of consciousness" release "the shadows of the past," a stream of memories delivered in a single flowing sentence half a page long. Edith's dying Victoria echoes this, in abbreviated form; old Beau Nash, in her *Bath,* sees the past float by in the same way. This conceit, or technique, of the time slip was not unique to Strachey even in 1921; and Virginia Woolf took it to virtuoso heights in *Orlando.* The point is only that Edith's "frequent and inevitable obligations" to Strachey are not confined to points of narrative in her book on Victoria. She would not have acknowl-edged this stylistic debt. In the 1940s, she made scornful reference to Lytton Strachey's "nibbling rat-like little books," and considered his *Elizabeth and Essex* "vulgar and *odious.*"

Experienced Edith watchers, however, saw the connection all too clearly. Wyndham Lewis wrote to Geoffrey Grigson about "the old Jane's" latest work: "It seems to be (am I right?) such a *barefaced* crib as to be almost disarming.—But cribbing should be put down somehow, what!?!"[9] Nevertheless her book sold and sold. There is room at least twice in every generation for a nonacademic study of the major historical figures. Edith hit that particular market with *Victoria of England* for the first but not the last time. Richard de la Mare of Faber's was "half off his head with excitement," she told Osbert.

16
A Youthful Silenus
1936–1937

One of the *New Verse* poets Edith had held up to ridicule—without naming him—in *Aspects of Modern Poetry* was the twenty-year-old Dylan Thomas. He was very angry, writing to Glyn Jones in December 1934: "Isn't she a poisonous thing of a woman, lying, concealing, flipping, plagiarising, misquoting, and being as clever a crooked publicist as ever. . . ." He had protested against the use of his "absurdly criticised" poem in her "latest piece of virgin dung" to her publisher Gerald Duckworth, who replied to the effect that "so many protests of a similar sort had been received, that he could, as yet, do nothing about it." It was hoped, said Dylan, that Duckworth would "have to withdraw the book."[1]

At about the same time, in Levanto, Edith read Dylan Thomas's recently published *Eighteen Poems*, and wrote to John Sparrow that the young man "ought to be dashed off to a psychoanalyst immediately before worse befalls; then if he would afterwards spend ten years in thought I am not sure that he would not produce some good lines."

John Sparrow was a friend of Geoffrey Grigson's, and Geoffrey Grigson was a friend of Dylan Thomas's; and all three had been on holiday together that year in the west of Ireland. One of their pastimes there had been to set up big white pebbles with faces crayonned on them, and to fling other pebbles at them until they cracked into "literary nothingness"—for all the faces were authors'. Edith's was one of them.

The young Welshman had been aware of Edith's poetry since he was a teen-ager at Swansea Grammar School, where he had contributed an essay on modern poetry to the school magazine. His comments then were less crass than those of many critics thrice his age. Edith Sitwell's poems, he had written in 1929, "are essentially feminine, with their shrewd grasp of detail, their sudden illuminations, and their intensity of emotion, and it is the more insignificant mannerisms of her femininity that make her poems difficult."[2] Under the influence of her mockery of him, and of Grigson, he now threw stones.

The following year Edith changed her mind about Dylan Thomas. In an article in *Life and Letters To-Day* in December 1935, she discussed a group of the younger poets, including William Empson and Louis MacNeice, and picked out Thomas, "a still younger poet," who seemed to her "to show most remarkable promise. He has not found himself yet, for he is tangled in a perfect web of complexes, mainly about the human body."

During the winter in Spain, at San Felíu, her *Victoria of England* out of the way, Edith had time and inclination to quarrel with Grigson in the letters columns of the *Observer* and to make plans for meeting the new poet. "I want to ask him some questions, and give him some advice," she wrote to Robert Herring, editor of *Life and Letters To-Day*, on January 27, 1936. Back in Paris, she began planning her next Sesame party; it was to be on February 8, she told Richard Jennings, and she wanted him to be there to meet "the young Dylan Thomas": "I haven't the slightest doubt that if *only* he'll get rid of his obscurities, he is the coming poet. And I do want him to be helped on to the right path." Before the party, she wrote to Dylan himself, saying, "I do not remember when I have been so moved, profoundly so excited, by the work of any poet of the younger generation."[3]

Dylan Thomas, flattered but alarmed, arranged to meet Robert Herring in advance of the party. "You can tell me all about Miss S.," he wrote from 5 Cwmdonkin Drive, Swansea, at the end of January. "She isn't very frightening, is she? I saw a photograph of her once, in medieval costume. . . ." Since he had not yet met Robert Herring either, he described himself: "short with bulging eyes, a broken tooth, curly hair and a cigarette."[4] He was also a heavy drinker.

That was not the Dylan that Edith perceived at the Sesame party: "The first time I saw him I felt as if Rubens had suddenly taken it into his head to paint a youthful Silenus. He was not tall, but was extremely broad, and gave an impression of extraordinary strength, sturdiness, and superabundant life."[5] Dylan Thomas stayed sober until after the party—"More dukes than drinks" was his comment.

Edith had given him a public ovation the previous week, in the February issue of the *London Mercury*, in an article called "Four New Poets" (the other three were Empson, Ronald Bottrall, and Archibald MacLeish). For years the *London Mercury*, edited since 1919 by their old butt J. C. Squire, had been anathema to the Sitwells; but by the autumn of 1934 Squire, ineffectual now and alcoholic, had drifted away. The editorship was taken over by R. A. Scott-James, who made an intense but unsuccessful effort to pull the paper together. It did not survive for long. But during the short period of the new editorship, Edith wrote for the *London Mercury*: notably, her "Some Notes on My Own Poetry," by which she set great store, appeared there in its original form, in March 1935.

Edith was delighted by Dylan Thomas. She wrote in her autobiography of his "warmth, charm, and touching funniness." She said she had "never known anyone with a more holy and childlike innocence of mind. The exuberance of his strong physique, of his strong physical life, never blurred or marred that." Thus she waived the unreliability, the drinking, and the girls. When she was asked in a BBC interview how Dylan had behaved at their first meeting, she replied: "Beautifully. I've never seen him behave anything but beautifully with me. He always behaved with me like a son with his mother."[6]

For Edith was now fifty years old. She could love and encourage and court and be courted by clever young men, and could warm herself in the vitality of "strong physical life," without worrying, as she had used to in her old-maidish way, about her "reputation" and whether she was causing gossip. This was a release. The acute stage of her passion for Tchelitchew was over (though not her love for him, which in spite of what she sometimes said was never killed). She had a new injection of confidence from her success with *Victoria of England*, which made her able to give again. Dylan Thomas enchanted her, both in his person and in his poetry: the richness and sensuousness of his language, his mythical/religious preoccupations, the musicality and "intensity of emotion" that as a boy he had recognized in her own poetry, all delighted her. This, and from a young person, was the "pure poetry" that she herself lived by.

And he? Thomas's attitudes towards Edith, wrote his biographer Constantine FitzGibbon, "were those of affection and gratitude. Although he had no overwhelming admiration for her poems, he would frequently include them in his later broadcasts of verse"; and he read them beautifully, and brought her new admirers. "Once they became friends," wrote FitzGibbon, "he never again wrote unkindly about her in his letters." There are reports, however, of his having spoken unkindly of her in his cups. The writer Jack Lindsay, who came to know both of them well, thought that "Dylan liked Edith Sitwell and knew that he owed much to her," but he never heard Dylan Thomas give any unqualified praise of her work. "Despite certain deep kinships with his own poetry, it put him off with what he felt its uncurbed magnanimity."

(Lindsay is referring to her later poetry.) "I think perhaps he felt the need to guard himself against Edith's work precisely because of the elements of kinship," Lindsay wrote.[7]

Nevertheless, after Dylan died there remained a photograph of Edith pinned up on the rough wall of his last writing place, the shed at Laugharne—until the place was cleaned up and made a place of pilgrimage, when everything was changed.

Over Christmas 1935 and into the spring of 1936 Edith, with Helen and Evelyn, rented a house in San Felíu, instead of going to the hotel. There was no maid, a wonderful wild garden, and "une foule de pouces [puces] dans mon lit!!!!," as she informed Choura. She loved the place, but "Woosh! the *boredom!*" she complained to Georgia. "Someone we know, who has always been a bit of a raconteuse, has now developed the art to such a pitch . . . and in addition, her sister is now going deaf," which meant that Helen, the raconteuse, was compelled to tell her stories twice over. "God bless our happy home," said Edith wrily. She was torn between irritation and love. Helen's illness was taking its natural course, slowly. "She has had such a *wretched* life, poor woman."[8]

Edith was trying to get started on the project that had been in her mind for some time—a novel. She had made lots of beginnings, at different times, which generally involved two girls—a pretty, spoilt one and a homely, loyal one. Sometimes they were Spanish, sometimes Italian—Bianca, Vittoria, Pepita . . . . Betrayals, skeletons in family cupboards, desertions, ghosts, bloody murders, were sketched out. The story line settled down into a preoccupation with Lily and her loved boy-cousin Laurie and their unloving grandparents. Lady Ida was in there, in many guises. Her voice, speaking of her husband, rings clear: "Of course, darling, what I would *really* like would be to get him certified and shut up in an asylum." Lady Ida also unwittingly provided the script for a fragment of abortive classical drama preserved in Edith's notebooks:

ELECTRA: Do you want anything, mother.

CLYTEMNESTRA (*fretfully*): I know there was something I wanted, Electra, but I can't remember what it was. Could you shut the door, darling. There is such a draught.

ELECTRA: The ghost-wind blowing. [In fact, Orestes, offstage.]

Clearly there was no future at all in any of this. When she got away from her own family, and into a fictional account of the life of Jonathan Swift, what was to be her novel began to take shape.

At the same time she was turning out a great deal of journalism. Between 1935 and 1937 she wrote regular feature articles for the *Sunday Referee*, of a kind that can be deduced from their titles: "People I Meet in the Train," "What Is Slavery?," "Let's Scrap Parliament," "That English Eccentric, Edith Sitwell." The fact that she had written so little poetry in the past seven years was masked by the appearance from Duckworth of her *Selected Poems* in June 1936—cashing in perhaps on the success of *Victoria of England*—including a revised version of her "Some Notes on My Own Poetry." The selection contained only two new poems, both written the year before—"The Fox" and "Prelude" (first published in the *London Mercury* in June 1935). Kenneth Clark has seen "Prelude" as "of crucial importance, for it introduces the fundamental changes in her later poetry":

> First, the lines have an entirely different movement. Gone are the rhythms of the Chinese wall-paper, gone the decorative details, the diminutives, the pretty Christian names, and gone, thank God, the tom-tom beats of darkness . . . the new vision requires an ampler style, a rhythm capable of sustaining simple, passionate and prophetic statements of belief.[9]

The closing lines of "Prelude," as Clark pointed out, reappear almost in the same form in her published novel, and in her poem "An Old Woman" (1942). Clearly their meaning "is of unusual import to her." They express a faith in a unifying life-force of light and growth:

> The man-made chasms between man and man
> Of creeds and tongues are fill'd, the guiltless light
> Remakes all men and things in holiness.

Her position in the canon of modern poetry seemed further stabilised by the inclusion of six of her poems, or sections of poems, in *The Oxford Book of Modern Verse*, an idiosyncratic volume compiled by her old champion W. B. Yeats, now nearing the end of his life. He wrote to her on December 3, 1936, thanking her for not exacting any payment for her contributions; the Oxford University Press had given him a budget of £500, which he had exceeded by more than £200, "which I am given to understand I shall have to pay out of my royalties."

He also asked her if he could have her early poem "The King of China's Daughter" illustrated and set to music for one of the "broadsides" published in limited editions by the Cuala Press, run by his sister. "You will be in tolerably good company." The poem was set to music by Arthur Duff, and the broadside published the following year. Yeats, who never had much money, paid Edith £1 for it.

In his introduction to *The Oxford Book of Modern Verse* Yeats wrote:

Edith Sitwell has a temperament of a strangeness so high-pitched that only through this artifice could it find expression. One cannot think of her in any other age or country. She has transformed with her metrical virtuosity traditional metres reborn not to be read but spoken, exaggerated metaphors into mythology. . . . Nature appears before us in a hashish-eater's dream.

The dream, he said, was double: in one of its aspects a perpetual metamorphosis "that seems an elegant and artificial childhood," and in another "a nightmare vision like that of Webster, of the emblems of mortality."

Recognition in an Oxford Book from the poet Edith considered to be the greatest of her time was worth much. Honesty demands the caveat that Yeats included in this collection lengthy contributions from one or two other women—Dorothy Wellesley in particular—who had endeared themselves to him, but whose writing was nowhere near as good as he chose to think it. The sentimental attachments of the aging Yeats tend to discredit his selection in this volume. But Edith is not to be included in this category; they had known one another for years, but there was no regular correspondence between them, and they were not even on Christian-name terms.

There had been an awkward hiatus after Edith's initial happy meeting with Dylan Thomas. He made contact again that September of 1936, writing from Swansea on the second:

I know I couldn't have expected you to answer my letter of so many months ago. I was dreadfully rude, not turning up or anything, and I do understand about your not answering my silly letter of apology. But I hope you're not cross with me really. . . . You're still a great encouragement to me — and always will be — and I do appreciate it.[10]

It may have been no coincidence that he made this filial gesture of conciliation a week before the publication of his next book, *Twenty-five Poems*. (Nor can he have been entirely disinterested when, in August of the following year, asking her to help him get BBC work, he added: "I should enjoy very much reading some of Sacheverell Sitwell's poems, if the BBC, and he, some time allowed one. . . .") Edith was "not cross with him really"; she reviewed his book for the *Sunday Times*, rather late, on November 15.

Writing eighteen months later to Henry Treece, Dylan himself said that Edith had in the *Sunday Times* made "a few interesting mis-readings, or, rather, half-readings" of his poems. He had not meant in "A Grief Ago" that the grave was, as she suggested, a gentle cultivator, but "a tough possessor, a warring and complicated raper, rather than . . . an innocent gardener." Elsewhere, the half-veiled loins and wombs of his imagery passed unnoticed or unacknowledged by her. Her analyses seemed to him "very vague and Sunday-journalish."[11]

However, even though his quality was also being recognised by other critics, Edith had seen to it that no member of the reading public could now fail to have heard of Dylan Thomas.

The September that Dylan had written his placatory letter, Edith, in London, had been getting bad news from Paris. Helen now had inoperable bone cancer. On Edith's return to Paris, life in the rue Saint-Dominique was ever more oppressive. Evelyn got on her nerves. Edith had made some hundreds of pounds out of *Victoria of England*, which now dwindled away keeping the flat going and paying for Helen's radium treatment. They were back in the poverty trap.

Pavlik was in Paris too; and in October he began painting Edith again. His attachment to Charles Henri Ford had not cancelled the fascination of Edith as a model. "This time it is a straightforward portrait," Edith reported to David Horner, "and I am frightfully pleased with it. . . . He is mournful but good." This was the "Sibyl" portrait, bought by Edward James and now in the Tate — a full-length seated figure in a bulky brown habit with a huge amber cluster on her breast; the light hair shoulder-length, the old-young face showing the skull beneath the thin pale skin; the fine hands well in evidence, holding paper and a great quill.

Edith still would have nothing to do with Ford; and so, with no Allen Tanner to act as liaison officer, her contacts with Pavlik away from the easel were limited. Edith refused to accord even diplomatic recognition to Ford until after they were all separated by the war; as late as June 1939 she was pouring out her disgust that Pavlik had taken Ford to England with him, in a letter to the abandoned Allen:

> I could not believe *anybody* could be guilty of such disregard of both your and my feelings. . . . I cannot tell you what I feel at the creature being introduced to my country people,—to all the people I know. . . . I am so angry at the thought of this perfectly worthless parasite, with no gifts, and a thorough slum-type, throwing his weight about in England. . . .

If it had not been for the fact that it would have ruined Pavlik's prospects in England, she would have got Ford "chucked out of every house because of that book [*The Young and Evil*]." And Pavlik had "absolutely no delicacy; he even went so far as to write: '*Nous* parlons souvent de toi avec Edward [James]!'"

After spending Christmas 1936 in Spain—which she and Helen had to leave in a hurry because of the civil war—Edith consulted her doctor, now Lord Dawson, the King's physician, who told her she was suffering from exhaustion. News of the horrors in San Felíu followed them to Paris. "The doctor at San Felíu has certified Helen's friend the priest, and another priest, insane, and has got them in the hospital . . . in order to save their lives," Edith reported to Georgia. "The reds caught 20 priests at a village near San Felíu, where they were in hiding . . . saturated them with petrol and burned them."[12]

In the rue Saint-Dominique, Edith made at last a serious start on what was to be the novel *I Live Under a Black Sun*. She told Georgia that writing it made her weep; "I am hardly fit to be seen, when I emerge from it. It is rough stuff, and no doubt about it."[13] In February 1937, not long after their return to Paris, Edith decamped again with Helen, to Levanto, since the noise in Paris made it impossible for her to work, and Helen was better in the warmer climate. They stayed till June.

From Levanto Edith continued her campaign for Dylan Thomas. She had sent a copy of his *Twenty-five Poems* to Yeats in Dublin before she left Paris. Now she enlisted Richard Jennings, since "I've simply *got*, (if it is humanly possible) to find a job for 22-year-old Dylan Thomas. . . . That wretched boy is living on what he can earn by his poems and stories, and he realises he can't go on like it any longer. He has, too, come to a proper sense of the error of behaving like an undergraduate." She pulled every string she had; she even asked Victor Gollancz to give him a job. But Dylan was hard to help. Soon she was telling Jennings that he was "heading for having his ears boxed. . . . *What* a tiresome boy that is, though a very gifted one. Having given us all trouble, caused me to write to you and to write dozens of letters to busy people who must now curse the name of Sitwell—he has disappeared again,—disappeared without leaving a trace. . . ." Did she but know it, Dylan was in purdah at his parents' home in Swansea, nursing himself through a venereal infection.

Edith sent him a cheque for his wedding to Caitlin Macnamara—whom she had not yet met—and he wrote a decent thank-you letter from Cornwall on August 20; they had bought with the money everything "from knives and towels to a Garbo picture, and paid off the clamourers." He still needed a job, though; perhaps she could help him—again.

But Edith's heart was now in her novel. She was writing, and then copying out, four thousand words a day. By evening, she told Margery Beevers in April, "I am honestly so tired that all I can do is to lie on my bed with my mouth open,—neither reading nor thinking, just lying there." It was going well, she told Geoffrey Gorer's mother in May: "It is the only prose book (excepting for criticism) that I've ever been pleased with. (I mean, *naturally*, the only prose book of *mine*!!!!)"[14] She started work by six o'clock each morning—in bed, a habit that was becoming unbreakable. The hotel had deteriorated—"the food is worse, the noise awful, and it is infested with gibberingly appalling people." Since Helen was now completely bedridden, the appalling people cannot have seen very much of either of them.

She could not afford, Edith told Georgia, to come to London for Whitsun, having received "a severe letter from the Bank." But shortly after she and Helen had returned to Paris at the end of June 1937, Lady Ida fell ill, and was brought back from Montegufoni to England. Edith had to go over. Her mother died in mid-July, and was buried at Weedon Lois, near Weston. There was also a memorial service at St. George's, Hanover Square, in London. The subheading to the obituary in the *Times* on July 13—which made no reference to her short spell in Holloway Jail—was "A Great Lady of Yorkshire."

Edith took it all with cold calm. She showed no emotion, because she felt or dare feel none. She did not go to the funeral, and the day after was at the Sesame Club, writing baldly to Choura, "Elle est morte il y a deux jours." She said she was exhausted, and had had to spend all day listening to her father crying, "etc." Did Sir George, then, cry when his wife died?

Did he, after all, love her? He had been very much in love with her once, when she was a mere child in the schoolroom. It had been a wretched marriage, held together by propriety and property, and stimulated chiefly by animosity and misunderstanding. Lady Ida had never grown less self-indulgent or less silly, or less enchanting to those who found her so. "The boys get their brains from me, of course, but I can't think where Edith gets hers from." To put it mildly, as Harold Acton characteristically has done, "It was painfully evident that she failed to understand her distinguished daughter or appreciate her poetry."[15]

But she did inspire affection, and not only her sons'. In her latter years at Montegufoni she used to forward her bills from the tea shops and bars of Florence to Harold Acton's father, because she did not dare show them to her husband. And Arthur Acton paid up for her double-double whiskies from Doney's in the Via Tornabuoni, because he could afford it, and because he liked her.

Sir George, hypochondriacal but durable, was packed off back to Montegufoni in the care of a new, male companion-secretary, Francis Bamford, who was to "take Mother's place," as Osbert told him. The younger Sitwells had Renishaw to themselves again. Edith told David Horner, when the summer was over, that "Renishaw was more perfect than ever this year. Not even the Baronet's brief descent could do anything to spoil it." Unloving parents had made her a doggedly unloving middle-aged child.

Maturity, however, had its compensations. Edith may have been unappreciated by the young intellectuals of the 1930s, but there was *The Oxford Book of Modern Verse*, and an invitation to all three Sitwells to give the Lord Northcliffe Lectures on Literature at University College, London, that October. Edith spoke on "Three Eras of Modern Poetry," and all the lectures were published by Macmillan under the title *Trio: Some Aspects of National Genius* a year later. In August Edith had lectured for three days at a summer school in Cambridge, with Humbert Wolfe and Middleton Murry; the prospect, she had told Richard Jennings, was unattractive:

Umberto won't speak to me because he thinks I've egged on Siegfried Sassoon to tease him, and Middleton Murry won't speak to me because Osbert called him Muddling Moral. . . . I remember when Siegfried wouldn't speak to me for two years,—indeed he cut me dead at a party,—

because Osbert had mistaken an enlarged photograph of W. J. Turner for a map of Vesuvius.

Not much had changed, it seems, since Edith had regaled Arnold Bennett with horror stories of the "poetry scene" back in 1924. Except these combatants were now veterans, and their battlefields a little off the centre of the stage.

17

Under a Black Sun

1937–1939

Edith's novel *I Live Under a Black Sun* came out on September 27, 1937. For this book she was "leaving the Egg and going Golly"—i.e., leaving Duckworth and going to Gollancz. (Doubleday brought out an American edition the following year.) Victor Gollancz had been negotiating with Edith for a book since 1935; the first idea had been that she would write a life of the actor David Garrick for him, but she asked him to accept instead her idea of a novel based on the life of Swift, which, as she told Norman Collins of Gollancz in February 1935, she had been wanting to do "for three years."

Edith had great hopes for the success of her novel, which had been written with such concentration and commitment. It was an uncommercial novel with an uncommercial title, taken from a line of poetry by Gérard de Nerval; but Edith, after considering calling her book *Black Sun, Dark Sun,* and *Nowhere to Go,* finally settled on the unwieldly *I Live Under a Black Sun.* It achieved a minor succès d'estime—but not as great or as lasting a one as that enjoyed, for example, by *Nightwood,* by Charles Henri Ford's friend Djuna Barnes, which had been published the previous year with an introduction by T. S. Eliot.

The blurb unaccountably related Edith's novel to Virginia Woolf's *The Years,* presumably because it was her most recent, and had sold well. But Edith did not traverse long passages of linear time, as did Virginia in *The Years* and in other of her novels. Edith took the lives and characters of Jonathan Swift, and of Stella and Vanessa who loved him, and some of what Swift wrote, and she transposed all this material in time to the First World War and its aftermath.

She was powered in the writing of it by two main preoccupations. The first was the situation in Europe: the poverty and hopelessness that she had seen for herself in the streets of Paris and London and Sheffield over the past ten years, and the rise of the dictators. "It is an allegory, in a sense," she told Raymond Marriott in February 1939 (he was then a struggling journalist, and one of her lame ducks). "The reason I put Swift into modern clothes is because the spirit of the modern world is power gone mad. And Swift was power gone mad."[1] She was even more specific to E. M. Forster, when she sent him a copy of the book—"with some trepidation"—on October 1, 1939: "But I beg you to believe that I *don't* consider it a novel. It is an allegory."[2]

In her novel Edith evokes the despair of those without power even over their own lives—a homeless girl, for example: "Nothing was left now but want, like a cruel rat eating down to the heart. Soon the heart too would be gone; but even then, want would not desert her; it would remain, gnawing there, till no flesh was left on the bones, till there was neither hope, nor memory, nor, at last, even the will to die." Bleaker still is her final page, where Jonathan Swift—or Jonathan Hare, as she calls him—sits in his empty room in catatonic madness, dropping bread on the floor from one stiff hand, not moving his eyes or his head, while, in the wainscoting,

> the civilisation of the mice, upheld by war, was being made safe for posterity. Rather than share the piece of bread that had fallen from the giant's hand, they were willing to be wiped out. Squealing and shrieking among the dust, they rushed to destroy each other.
> And outside, his paw outstretched, the cat was waiting, watching.
> Let them fight. Let them destroy each other.
> Then will come Darkness.
> Darkness.

It is powerful, visionary writing, and it is not the writing of a light-minded—or lighthearted—person. It is the writing of someone who sees no relief before the grave, and even that relief is negative. The quasi-religious faith of the poem "Prelude," with its imagery of light, has been extinguished.

The second main theme is unrequited love, on which Edith had become an expert. Her Jonathan Swift/Hare is unable to commit himself to a woman because of his knowledge that he has inherited madness—a common enough interpretation of Swift's behaviour. But Edith complemented this with an account of his attitude towards women which was near enough to Tchelitchew's: "Womanhood was to him a symbol of nature, a monstrous creative force that, in order to create, was willing to destroy all previous life and forms of creation—a force more terrible when it was overlaid by civilisation than when it was rank and naked." Yet "when he was poor or out of Fortune's favour . . . he would pursue and inhabit the heart of a woman, seeing in the ultimate death of all her natural impulses only the result of his mysterious power." So had Tchelitchew dealt with Edith.

Edith's Stella/Anna figure is the woman who sacrifices herself for love. She has devoted "my whole life, the whole of my existence, *all* my thoughts to Jonathan, for years now. . . . My life has been given up to helping him make *his* life." She is growing older: There are "little lines round the corner of her mouth" now; there are "depths of hollow darkness about her, behind the vast black blaring shadow of her eyes," and in the "large beast-furred mole near her lips, that belied the tiptoeing life that she had led for so many years." For Jonathan has told her the truth: "There are certain things for which most women hope—things that mean nearly everything in life to nearly every woman, that you must give up for ever, for they will never be yours—hopes, wishes, which belong to one side of your nature." In return for this sacrifice, "I will give you everything I have it in my nature to give. You will be the only woman in my life whom I will call my friend."

That might have made the sacrifice worthwhile. But Jonathan betrayed Stella with Vanessa (Essy, in Edith's book). Essy personifies the frantic, craven side of love: She is "violently and irretrievably" in love with Jonathan, "beyond control." The frenzy of letters written, of replies awaited, the unchecked reproaches and pleadings of a love where pride has been abandoned, are played out by Essy with Jonathan, who is filled with distaste by the spectacle. He tells her that she has "begun to develop misery as a habit": "You have allowed it to grow on you, developing it of your own free will until it has become a necessity to you. It is no longer an emotion or a feeling, but something you indulge in as the poor indulge in sorrow because it is their only luxury." Edith was one of those women who have found that even an unanswered love is preferable to the renunciation of love; self-awareness, or the affectionate home truths of Stella Bowen, could describe but not modify.

It is curious on how many points Edith's relation to Tchelitchew echoed the historical record of Swift and his two women. Swift would never see Stella alone ("What—alone with Sitvouka? . . . *I should be raped!*"), and Stella had an older companion, Mrs. Dingley, with whom she lived, as Edith lived with Helen. Vanessa lived with her sister, who became mortally ill; when she dies, Vanessa/Essy in Edith's novel says to herself: " '*This* will bring him back to me.' She had sunk to that." Helen's death was still in the future when Edith wrote that scene; it did not bring Pavlik back to her.

These parallels and interpretations are interesting for the student of Edith's heart and mind, but tell nothing objective about the quality of the novel. The passages quoted suggest an intensity and a level of feeling, and sometimes of insight, that are impressive. But that is not the whole story. Edith had no gift for dialogue whatsoever. As soon as two characters strike up a conversation they become stilted and unreal. And her lyrical, poetic passages sit uncomfortably in their contexts; one would need greater skill and greater self-criticism than Edith possessed at the time to get away with it.

Where she is very acute is in descriptions of psychological states and close-range observation of behaviour. She can empathise with a mother on the loss of a child—increasingly in her work, having suffered "the death of all her natural impulses," Edith mourned, by identification with bereaved mothers, the child she had never even conceived. She is very good too on the grating presence of Anna's constant female companion, her wearisome emanations "enveloped in, and then escaping from, the density of bosom, mind, hair, and personality. . . ." This companion at tea is well observed: She "ate a good deal, but in doing so preserved, throughout, the appearance of one who was per-forming a public duty, quietly and resolutely, against her will." And Edith captures the inimitable gentility of an elderly dressmaker who talked about another elderly dressmaker "as 'my friend,' as though one could only have one friend." There are refined shades of Evelyn Wiel in these inescapable females.

The final impression left by Edith's novel, however, is one of confusion of intent and execution; prophetic utterances, social observation, rustic flights of fancy, psychological insights, modern sensibilities, twentieth-century events, eighteenth-century usages and quotations, have the reader constantly adjusting his viewfinder. There is no sense of place at all. Everything that is not in a slum in the suburbs of hell seems to take place in a pleasantly wooded area of the moon.

The same kind of thing could be said of some of the plays of Shakespeare; and nothing of this would matter at all if someone seemed to be in charge. But Edith had no perspective, and was as embroiled as her readers. She put all of herself into the book. "I felt as if I had been through an earthquake, after I had written it,"[3] she told Raymond Marriott. After such massive tremors, a more experienced novelist might have let the dust settle, and then set to work sorting out the fallen masonry. Edith just sent it off to Victor Gollancz. He received it with enthusiasm—"a truly exquisite book"—and paid her £350 for the British and American rights.[4]

Edith was disappointed by the way her novel was received. The critics were not sure how to take it. Evelyn Waugh in *Night and Day* (October 21, 1937) was among those who took the trouble to try to come to grips with it, and succeeded rather well. The novel "defied cursory treatment," he wrote:

> The date of the story has no importance. . . . Elsewhere Miss Sitwell has shown herself a master of "period." It is easy to imagine with what deft and significant touches she could . . . have given us a historical background to the life of Swift; perhaps it is not impertinent to think that she may have begun with some idea of a historical novel. . . . But the tragedy and the mystery of Swift were too potent for such treatment; she seems to have seen deep into his tortured soul, to horror lurking beneath horror, into a world where costume and decor become meaningless. It is a terrifying book.

Apropos of the horror—William Empson, to whom Edith sent the book, complained to her from Hanoi in April 1938 that she made Swift's pathological misery seem "normal and typical"; and it is true that in Edith's novel his despair does seem but one expression of the whole world's despair.

The Times Literary Supplement's reviewer (October 2, 1937) commended the "eccentric and lively" minor characters. Her young country boy who goes to the war is adapted from her description of the young Rimbaud in her introduction to Helen Rootham's translations. Her own father, Sir George, stalks through the book, disguised as Sir Henry Rotherham, and Wyndham Lewis is there, masquerading as Henry Debingham. Edith's original name for this character had been "Ratney Pierpoint," which was an amalgam of the names of characters in Lewis's *The Apes of God*. The lawyer H. F. Rubinstein, who read her novel for libel risk on behalf of Victor Gollancz, wrote to the publisher: "Wyndham Lewis is a dangerous person. I speak from experience. I suggest, therefore, that no loophole should be allowed him to make trouble." So the name was changed. Edith described the character with the very words and phrases she had used in her unpublished essay on Wyndham Lewis.

The *TLS* review ended on a downbeat. The novel was "very uneven"; "The general impression, perhaps deliberate, is of no period in particular. . . ." Jonathan remained "an insubstantial, half-legendary figure throughout most of the book."

Edith did her best to be pleased with the "most generous" reviews. "Poor Mr. [Edwin] Muir is a strange example," she told Victor Gollancz. "I love the way in which he did me up in a tiny parcel with that inconsiderable man Dickens and threw us both away with a wince." Twenty-five hundred copies had been sold by the end of the first ten days, which was very good, Gollancz told her. Four thousand copies were printed, of which 3,898 finally sold—a nice piece of editorial judgment.

Edith was back at the rue Saint-Dominique for Christmas 1937, to find Helen much worse. She now had to be lifted out of bed and lifted back again when the bed was made; the pain this small disturbance caused her made her faint. A bad cold was visited on Edith; to avoid the risk of infecting Helen, she spent a few welcome days on her own at the hotel; but then she returned to the flat. There could be no visitors there now. To see Choura, Edith would slip out for an hour at lunchtime, usually to the Brasserie Universelle in the rue de l'Odéon. In the flat, she worked on a radio play—about Beau Brummell—called *The Last Party*, and started a new novel for Victor Gollancz, with a violent death in the first chapter.

Life narrowed down almost to nothing in the months before Helen died. Edith was barely writing letters. She explained to Victor Gollancz that Helen was "dying in this flat, inch by inch, of cancer of the spine and hip, liver and kidneys. The flat is very small, and the sounds one hears are unbearable. And one is so overwhelmed with pity." That was in March; and there were still, though Edith would not have believed it, another six months to go. Her beloved cat was the only encouraging piece of life in the small and stuffy rooms.

Edith went briefly to Renishaw during the summer. While she was there she had a visit from Henry Moat, Sir George's old servant, who reported loyally to his ex-employer at Montegufoni: "I was pleased to see Miss Edith there too. I think she gets more aristocratic-looking every year, and her beautiful manner, so different from these painted hussies who are filling up all over."[5]

But Edith was only just holding on. She did not even answer letters from Dylan Thomas. On June 1 he was writing to Henry Treece saying that he was not sure whether Edith "likes me, personally, now or not. I have the idea she's offended, but this may be incorrect. I wrote her some two months ago at her Paris address, but have had no answer." Perhaps, he added, she too had become lazy or bad mannered, "but this I doubt extremely."[6]

Helen, who had taken so many months and years to die, found it hard to slip out of life at the very end:

> Three days before she died, some good religious friends of hers came and sat beside her, and called her. She seemed to be dying at the moment. But she revived because of that. Afterwards she said to me, with a frightful despair, with infinite bitterness: "You know Edith, I was in such peace. I was just going. And that *poor good fool* brought me back."[7]

When she finally went, in October 1938, the effect on Edith was catastrophic. Helen's death was a relief and a release; it was a release not only from ten years' anxiety and obligation, but also from the mechanism by which she had smothered her feelings. The violently ambivalent emotions she had suppressed on the death of her mother merged with her equally ambivalent feelings about Helen, and the incoming flood, in the months that followed, engulfed her. Grief for a wholly beloved person is simpler to live through. Edith's complex grief was mixed with the gratitude and resentment of years. "She was like a mother to me," Edith wrote to John Lehmann of Helen, over five years later. And Helen took with her so much of the past. Edith was no stranger to depression or to periods of near-despair, but she did not usually let anyone see them. Geoffrey Gorer, who had been in touch with Edith even in her most agonized times with Pavlik, never saw her show her unhappiness openly, except on the death of Helen.

There was also the frightening practical problem of where and how she would now live. Though Helen had become a burden, she had been Edith's home companion for more than twenty years. Events in Europe in the autumn of 1938 made it doubtful whether France was going to be a good place to stay; in a desultory way, she began putting her belongings in some order. In any case, to share a home and a life with Evelyn Wiel had no attraction whatsoever.

She went over to London in November to see Massine's ballet *Nobilissima Visione*, which Pavlik had designed. But Ford was with Pavlik; and he was surrounded now by his rich admirers, as Ford wrote to Parker Tyler, "Lady Cunard, Sir Kenneth Clark, Lady Juliet [Duff], Lord Berners, Baron de Gunsburg." As for Edith, depressed and in mourning for Helen:

> With unflinching eye . . . the artist inspects the voluminous black gown being worn by his friend, thinks it badly cut and informs her of his opinion, adding as if for a clincher, "It makes you look like a giant orphan." The lady's gowns have become a permanent issue for Tchelitchew,

and will never cease concerning him so long as she is in sight . . . everything, and especially mourning perhaps, should be done well.[8]

Edith went on living, indecisively, with Evelyn over the new year and into 1939. Osbert had set off with David Horner on a German cruise ship to Guatemala; Sacheverell and Georgia and their two sons—the second, Francis, was born in 1935—were at Weston. Edith wrote to Raymond Marriott from the rue Saint-Dominique on February 26 that she could not wish Helen back: "She suffered six months of unspeakable torture, and as she was nursed in this tiny six-room flat, both her sister and I were worn out. What I *am* suffering from is delayed shock. One gets over that. . . ."[9] What she could not get over, for many months, was Pavlik's lack of concern for her, as she told Allen Tanner, writing from her customary retreat at Levanto in June 1939:

> I cannot help knowing this: that all last autumn, I was very poor and unutterably lonely and unhappy, and I did not see how I was going on with my life. *And P. left me to it*, whilst he went rushing about with that parasite. . . . I might have been absolutely alone in Paris, and I can't forget it.
>
> Now, of course, he wants me to write to him, because he is in England, where my name has a certain glamour.

In some quarters the glamour of her name was insufficient. Nineteen thirty-nine was the year in which Sir Arthur Quiller-Couch, then seventy-seven, updated his 1900 *Oxford Book of English Verse*, and he did not include Edith among the moderns. (It is possible she excluded herself by opposing any selection of her work he might have made.)

Earlier in the year her agent had tried to solve her financial problems by fixing an American lecture tour. Geoffrey Gorer's mother was already in the United States: "*What* fun we will have,"[10] Edith wrote to her in March. "Moby Dick, the maid, and I" had all been having flu. (Moby Dick was Evelyn Wiel.) But the project fell through. The conditions laid down by Colston Leigh, the American lecture tour agent, terrified her: "I cannot *possibly* lecture *excepting from manuscript*": "They say I must not lecture from manuscript, but if they won't let me, then I can't go. I have no memory at all, and my lectures are highly complicated. . . . They must think I'm not an artist but a trick cyclist."[11] In any case, she said, she had only wanted to go in order to get away from Moby Dick for a bit.

When Germany invaded Poland on September 1, 1939, Edith was in Levanto, working on the compilation of an anthology for Victor Gollancz. On receipt of a telegram from Osbert, who was also abroad, she went straight home to Renishaw, getting there before him. She left behind her in Paris nearly all her possessions—her books, her notebooks, her Tchelitchew paintings and drawings, her letters and papers, her cat—and Evelyn Wiel. War had made her decision for her. She never went back to 129 rue Saint-Dominique.

18

War
1940-1943

Edith felt the war chiefly as a dreadful waste—of life, of talent, of time. "Oh really!" she wrote to Anthony Powell, when he was called up in December 1939. "The unceasing misery, wretchedness, and, in minor ways, the boredom! The waste of time! . . . How far away everything that we once enjoyed seems!"[1] In the spring of 1940 the Vic-Wells Ballet came to Sheffield, "so Constant [Lambert] and Freddie [Ashton] and Bobbie [Helpmann] have been here," she told Georgia. "It is so dreadful seeing all these poor young men on the brink of this ghastly catastrophe."[2]

There was little that Edith, impractical and over fifty, could contribute—it seemed then—to her country at war. She told Lady Violet Powell, Anthony Powell's wife, in January 1940:

> I have no news whatsoever. Life is just one long grumble, with intervals of freezing, and of conversations with the wives of Majors.—Osbert has become a magistrate, and has learnt a lot of fresh frightful language in the cause of his duties, but even that doesn't seem to help much. I knit, and try not to listen to the wireless, and there one is.[3]

Edith, so undomestic in most ways, had always knitted: long, rather shapeless cardigan jackets for herself and Helen, in the old days. Now she knitted socks and pullovers for everyone—for David Horner, who had joined the RAF, for Sachie, for Alec Guinness (who had married Merula Salaman, a connection of the Sitwells and "a most sweet young creature," the year before the war broke out), for the Guinnesses' baby. She knitted all through that first winter of the war, as she and Osbert settled down to life together, enclosed in the great house where, although it was "home," there was no familiar daily routine at first: They had never lived there for more than a few months at a time, and nearly always in summer. Osbert was forty-six, and in uncertain health. There was still no electricity at Renishaw; knitting and reading and writing were done by oil lamps when the short winter days' light failed. The house was bitterly cold in spite of roaring coal and log fires both down- and upstairs. The firewood, Edith complained to Georgia, seemed "made entirely of toadstools and of sponges." The bathroom was inconvenient and chill.

Osbert and Edith, as if in an increasingly harmonious marriage of convenience, evolved their way of life. Osbert's soldier-servant John Robins and his wife looked after them. The companionship of her "dear old boy" was sweet to Edith. Writing to Evelyn Wiel in October 1942 after an enforced break in correspondence, she said: "I have been, all this long time, in the country with Osbert. What a wonderful nature he has. . . . I knit and I write."[4] Neither brother nor sister appeared downstairs before lunchtime. Edith often remained cloistered for even longer, until five in the afternoon. She read and worked in her room on the first floor, usually in bed. Once established, this routine lasted all through the war. "Nobody ever comes down to breakfast," she wrote to Eliot on July 1, 1945, to entice him to come and stay. "People disappear for hours on end if they want to. . . . They go away to work, if they feel like it, or for siestas that last for hours." It was disconcerting for a visitor who expected conventional entertainment, but it pleased most: "They have done what I most hoped they would do—left me alone for the afternoon," Evelyn Waugh wrote to his wife, Laura, in June 1942.

Waugh was one of the many serving in the forces who found Renishaw a curious oasis when on leave, or when stationed within visiting distance. The house was shabbier outside, he told Laura that summer, "with the lawns grown long & the hedges ragged so that you might think the house deserted. . . . " The formal flower gardens were given over to growing cabbages; all through the war, the food at Renishaw, self-supporting as far as vegetables were concerned, was fresh and good. The neglected exterior of the house belied what was within, in summer at least: "There everything is open; no evacuees or billeted soldiers; no dust sheets except in the ball room. Banks of potted plants & bowls of roses; piles of new and old books and delicious cooking . . . ."[5] There was also, Waugh told his wife, "an extremely charming artist called Piper staying here making a series of drawings of the house."

John Piper, who was working as a war-artist, was in his thirties; he was a great friend of Geoffrey Grigson, who let Piper know that he thought his Renishaw contact was an unworthy piece of social climbing. But for Piper, the stays at Renishaw were a welcome respite from the war; Osbert paid him generously for his work, and admitted him to a world of sophistication and knowledge that enlarged his own. Osbert had begun his own major work in the enforced seclusion of Renishaw: He had embarked on his great five-volume autobiography, that universal mythology of Sitwellism, and he wanted John Piper to provide the illustrations—the originals of which he hung in the great hall at Renishaw. It was patronage in the grand old manner, and brought nothing but benefit to the artist. Piper fitted in easily and, not looking for trouble, found none.

The only person who was not so pleased, apart from Grigson, was David Horner, who resented his "own" room at Renishaw being given over to Piper on his visits. Horner was at the Air Ministry in London at the beginning of the war, but soon was posted as Intelligence Officer to a station at Watnall Chaworth, within easy reach of Renishaw. This was a comfort to Osbert, though the relationship between him and Horner was not now always so easy. Nor was the one between Horner and Edith: Some painful scenes took place during one of his visits in the early months of the war, about money troubles—either hers or Sacheverell's—which forced her to write one of her rare apologies:

> I am horribly ashamed at having made that maddening scene when you had come over here to have a rest, dead tired as you are. . . . Also poor Osbert gets all Sachie's worries and it was too bad of me to make a scene. . . . It is to be ascribed partly to the fact that I get terrified, as I cannot understand business. I won't do it again. You shall have a tearless Thursday and Friday I promise you. . . .

She managed to get on with him, since she had to, and David, because he had to, managed to get on with her. But she found his almost constant presence boring, irritating, and a strain. Sometimes, during the war, when Edith expressed frustration and confessed to violent—even murderous—impulses, it was because of David Horner. But no one could have guessed it. She concealed her feelings totally, which made them all the harder to bear. Almost the furthest she would go, in a letter, was to Georgia, and even then she wrote obliquely: "If you knew how difficult it has been sometimes not to be irritable under the Circumstances."[6] To the world she showed nothing, out of loyalty to Osbert. David had become to all intents and purposes one of the family.

There was disruption at Weston, late in 1941, when Sacheverell, now over forty, became adjutant of the local Home Guard. Edith resented this demand on her brother's time and energy. "A ghastly worry," she wrote to him. "No words can even say what I feel about it! . . . I feel sadder and sadder. There is hardly anything left that is worth while."[7] Relations between Osbert and Sacheverell were distant now, even strained, because of disagreements and disappointments about money; when Edith went for a week to Weston, she went alone.

John Piper, who only saw Edith when she appeared downstairs towards the end of each day, found her cosy and sisterly. In the evenings, while Edith knitted, they played records—Debussy—on the wind-up gramophone. What did shake Piper a little were the "huge glasses of neat gin" consumed. Alcohol, at Renishaw, was one way of allaying the anxiety and loneliness and boredom of life during the war. Edith's dependence on alcohol gradually established itself, unremarked, during these years.

The winters were worst. Both Osbert and Edith had a neurotic fear of catching cold, and Edith would trace back each carrier of the dreaded cold germs with a rage more applicable to those guilty of criminal assault. An undated letter to John Lehmann is typical: "One of the ladies who 'obliges' arrived last Saturday week, just looked at Susan [Robins's wife], sneezed at her—and retired, like a Naiad in a Fountain." So the whole household came down with colds. "The house echoes with the lion-like roarings of Robins clearing his throat, and is damp with the tears and sighs of Susan—oh, I could *wring everyone's neck.*"[8]

Anthony Powell spent a week's leave at Renishaw with his wife in the winter of 1942, "snow on the ground, the statues of the Italian garden clad, appropriately for wartime, in their seasonal garments of sackcloth." In her letter of invitation, Edith had written: "Three bombs have just fallen outside the window (well, *almost* outside . . . relatively speaking) . . . our first for some time. I wish the brute would go away. He is just coming back again. . . . I am stupider than ever, and have no spirit left to say Bo to a single goose."[9]

During the visit, the Powells and Edith decided to go into bomb-torn Sheffield. Before they left, Osbert—who was far more *au fait* with all household arrangements than Edith—drew Lady Violet aside. "We're a little short of food," he said. "Don't bother Edith about it." They were to call on a certain fishmonger, who could sometimes be persuaded to let them have a salmon. The fishmonger project came up during the short car drive to Sheffield; Lady Violet gave Edith a summary of the various ways of cooking a salmon so as to eke it out as far as it would go, ending up, "Then you make the tail into kedgeree."

For this foray into town Edith Sitwell had gone to some trouble in her outfit, which included a high cylindrical hat, something between an archimandrite's and that of a Tartar horseman in *Sohrab and Rustum*. She was a person who would never have deliberately jumped a queue, but, her head full of her brother's instructions, Violet's words on the culinary uses of salmon, she swept forward, disregarding the people waiting patiently outside, and seized the fishmonger . . . by the hand.

She asked him how he was. She asked after the well-being of his family. She told him he was looking well. She had come to ask him, she said, " 'whether by any chance you have a salmon? *We want a salmon for making kedgeree.*' . . . The fishmonger went pale. Had the days of the Bourbons returned? Lucullus himself might have thought twice before devoting a whole newly caught salmon to kedgeree; anyway while Rome was at war."[10] The fishmonger nevertheless produced a salmon, which was left behind in another shop where they were buying something else; it was put on a train, and reached Renishaw in time for dinner. (This anecdote of Anthony Powell's has a backwards echo. Long before the war, her old target J. C. Squire had contributed to *Punch* a ballad based on a chance remark overheard at a party: "I once saw Edith Sitwell buying fish . . . .")[11]

Sheffield bore the brunt of several air raids; after the second, in summer 1943, Edith was again in the town, but alone. "There was a silent Fair, unspeakably squalid and miserable in the grey drizzle, camped in a space where once houses had been, felled by the bombs. . . . Sheffield has no inside, none."[12] On this occasion, Edith did not leave her shopping behind; she went straight home without having had the heart to do any shopping at all.

In January 1942, in the third winter of the war, Edith was writing to Mrs. Gorer in America that she was tending to regard life "—excepting for the unspeakable horror and disaster of it,—as a railway journey which has to be undertaken. But when one thinks of the thousands and millions of wrecked lives . . ." To Georgia she wrote that she felt "older and older every day,—and so deadly uninterested,—excepting for the feeling of horror one has the whole time."

One of the many wrecked lives was that of Evelyn Wiel, stranded in German-occupied Paris, alone and penniless. Edith had arranged to remit through Coutts' Bank the sum of £10 a month to Evelyn, ostensibly for looking after her cat, now fourteen years old. But that January she received a telegram about Evelyn from a stranger: *"Envoyer d'argent d'urgence. Situation désespérée."* "It is a nightmare horror," Edith wrote to Anthony Powell. "I can't get at her."[13] Since the fall of France—Paris had been occupied since June 1940—not a penny of the money had got through to Evelyn; and letters could only be sent through the Red Cross, routed via neutral countries.

Edith went into action like a lion when the telegram came. She wrote to the Red Cross, to the Foreign Office, to the Trading with the Enemy Department of the Board of Trade, setting out Evelyn's pathetic circumstances and begging for permission to send her money: "She has not a penny. She is entirely destitute. . . . She is a lifelong friend of mine, and I have supported her for years." She spelled out Evelyn's marital circumstances, her age, and her ill health: "She has had the worst possible internal operations. . . . She has also burst varicose veins, has open wounds from the toes of both feet to her knees, and is lame." Osbert wrote letters too; while Evelyn's brother, Ernest Rootham, a solicitor in Barnstaple, would take no interest in his sister's plight.

Edith received a desperate letter from Evelyn, who thought herself abandoned. Edith wrote back in a fever of reassurance: "I miss you every hour of every day. . . . Darling, I would *never* desert you. *Never*. . . . How well I see the rooms in the flat. I dream, continually, sometimes every night, for weeks on end, that I am back in the flat." Edith's dreams of being back in the rue Saint-Dominique were nightmares. But Evelyn, maddening and limited though she was, was part of Edith's past and never to be abandoned. Her hopeless dependency clawed into Edith's loving heart. And then there was the cat: "And then I wake up in an agony of mind, wondering how you are, and how my darling little angel, whom you do not mention, is. . . . Does that mean he is dead? I long for him, and love him, with all my heart, and always shall, all my life!"[14] The cat was still alive. In a codicil to the will she made that May, Edith wrote: "I wish my cat now in the charge of Madame Wiel to be amply and generously provided for and taken care of, as I could not die easy if I thought he was not in proper care."

If this were the whole story of Edith's wartime experience—the story of a distinguished middle-aged writer anxiously sitting out the war with her brother in their family home, worrying about the safety of their friends—it would not be remarkable. But this is only the underpinning of the story. There were three factors at work to give Edith's war another dimension, for both herself and others.

The first was Pavel Tchelitchew. On September 7, 1941, Edith was writing to Alec Guinness that Pavlik said Auden had had "a terribly offerly Flop" in America: "His letters—he usually writes to me once a week—are perfection."[15]

Other people might still agonize over their relationships with Pavlik— Geoffrey Gorer, for example, who was writing to Edith from New Haven, Connecticut, in August 1941 that he "found it very difficult to forgive the way he has treated Mother. . . . When she had money to buy pictures he was full of empressement; but now, when she has none, not even a card for a Christmas greeting, or any other sort of attention. . . . I think he has turned out into a very fair weather friend." Fond though she was of the Gorers, these words can only have reinforced Edith's new sense of security. Had she not always said that Pavlik would one day know who his true friend was?

They had not seen each other to say good-bye when war broke out; she had speeded back to Renishaw, and Pavlik to New York. But he had written to her from shipboard at the beginning of September 1939; and from then on they corresponded regularly and copiously. The hundreds of thousands of their written words are, as has already been remarked, locked up and inaccessible until the year 2000. Parker Tyler had access to them when he wrote his life of Tchelitchew, since Edith was alive then to give her consent. It is only from his pages that the nature of the letters can be deduced.

Edith, with an ocean between them, became once more Pavlik's "spiritual confidante." There was a renewed rapport, as intense as in the earliest days of their friendship. For her, it was a miracle. She was again his Delphic Oracle, his Dame Blanche, the Sibyl of his 1937 portrait of her, the "bee-priestess"— honey is liquid gold. He wrote about himself, and his moods. He said he dreamed about her. He wrote about his work, and his ill health. He gave her the reassurance she needed: "No no my dear, don't be childish, you are my greatest friend of heart and brain." And "Edith my dearest friend you are like an enormous heart who is also an ear and an eye to read through my madmans [sic] thoughts."[16]

They both grew dependent on the correspondence, fussing about mailing dates and letters lost or not yet received. Both inclining to paranoid states, they compared notes on insults and humiliations borne. Pavlik told her that her trials and troubles had made her grow into a "Great Oak." They vied with one another in pillorying mutual acquaintances. They discussed at length Pavlik's chief preoccupation—the mystic function of anatomy, and the way in which every form found in nature had its counterpart in the human body.

And Charles Henri Ford? They made jokes in their letters about "pretty young men," of which Edith said she knew a number who "ought to be hanging out their lingerie on the Maginot line." Pavlik gave her oblique reassurance. "Sex is not love, no it is contrary to love—it is a sort of madness like gloutonnerie, like cleptomania." He told her, "I have no friends beside you, no real friends."[17] The result was a softening of Edith's attitude. She reviewed a book of Charles Henri Ford's poetry favourably in *Life and Letters To-Day* in October 1940, and they began to correspond warily: "Dear Miss Sitwell . . . ," Ford wrote praising her poems; he asked if he might dedicate his translations of Baudelaire to her.

The sustaining flow of letters from Pavlik continued all through the war, and for three years after, until they met again.

The second and most important element of Edith's wartime experience was the poetry that came out of it. This was not unconnected with her correspondence with Pavlik; for the themes and topics they discussed became part of her poetry, and it is possible that without the stimulation and emotional heightening his letters gave her she would have felt too depressed and discouraged to find her voice. The third new element, which was new friendships, grew out of her poetry; for her poetry touched hearts and minds and brought people to her. She summed it all up in a letter to Evelyn Wiel written just before Christmas 1944; if her account sounds simple, even naive, it is because she was tailoring it to her rather simpleminded correspondent:

I have new and *much* nicer friends. . . . My great new friends are Stephen Spender, the poet, and his wife; and John Lehmann [Rosamond Lehmann's brother—the editor of *New Writing*]. Besides Bryher MacPherson, whom I have told you about. . . .

Writing? Poetry all the time. My new book of poems, published in August, has sold 5000 copies already, 2000 more are being printed—which means they are certain to go. My previous book of poems, printed in 1942, went into 4 editions! They now say I have taken Yeats' place. But of course the pipsqueakery are still squeaking. It would mean my poetry was dead if they didn't. My poetry is now incredibly bigger than it used to be.[18]

It was all true; how had it come about?

The new friendships and the new poetry grew up together out of the horror of war, as the wild clematis and rosebay willowherb grew and flowered on the bomb sites in the cities. Edith was writing to Geoffrey Gorer—in America—in October 1940 that she had been "muffled in a kind of grey horror, a sort of nightmare in which I have found it difficult to move. I write poetry, because that is my natural function, and I spin it out of myself as a spider spins thread out of itself, but that is all."[19] She told him she had become "great friends" with Alec Guinness, now serving in the Royal Navy; he became one of her regular correspondents.

Another wartime friend, who played the part of fairy godmother to Edith ever after, was the novelist "Bryher." Bryher Ellerman, the wealthy daughter of shipping magnate Sir John Ellerman, was seven years younger than Edith. She had been married to Robert McAlmon for a few years in the 1920s, and afterwards to Kenneth MacPherson, the Scottish writer and authority on the cinema, with whom she published the magazine *Close Up*. When the war began she was sharing her life with the poet "H. D."—Hilda Doolittle, the ex-wife of Richard Aldington. Short, blue-eyed, bereted, and immensely energetic, Bryher was capable of an intense devotion that her practical personality and manner prevented from becoming sentimental. Thornton Wilder said to Gertrude Stein: "Bryher is Napoleonic, she walks like him, she talks like him, she probably feels like him."[20]

This female Napoleon had made her home in Switzerland; but she deliberately chose to be in London when England was at war, sharing a flat in Lowndes Square with H. D. Her patriotic gallantry brought her close to the Sitwells: "Osbert's friendship and Edith's love," she wrote, got her through the war. Bryher provided the financial backing for *Life and Letters To-Day*, which Robert Herring edited and for which Edith wrote; when its offices were bombed in 1940, Robert Herring took refuge at Renishaw, later renting a house in the adjacent village of Eckington and editing the magazine from there. Bryher went up to see them all.

It was during this visit to Renishaw that my friendship with Edith began. I had met her a few times, always in the midst of a crowded tea party, in the apartment in Bayswater. Now, and Edith herself could not have realized how much it meant to me, once the visitors had left she read me poems, sitting outside on the terrace in the pale October sunshine. . . . Even now, more than twenty years after the so-called peace, Renishaw is a circlet of golden moments uncovered from a temple's dust.[21]

After this first visit she went again and again. Bryher looked straight through the flamboyant, eccentric Edith, which was all that those hostile to her saw, and perceived, with the eyes of love, her essence: "Poetry to her was as the nun's dedication in the Middle Ages and she tolerated no pretence. Perhaps this was why she had so many enemies."

> Whenever I think of Edith, it is summer at Renishaw. We seldom obeyed Osbert's instructions to sit out of doors but stayed instead just inside the doorway that led to the terrace. . . . There Edith used to read me Shakespeare, the old ballads and if I pleaded very hard, her own poems. Her voice, the air, an ornament of her dress, all seemed golden. . . .[22]

Like Allanah Harper twenty years earlier, Bryher found no way to express her feelings to Edith. "Others to whom she read her poems were able to find the right words to express their gratitude. I had been trained to silence and could only feel. . . . All of us have our assigned tasks and mine was to be a messenger." Bryher was full of resource. When warm clothes were hard to come by during the war, she obtained a sack of camel clippings from the Zoo and had them spun into yarn in Scotland, and made up into jackets for herself and Osbert. Her admiration and love for Edith was expressed not in words, but in unequivocal chequebook generosity.

Edith's financial situation at the beginning of the war was parlous. She wrote to her agent in autumn 1941 unwillingly accepting poorish terms—no advance on 10 percent royalties—for her new poems, *Street Songs*, since "the publication of a new book by me, after a lapse of years, should, if properly handled, attract the greatest attention and obtain a most favourable sale" (as indeed it did).[23] She was also negotiating with Macmillan for what was to be *Fanfare for Elizabeth*. "I *cannot* go on being supported by Osbert; it simply is not fair on him, and it is most painful for me. I *must* earn money: I must pay my way."[24]

Perhaps these were the circumstances that had provoked the tears for which she apologised to David Horner. Not long afterwards, she was writing to Alec Guinness that she was hoping to be given—"yes, given"—a house in Bath. "It is very like a Tchekov play, the idea of the house in Bath. Either one will go on talking about it for ever, and not buy it,—or will buy it, and not have the money to live in it."[25]

Bryher did buy the house in Bath for Edith: 8 Gay Street, a pretty little house that had belonged to Dr. Johnson's Mrs. Thrale when she was Mrs. Piozzi. Edith never lived in it; for the rest of the war, since it was unoccupied, it was requisitioned by Bath Corporation, who paid Edith £282 5s. 5d. in compensation afterwards; she sold it in 1949, without ever having spent a night there. But it had been a sound investment, as all Bryher's were. Bryher's saintliness was that of St. Teresa of Avila.

The house did not solve the income problem; in 1943 Edith's overdraft stood at £3,000. But gradually things improved. In 1944 Osbert gave her £1,000 of 3-percent Defence Bonds, which she redeemed in 1955; and at the end of the war in 1945, Bryher made a Deed of Covenant for seven years which gave Edith £41 13s. 4d. per month, less tax. More importantly, she began to make money from her poetry. At the beginning of the war, she had plugged on with her second novel; but as she began to write poetry again, it slipped into the background; no more was heard of it.

The publication of *Street Songs* was a turning point in Edith's life as a poet; it justified the otherwise rather ludicrous action taken by the Sitwells the previous year. Immediately before *Street Songs* Edith had published three anthologies to keep the pot boiling: *Edith Sitwell's Anthology* came out from Gollancz in January 1940 (she was paid £500 outright for it); *Poems Old and New*, from Faber, in October 1940; and *Look, the Sun!* (which "I *pretend* is an anthology for children. But of course it isn't," she told Merula Guinness[26]) from Gollancz in September 1941, which brought her another £100. It was the first of the three that caused the trouble.

Hamilton Fyfe, reviewing *Edith Sitwell's Anthology* in the Sunday paper *Reynolds News*, took the opportunity to give his views not only on the book, which he quite liked, but on the Sitwells, whom he dismissed as "literary curiosities of the nineteen-twenties," suggesting that energy and self-assurance rather than talent had been responsible for their success and, most injudiciously, that "now oblivion has claimed them, and they are remembered with a kindly, if slightly cynical smile." It was this sentiment that made the Sitwells' solicitor, Philip Frere, agree that there was a prima facie case for libel.

The case briefly brought the trio together again. "Georgia will have told you," Edith wrote to Sacheverell, "that we are demanding £500 *each* from

Reynolds. We shan't get as much, of course, but they have to be taught a lesson."[27]

The defendants offered the Sitwells £150 each, and costs, to settle out of court; they turned the offer down. Their case was that Fyfe's words meant "that they were persons of no literary ability, whose arrogance and conceit constituted their sole claim to prominence," and that they had therefore been "seriously injured in their characters, credit, reputation, and in the way of their profession." The object of bringing the case at all, they announced, was "to prevent newspapers from libelling artists."

The case was heard before Mr. Justice Cassels in February 1941. All three Sitwells did well in court. Edith pointed out that, so far from being claimed by oblivion, she had written or edited nine books since the publication of *Alexander Pope* nine years before, which was the point Hamilton Fyfe identified as her last noticeable effort; he had made no mention of the subsequent and very successful *Victoria of England*, let alone the rest. When the counsel for the defence accused her of courting publicity, she replied: "I have advertised my books in the way that all tradesmen advertise their wares." The peccant Hamilton Fyfe looked in court like "some sort of insect," she wrote to Christabel Aberconway afterwards, and as for herself: "I gave what I consider a really beautiful performance of a sweet, sunny-natured old lady, stinking with lavender and looped with old lace, in whose mouth butter, even in the palmy days when it could be procured, would not have melted."[28] Daniel Macmillan, for the publishers, was a witness to the value of the Sitwells' literary work, as were Mr. Wilson of Bumpus's book shop, Arthur Waley, and Charles Morgan. The Sitwells won their case, and were awarded £350 each plus costs. Hugh Walpole wrote to the *Daily Telegraph* on February 14 to say that all writers should be grateful to the Sitwells for their action, and the *Times* published a facetious leading article on the subject:

[The Sitwells] will not claim to be exempt from the sentence of Holy Writ: "Our names shall be forgotten in time, and no man shall have our works in remembrance." But, if Sainte-Beuve rightly defines a critic as one whose watch is five minutes ahead of other people's, yesterday's judgement is a salutary warning that the habit may be expensive.

Some of what were to be Edith's best-known war poems from *Street Songs* were published before the book came out—"Any Man to Any Woman" and

"Street Song" itself in *Life and Letters To-Day* of April 1940 and January 1941, respectively, and "Still Falls the Rain" in *The Times Literary Supplement* of September 6, 1941. The book itself came out from Macmillan in January 1942. There was a rather modest first printing of fifteen hundred copies; it went through three more editions in five months. As John Lehmann wrote in *A Nest of Tigers*, "The hour and the poet were matched." She was one with her time, speaking for her time, as she had not for thirteen years, since *Gold Coast Customs*.

Street Songs brought to her feet the halfhearteds: Cyril Connolly, who asked her to write for *Horizon* (though a *tour d'Horizon* will show that she did not start out as a regular contributor), and above all Connolly's co-editor, Stephen Spender. Writing to Mrs. Gorer in March 1942 about the "really terrific reviews" that *Street Songs* was having, Edith said that Spender, "who never, I think, cared much for my poetry, now says the poems are extremely beautiful."[29] He had written about them in *Horizon* and in the *New Statesman*. Spender was reverting to, rather than reversing, his former opinions, for he had read her early poems as a schoolboy, and had been "immediately attracted by a poet who transforms everything into pure hard images"; his own early efforts "were often their imitators," just so long as he inhabited the pre-Auden "poetic world outside everyday life."[30]

He had moved on—into politics, introspection, psychoanalytical theory, painting. In 1941 he made his second marriage, to the pianist Natasha Litvin, and both Spenders appreciated Edith's generosity and "sensitive sympathy"—"her own well-being was bound up with that of her friends"—and her lethal gift for repartee. Since she was mostly at Renishaw, and Spender in London—and, in the years just after the war, often abroad—the friendship was largely a pen friendship. They wrote about their own and each other's work, without too much mutual back scratching. His "Lines for Edith Sitwell"—a public tribute to their friendship—appeared in *Horizon* in July 1943; Edith's "Song of the Cold" is dedicated to Natasha Spender, and her "Harvest" to Stephen.

John Lehmann has commented how one of the curious side-results of the war was that it became a "great feast of reading." Literary magazines "were read with a fierce love and enthusiasm such as perhaps no magazines in our century have been read before or since."[31] Edith's poems were part of the feast. Other feasts, particularly for those trapped in the danger and stagnation of big cities, were music and the performing arts, oases of pleasure and reminders of worlds elsewhere. The Griller Quartet, after playing in Sheffield, came to Renishaw Hall in October 1943, and gave a private performance for the Sitwells and their visitors—they played Mozart, Bloch, Brahms, Haydn, and Benjamin Britten. Edith signed up with C. Day Lewis, Walter de la Mare, T. S. Eliot, Louis MacNeice, and Stephen Spender in the Apollo Society, founded to "revive the neglected art of reading poetry and to show that music and poetry can be regarded as complementary." And in February 1943 Osbert was asking Bryher to persuade H. D. to give a new poem for a very special reading he was organizing "to keep the arts alive."[32]

For this reading, Edith and Osbert chose the poets and rehearsed and timed them beforehand. Dorothy Wellesley, Edith told David Horner on March 28, was "being beyond any words tiresome. . . . Practically every day I get letters worrying me about something. She sends me all the tripe she writes. . . ." How on earth did Yeats put up with her? Edith wondered. "Honestly, you know, the old man's mind must have been going for him to think her any good at all as a poet." (Edith invited her only because she wanted another woman involved—but not one who could steal her poetic thunder.)

The great reading—the profits from which were to go to Lady Crewe's French in Britain Fund—took place in the Aeolian Hall on April 14, 1943; the revue artist Beatrice Lillie was the programme seller. In the front row sat the Queen and her two young daughters, wearing mittens. The poets read in alphabetical order: Edmund Blunden, Gordon Bottomley, Hilda Doolittle, T. S. Eliot (who read the "London Bridge Is Falling Down" section of "The Waste Land"), Walter de la Mare (who read "The Listeners"), and John Masefield.

During the interval that followed, Dorothy Wellesley created a diversion. She was very drunk. Bryher described the scene:

> Various gentlemen were making efforts to persuade her to retire but instead she turned on one (so elderly, so respectable) and thinking it was Osbert, began to whack him heartily with her stick. . . . People lost their heads, nobody knew what to do. Beatrice Lillie, dropping her programs, took control and led the lady firmly from the aisle just before the solemn return of the regal procession.[33]

The respectable elderly gentleman was Harold Nicolson. The second half of the programme followed, beginning with Nicolson's wife, Vita Sackville-West

("The poem was perhaps a little long," thought Bryher); then "Edith stepped forward as if from some great tapestry to give us 'Anne Boleyn's Song' as only she could read it and at that moment it became not only a poem of memory and loss but also of the rise and fall of an epoch that exactly fitted the times."

19
Life and Death
1943-1944

After the great reading Edith was unwell, with low blood pressure and an uneven pulse, and a feeling of intense frustration not unlike Dorothy Wellesley's. "The awful thing is," she wrote to David Horner on June 18, 1943, "I may quite easily soon commit a murder. . . . I have an almost insane longing to do a physical violence on certain people." Renishaw and its atmosphere were beginning to get her down. And by December the statutory colds and coughs had enveloped the household, with no diminution of Edith's blocked aggression, as she explained to Natasha Spender: "The watchdog won't allow anybody to cough: and if anybody *does* cough, he barks for about 19 hours. . . . I wear gloves, and keep my hands folded in my lap (excepting when being a ministering angel)—for if I unfolded them I might strangle somebody."[1] Most of this murderous tension was caused by the quite extraordinary circumstances surrounding the last days of her father, Sir George Sitwell. His behaviour, she wrote to the Greek poet Demetrios Capetanakis in August 1943, "has brought down on our heads worries so appalling and devastating (and a disgust, a nausea which nearly chokes me)" that it was impossible to work.

Sir George had elected to stay in Italy when war broke out; when he fell ill, he was befriended by a Swiss, Bernard Woog, an ex-employee of the bank in Zurich where Sir George had deposited his money. Woog's wife, Olga, had been born Chandos-Pole, from a family connected with and well known by the Sitwells, with a house not far from Renishaw. When the Woogs moved back to Switzerland, Sir George went with them.

The first intimation of anything untoward was in September 1942, when they heard that Sir George, now over eighty and in a feeble state of health, was planning to marry a German widow and settle on her £500 a year for life. This marriage did not take place, much to the relief of his appalled children; but they were uneasy again early in 1943, when it transpired that not only had Sir

George been drawing very heavily on his Zurich account, but he had given power of attorney to Bernard Woog.

Sir George died at the Villa Fontanelle in Porto Ronco, Locarno, on July 8, 1943; and the contents of his will did nothing to ease the tension between his two sons. Osbert had become Sir Osbert; and Renishaw and Montegufoni (originally bought in his name) now belonged to him. But he was left little money. This lack was mitigated by the legacy of £10,000 that he had just received from the late Mrs. Ronald Greville, the wealthy, widowed society hostess and daughter of a Scotch millionaire, who had taken Osbert up as a very young man just after the First World War and who did not at the end let him down.

Sir George's original bequest of £1,000 a year to Edith had been cut by a codicil to £60. Sacheverell's share too had been cut. What remained of Sir George's fortune was to skip a generation and go to Sacheverell's sons, Reresby and Francis. There were, belatedly, a few further benefits from his death: in 1948 Edith received £6,454 of Canadian Pacific Railway 4 percent preference stock and some Swift International shares, originally part of Lady Ida's estate.

The will was bad enough; but in the spring of 1944 they found out just how little remained of the money in Sir George's Swiss account. "£78,000 had gone," Edith told Stephen Spender in June 1944. "The last £10,000 was settled on his host, although he had declared, three months before, the old man unfit to make a will."[2] Edith, writing to her friends about her father's death, used impersonal phrases ("the old man") in every case, whether for fear of the censor or of incurring a libel action, from lack of filial feeling, or from a sense of melodrama. She had already written to Spender in May telling him "a story about an old man of 82, very tyrranical [sic], very obstinate, distrusting his own family, trusting every fraud, —plotting and plotting to get his eldest son's inheritance away from him, (partly for his own use, partly to leave to his grandchildren and problematic future heirs)."[3] As a result of that plotting, wrote Edith, the old man himself fell "into an unspeakable trap. . . . I see a shabby old tiger tamed in a circus; and an old man-eating tiger fighting, in an appalling bloodfight, a horribly spry youngish jackal. The jackal won. So far."

Edith decided that Woog had got Sir George's money off him, and then—to put it delicately—hastened his death. She came to this conclusion either via a projection of her own violent impulses, or just because she had an imagination that ran readily along such lines, having, as she did, a strong taste for criminology and murder stories.

Edith carried Osbert with her in her belief. Osbert got his secretary, Miss

Andrade, to take a letter from Sir George to a medium, whose baleful interpretations of the letter's emanations fed their morbid fears and hopes. Accounts of the old man's last days provided detail for Edith's imagination to work on, as in a letter to Evelyn Wiel of February 1945:

> Certainly there was coercion. But what else? What was the end? . . . Your friend and her brother got the most horrible letters . . . giggling and triumphant, and oh so friendly. One letter received just after the old man's death, said "The false teeth the nurse ordered have arrived." Fancy false teeth coming for a man who has been cremated![4]

And "once the old man got away from his guards into the garden (weak as he was, —just before his death). There was a ghastly scene before he could be got back into the house." He had brought it all upon himself because of his "wicked hatred of his eldest son, who is a most *noble* character," and who showed only "unresenting dignity over the *appalling* injury that has been done to him." Sir George had "played ducks and drakes" with Sachie's money too, and lost it all. "And now the old man is dead, the money gone. . . ."[5] Nothing of course could be done. Woog retained his legacy; and some of the unaccountable losses turned out to be the responsibility of the bank.

Small wonder that in October 1943 Edith was writing to put Laurence Whistler off, since domestic problems were so bad that she "couldn't ask anyone to come and see us."[6] Small wonder that when Arthur Waley, whom she loved, came to stay, she particularly resented the presence of his mistress, Beryl de Zoete, whom she could not stand. Beryl had a habit of sending them visitors as unwelcome as herself: "She has an invariable flair for the people one least wants to see," Edith complained to Mrs. Gorer.

Nor was this all Edith had to contend with. In view of Osbert's mammoth project of writing a five-volume autobiography, Edith was eschewing autobiography for the moment, since "much of our material would clash," as she explained in March 1943 to John Lehmann, who wanted something of hers along these lines for his *New Writing and Daylight*. Sacheverell was then working on what was to be his book of personal impressions, *Splendours and Miseries*; Edith had read much of the work in progress, and thought it one of the best things he had done. The book came out in December 1943, and Sacheverell, in a final chapter called "Songs My Mother Taught Me," was not inhibited by his brother's work: He wrote about childhood, and about their mother, in the most tender, lyrical terms.

Coming on top of the misery and melodrama attendant on their father's death, Sachie's extended hymn of love to the mother who had rejected Edith was just too much for her. She railed to David Horner in December, "She is represented as a gentle sweet woman brimming over with mother-love. . . . I really haven't any words to say what he has done to *me* by that chapter." Sachie had succeeded in "leaving me alone with the hell of my childhood," seemingly conveying "that it was all *my* fault." He "raised up the whole of my childhood and youth . . . and has succeeded in fusing into my mind the whole of the way in which Father, as well, has behaved."

The pain lasted all through Christmas 1943; on January 6, 1944, Edith was writing to Stephen Spender with greater control, having persuaded herself that Sachie had distorted the truth out of his own need.

> I've been very unhappy. . . . Poor Sachie—who would do anything in the world rather than cause me a moment's pain—created for himself (simply because he has been extremely unhappy in some ways) a wonderful dream-mother who understood everything . . . the facts were sadly and terribly different. Though nothing did fall on him, actually: the horror was all mine.[7]

The truth is that there is more than one truth—even, mercifully, in relation to so inadequate a person as Lady Ida. Sacheverell was telling *his* truth, as even Edith acknowledged here; and who is to say that there was no shred of another truth in the construction Edith put on it? "But what with all the dreadful memories, and the realisation of how unhappy he must have been, to have made this dream picture, I've been feeling pretty grim." What made her really unhappy was the renewed sense of personal failure and rejection. To make fun of the despised "Gingers" all together, to fight a common enemy, was one thing. To feel she had all along been on her own in her despair, outside a magic circle, was something quite different. Nor is it strange that in her mid-fifties she should feel herself "left alone with the hell of her childhood." Increasing age makes the past real and near again; and Edith had no buffer between herself and her childhood, no home that she had made, no children of her own with whom and for whom to compensate for her own early unhappiness.

Osbert, aware of this crisis and closer, during the war, to Edith, was more understanding and circumspect when he wrote about their childhood in his autobiography, without betraying his own vision of Lady Ida. When his first volume, *Left Hand, Right Hand!*, came out in 1945, Edith wrote to Stephen

Spender: "In this wonderful book, I feel that something has been made of my parents' useless lives. And I remember that I shall never see them again. And that I am intensely proud of the book."[8]

Those whose lot was harder than her own were never far from Edith's mind; all merged in the sense of general suffering. Friends died, and were mourned: Demetrios Capetanakis, John Lehmann's close friend, who died not from gunfire but leukemia; Laurence Whistler's wife, who died in childbirth three months after his brother Rex—who had painted a small and beautiful portrait of Edith in the early 1920s—had been killed. A soldier, unknown to Edith, with literary aspirations—a Gunner Rhys—wrote her an eloquent complaint about conditions in the army that touched her heart; she sent it on to John Sparrow, now at the War Office, who took a more robust view: "I should be very much surprised if he were a good poet—judging not by his prose style but by the quality of emotion displayed in his letter. There! Edith! I am sorry. I think that you are, as ever, far too kindhearted and noble."

Towards the end of the war, in the summer of 1944, her cousin Veronica Gilliat's son was killed. "I think it quite probable she will go mad,"[9] Edith told John Lehmann on August 28. The shock and horror "shrivel one's emotions, and, too, in a strange way, one's language." Shock and horror reached even nearer home that summer, to Renishaw itself, where one of the maids, now in the W.R.N.S., heard a week after her wedding that her young husband was missing. Edith, sitting with her, worked on her poem of suffering and death, "The Song of the Cold."

Earlier, in 1941, there had been Virginia Woolf's suicide; in her letter of condolence to Leonard Woolf Edith had written, "Perhaps the day will come when we shall think 'at least she was spared seeing people sink lower and lower,—and all the new desecrations and shames,' but at the moment that doesn't help at all." Not that Edith was now among those who had the highest opinion of Virginia Woolf as a writer—"not an important artist at all," she had said airily in a letter to Demetrios Capetanakis. In print, in *English Women*, she extolled Virginia Woolf's brilliance and her radiant personality, but said of the characters in her novels: "I do not think that they tell us the secrets of their hearts. . . . They do not live dangerously, the great adventures are not theirs." Virginia Woolf, for her part, told J. R. Ackerley, the literary editor of the *Listener*, on October 4, 1940, that "the Sitwells, as a family, bore me."[10]

Edith was not a great admirer of Leonard Woolf, either, and later encouraged John Lehmann when he was thinking of leaving the Hogarth Press:

> I am perfectly sure you are right to strike out on your own, and to leave all the deadening Hogarth influence behind you . . . wrong, and maddening for you to be hampered by Mr. Woolf's crotchetiness and small outlook and timidity. I have always felt that about him. He has got all the Puritan Fathers' makeup, but without their fire and resolution and courage.

But by that time she was much closer to John Lehmann than she had ever been to Virginia or Leonard Woolf.

He had still been "Dear Mr. Lehmann" when he wrote to her after the publication of her *A Poet's Notebook* in spring 1943, asking her to write for *New Writing and Daylight*. Lehmann himself wrote in his autobiography that "to most of us in London it seemed, when *Street Songs* was published early in 1942, that another great event had happened in English poetry."[11] Soon he had become one of Edith's most trusted friends and professional allies, and a constant correspondent. He understood what she was trying to do, and as an editor he could help her to present her new poetry as and how she wanted to. Nor was the traffic all one way: She discussed his own poetry with him, and was endlessly encouraging.

Others writers too now seemed sympathetic to her, where previously she had withdrawn her skirts: Henry Reed, who wrote appreciatively about her in *New Writing*; Louis MacNeice, whose poetry she now found "superb," whereas in her Northcliffe Lectures she had condemned it as "sticky in texture, or disintegrated, gritty and sabulous." Decades earlier, she had said to the painter C. R. W. Nevinson, who had done a portrait of her, "I always felt that success would be the one thing that would do me good." Certainly her wartime success made her less defensive towards other poets, less ready to fly into attack—for a while. Now she was seeing Roy Campbell again, whom she had met as an undergraduate long ago; and she was patching up her quarrel with John Hayward.

There was one brief and vivid wartime friendship that was terminated prematurely by death. In 1942 Denton Welch was an aspiring writer of twenty-seven, a semi-invalid after a serious accident seven years earlier when a car had run into his bicycle. The accident left him frail both physically and emotionally:

Denton Welch was introspective, fastidious, unstable, and gifted as both a painter and a writer. In August 1942 *Horizon* published an account he had written of a visit to the Sitwells' old friend the painter Walter Sickert. Edith wrote to the young author, out of the blue, one of her long, openhearted letters, telling him that she and Osbert had "laughed till they cried" over his article, and that he was a "born writer."

She sent him a signed copy of *Street Songs*, and arranged to write the foreword to his first book, *Maiden Voyage*, which was about to be published and was now to be dedicated to her. "It's a wonderful event in one's life, when one's first book comes out," she wrote to him on October 25. "My first book was one of five pages; it had dark brown paper covers, and I paid £5 10s. — a vast sum to me at that time, to have it published." This was *The Mother*; it had cost 6d., "and it is now worth anything up to £10 a copy! Isn't that strange?"[12] Denton Welch wrote in his journal on October 31: "It is so funny, so winey, so toxic, always to be hearing fine things about one's attempts from someone famous. How much she says with no fear of using words full of feeling. There is beauty in someone being generous, even if it should lead to difficulties of misunderstanding and withdrawal."[13] That Christmas he sent her a topaz ring.

In April 1943, Edith sent him a telegram bidding him to lunch at the Sesame Club. He had to come up from the country, but was there in good time, as nervous as a cat: "Into the drab hall of the Sesame Club, basket chairs, ugliness," he wrote in his journal afterwards, "in a fright that I might not recognize Edith Sitwell":

Then the tall figure dressed all in black, black trilby, Spanish witch's hat, black cloak, black satin dress to the ankles and two huge aquamarine rings. Wonderful rings on powder-white hands, and face so powder-pearly, nacreous white, almost not to be believed in, with the pinkened mouth, the thin, delicate swordlike nose and tender-curling nostrils. No hair, I remember no hair at first. The rings, the glistening satin, and the kid-white skin.

They had drinks in the bar, then went in to lunch. She talked about his writing.

"Now I think is the time for you to do something violent and vulgar," she said.

The words struck a bell in me.

"That's what I'm longing to do," I said. . . .

"I will tell you what your danger is; it is your ingrowing toe-nail. Everything in, in, in."

She bent her very dignified head and brought her two hands up to it in movements rhythmical, swirling, in-turning.

After lunch Osbert appeared, by arrangement, and joined them. "Edith Sitwell began a remark, but her brother followed closely with one of his own. She leant back, silencing herself at once. It was as if she left him to talk and be amusing, now that he had come."[14]

They did not meet again. Edith sent Denton Welch her new books as they came out, and she invited him to the Sesame Club again, but his health deteriorated and he was never well enough to come. He died at the end of December 1948. Edith was in New York at the time. "Poor little Denton, I am filled with sadness about him," she wrote to John Lehmann.

It had been the publication of *Street Songs* that brought Edith back into the limelight, and made her honoured in her own country as never before. Her other major wartime collection, *Green Song* (the title poem, dedicated to David Horner, had appeared in *Life and Letters To-Day* in December 1942) came out in August 1944; Macmillan was not overestimating the demand in its first printing of five thousand copies. The American edition, brought out by Vanguard, was embellished with a Tchelitchew portrait of Edith as a frontispiece.

Between these two important collections Edith's renewed fertility flowed into other, minor channels, and there was a performance of *Façade* at the Wigmore Hall in May 1942. She contributed *English Women* to the list of titles Collins produced in the "Britain in Pictures" series, edited by W. J. Turner—a series of short books with texts by distinguished authors written as a patriotic duty, for a flat fee of £50, on aspects of British history and culture; in the climate of war they were extremely popular and sold very well. *English Women*—which Edith called her "propaganda book"—was not a demanding commission. It consists of brief pieces—only a few hundred words each—on figures from Elizabeth I onwards: travellers, actresses, philanthropists, writers. It is written in a lively manner, though the figures are rather arbitrarily chosen and treated. The most notable piece is on Elizabeth I, with whose personality Edith felt she had a strong affinity, and whom she grew to resemble physically.

Elizabeth was, she wrote, from some points of view barren and from some "infinitely fertile": "That high courage of the lion, and the lion's heart, the lion's rages, contrasted with the subtle mind; that 'pride of the peacock which is the glory of God,' coupled with the knowledge that it was the Queen, and not the woman, that was loved. . . . " In her notebook draft of this passage she called Elizabeth I "this Queen Bee of all Queen Bees," in anticipation of the title she would give to her book about her, *The Queens and the Hive*, nearly twenty years later. "Bee-priestess" was one of Pavlik's names for Edith herself.

Some Englishwomen get short shrift from Edith in her "propaganda book." "I find it difficult to read her works at this time," she says of George Eliot. Great sympathy is shown towards two women who made their brothers the objects of their devotion—Dorothy Wordsworth and Christina Rossetti—and towards their respective, respected Williams. Edith thought that Dorothy's attachment to Wordsworth was entirely natural and commendable, and that Dorothy was in love with Coleridge "without knowing it." As for Christina Rossetti, "Goblin Market," she wrote, was "perhaps the most perfect poem written by a woman in the English language."

In April 1943 Macmillan published *A Poet's Notebook*, which was warmly received by critics who in other times might have noted the inclusion of some well-worn material from her *Alexander Pope*, from her introductions to *Edith Sitwell's Anthology* and *The Pleasures of Poetry*, and from the ill-fated *Aspects of Modern Poetry*. But principally the book is a collection under subject headings of aphorisms and quotations about poetry, and also about music and painting, by practitioners of these arts. All the quotations had been copied out by Edith at some time in her working notebooks, and for this reason the book has a very intimate air. The pieces quoted have impressed or moved her, and the reader is moved at second hand by the intensity of feeling, the dedication, the oil-lamp whiff of the autodidact's solitary hours, over long years spent reading, responding, copying out. *A Poet's Notebook* is a far finer gauge of the quality of Edith's aesthetic and critical sense than are any of her more finished displays of assessment and technical analysis.

She compiled another anthology during 1943, which came out as *Planet and Glow-Worm: A Book for the Sleepless* in March 1944. *The Times Literary Supplement* was among the periodicals in which her new poems were welcomed; "Heart and Mind" first appeared there, in June 1943. And in the summer that *Green Song* was published, Edith and Osbert both became Fellows of the Royal Society of Literature.

If one adds to this great increase of Edith's creative activity the public readings, the generous friendships, the copious, supportive letter writing, and the hospitality given at Renishaw and at the Sesame Club to writers, painters, poor relations, and friends on leave or in need, it becomes evident that during the war she embodied in her own life the new hope that swept through her work. Now she tells "Tales of the old world's holiness, finds veins of ore / In the unripe wheat-ear," as she wrote in "Invocation," the Yeatsian poem she sent to John Lehmann, which is dedicated to Alec and Merula Guinness and included in *Green Song*:

> I who was once a golden woman like those who walk
> In the dark heavens—but am now grown old
> And sit by the fire, and see the fire grow cold,
> Watch the dark fields for a rebirth of faith and of wonder.

Her novel had ended in sterile darkness. Now she felt the influence of a benign life-force that she sometimes called the Sun, "the first lover of all the world."

Bryher, in her dry way, spelled out the purely practical contribution the Sitwells made to Britain at war:

> During the war when writers were considered "useless mouths," Osbert and Edith had fought to keep a skeleton of the arts alive. They gave parties to help the strays among us, they assisted those who were suffering not only from lack of funds but extreme isolation, and although they did not agree with their views, they did their best to keep conscientious objectors out of prison.[15]

An example of Edith's attitude to conscientious objection was the gently astringent way in which, while trying most energetically to find "safe" civilian jobs for Raymond Marriott and his friend George Bullock, she had ended a letter in October 1939: "I wonder if there is not some national work which would not harm your conscience as pacifists?—Pacifists in the last war did work for the nation."[16]

Bryher ended her praise for the Sitwells' own "work for the nation" with the reflection that "a few intimate friends apart, nobody thanked them when the war was over." But it was not quite over yet.

20

The Terrible Rain
1944-1946

In August 1944 news reached Renishaw that Montegufoni was safe. It had been neither bombed nor blasted. It had been sequestrated by the Italian government and used as a repository to store some of the greatest paintings from the Uffizi and Pitti galleries in Florence, and from churches and museums all over Tuscany, watched over by Sir George's old agent, Guido Masti. As many as two thousand refugees shared the castle with the paintings. The novelist Eric Linklater, with the Allied forces advancing on Florence, was the first British officer to go into Montegufoni. With a small detachment he came through the vineyard and up the terrace, and entered the Sitwells' castle through a French window. He saw what looked like a very good reproduction of Botticelli's *Birth of Venus* propped up just inside—it was the real thing. The *Primavera* was there too, and the great Madonnas of Cimabue, Giotto, and Duccio, Piero della Francesca's Duke and Duchess of Urbino, and Uccello's *Battle of San Romano*. The Germans had turned out the refugees and occupied the castle; they had used a circular Ghirlandaio, face upwards, as a dining table, but no serious harm had come to anything else.

In London, the summer of 1944 was ruined by the buzz bombs, the V-1s, which were a strain hardly to be borne in the fifth year of the war. Everyone was tired; "apart from the very young," said Bryher, "few of us *wanted* to live." The sense of lost years was in everyone's mind as the war drew to a close; Bryher wrote that "it was only routine that was holding us together and once it broke . . . everything snapped. People quarrelled mercilessly with those for whom they had made great sacrifices and the worst in us all came to the surface."[1] It was the same at Renishaw, as Edith indicated to William Plomer on September 5:

> Nobody to whom one writes answers any letters,—but strangers from all over England send me poems. The bell-ringers are practising, and it is

raining like a cloud-burst. Susan (Robins's wife) is crying because the gardener (whom she hates) has sold somebody else whom she hates some tomatoes. He did this weeks ago, but she has only just found out.

Complaints of another sort reached Edith from the other side of the Atlantic. Geoffrey Gorer wrote to her from Washington in October that Pavlik, in New York, was

> completely tied up in his very elaborate social life, which cannot possibly be disarranged to give an hour to an old friend. This may sound bitter, and I think it is rather; but I also think New York has had quite a disastrous effect on him, on the one hand encouraging his social proclivities and *Vogue* appurtenances (once he couldn't see me because he was dining with Cecil Beaton . . .) and on the other developing all sorts of very pseudo and pretentious mysticism, chiefly I suppose under the influence of dear Charles Henri.

Amid the rigours of world war, the familiar song has a tinny ring. Edith herself was still hearing regularly from Pavlik. In 1945 she published a poem called "The Two Loves" in *New Writing and Daylight*, dedicated "To Pavel Tchelitchew and his work in progress," in which she expressed some of the nature mysticism which he discussed not only with Charles Henri but with her:

> And great is the heat of the fires from elementary and terrestrial nature —
> Ripening the kernel of amethysts in the sun of the peach —
> The dancing seas in the heart of the apricot.

In the relative security of her long-distance communion with Pavlik, she put into "The Two Loves" her understanding of his fear of the female, and her own sublimated love:

> And the lover seeing in Woman the rankness of Nature, —
> A monstrous Life-force, the need of procreation
> Devouring all other life . . . or Gravity's force
> Drawing him down to the centre of his earth.
>
> . . .
>
> I see Christ's wounds weep in the Rose on the wall.
> Then I who nursed in my earth the dark red seeds of Fire —

The pomegranate grandeur, the dark seeds of Death,
Felt them change to the light and fire in the heart of the rose. . . .

The bomb-ridden summer of 1944 saw Edith at another famous reading
behaving with a courage and panache that became, in the telling and retelling
of the story by those present, legendary. She, Osbert, and Sacheverell were
giving the second of two readings from their own work at the Churchill Club
in London. This was a club for Allied officers set up in Ashburnham House,
part of Westminster School, which had been evacuated for the duration. The
club was run by Randolph Churchill's then wife, Pamela.

The room was crowded with officers—British, Canadian, American—and
with friends. The Pipers were there, and John Lehmann. Osbert read first, and
talked a little about his work in progress, the autobiography. Then it was
Edith's turn. What happened is described by one of those present, Donald
Sutherland:

She had not been reading for many minutes when an air-raid siren
sounded its warning, at that period an indication that enemy flying
bombs had crossed the coast. . . . Edith Sitwell was reading her poem
"Still Falls the Rain" with its sombre repetition of that phrase, and its
inspiration the raids of 1940. By now one could hear the sinister throb of
the approaching buzz bomb, but she read on

"Still falls the Rain
In the Field of Blood where the small hopes breed. . . ."

Suddenly from the Dean's Yard outside, the shrill whistle of the Warden
sounded, warning all who heard it to take shelter.[2]

There was, not unnaturally, an "audible restlessness" among the audience, but
Edith read on as if nothing were amiss, and no one dared to make a move. "It
was a magnificent performance," wrote John Lehmann, "worthy of a British
admiral coolly dictating orders from the bridge in the middle of a naval
engagement. She held the whole audience in the grip of her discipline. . . ."[3]
The bomb grew louder and louder; it came very close; the windows of the
room were all wide open, and it seemed the bomb might come straight in on
them all:

As the bomb came overhead, its engine died and one knew with the relief born of experience that with its load of death and destruction it must glide on beyond the immediate vicinity. Edith still read on, coming finally to her last line,

"Still do I love, still shed my innocent light, my Blood, for thee."[4]

As she finished, the bomb exploded, perhaps a mile away. There was deafening applause, "a mingling perhaps of relief with appreciation." "It was never revealed," added Donald Sutherland, whether Edith "had failed to hear the Warden's take-shelter warning, or whether deliberately to avoid the panic of her audience trying to make a hasty retreat from a crowded room she had courageously chosen to ignore the Warden's warning."

Edith did reveal precisely what she had felt, in a letter to Evelyn Wiel:

I had just stood up to read a poem of mine about the 1940 air raids, when the warning went, and then the chug-chug-chug of the V-1 bomb, and the whistle blew. Which is the signal of imminent danger!!! I must say I *did* feel rather old-fashioned, as the thing was just over the roof, where it remained chugging about *throughout* the poem!!! However I continued to read as if nothing was happening, and the thing by a miracle went away. But of course some other poor wretches got it. I tell you this because it seems part of daily life, and you told me to tell you daily life.[5]

Communication with Evelyn—and with Choura, whose husband had died—became easier after the liberation of Paris that autumn; they all watched scenes of the familiar streets crowded with soldiers and civilians on the cinema newsreels, and old memories were stirred. Now Edith could pour out her concern and reassurance to Evelyn in long letters. She told her again of her recurring dreams of the rue Saint-Dominique, and still "I miss you every day of my life." She was going to send Evelyn £16 a month. Evelyn, in her turn, poured out a torrent of affection and complaint. There is a touch of asperity in some of Edith's responses: "Shabby? Poor darling.... But let me tell you, everyone is shabby here, because of coupons!! I, being immense, can have no new clothes, and look like nothing on earth."[6]

Edith was in London for a long visit in the autumn of 1944, after the Churchill Club reading. She gave a great many Sesame Club parties, sometimes in collaboration with Osbert—"giant tea-parties" and lunch and dinner parties where Lehmann and the Spenders were among the most frequent guests. Amid the dowdy and sometimes disapproving feminine respectability of the Sesame Club's membership, Edith was "as out of place as a hoopoe among starlings,"[7] John Lehmann thought. But the club, even during the war, had a good chef; the entertainment was very much grander than it had been at Pembridge Mansions. Her large parties were not, Lehmann went on, "the ideal occasions for getting to know Edith," even though there was a "lottery excitement" as to who one's fellow guests were going to be. Some of her most affectionate and oldest friends—William Walton, the Kenneth Clarks, T. S. Eliot—preferred not to come to the "giant tea-parties," now or later: "I will come and see you any time," said Walton, "but not those awful friends you surround yourself with."

Maurice Bowra, who had written with great understanding about her poetry, was a regular guest; from him and his books Edith learnt a great deal that interested her about the poetry of Valéry and "that extraordinary electric battery" Apollinaire. It is surprising that Helen's conditioning, and her French connections, had not thoroughly familiarized her with these writers already. Edith's reading was wide but haphazard; Helen had been her only teacher, and their choice of literature had been arbitrary. In 1937, when Edith was working on her anthology for Gollancz, Norman Collins, Victor Gollancz's right-hand man, had written in an internal memo that he was "quite amazed to find what poems she considered to be little known, and she admitted that it was only comparatively recently that she has really read anything! She spoke of Keats's "Hyperion" and Blake's Lyrics as being things that no one has read." He should not have taken her so literally. Edith had read all Keats as a girl, and was quoting Blake in the 1920s. She wanted poetry in general, and her anthology in particular, to be popular in the true sense of the word—and a spot-check of the passersby in an English high street would not, then or now, produce many instances of familiarity with Blake, or even with Keats. Yet there is a sense in which what Norman Collins said was true. It is also true that, among specialists, she was boxing above her weight.

John Lehmann introduced her to the work of Hölderlin now too; and she, for her part, used her "great new friends" to try to find a publisher for a new protégé, José Garcia Villa. He was a Filipino living in New York who had sent her his poems, some of which, she told Spender on September 8, 1944, "are really *lovely*," and some "so awful that my blood turns to blocks of ice in my veins."[8] The fact that he was a Filipino caught Edith's imagination; she enjoyed the fantasy that he was some kind of magic iguana, and wrote to

Georgia that "it is so extraordinary to think of this presumably minute, dark green creature, the colour of New Zealand jade, spinning these sharp flame-like poems out of himself. Of course some are bad. . . . "9

She wanted Spender to get one of Garcia Villa's poems into *Horizon*; but it was not until May 1949, only a few months before the magazine ceased publication, that his poems—seven of them—appeared in its pages. (The most remarkable characteristic of Garcia Villa's poems is the presence of a comma between every single word of every single line, resulting, as he claimed in his prefatory note, in "a lineal pace of quiet dignity and distinction.")

Osbert had spent Christmas at Badminton, "clamped to Queen Mary and I can't get at him," as Edith complained to Natasha Spender; and to Georgia: "I am going to spend *mine* in bed." All through the war Osbert had been summoned at intervals to amuse the old Queen, sequestered with the Sitwells' Beaufort cousins at Badminton for the duration; the Christmas visit, Edith informed Stephen Spender, "apparently entails wearing a paper cap and being very jolly."10

Edith herself was working on a book about Shakespeare, and worrying about the sabotage efforts of the "pipsqueakery": James Agate had been making fun of Osbert, and she defended her brother and vilified Agate in a review of Osbert's *Noblesse Oblige*, the offending work, in *Horizon* that January. J. R. Ackerley had deprecated Demetrios Capetanakis in the *Listener*; Julian Symons had criticized her own poetry as being "removed from life"; in fact, she wrote to Lehmann while Osbert was being jolly with Queen Mary, "The dregs of the literary population have risen as one worm to insult me"—phrasing, as John Pearson has written, "that only Edith could have used."11

Yet both Osbert and she had experienced a renaissance of their writing lives during the war; Edith had against all odds responded to horror and social isolation with a flowering of feeling and expression, and reaped a harvest of recognition. In her wartime poetry she spoke for those without a voice. She had become a revered and a formidable figure. The new generation of British composers, looking for words to set to music, turned to hers: In 1944 "The Weeping Babe" was set by Michael Tippett, and "O Ye Forgive" by Elisabeth Lutyens. And vicariously—"Helen would have been so happy," she wrote to Evelyn Wiel in February, "because the most lovely settings of her translations from Rimbaud have just been done by a young composer who is Willie Walton's runner-up . . . oh his name escapes me for the moment: he is terrifically famous too—Oh yes, Benjamin Britten."12

When the war in Europe was finally over in May 1945, Edith, at Renishaw and far from the scenes of communal rejoicing, felt only that emotional exhaustion which Bryher had described as widespread the previous autumn. At the beginning of the war, it had been the sense of waste that had oppressed her. Now, she told John Lehmann, she was *"beyond* registering anything . . . if one once begins to think of the young lives! Believe me, one would go *raving mad!"* She walked about, she said, "with tears in my eyes."

On September 10, 1945, Edith and Osbert gave a reading in the Royal Pavilion at Brighton. In the audience was Hubert Nicholson, a young left-wing writer with whom Edith had corresponded. She was wearing for the occasion, as he has recalled,

> a black, voluminous dress with a dark fur, but she enlivened the effect with a scarlet turban and the largest jewels I had ever seen. . . . Her face, like her figure, had grown softer and vaguer over the years. Her small mouth was pursed and her tiny eyes seemed to fade away entirely. Having broken a toe, she had to read sitting down. . . . But even her voice had faded and was sometimes barely audible. She couldn't, in any case, manage the mike.[13]

The truth was that she had been shocked. She has described that day herself: how she and Osbert went to Brighton by train, and in the train Osbert leaned over and handed her the *Times*, pointing to a paragraph in it—"a description by an eye-witness of the horror at Hiroshima": "That witness had seen a totem pole of dust arise to the sun . . . a totem pole . . . the symbol of life, the symbol of creation. From the moment of reading the paragraph, the poem began in my brain and blood."[14]

But she did not begin to write her first Hiroshima poem—"The Shadow of Cain"—until April of the following year; Hubert Nicholson reviewed it in *Adam* when it was published.

The sequence of glorious forays to London followed by withdrawals to the chilly seclusion of Renishaw was a feature of Edith's postwar years—a recipe for mood swings of the most extreme kind. Her visits to Sacheverell and Georgia at Weston brought unalloyed happiness; but they were only visits. She did not consider living in her house in Bath, and sold it in 1949. "Of course I understand about the Bath house," Bryher wrote to her from Switzerland in September of that year; "everything in England has changed so much since those early war times when we thought of it." She enclosed a "small cheque," which was not small, for Edith's birthday, as she always did.

In November 1945 Macmillan had brought out *The Song of the Cold*, which, though it was principally a collection of her already published recent poems, brought Edith further tributes. The title poem, first published in *Penguin New Writing*, was dedicated to Natasha Litvin (Spender). Cyril Connolly was now an ardent convert to her poems. He had used her "Euridice," which she had dedicated to John Lehmann, as the lead piece in *Horizon* for August 1945, and now wrote to say that "Natasha's poem"—"The Song of the Cold"—was "a staggering poem, like a symphony composed around one single octave," and that he had seen Maurice Bowra in Oxford, who said Edith was "writing now the greatest poems of our time." Connolly even asked Edith to be his literary executor; this was a very eccentric request, but a measure of the nature of her new standing.

Connolly also told Edith in a later, undated letter from Malaga, "I think your habit of dedicating all your poems may antagonise some reviewers by suggesting a coterie of 'best people' from which they are excluded." Other of her literary habits exercised other friends and admirers. In April 1946 Spender published an article in *Horizon* entitled "Poetry for Poetry's Sake and Poetry Beyond Poetry": Edith's was of the former kind, he said. "Her greatness really lies in her ability to project the growth of her whole personality into her poetry," and to reveal "the interior life of the spirit." Without questioning this greatness, Spender did, however, try to come to grips with what every serious reader of Edith's poetry has to be concerned about: the repetitiveness of her later work.

Earlier, in a praising review of *Street Songs* in *Horizon* (February 1942), Spender had referred unequivocally to the "monotonous themes and mannerisms which have now become literary vices." The Ape, the Tiger, the Lion, the Sun, the Bone, the Cold, the Rose, Ixion's wheel, the Fall of Man, the heart of man, "I, an old man," "I, an old woman," gold, wheat, honey, blood, "the road from Nothing to Nowhere," "the terrible Rain"—the phrases and images, even whole lines, recur—the code and cipher of Edith's obsessions.

Her own explanation, or defence, was that if something has been expressed as perfectly as possible, an alternative form of expression would necessarily be imperfect, to which the answer can only be: Why express the same thought more than once? But Edith Sitwell came to poetry through music and through the music of words. It is the familiar character of a composer's musical phrasing, intervals, and—to use that favourite term of Edith's—texture, that tell even a technically inexpert ear whether a piece is by Prokofiev, Brahms, or Britten. A painting is recognised as its creator's by a familiar palette, customary techniques of composition, even by often-repeated themes. Variations on a theme, in either music or painting, are not in themselves signals of weakness or of failure in inventiveness—very often the reverse is true. Edith felt for poetry in the same way.

But according to the conventions that have grown up around the art of words, repetitiveness is at best rhetoric, and at worst repetitiveness and no more. For readers and critics for whom this seems true—and that means most people—Edith Sitwell simply published too much. Phrases and images that seem startling and strong the first time are not only diminished in their second and third appearances; the proliferation dilutes even the memory of that initial impact. Yet the very fact that her familiar emblems, from her wartime poetry to the end of her life, carry so consistent a message, or myth, means that one can speak of the "music" of Edith Sitwell as one can of few modern poets. Spender called her war poems "prodigious hymns"; and their recurring rhythms, rhymes, resolutions, are like the Psalms, or passages from the Old Testament: incantatory, secure in their base, locked in a system of symbol and reference for which there is no more adequate word than "religion."

Frederick Prokosch has suggested why and how it was that for so many people Edith seemed to be writing, as Kenneth Clark said, "the greatest poems of the war." There was, in those emotionally heightened years,

> a powerful reaction against Auden, and a resurgence of traditional influences, of traditional imagery and metrics. . . . Two figures seem largely associated with this tendency: Dylan Thomas and Edith Sitwell. Both are cryptic, incantatory poets (in their recent work) and both employ a highly developed system of symbols quite unlike Auden's, quite removed from everyday life, highly nostalgic and almost archaic; both are superlative craftsmen. [15]

The new romanticism was not sustained by Edith and Dylan alone. The group calling themselves Apocalypse—Nicholas Moore, Henry Treece, J. F. Hendry, G. S. Fraser—published their significant anthology *The White Horseman* in 1941. They were against the machine-age influence on poetry, and hopeful of myth as a means of integrating personality. Edith belonged, with them, to Dionysus, not Apollo. And the impulse that permitted her to repeat lines and phrases like mantras, combined with her incantatory "copying out" method of composing, meant that although the spirit of her wartime poetry was very different from that of, say, *Bucolic Comedies*, the essential drive was the same: the music and the magic of words. She wrote to Maurice Bowra, of *Street Songs*: "It is a dangerous thing to say, but I can say it to you. Sometimes, when I begin a poem, it is almost like automatic writing. Then I use my mind on it afterwards."[16] Edith wrote of one of her poems that she took most seriously, "Gold Coast Customs," that "down to the sixth verse the poem is obviously nothing but abstract sound—abstract, but I would like to think significant."[17] While this approach to writing is exciting and stimulating in her early poetry, such an arbitrary grab for significance in ambitious poetry of life, death, war, anguish, original sin, redemption, and spiritual rebirth makes one uneasy. The poet may turn up a jewel; or he may just churn up, for the tenth time, the stale and shallow waters of his overfished subconscious.

The most celebrated of her war poems is probably "Still Falls the Rain," the first poem in *Street Songs*:

Still falls the Rain—
Dark as the world of man, black as our loss—
Blind as the nineteen hundred and forty nails
Upon the Cross.

Still falls the Rain
With a sound like the pulse of the heart that is changed
    to the hammer-beat
In the Potter's Field, and the sound of the impious feet
On the Tomb:
        Still falls the Rain
In the Field of Blood where the small hopes breed and the human brain
Nurtures its greed, that worm with the brow of Cain.

Still falls the Rain
At the feet of the Starved Man hung upon the Cross,
Christ that each day, each night, nails there, have mercy on us—
On Dives and on Lazarus:
Under the Rain the sore and the gold are as one. . . .

"With religious poetry there is no room for the imagination," Edith wrote to Stephen Spender on April 9, 1942. "Imagination would make me a liar."[18] In this particular poem, " 'The nineteen hundred and forty nails upon the Cross' was my way of concentrating my feeling of the appalling cruelty of that waste!—All those years!" When Julian Symons undertook to be tough about this poem, he wrote: "Is it merely pernickety to point out that rain is itself not black nor even dark, and that even in its symbolic meaning (Rain = bombs) black does not seem a right or powerful word? Is it impermissible to ask why the nails on the cross are called blind, and to wonder how they could possibly see?"[19] Yes, it is merely pernickety. There is fiercely powerful imagery that is not literally or easily explained: What about Shelley's "white radiance of eternity," or Yeats's "gong-tormented sea"? But Symons is, obliquely, onto something that is important—the fact that Edith Sitwell wrote loosely, accumulating imagery under the influence of "inspiration," or suggestion, or association (however precise she was technically), and that she believed poetry should be written that way, imprecisely and instinctively. In December 1943 she wrote to Demetrios Capetanakis, "I think Keats was one of the greatest poets ever born in England; he was born for poetry as a race-horse is born to race." But, she said, he was short on intellect. "The fact that he had no brain didn't prevent him, in the slightest, from being a great poet. People *will* mix up poetry and intellect."

The point may be—if we overlook her underestimation of Keats—that the great poet can achieve intuitively, by a shortcut, the same vision that the intellectual glimpses dimly, and that he smudges further in his efforts to reach. But it is a question of horses for courses: Edith, when she dealt with the vast metaphysical universals, moved off into soft-focus mythology. It is when she takes a more limited subject that her vision has precision. When she is simpler, she is greater; as in "Any Man to Any Woman," from *Street Songs*:

> . . . And so I love you till I die—
> (Unfaithful I, the cannon's mate):
> Forgive my love of such brief span,
> But fickle is the flesh of man,
> And death's cold puts the passion out. . . .

The poem ends with a traditional lyric image:

> —A rainbow shining in the night,
> Born of my tears . . . your lips, the bright
> Summer-old folly of the rose.

She casts a spell—as do Walter de la Mare, Dylan Thomas, W. B. Yeats. Resist it, or succumb to it. There is no final quantifying of the strength of spells: Either they work or they do not. John Russell has told how Logan Pearsall Smith had by his bedside a "revolving ark" in whose shelves he kept his reference books. On the top, he placed selected new books—selected either for their extreme goodness or extreme badness. "With rising excitement, therefore," wrote John Russell, "I noted one day upon this dangerous shelf a copy of Miss Sitwell's *Green Song*":

> My host said "That's a very remarkable book. I had no idea there was poetry of that kind in the world any more. She's a real poet. When I first read those lines—how did they go?—
>
> > I who was once a golden woman like those who walk
> > In the dark heavens—but am now grown old
> > And sit by the fire, and see the fire grow cold
>
> I said to myself, 'There's the old voice of poetry, the old incantatory magic come back again.'" He paused for one of those coughs which marked, as it were, the bar-lines of his conversation. "'Yes,' I said to myself. 'Why yes—if that doesn't beat the bugs!'"[20]

Self-doubt always lay in wait behind Edith's success, and the habit of unease was not easily abandoned. Nor were old friends abandoned, now that, it seemed, she had come into her kingdom. At Christmas 1945 Evelyn Wiel made the first of what were to be regular visits to England. She came at Edith's expense, and at Edith's expense she was entertained. They stayed together at the Sesame Club, where Evelyn, provided by Edith with suitable clothes, enjoyed all the parties.

But Edith's loyalty to friends was occasionally misdirected. In 1946 Roy Campbell's *Talking Bronco* appeared, satirising, in the composite figure "Macspaunday," those left-wingers who had never taken up arms for their ideals. Spender and Day Lewis, two limbs of Macspaunday, were angry, but decided to take no action. Edith was rather too ready to fly into battle on their behalf. Day Lewis, who was then living with Rosamond Lehmann, wrote to Spender: "Edith, from who Rosamond received an indignant letter today, is girding herself up terrifically for the fray; if we are not careful, we shall find ourselves caught up in one of those Sitwell Charges of the Light Brigade: I must try to gag her somehow."[21]

Easter 1946 saw Edith gathering the faithful at the Sesame again—the Louis MacNeices and George Barker, the Henry Moores, and of course Lehmann and the Spenders—"you and Natasha with whom all parties of mine begin. I mean you are the centre and then I spread outwards."[22] At Renishaw she had written almost nothing. Periods of sterile melancholy assailed her there, which only copious letter writing alleviated. But just before Easter, while still at Renishaw, she had heard John Lehmann talking about her poetry on the wireless, and hope returned. "What have you not done for my poetry!" she wrote to him on March 28. "I think when I die I shall have to have inscribed on my tomb, 'She is still grateful to John Lehmann!'" Edith had needed "heartening": "I get fits of terrible depression. . . ." His broadcast had "made me feel poetry will soon come alive in me again." And she asked him to tea at the Sesame for April 10—"that is, if we don't have to go to a committee meeting about that ridiculous Poets' Reading."[23]

For Osbert, the major event of spring 1946 was his first visit to Montegufoni since before the war; he went with David Horner, opened up the house and took possession of his inheritance, and exorcised the ghost of his father. For Edith, there were two major events that spring. The first was that immediately after Lehmann's broadcast she was able to write again, and began working on "The Shadow of Cain." (As Dylan Thomas had said to Anthony Powell at one of her parties, "If poetry was taken away from Edith, she mightn't die, but she'd be bloody sick"—[24] and, recently, she had been bloody sick.) And the second was that Dylan Thomas himself re-entered Edith's orbit, bringing with him Caitlin, and comedy.

21

Postwar Fanfare
1946-1947

"That ridiculous Poets' Reading" was at the Wigmore Hall on May 14, 1946, organized by the Society of Authors. Queen Elizabeth and the two princesses were there again; and the readers were John Masefield (the Poet Laureate), Cecil Day Lewis, Walter de la Mare ("who is now very sweet (as ever) but definitely non-compos," Edith had written to David Horner after the committee meeting on March 14), T. S. Eliot, Edith Sitwell—and Dylan Thomas. Edith told Denys Kilham Roberts, of the Society of Authors, that she thought Dylan's recital of Blake's "Tyger" was "one of the greatest, the most impressive, the most truly wonderful things I have ever heard or witnessed."[1] She was, as ever, indulgent; Dylan's inordinately emphatic delivery, punctuated by long silences, was due to the fact that he was not sober.

Dylan had written to Edith six weeks before, on March 31, from the house in Oxford that he and Caitlin were renting from A. J. P. Taylor. His long letter was a masterpiece, a bravura flight of self-reproach and conciliation. He began by saying how much he regretted the "nine or ten years" that had passed since they had met, and how he had missed asking her advice about his writing:

I think that, in some way, I offended you, through some thoughtless, irresponsible written or spoken word, on some occassion [sic], those nine or ten years back. And I can't forgive myself that I can't remember what, exactly, the offence was, how crude or ignorant. Whatever it was, it seemed to stop, as though for ever, our writing to one another, let alone our meeting. May I say, now, as I know I should have said many years before, how sorry and, inarticulately, more than that, I am that some minor (oh, I hope so, minor) beastliness of mine, presumption, conceit, gaucherie, seeming-ingratitude, foul manner, callow pretension, or worse, yes, indeed, or far worse, interrupted our friendship, just beginning, and lost for so long, to me, the happiness and honour of being able to send my work, as it was written, to you, and to write to you of the never-ending-circling problems and doubts of craft and meaning that must always besiege us. If my apology, true as my love of your *Song of the Cold*, reads to you as stiltedly as, quickly writing, it sounds to me, I'm sorry again and can only say how hard I find it to move naturally into the long silence between now and nine beautiful, dreadful, years ago.

That is only one-quarter of the whole letter.

Of course he heard from her. And after the Wigmore Hall reading, Edith included Dylan and Caitlin Thomas in the "awful" dinner party she gave for all the participants, and a few more, at the Sesame. She wrote a great many letters after this party; and the precise nature of its disastrousness can be pieced together. Dylan, naturally, grew no more sober as the evening progressed. "D.T. was good as gold to *me*," she wrote to David Horner at Montegufoni on May 29, but he

suddenly felt an inescapable urge to fly at Tom Eliot on the subject of Milton. He muttered across me to Tom—"I'm surprised we were *allowed Milton*, this afternoon, I thought he was dead." Then in a tone of unspeakable scorn "*Dislodging* Milton with very little fuss. . . . "

Tom said mildly: "I can't be held responsible for what Leavis says." "Well you ought to *stop* him," said D. "And look here. Why does a poet like you publish such *awful* poetry. *You know* it's bad . . . . "

Worse followed with the pudding. Caitlin Thomas spilt some ice cream on her arm and ordered her neighbour, John Hayward, to lick it off. (Hayward, in his wheelchair, was beside Edith, with Sacheverell on her other side.) He refused. Caitlin insisted. Hayward said "he would lick it off any other part of her body but *not* in the dining room of the Sesame." "Mother of God!" she replied. "The insults of men! You great pansy!"

The Sesame had seen nothing like it. In the end Caitlin was led out of the dining room. Edith wrote apologising to Hayward for the "mixture of ennui and shock," and for the fact that Eliot too had been "exposed for a moment—but happily only a moment—of tiresomeness": "It worries and distresses me so terribly thinking of that wonderful creature losing friends—(which he *will* do)—through her. He worships her. He said to me that he would love her whatever she did. He won't lose *my* friendship—but of course I can't inflict that on my other friends. It is so sad."[2] Edith forgave Dylan everything; he was never in the wrong, and her romantic young-old heart was amused and impressed by his love for Caitlin: "He would sit beside me, just looking at her. 'Isn't she beautiful?' he would say. And I would answer, 'Yes, my dear boy, she is.' 'You know, Edith, promiscuity is not important.' 'Of course not, my dear boy. Perish the thought!'" She expanded to Stephen Spender, on May 29, on the general problem of husbands and wives—Arthur Waley having recently announced that he and Beryl de Zoete were not going to get married.

> But having had one experience of Mrs. D.T. I think A[rthur] was right. If a female, no matter how aged, wishes to see D., it means taking on Mrs. D. also, because otherwise Mrs. D. could justly complain she had been insulted. She has a *right* to come. How lucky men are. A man can perfectly well omit asking his man friend's impossible wife.[4]

The reconciliation with Dylan Thomas survived the dinner party in only a fragile form. By July Edith was telling William Plomer that Dylan "has wandered away from me again and renounces me and won't have anything to do with me."

This did not prevent Edith from continuing to help him. She was that year the chairman of the committee administering the Society of Authors' Travelling Scholarship Fund. (The money was actually put up by Bryher, whom Edith referred to as the "Anonymous Donor.") Dylan was granted £150, and decided on a trip to Italy, whence he wrote charmingly in April 1947 to tell Edith he was "grateful to you [for] every warm, blue minute, every orange and olive tree, every fir on a hill."

Edith spent most of the summer of 1946 at Renishaw, working on *A Notebook of William Shakespeare* and finishing "The Shadow of Cain." William Plomer pleased her in July by giving a radio talk on the Sitwells, but since it was on the Overseas Service she could not listen in. That August she was invited to take part in a poetry reading and discussion at the "Red" Unity Theatre by the young poet Maurice Carpenter. Edith, looking at the names on the list of her co-panellists, had an acute access of paranoid grandeur—a sense of being threatened that manifested itself as outrage. She hit out, replying to Carpenter on August 5:

Mr. [Dylan] Thomas is a young poet of genius, and Mr. [W. J.] Turner is a well-known and practised poet, but Miss [Anne] Ridler, though, I believe, a nice young person, is not qualified to discuss poetry with me. And Mr. [Roy] Fuller, to whom the last clause of the above sentence also applies, not only writes verses which to my mind are of no consequence, but has also had the presumption to be impertinent to me.

To ask me to discuss poetry with them is like asking Sarah Bernhardt to discuss the art of acting with some nice—or nasty—young person who has appeared twice in some remote and sparsely-peopled, dusty provincial theatre.

One hopes they will get on—but—well, *you* know.[5]

This shocker of a letter was her immediate response to her unformulated fear that, as in the 1930s, a new tide of alien poetry and alien poetic ideals was preparing to sweep her away again with the wrack. She was King Canute, as every aging artist must be in his heart. A more calculating person would have dissimulated. Not she. And she had, now, so much to lose. She was not to lose it yet.

Maurice Carpenter, to his great credit, was courteously persistent, and twelve days later Edith was telling him, "Of course I would not wish poor Mrs. Ridler to be disappointed."[6]

Fanfare for Elizabeth, Edith's prose book about the youth of Queen Elizabeth I, had been planned and written over a dispiritingly long period. She had begun working on it during the early years of the war—the poem "Anne Boleyn's Song" was a spin-off of her reading—and extracts from the book were published in four issues of *Life and Letters To-Day* during 1945. The project was undertaken "because I *had* to make money," before it became clear that money was going to flow in, and energies flow out, on account of her new poetry. In the event, her fame as a poet increased the public expectation already aroused by the popularity of *Victoria of England*, and the publication of *Fanfare* in September 1946 fulfilled everyone's hopes, including her publisher's—Macmillan made a justifiably optimistic first printing of twenty thousand (though American Macmillan, who published earlier, in July, printed only ten thousand). Edith was again among the best sellers. Alexander Korda paid £200 for the film option, which he later relinquished; but that was not the end of hopes of *Fanfare for Elizabeth* becoming a film.

The interest of film tycoons in *Fanfare* is not hard to understand. This short book is by far the best of Edith's "potboilers." What Rylands called her "post-impressionistic" style of writing, familiar now from her previous historical books, was wielded here with a lightness and swiftness that is highly cinematic, as for example in a passage describing Anne Boleyn and her jealous fears: "She could not walk down a gallery of the Palace but unseen watchers peered at her through the half-open doors of rooms she believed to be empty. . . . But she said to herself that all her enemies had been overcome, one by one." Had she not even destroyed the power of "that shadowy masked beauty whose ascendency over the King had once threatened her — but whose name, so utterly was she overthrown, has not even come down to us? . . . We see only some glimpse of that lovely laughing face, and then it is gone, as if bright great leaves had cast a network of shadow across it, darkening it and hiding it from our view."

Since when *Fanfare* ends, Elizabeth Tudor is only fifteen years old, the story of her parents' marriage and of her successive stepmothers dominates the book. The characters of Henry VIII and of his wretched wives are vivid, in Edith's peculiar vision of them, to the point where it would be difficult for a very young person who had read this book ever to see them subsequently in any other light. The sickening atmosphere of poverty in the "shamble-smelling, overhanging streets where the Plague breeds"; the equally sickening threat of death in the great palaces of Greenwich and Hampton Court where the King's will ruled; the velvets, the gold embroideries, the potions, the books and music, the gossip, intrigue, corruption, whisperings, rantings, grief, guilt, terror — if a professional historian would learn nothing he did not know from these evocations of Edith's, and from her well-chosen quotations, the nonspecialist is made to experience something more vital than most historians can provide.

Elizabeth herself is "a sad little girl . . . in a world that would never understand her," overshadowed by multiple deaths — particularly the deaths of three women close to her: her mother, Anne Boleyn; her stepmother Jane Seymour; and yet another stepmother, "the lewd, sly, pitiable little ghost Katherine Howard." The grim fates of these three young women, Edith wrote, "were to alter the whole of Elizabeth's life. . . . They were to affect her sexually, laying the chill of death on her hot blood. . . ."

Edith made of the events into which the misunderstood, neglected, too-articulate princess was born a "Sophoclean tragedy of passions, faiths, lusts, ambition that had the fever of lust. . . ." She also made it into a fairy story, with cruel stepmothers and wicked uncles. She described the christening of the infant Elizabeth, attended by good and wicked fairies, as if it were the beginning of the story of the Sleeping Beauty; and Elizabeth I, like the Sleeping Beauty in Edith's poem of that name, was never claimed and awakened by the Prince. Edith in her book identified herself as a child to some extent with the lonely young princess. Even more did she identify herself with the mature Elizabeth, the Virgin Queen; she had written in *English Women* of "this strange contradiction of a woman whose life, seen from one aspect, was barren, seen from another, infinitely fertile."

The end of 1946 brought Edith her customary bout of nervous depression, and she cast about her seeking whom she might devour. She overreacted to reports of an adverse criticism of the Sitwells made by Lawrence Durrell. A chain reaction of grievances brought back old angers—bubbles rising, one after another, from a rank spot in the pool of memory. It was in moods such as this that she scribbled "blacklists" in her notebooks, as, for example:

Person who insulted Sachie under heading of Sir Patchwork Quilt.
Person who insulted me by letter.
Person whom Kingsley Martin allowed to re-insult me in *New Statesman*.

These "persons," for being unnamed, take on a mythic quality.

She recalled that winter Noel Coward's perfidy of more than twenty years ago, in exaggerated terms. She heard that Geoffrey Grigson had been invited to speak at the Sheffield Literary Group, and asked Osbert to write complaining of this disloyalty; she disliked the implications of a talk Grigson gave on the BBC, and had him sent a solicitor's letter. Grigson wrote to her personally on December 9, 1946, with considerable restraint and dignity: "You will agree that if a critic holds his views strongly enough about any kind of book, etc. he has a right, if not a duty, to express those views. I should not grudge that right to you, (indeed how many times have you exercised it!). . . ."

He told her she should not fear; he was preparing no major attack: "No, I have had my say." As one approaches middle age, Grigson wrote, "one realises the priority of affirmations beyond attacks." He ended by suggesting that both he and Edith could perhaps "agree upon keeping, for the future, our judgments relating to each other's work to ourselves."

These were soothing words. And in January of the new year, 1947, Edith went to London to read in a BBC broadcast of *Façade*—"I *do* feel like it!!!" she wrote to Georgia with heavy sarcasm. But the trip prised her out of the winter gloom of Renishaw, where reality was not always easy to recognise.

The Shadow of Cain, the first of Edith's "three poems of the Atomic Age," was published on its own in book form by John Lehmann, now running his own publishing house, in June 1947; it was dedicated to Maurice Bowra. The book's reception confirmed her position as a modern seer, the interpreter of suffering humanity. "The first two pages," she herself said, "were partly a physical description of the highest degree of cold"—always Edith's hell— "partly a spiritual description of this."[7]

> Under great yellow flags and banners of the ancient Cold
> Began the huge migrations
> From some primeval disaster in the heart of Man.

She said the poem as a whole was about the second Fall of Man, "the gradual migration of man (the final separation of brother from brother, of Cain from Abel, and of the rich from the poor) . . . towards the final disaster, the symbol of which fell on Hiroshima."[8]

In the July 1947 issue of *Horizon*, which contained Edith's poem "A Simpleton" and an extract from Osbert's autobiography, was a long article by Kenneth Clark entitled "On the Development of Miss Sitwell's Later Style," revealing a very close knowledge of her work, both earlier and later. His conclusion was that in *Street Songs* and *Green Song*, "those who care for poetry recognized a true poetic and prophetic cry which had not been heard in English poetry since the death of Yeats," and that *The Shadow of Cain* confirmed her as having written "the greatest poems of the war." Cyril Connolly himself wrote in his "Comment" column: "In the light of the comparative failure of the 'progressive' movement of the last few years to rise above intelligent political journalism into the realms of literature, we must look elsewhere, either to the mad and lonely, or to those who have with a certain angry obstinacy cultivated their own garden." "Among these," he said, without making it absolutely clear whether he was including them among the mad and lonely or among the cultivators of their own garden, "the Sitwells shine out. . . . And so this number, at the risk of the inevitable accusations that we support a literary clique, is wholeheartedly dedicated to them."

That autumn Edith treated Evelyn Wiel to a few weeks at the Branksome Towers Hotel in Bournemouth—a resort that was to become one of their regular refuges. As a result, Edith's Shakespeare book was still unfinished. Just before Christmas she made a new friend, Ian Fleming, not yet the creator of James Bond, but working on the *Sunday Times*. They had found a common interest of a rather tenuous kind in Paracelsus, the early-sixteenth-century physician and chemist, whom Edith was reading on account of Pavlik's current obsessions. Her correspondence with Pavlik about Paracelsus had its effect on her poetry, which often borders on the bombastic—in a literal sense, since Paracelsus's real name was Bombast, whence the adjective. Ian Fleming had once translated an essay by Jung on Paracelsus; he and Edith seriously but inconclusively discussed working together on a monograph on him, with Edith writing it and Fleming producing the bibliography.

Edith never enjoyed Christmas, always spent at Renishaw, generally with David Horner in attendance. This year she had "blinding headaches—due to oil lamps with as much light as that given by a cigar," she told Lehmann on December 11. She wrote to William Plomer semi-ironically on December 29 that she was beginning to believe in "previous existence":

> I am certain that I imprisoned three old women, and did them to death slowly by sheer *boredom* and selfishness. And when I said did them to death, I *mean* did them to death. It must have gone on for years and years and years, and they must have died of slow strangulation eventually under a cosy feather bed, held down by me.

The three old women sound like a version of the three queens who, in her *Fanfare for Elizabeth*, were to "alter the whole of Elizabeth's life." They are also maybe the three Norns who haunt the last page of her bitter autobiography. Boredom was Edith's great enemy. In the boredom that engulfed her at Renishaw and at Montegufoni, her fantasy turned to the macabre. Boredom as a motivation for murder was an idea long familiar to Edith. More than twenty years earlier, in 1924, she had published in *The Golden Hind* a short story called "Undergrowth." It is about two sisters. The younger opts for danger and excitement and comes to no good. The elder stays at home, where there are no temptations but no stimulation, and commits a double murder from boredom and apathy—she kills the two children of a servant girl. She is not found out, but her sister, returning home, guesses what has happened, and the two of them, with their different guilts and failures, live together in silent complicity, not unlike the two sisters in Christina Rossetti's "Goblin Market." "Undergrowth" expresses a conflict that Edith never resolved. In the world, energies are dissipated and morals corrupted. But social isolation is, in a different way, equally destructive.

Edith, for pleasure and relaxation, read lurid thrillers and detective novels. Murderous fantasies had flickered in her since she was very young. The atmosphere of Renishaw in winter aroused the old black thoughts that loneliness and alienation as a child had fostered. She felt, she said to Lehmann, that she was hallucinating, because she had been reading nothing but Blake. "A heavenly hallucination, but making one feel rather dotty."

The gloom was lightened vicariously by the news that T. S. Eliot had been awarded the Order of Merit, the highest civil honour, in the personal gift of the sovereign, as part of the New Year Honours List. Edith wrote to him straightaway, on New Year's Day: "I had never hoped to see the greatest poet of our time properly honoured and reverenced. Well, I have."

22

Left Turn
1948

Jack Lindsay, son of the Australian artist Norman Lindsay, was born in Melbourne in 1900, and came to England in 1926. He was a Marxist and a polymath, and therefore out of the mainstream of British literary history and British literary society; the British welcome no more than a token flirtation with the Communist Party in their major writers, and prefer the scholarship of their scholars to be limited to one well-fenced field. Jack Lindsay was the author of so many books at such frequent intervals that Edith, in the end, had to instruct him, through her secretary, to stop sending them to her, as she could not possibly read them all—and so ended an intense literary friendship. But that was nearly fifteen years later, when she was old and tired.

In early 1948 Lindsay reviewed "The Shadow of Cain" in *Our Time*, and gave Edith the injection of reassurance that she needed, over and over again, to lift her out of dejection. She wrote on February 2 to thank him for the happiness and help he had given her:

> This happiness, and this encouragement, and this profound and wise understanding of all the implications in the poem, have come at a time when I have been finding it almost impossible to work, and have been feeling a strange *bereavement*—I suppose owing to the increasing menace and stupidity of the world. You might almost have timed this essay to the exact moment when it would be the greatest help to me. For it has made me begin to write again.

They began a correspondence, a conversation by post. Only four days later she was telling him, "It fills me with excitement to hear that you are contemplating the possibility of writing a much longer and more detailed study of my work...."

Although they had never met, Lindsay had seen her, twice. The first time she was standing outside the Unity Theatre, where she and Hugh MacDiarmid were to talk about poetry. "She had expected someone to be waiting for her and could not bring herself to walk in unannounced. . . . I wondered what strange proletarian den she had imagined she was intruding on."[1] So she stood outside in the cold, like someone waiting to be interviewed. She was used to more ceremony than the Unity Theatre went in for. She never got over her shyness and self-doubt—hence her reliance on the props of ceremony, and hence also her voracity for praise, which, as Lindsay has written, "for a moment dulled the ache of doubt." But in this Edith was not so very different from most artists and performers. The difference is only that pride and worldly wisdom make most people conceal from others—and sometimes even from themselves—not only the ache of doubt but the voracity for praise.

The second time Lindsay saw her was at the christening of the Carpenters' baby, where he watched as "the baby squirmed in Edith's inexpert grasp and nearly fell into the font," and no one was introduced to anyone else.

They finally met for lunch on March 24 at the Sesame Club. Lindsay brought his wife, Ann, with him. It was the first of many meetings, intense and frequent for the first five years, and then less so. Edith enjoyed not only his understanding and appreciation but the intellectual tuition he gave her. He introduced her to Lancelot Law Whyte's *The Next Development in Man*, which impressed her, and she asked him to bring Whyte to meet her, which he did. "I wouldn't speak," she wrote to Lindsay beforehand, "but I should listen to you and him talking. Silence is one of my few gifts." Lindsay dedicated his *Life of Dickens* to Edith; and she gave him the poem "Street Acrobat" for the ill-fated quarterly *Arena*, in which he was involved. "You are one of the only two people who know what my early poetry means,—Arthur Waley is the other," she told him. "And you are the only person who knows what 'The Shadow of Cain' means. . . . You might have been the mind and heart that wrote it."

That being so, one does well to look at some of what he has said about "The Shadow of Cain" and her later poetry. He saw the figures of Cain, Dives, Lazarus, Christ, as she recurringly used them, as "basic symbols of the human condition and the forms of social struggle that make up history." He noted her themes of "elemental death and renewal":

The battle of men is realised, not as something projected on to the detached screen of the universe, but as a storm of potencies which reaches everywhere. . . . A form of pantheism? Yes, but not quite according to the definitions in the manuals of philosophy. . . . The philosophic affinity is rather with Marx. . . .[2]

Lindsay saw Edith, in Marxist terms, as a poet of revolution. (He tended to see every poet he admired as a poet of revolution.) She accepted his interpretations; she saw no conflict between Christ and Marx. "Gold Coast Customs" is among other things a political poem.

But Edith consistently and firmly resisted all pressure towards party politics. No one could be a poet, she told Lindsay, who "did not care for great human problems"; but "I am unable to understand the mechanics of politics." What she meant was that politics in the narrow sense seemed to her irrelevant and boring.

Nevertheless it was a new and intoxicating experience to be hailed by a section of opinion to which she had hitherto been alien and inaccessible, if not totally insignificant—the extreme left. "You say you are outside all [literary] cliques," she wrote to Lindsay. "My God, so am I! . . . But, as you say, it adds to the up-hill aspects. . . . I know, for nobody would have anything to say to my poetry for years—indeed, until 1942! Meanwhile, all the 1930 boys in their brown shirts with Liberty in large red letters all over them, were scratching each other's backs and rolling each other's logs like anything." Ann Lindsay read "Gold Coast Customs" aloud at a Hampstead gathering where Harry Pollitt, General Secretary of the British Communist Party, was present. " 'Aye, the lass's heart is in the right place,' he commented, nodding his head and taking a good swig of beer."

But communism was not the answer for Edith. She remained "a little outside life," even in the context of the mandarins among whom she belonged by birth and custom. The hundredth number of *Horizon* in April 1948 carried her poem "The Coat of Fire"—a pre-Lindsay poem of despair for the sins of the world. Connolly wrote in his "Comment" column that "six eminent poets" had been asked to contribute a new poem to the centenary issue, but the others had nothing ready. Edith Sitwell, he pointed out, was the only full-time poet; the other five were "hardworking officials, publishers, teachers etc." It was not a rebuke to Edith, but an excuse for the absence of the others. Nevertheless his remark points up one of the many systems of tensions within which she existed. She never had any money, but she lived, footloose, among those who had. She did not do the world's work, but her "heart was in the right place" for Pollitt and others like him.

The system of tensions—between heaven and hell, life and death, the timeless and the actual, the rich and the poor—that Lindsay saw as the force behind her poetry he also saw in herself, though he did not say so explicitly in print, and not to her. A convinced Freudian, he noted that she had read Nietzsche, Hegel, Goethe and the German nature philosophers, Jung (in fact, she first read Jung only in 1946)—but not Freud. He saw her as a sexual person; he sensed her "hunger for life," and it was the sensual element in her poetry that had first attracted him to it. He saw too, as he got to know her, that her instinctive, spontaneous self was much stronger than the intellectual one. He saw how self-conscious she was physically, imprisoned in an imperfect body; her sexual self, it seemed to him, lived in a separate sphere. Only in her poetry did everything meet, and she was able to express herself fully. To reject her poetry was to reject Edith, in a more absolute sense than is usually the case with writers.

Lindsay, like John Lehmann, was one of those friends who prolonged her writing life. He was aware of his role. The horrors of war had given her a poetic vision, "but with her failing strengths she felt herself unable to sustain this vision. What she gained from me was the capacity to sustain it and to reach the clear definition of 'A Song of the Dust,'" which was, he has said, written in "direct response" to the Lindsays' own enthusiastic and emotional accounts of what they had seen and heard on a visit to the USSR in 1949.[3] (He later modified his opinions about the Soviet Union. And it is likely that what Edith responded to was the Lindsays' idealism and hopefulness, rather than to the substance of their travellers' tales.)

The last thing she would ever have wanted was for Lindsay, or anyone else, to explain her private self, either to herself or to the world. She was very well defended against such attempts, and was opposed to every sort of invasion of privacy, as she saw it, and not only on her own account. Writing to John Hayward on June 30, 1946, about what she felt as Shakespeare's "sexual bitterness," she said, "Is it not wonderful how he kept all his private life from the prying eyes of Ben Jonson."[4] In December of the same year, "a young American" came to see her who was writing a book about W. B. Yeats. This was Richard Ellmann—the book, *Yeats: The Man and the Masks*, was published in 1948. After Mrs. Yeats had sent him to Renishaw, Edith told John Lehmann:

> I wonder if she has any idea of what he is *really* up to! His one interest . . . is exactly what terms Mr. Y was [on] with Mrs. Maud Gonne and others.

He says he is going to base the book on the effect this had on his poetry!!! oh, oh, oh! Is it not *awful* that every great man has got to be exhumed and nailed down at the cross-roads with a stake through his heart? . . . The young man was quite well-intentioned.[5]

The personal pronoun *I* occurs in Edith's poetry less frequently than in the work of most twentieth-century poets; indeed, one of her most usual complaints about other women poets was the claustrophobically personal and confessional nature of their work. But she was not so self-deceived as to deny the link between art and autobiography. She put her point of view clearly enough in a letter to Olivia Manning on May 15, 1952:

Most great poetry comes through the personal becoming universal. I did *not* say that poetry should not be written about personal emotions. What I said was that these must be transmuted so that when I write a love poem I am not a woman writing about her individual love for Mr. Jones or the Duke of Malfi, but a woman writing about her love for a man (and hence every woman's love). If one has no personal emotions, one isn't a poet, — or a human being.

If one is writing a love poem, it is *love* of which one should be writing, not one's approaching marriage to Mr. Jones, — or the fact that he has broken off the engagement. But to write great poetry, one must *experience*.[6]

May 7, 1948, was, Edith assured Professor Bonamy Dobrée of Leeds University (who had been so scathing about the Sitwells in the past) the "proudest and happiest day of my life—quite unflawed by anything. . . . Even my shyness couldn't spoil the day."[7] Leeds, not far from Renishaw, had made her an Honorary Doctor of Literature. She was now Edith Sitwell, D. Litt. "My dearest future doctor!" Pavlik had written when he heard the news, "I can't tell you how happy I was to hear about you becoming a doctor because if there is anyone to be called one on account of one's wisdom, you are certainly *the one*. Cecil [Beaton] just said: 'She ought to be the Poet Laureate because she is it already.'"[8] When he painted her portrait again, he said, it would be as a Muse and not a Sibyl. But he did not paint her again.

All Edith's correspondents were apprised of her new designation. "O William," she wrote to Plomer on May 19, "how cruel you are! You *never* put D. Litt. on my envelope." In June another great university of the north of

England, Durham, doubled her pleasure: Now Dr. Sitwell was "D. Litt., D. Litt." on all correspondence.

In October 1948 her long-brewing *A Notebook on William Shakespeare* was published by Macmillan. She had talked around the subject widely—with Stephen Spender and the actor John Gielgud particularly, on *King Lear,* which was the play that meant most to her—and many sections of the book had been appearing in periodicals over the past three years. She dedicated the book to Arthur Waley and Beryl de Zoete, and described it in her foreword as "a series of notes, which are not to be considered as essays, but rather as running commentaries on certain aspects of Shakespeare." Her most personal and characteristic chapter, "A Hymn to Life," stresses Shakespeare's life-giving earthiness: Characters such as Falstaff are "lumps of the world," are "still alive from the roots, a part not yet cut off from universal nature," and have a "gross physical enormity of sensation which approaches a kind of physical godhead." These images reflect the images of her poetry of the same period, as in "The Canticle of the Rose," published in *Wake* the same year:

> I rise upon my stem,
> The Flower, the whole Plant-being, produced by Light
> With all Plant-systems and formations. . . .

(During 1947 and 1948 she had copied passages from Lorenz Oken's *Elements of Physiophilosophy* into her working notebooks: "An animal is a flower without a stem"; "The plant is an animal retarded by the darkness, the animal is a plant blossoming directly through the light, and devoid of root.")

Shakespeare, she wrote, "is like the sun, that common-kissing Titan, having a passion for matter, pure and impure, an energy beyond good and evil."

Edith sent an advance copy of the book to Ian Fleming at the *Sunday Times*, who in thanking her wrote, "Incidentally, please tell me who you would best like to review it for the *S.T.* and I will use my small weight with the literary editor."

The Times Literary Supplement's reviewer, anonymous of course—but in fact George Rylands—praised her Shakespeare book's "delicate fancies and crowding appreciations," its "perceptions communicated in the post-impressionistic manner which she has made peculiarly her own." His tone was genial, a little condescending, and ended with "a note of reproach if not of rebuke": The book was announced as a companion volume to *A Poet's Notebook*—"Is not this a disingenuous way of stating the fact that more than a quarter of the previous volume is incorporated here, often with hardly the change of a word . . . ?"⁹

Be that as it may, Edith's fresh appreciation of Shakespeare as, in Ryland's words, "the lover and giver of elemental life" sprang from her fertile wartime phase that Jack Lindsay's recognition was prolonging in her. The most important of her poems published in 1948 were the second and third "Poems of the Atomic Age," both much shorter than "The Shadow of Cain": "The Canticle of the Rose," which was dedicated to Geoffrey Gorer and written, as she told William Plomer, after reading that new vegetation was beginning to sprout at Hiroshima; and "Dirge for the New Sunrise," first published in the *Quarterly Review of Literature*. The liberating fertility also gave bite to her comments, in the Shakespeare *Notebook*, on Isabella in *Measure for Measure*, the girl who refuses to sacrifice her chastity to save her brother's life. Isabella, wrote Edith, was an "unconscious hypocrite": "Cold and repellant Isabella tells herself that her natural repulsion against the loathsome attempt of Angelo, is not a natural repulsion, but a horror of sin as sin. Yet she does not scruple to lie and cheat." This is a more interesting objection than the more common modern antipathy to Isabella's selfish virtuousness.

John Lehmann was to reissue her novel *I Live Under a Black Sun* in his Holiday Library series in the autumn of 1948. Edith was very pleased; it was her "ewe lamb." But she barely earned her £100 advance.

Fortunately something new and exciting was afoot when the Lehmann version came out. Everything was drawing her—and Osbert—to the United States. Edith had been "Dearest Edith" to Charles Henri Ford for over eighteen months; her name was on the letterhead of *View*, the magazine he edited. In May 1947 he ended a letter with "Best love, dearest Edith—I wish love could work more wonders." One of the wonders love might be expected to work was the reunion of those long-separated friends, Edith and Pavlik. There was a question of her going to Paris when Pavlik had an exhibition there; but both parties nervously drew back from Paris as the place for the momentous reunion.

Edith never did go back to the rue Saint-Dominique after the war to claim her books, letters, notebooks, and manuscripts—not even to claim her Tchelitchew paintings—in spite of her constant contact with Evelyn, and in spite of Evelyn's own constant crossings of the Channel. This avoidance is a measure not only of how unhappy she had been there—her nightmares about the flat continued—but of how completely she was without that dependence on personal belongings, household gods, familiar bits and pieces, that for most people mean security and a sense of identity. She felt no need of a "setting." As Elizabeth Salter has written, "The woman who had made an artistic tour de force out of her appearance never cared about, if indeed she ever looked at, a piece of furniture, the colour of a room, the pattern of a carpet."[10]

If Paris held no attractions, America with Osbert did. Charles Henri Ford was involved in negotiating a lecture and reading tour, to be organized by the Colston Leigh Bureau, at the end of 1947. Edith's limited knowledge of Americans was not encouraged by the way the tour seemed to be planned. "Oh dear! Our rhinoceros-like lecture agent in America has just insulted the American Poetry Society," she wailed to Jack Lindsay. Colston Leigh had told the Society "they'll have to pay Goodness knows what before they are allowed to as much as get a look at me." She ended this letter with a characteristic cry set in a new key: "The whole Continent of America is up in arms against me." She was nervous; this was half a joke, half a preempting of adverse criticism.

She would of course need new clothes for her public appearances. Her wardrobe for the tour was provided by Nina Astier, a couturière in the King's Road, Chelsea. Edith was at Montegufoni for Christmas 1947, and wrote from there in January 1948 to Madame Astier asking her to make some "lovely new clothes" for America:

> I think I had better have a new evening dress (please will you get some patterns of brocade from Liberty)—a black woollen dress for day, and a short velvet coat, and a black dull satin. *No* braid on the woollen dress please, as I like them very plain,—also I would like this rather shorter than usual—as short as you made the one before that with the braid.
>
> And please will you not cut the dresses too low at the neckline, as I always have trouble with my petticoat and vest showing. I would like them cut in a round just below the collar-bones.[11]

She had got so thin, she told Madame Astier, "you would hardly know me—(thin for *me*, I mean!) I took my measurements round the hip-line, holding the measure rather tightly round my petticoat,—and it was 40½ inches." Pavlik, when he heard she was definitely coming, sent his "bee-priestess" some black-and-gold-striped material that she then had made up into an evening dress.

Before she left for the United States, Edith met Wystan Auden for the first time; Natasha Spender brought him to luncheon at the Sesame. Edith's opinion of Auden had been forcibly modified over the past few years. He and the other Macspaunday poets—all of whom were by now friendly with her—had taken over in the 1930s, and no one had followed up her lead; Auden had epitomized everything she stood against in poetry. She had retailed *con brio* all derogatory remarks about him, as poet and person, writing, for example, to Robert Herring during the war: "I've just had a letter from Pavlik who seems to have taken a dislike to Auden. To read his poetry, he says, is 'choos' (just) 'counting mackintoshes in large warehouse.' . . . Nor does Mr. Auden's face escape censure: 'Choos large disaster, badly carved Roquefort cheese.'" Yet Edith had had to recognize him, however grudgingly. In her second Northcliffe Lecture she had called him "a fine poet, though a minor one," while dealing a knockout blow to one of his best-known, now classic, lyrics, "Lay your sleeping head, my love, / Human on my faithless arm": "It has a certain beauty," she had said, "yet it is full of outworn clichés. . . . Cliché after cliché." But she could not hold out. After reading *For the Time Being* towards the end of the war, she had written to Georgia: "You know, the awful thing is that a great deal of Auden's new book is *extremely* good. Which is a shock."[12] Now at last they had met; and she told Stephen Spender, "I cannot tell you how much I liked him, and what a feeling of *reality* he gave me."[13]

Both Auden and Spender could tell her what to expect in the United States. The American literary world was also being prepared for Edith. Maurice Bowra had written a monograph on her poetry, an Anglo-French production that came out from the Lyrebird Press that summer; Vanguard in New York published an anthology of her poetry, *The Song of the Cold,* to coincide with her visit (she jotted in her notebook later that it sold 3,483 copies in the first year); and José Garcia Villa edited *A Celebration for Edith Sitwell,* published by James Laughlin at New Directions. Tchelitchew's "Sibyl" portrait of Edith was on the cover of *A Celebration*; the volume consisted of essays on her work by Stephen Spender, Maurice Bowra, Frederick Prokosch, Horace Gregory, Jack Lindsay, John Piper, Kenneth Clark, Gordon Bottomley, John Lehmann, Arthur Waley, Charles Morgan, Richard Church, John Russell, and L. P. Hartley, with a "Reminiscence" by Osbert, Gertrude Stein's prose poem "Sitwell Edith Sitwell," and Yeats's sonorous letter to Wyndham Lewis—a royal muster of witness—plus ten of her own poems.

Edith and Osbert, and David Horner, set sail on the *Queen Mary* in October 1948. Just before leaving, Edith wrote a last letter to Stephen Spender: "I dread, and am terrified of everything. But I suppose one can get used to anything. . . . The only thing I look forward to, in America, is seeing you, and to seeing Pavlik (whom I have not seen for ten years!)."[14]

23
Pyrrhic Victories
1948-1949

Edith wrote in her notebook:

> This city is as beautiful, as strange, as full of wonder to a European as
> any fabulous city of the ancient world—as Babylon, Thebes, Palmyra.
> I suppose it is one of the four most beautiful cities of our present
> civilisation. By strange, I mean unaccustomed—for its life is intensely
> friendly. Its skyscrapers are as delicate in design as they are strong.

Edith, like most Europeans, was prepared for the vitality of New York and
the friendliness of Americans; and Pavlik, in his last letter before she sailed, told
her that she would find New York "very childish and very exhilerating [*sic*],
also very trying"—all of which was to prove true. But she was not prepared for
the beauty of Manhattan, at its most startling in the lucid sunlight of early
autumn—a beauty rarely sufficiently stressed, perhaps because there is so much
else. "My first impressions of New York was [*sic*], overwhelming. Everybody
appeared to be young. It was not possible to believe that people so alive could
ever be old," she wrote in her autobiography. Her first visit brought her
extremes of personal triumph and personal desolation entirely in keeping with
the extremes contained within the unique city.

Pavlik had an access of nerves when it was time to go and meet Edith and
Osbert at the ship. If it had not been for the encouragement of Charles Henri
Ford and Kirk Askew of Durlacher, Pavlik's dealer, whom Edith had already
met in London, he would not have gone to the docks. Pavlik was enjoying
considerable fashionable success in New York, and had been able to arrange
for Mrs. David Pleydell-Bouverie and Mrs. Vincent Astor to provide tax-
deductible funds for a suite at the St. Regis Hotel for Edith and Osbert. So
they were well placed, on the corner of Fifth Avenue and Fifty-fifth Street.

And by chance, English friends were also on the East Coast at the same time, profiting from the postwar wave of pro-British feeling that brought British writers, academics, and entertainers over the Atlantic to have the time of their lives; in autumn 1948, Stephen Spender, Harold Acton, Geoffrey Gorer, Cecil Beaton, Evelyn Waugh, and Maurice Bowra were all in the United States for their various purposes, as well as the Sitwells.

The first social engagement for Edith and Osbert was a dinner party given by Mrs. Pleydell-Bouverie and Mrs. Astor. The other guests were Lady Ribblesdale (Alice Pleydell-Bouverie's mother), Monroe Wheeler of the Museum of Modern Art, Lincoln Kirstein of the New York City Ballet and his wife, Fidelma, Pavel Tchelitchew, and Charles Henri Ford. Straightaway it was clear that Edith's reunion with Pavlik was not going to work out as either of them had imagined. They had both aged: Edith was now sixty-one. For ten long years their correspondence had been an outlet and a solace to them both. An idealized Edith had written weekly to an idealized Pavlik, as he to her; apart, they had met in an area without conflict, speaking directly to that part of the other which each needed. It was fantasy, but only in the sense that reality for both of them was infinitely more complex and cluttered.

At the dinner, Edith wore the dress made from the gold-and-black-striped material that Pavlik had sent her. She did not look as he had imagined his bee-priestess would look in it. He told her he did not like the way the dress had been made up, "and neither his voice nor conversation can hide his irritation."[1] He talked a great deal at dinner, but not to her.

The one moment he had been longing for was the moment when he would be able to show Edith his major work, the painting *Hide and Seek*, which had been bought for the Museum of Modern Art. He had shared with her, in his letters, every stage of its conception and execution; he wanted to stand beside her in the museum and receive her acclaim and hear her praise. They had planned that moment for months.

But on the morning after the party, a depressed and discouraged Edith told him by telephone that her lumbago was giving her so much pain that she could not go to the museum with him. He therefore arrived at the St. Regis to lunch with her and Osbert in a disappointed and difficult mood. The nervous unease that his behaviour produced in Edith contributed to the disaster that followed. When finally they stood together in front of *Hide and Seek*, she found she could say absolutely nothing at all. She stood before it mute.

Silence is sometimes the most fitting tribute to a work of art, but it was not the one that Pavlik expected. He wanted a histrionic, articulate, overwhelming response. The next day he received a letter from her overflowing with all the praise that she had not given at the time. It was too late. Nothing went right between them from start to finish. They dined together after the debacle, and Edith tried to explain to him how shy she had felt, how inarticulate and at a loss. Pavlik could not believe this. He explained her silence to himself and Ford in terms that echoed his former complaints about her: "Her behaviour was caused by her overwhelming response to him as a man, a sex."

He extorted her devotion always, and when he got what he wanted he recoiled in disgust from the threat of engulfing femaleness — which was deduced, in a Freudian double bind, from either speechlessness or effusiveness. For the rest of Edith's visit he suffered from acute colitis.

Edith was undermined by his attitude. She was further undermined by a review of a book called *Poems of the War Years*, compiled by Maurice Wollman, that appeared in the *Listener* of October 14 and followed her to New York: "The later poetry of Miss Sitwell, here more than adequately represented by five poems, has been much praised, but after several readings the repetitive imagery, the golden Suns and Lions and Tigers and Roses and the garrulous talk of Time and Wisdom leave us finally with an impression of emptiness." This was not encouraging to read as she prepared to face her American audiences.

Cecil Beaton, who was staying at the Plaza, was visiting the Sitwells' suite at the St. Regis when Pavlik asked Edith to come and see him at his apartment, which was lovely, he told her, with the el going by outside and all the twinkling lights. Wary by now, Edith said she would have to think about it. Pavlik left, feeling insulted.

These constant failures to get on with each other face-to-face distressed them both. On October 26 Pavlik wrote to her repeating his invitation, and showing both a desire to patch up their differences and some insight into the causes of them. He was so used to her in her letters (he wrote in his idiosyncratic English) in which she was always "the friendly and wise receiver":

> The relations of our persons . . . always had surrounded by many others, are rather difficult, they are stript from their secrecy, we look at each other and make signs of silence and wait for the opportunity of writing to go back to our ten years happy. . . . It is most unfortunate that we have to do so but it is maybe better. Because, since ten years we have both grown very much.[2]

There was something else causing trouble between them, his letter suggested. The people who surrounded them whenever they met were all making much of Edith. She was in New York, he wrote, "to get glory, to get acclaimed," in a much larger and more "tumultuous" arena than ever was the case with painters. Pavlik was jealous—both of her and of the impact she was making. He was, he wrote, "a monk in a cell." But the place for the Sibyl, the Muse, was in the shadows, being the "friendly and wise receiver." He found it outrageous that he had to compete for her attention. But even had she opted for the role he offered her, she would soon have been repulsed once more by the inevitable emotional shift that transformed devotion into predatoriness in his eyes.

Pavlik was not deceived about the "glory" that Edith was receiving in New York and elsewhere. If the first and final phases of her trip were blighted by private disappointment, her public triumph was unexpected and total. The Sitwells' schedule was arduous—the lecture circuit took in the Middle West, and they addressed universities, women's clubs, and student societies, and gave public recitals. The fee to clubs and colleges was $1,750 per evening, of which the Sitwells took half. The agency, who took the other half, also carried most of their expenses. Osbert lectured on "Personal Adventures" and "The Modern Novel: Its Cause and Cure," Edith on "Modern English Poetry." More popular than the lectures were the public readings, "for it was the Sitwells *themselves* their audience paid to see," as John Pearson has written. "There was a crash audience at Yale, a sell-out in Boston, and in New York ten thousand stormed the Town Hall to hear them."[3] With a schedule so demanding, a success so overwhelming, and a social life to match, Edith had to put the Pavlik disasters into perspective.

She met Charlie Chaplin, and Greta Garbo—"a being . . . of the lily tribe, but with a human heart and mind";[4] she was taken up by New York's wealthy hostesses the Cushing sisters—Mrs. Vincent Astor, Mrs. Jock Whitney, Mrs. William Paley. Mrs. Pleydell-Bouverie gave a party for her in her mansion on the Hudson River to meet Marianne Moore. A friend of these wealthy women was Billy McCann, who was also an old friend of all the Sitwells—as a very small boy he had lived in Moscow Road, where his mother had taken a keen interest in the unusual visitors going upstairs to visit Edith and Helen Rootham. He was there at the introduction of Marianne Moore to Edith, and at other parties:

It was at Minnie Astor's mansion, on the Hudson, that Edith arrived, in full fancy dress too, in Vincent Astor's amphibious aeroplane, and I shall never forget the sight of Edith having to leave the plane, in the middle of the river, in the smallest launch I have ever seen; she nearly overturned the launch with her extraordinary luggage (two suitcases of books alone, and old-fashioned suitcases at that!) that she considered necessary for a long weekend—and only 80 miles from New York City. She had of course never flown before, but her endearing enjoyment of an adventure she had never experienced was so natural.[5]

Evelyn Waugh, in New York to settle a commission with *Life* magazine, wrote home to his wife on November 14 that "the Sitwells were rampaging about New York cutting a terrific splash but I kept clear of them." And to Nancy Mitford he wrote that Osbert had let his hair grow long, and looked like Einstein: "He and Edith (and Mr. Horner) are having one hell of a time. Every magazine has six pages of photographs of them headed 'The Fabulous Sitwells.' They have hired the Philharmonic Orchestra which in this town is something very big indeed to play while they recite poetry. Goodness how they are enjoying it."[6] Wyndham Lewis was sent some of the magazine photographs by a friend in America. Looking at these images of his old sparring partner, he observed: "She has changed since the days when I painted her portrait. She has now become a Van Eyck...."[7]

Neither Edith nor Osbert was in very good health; Edith had to have minor surgery for a nonmalignant growth in her throat just before Christmas. They spent Christmas in Boston, in deep snow, after the reading at Cambridge. On January 6, back at the St. Regis, Edith wrote to John Lehmann: "Dear me, how much I *do* like Americans. Anyone who doesn't must really be mad."

There was a press party given by Frances Steloff—"a frightfully important bookseller" and a "sage-green vegetarian," as Edith told Georgia—at the Gotham Book Mart on West Forty-seventh Street. Here Edith, like a queen, with Osbert sitting beside her, was photographed for *Life* surrounded by a glorious company of poets and writers that included Stephen Spender, Horace Gregory, Tennessee Williams, Richard Eberhart, Gore Vidal, José Garcia Villa, W. H. Auden, Elizabeth Bishop, Marianne Moore, Randall Jarrell, Delmore Schwartz—and, seated cross-legged and puckish at Edith's feet, like the court jester, Charles Henri Ford.

The climax of their royal progress belonged to Edith: a performance of *Façade* at the Museum of Modern Art. It was Monroe Wheeler's idea; and Mrs.

Astor arranged for Edith to have a new, gold brocade dress for the occasion. She found in rehearsal that she could no longer recite the fast, staccato "Hornpipe" without stumbling; David Horner, for this one poem, stepped into the gap. The performance was a sellout, with tickets priced at $35 each. The notices afterwards were ecstatic and reverential. Prausnitz conducted. Recordings were made.

Edith's success was not dust and ashes. She loved it. "That's the stuff to give the troops," she wrote to John Lehmann, enclosing the notices. It was in despair and outrage, or in desperate need for support, that her Waterman's pen flew over the paper late into the night; in this moment of triumph she did not crow and exult excessively through the mails. Harold Acton, who witnessed her progress, has written that "the Sitwells were welcomed in America as few poets have been in England":

> Though Edith was already fragile she put every ounce of energy into her recitals. Her Gothic appearance, her capes and gowns and turbans, her exquisite hands with huge aquamarines on the tapering fingers, fascinated the eye as her voice fascinated the ear. After the years of retirement at Renishaw it was physically fatiguing to shake so many hands and answer so many questions, yet I had never seen her look so happy.[8]

The happiness was real; but after *Façade* came reaction and anticlimax. It was noticed that she was tense and irritable, and increasingly reliant on Dutch courage to get her through her engagements. Soon she and Osbert would be going home. She had seen less and less of Pavlik; when she did see him, he spoilt all her pleasure in her success, accusing her of "basking with too gross and loitering an ease in the public eye."[9] There had been no more talk of his painting the "Muse" portrait. Everything was unresolved between them. If she left with things as they were now, their ten-year correspondence would hardly be likely to continue; the only result of the great reunion would have been the destruction of a friendship of more than twenty years' standing. She had loved no one as she had loved Pavlik. She told the novelist Glenway Wescott, who visited her one morning at the St. Regis, that she could not stand herself because she was so ugly. She took another drink, and the last days ran out.

A farewell dinner was given for Edith and Osbert at Voisin's. Pavel Tchelitchew and Charles Henri Ford were there, and Auden, Kirk Askew, Lincoln Kirstein, and David Horner. For once Pavlik did not hog the conversation; on the contrary, he seemed very subdued. Then towards the end he silenced everyone, exploding into a loud, hectoring monologue of complaint and criticism against Edith—he made a scene "of intentional humiliation," accusing her of preferring her rich vulgar new friends to her old friends, of being self-obsessed, of betraying the poet she had been, of every sort of unworthy and cheap and disloyal behaviour. All between them was now over. Edith, ashen-faced and shattered, said nothing at all. Nor did anyone else make any more than calming noises; no one, not even Osbert, counterattacked, and when the storm was over, the dinner drew to a close in a thinly disguised icy awkwardness—one of Edith's hells of the Cold. In this way they parted.

Tchelitchew was not remorseful. His true complaint, he told his friends, was that Edith was "not feminine enough." His biographer, Parker Tyler, wrote, "What he means is, 'not passive enough.'" Yet Tyler added from his own observation that Edith in New York seemed to him "the most majestic as well as the most feminine person I ever recall seeing." Tchelitchew told Ford that Edith had "neither intelligence nor heart." He regretted, he said, withdrawing his allegiance from Gertrude Stein all those years back and making Edith his Sibyl (forgetting, perhaps, that it had been Stein who rejected *him*). He wanted to slap Edith's face, he said, "and have her kneel at my feet and crawl like a worm." Perhaps it was in the hope of eliciting this effect that he wrote her a "conciliatory letter" before she sailed.

Back at Renishaw, Edith drafted letters to Pavlik in her notebook through the spring of 1949. "Dearest P, I have tried for weeks to write to you, but it has been too sad, and much too difficult. I wish now only to say that I must of course accept your decision to end a friendship that has lasted nearly a quarter of a century.... You will never see me again." In the final version, the one that she posted, she said:

> You must know in your heart that I have been a devoted friend to you.... It was a most terrible blow to me, coming to New York and finding you unhappy and then ill—really one of the most dreadful blows of my life. You gave me no opportunity of showing you what I felt but I really was shattered by it, as Osbert knew.

Pavlik did not reply for some weeks, Then she heard from him again, a "heartless and callous letter," on March 28. Again she wrote drafts of eight-page letters of self-defence and reproach, the first on the evening of the day his letter came:

Dearest Pavel—

I call you that since it is how you now wish me to address you. . . .

First, I have never, since I met you, put myself before you.

I knew, from the evening after we arrived in New York, that you had changed towards me. You could not even *pretend* to want to talk to me. And as the days went on, this was made even clearer to me. I quite understand. But I had been looking forward to seeing you for ten years. . . .

I do not know what you mean, when you say I turned my back on your left-wing friends, and spent my time with people you despise. It was Charlie [Ford] who brought M. Cocteau to lunch, and I thought you were Mr. Stravinsky's friend. . . .

Ever since I arrived, you have hinted, persistently, that nobody likes me. This is both unkind, rude, and entirely untrue. . . . Would it *really* give you pleasure if my next book in America had bad reviews? . . .

I have never made any claim upon you. I have neither the right nor the wish to do so. But you should be ashamed for ever of the letter you have written me, and of your behaviour towards me.

Among the drafts and versions there lies an envelope addressed to "Pavel Tchelitchew, Esq.," and scribbled over the address, "This letter is *not* to be posted." Perhaps he never read these words.

The two other people Edith most loved, her brothers, were also now the causes of distress, in very different ways. Before she and Osbert had left for America, Sacheverell had been unwell and unhappy. In July 1948, Edith told Jack Lindsay that she and Osbert were worried because "he suffers so *appallingly* from melancholy, owing to the way he has been underrated—(and I imagine owing to his having been at school when my mother was sent to prison) that he has now given himself an internal ulcer. He couldn't,—wouldn't—write poetry for ages."

Sacheverell's temperament, and his very private life, kept him out of the world's eye. The fact that Edith and to a lesser degree Osbert were public figures and attracted a great deal of attention both in their literary and in their personal capacities exacerbated his melancholy and sense of isolation. "He can't see that other people are underrated too," Edith told Lindsay, "and he hasn't got his sister's vulgar violence and natural arrogance and swank."

The American tour threw Sacheverell deeper into depression and increased the tension between Renishaw and Weston. Yet as Edith wrote to Lovat Dickson in July 1949, "we are one of the most devoted families that has ever been." Edith, Osbert, and Sacheverell loved each other more deeply than is usual with brothers and sisters. All three were "darling" and "my darling" to one another, and these were not just the "darlings" conventional to their class and period. They bled and wept for one another. The one weak link was between Osbert and Sacheverell's wife, Georgia, who found little in common: "Anyway our love for Sachie must always be our greatest link, though mine for him grows every year," Georgia wrote bitterly to Osbert in February 1950.

Strain between Osbert and Sacheverell was not due to lack of feeling. Osbert had been very unhappy and lonely when Sacheverell married and broke up their close early partnership; Sacheverell, in his turn, felt let down in later years by Osbert. It was money troubles that chiefly came between them. Osbert's attitude was paternalistic. Edith, who loved them both dearly, could not bear to be at odds with either. In this particular crisis, however, she was closer to Osbert.

After their return from the States, Georgia, who was worried about her husband and a tiger in his defence, let Edith and Osbert know that in her opinion they had contributed to Sacheverell's illness by going off to America without him. (When Evelyn Waugh asked them in New York, "Is Sachie joining you?" the reply was: "Alas. Sachie is High Sheriff of his county and therefore unable to leave the United Kingdom.")[10] After their second lecture tour, in 1949–50, Georgia wrote again to protest against his exclusion, and about their insoluble financial problems. Because it was Georgia who spoke out, it was Georgia who bore the weight of Osbert's paternalistic reproof. On February 13, 1950, he wrote to her:

> Misunderstandings accumulate. I have been horribly worried and made quite ill by the financial plight. No one likes to have to stump up £20,000 even when it is easy. I love Sachie: but he doesn't like facing facts. . . .Other grievances of mine (old ones) are that you should consider Sachie badly

---

*Sacheverell was indeed High Sheriff of Northamptonshire in 1948–1949; but a High Sheriff has only to inform the Lord Lieutenant if he intends to absent himself for a while, and unless a visit from royalty is expected, there is no problem; for ordinary purposes, the permanent Under Sheriff will serve.

treated because I did not take him to America. 3 is one too many for lectures. And I have to underwrite the financial position of the lectures, and cannot do so for three people. . . . I admire greatly your devotion to Sachie and the children, and hope now, when this is over, he will settle down and *work*. And that you will also settle down and learn how to manage his affairs for him. I am sure you could do it. . . .

Osbert showed this letter, and the letter from Georgia that it answered, to Edith. She copied both out carefully into her notebook before returning them to him. Osbert's tone to Georgia bears out Edith's remark of four or five years before to her sister-in-law, when she had written to Georgia that "he really regards himself as a kind of *parent* to the entire family. . . . When they meet, we must try to get both sides *not to mention anything unhappy*."[11]

These anxieties and estrangements were prevailing at a time when Osbert's health was giving cause for concern. It was not his brother's financial plight that was making him "quite ill." Ever since their return from the American trip he had been suffering from eye trouble, pains in the legs, and, increasingly, fits of giddiness. His illness, and her own heavy schedule, increased Edith's tensions. "I am finding it *fearfully* difficult to write," she wrote to Georgia. "In fact I am despairing about it at the moment. I have had a kind of commercial traveller's summer. . . ."[12] No sooner had she settled down at Renishaw than she had to go to London to rehearse for the first performance of Humphrey Searle's musical setting of "Gold Coast Customs" for the BBC; she shared the recitation with Constant Lambert. She was still "tired after America" (even though, as she wrote to Lehmann in the same breath, "that is the place where we all ought to go and live for a large part of the year"). "Rehearsing with music is ghastly tiring and nerve-shattering." The performance was on May 17, and the Sitwells' literary agent, David Higham, came to hear it: "As my wife and I waited outside the BBC to be let into the concert hall . . . I turned and saw Osbert in the queue before me. He had been in the States: we hadn't met for some months. He looked unusual, I thought, his face flushed, his hand shaking as it grasped the ornamental top of a walking stick."[13]

Osbert was in the early stages, still undiagnosed, of Parkinson's disease.

24
Rows and Reconciliations
1949-1950

Edith's personal success in America was reflected by increased public demand for her at home. "Every girls' school in the country has invited me to go and give away the prizes at the annual Jamboree," she wrote to John Hayward during her "commercial traveller's summer," at the end of June 1949. "And the BBC has asked me—twice—to speak for three minutes on any subject that interests me to the women of England."[1] She was also involved on an advisory basis with Robert Helpmann's script for his film of *A Midsummer Night's Dream*.

In addition, she was compiling an anthology of American poetry for John Lehmann. Her approach to this project was cavalier: "I shall be in fearful trouble with all the Americans for not putting them all in. I shall therefore say in my Preface that this is the First Volume only, and that of course they will all come in the Second. And then there will be *no* Second!"[2]

That summer she was also indirectly involved in what was to her an exhilarating row between Roy Campbell and Geoffrey Grigson. Roy Campbell had already quarrelled with Stephen Spender (they were among the various pairs of Edith's friends who must not be asked to the Sesame on the same day). Grigson had taken a sideswipe at Edith for writing about motherhood when she was childless. Roy Campbell retaliated with a ferocious review, in the *Poetry Review* of August/September 1949, of *Poetry of the Present*, an anthology edited by Grigson. It was an attack not so much of the book as of its editor:

. . . For Mr. Grigson, poetically impotent, suffers all the rages and infatuation of a cuckold at his own keyhole . . . both his rage and infatuation are aroused by watching other people romping, frolicking, and performing feats with the Muses that he can't perform himself. His rage is often completely self-contradictory—at its worst it verges on abject hypocrisy, as when he attacked Miss Sitwell for writing of childbirth although she is childless: yet he is always writing about the War; and his own War-record is about as virginal as Miss Sitwell's contribution to the birthrate.

This performance was headed "Moo! Moo! or Ye Olde New Awareness"; and Campbell went on to find more unpleasant reasons for Grigson's animus towards "imaginative, creative, dynamic writers like Dylan Thomas, Edith Sitwell, T. S. Eliot, George Barker."

Edith sent Campbell a telegram of congratulation, followed by a letter: "It needed a poet to do it," she wrote. Grigson wrote to Campbell to say he forgave him for his attack because "you have written some fine poems. You know I would not even bounce a ping-pong ball off your venerable nut." To which Campbell replied: "If I was young enough to fight for you I am young enough for you to fight."[3]

It nearly did come to a fight, outside the BBC in Langham Place. And Edith, who took an exaggerated pleasure in her own exaggerated version of the story, in which Roy Campbell physically attacked the archenemy Grigson on her sole account, was now on Campbell's side in everything, both literary and personal. "Roy Campbell was one of the very few great poets of our time," she wrote in her autobiography. She wrote too of his "great stature, build, strength and vitality," and of his kingfisher-blue eyes. "I have never known a more vitalizing companion, nor one who had stranger adventures." As for his politics (Campbell had fought for Franco in the Spanish Civil War): "He was never a fascist. But, a deeply religious man, he fought against the Reds in Spain. He believed, as I believe, that it is equally infamous to massacre priests, nuns, Jews, peasants and aristocrats."[4]

In September 1949 Macmillan published an anthology of Edith's poems from 1920 to 1947 entitled *The Canticle of the Rose*; the last section was a similar selection to that published in America in 1948 as *The Song of the Cold*. America also saw a version of *The Canticle of the Rose*, which was distinguished from the British edition by the inclusion of "Some Notes on My Own Poetry." Edith's anthologies of her own poetry, the British ones, the American ones, and the British and American variants under the same title, are a bibliographer's nightmare, particularly as in her later years she repeated or transposed lines and passages from one poem to another, altered titles, and revised continually. She expected full and considered reviews of each collection, although, in this case, there was only a passage of four years between the British edition of *The Song of the Cold* and *The Canticle of the Rose*. Her expectations were more justified in the case of the latter, since it included a large body of her early verse; it was advertised as containing "nearly all the poems Edith Sitwell wishes to preserve."

She was, however, disappointed. *The Times Literary Supplement*'s review on September 30 could have been written, and probably was, she told Horner, by a "dear old moss-grown, low-church clergyman . . . living in a Manse outside Aberdeen." In fact the review was by the editor himself, Alan Pryce-Jones. *Time and Tide* reviewed her poems along with a volume by Kathleen Raine, about whom the reviewer showed greater enthusiasm. Terence Tiller wrote critically of her book in the *Tribune*; he received a stiff letter of complaint.

The trouble was that no paper was likely to give priority to a book of poems (which was not actually a *Collected Poems*) all of which had been seen before, and all of which had, at the time of publication and since, received due attention and column inches. There was more to it even than that; the tide, which had flowed her way since 1942, was just on the turn.

Not in the United States, however. America had made her a star, and now wanted everything she could give. The reviews there of *The Canticle of the Rose* had none of the grudgingness of the British—they were "magnificent," she told Lehmann on December 19. "The *Herald-Tribune* gave it the *whole of the front page* and . . . two extra columns full of praise. The *New York Times* was also very long and laudatory." It confirmed what she had been feeling before these notices even came out—that only in America was she now properly understood. "I am so indignant at the way my poems (my work of nearly thirty years) have been treated, that I will never, *never* allow the British public to see one of my poems again." They would be published only in America from now on, she had told Lehmann on December 6.

Inevitably, communication with Pavlik in America was re-established, through Charles Henri Ford. Kirstein too kept her abreast of developments. Ford and Pavlik were in Paris in autumn 1949, where Pavlik was ill; he found Choura ill too, and the city he had not seen since before the war seemed disappointing and dreary. Pavlik had money worries again; and once more Edith agonised over his health and his pennilessness.

She had spent some time that summer hunting up all her old letters from him, since he had decided that their wartime correspondence was to be deposited at Yale—he had had this investment in immortality in mind for some time. By October 1949 all their letters were safely "in the vault" at Yale. Edith was still worrying and arguing with Pavlik about what restrictions should be formally put on access to the letters, and two years later consulted Geoffrey Gorer, who according to her will made in 1942 was one of her executors. His reply in November 1951 was this:

> For one thing, it is absurd to imagine that Pavlik will be remembered and you forgotten in a hundred years! And your letters are too individual and your vision too personal for it to be possible for any serious student to fail to identify you. . . . Also, I think let sleeping Pavliks lie. . . . If you really want to place restrictions on your letters write to the Librarian at Yale and send him [Pavlik] a copy—but it is no use arguing with a Russian about treachery. . . . Pavlik is *very* Russian: when he says "You [E.S.] are not interested in my work" he means "I am not interested in your work"—just like Vishinsky in U.N.!

And so the ban was put on access to both sides of the correspondence until the year 2000, subject only to the consent of Pavlik and Edith so long as they lived.

Charles Henri Ford was nearly as important now to Edith as Allen Tanner had been ten years earlier; and in 1949 she wrote a preface to his poems *Sleep in a Nest of Flames*. The claims of friendship—plus her only very recent familiarity with some of the material—had an odd effect on her anthology of American poetry, *The American Genius*. After Pound, Whitman was probably the American poet for whom she felt the most—"that basely slandered man," she had called him in *A Poet's Notebook*, "who was one of the greatest of all poets, that inspired and great soul who has been seen through the dirty eyes of little, mean, and meagre souls. . . ." When in September 1949 she sent Lehmann her proposed selection, he was for once less than wholly enthusiastic. He regretted, he wrote to her on September 12, that she had not in her introduction given her views on "the specific Americanism" of her selection. "Also, if you will forgive me saying so, I thought it ended rather abruptly." As to her selection, "I found myself out of sympathy with a great deal of Mr. Patchen's, Mr. Ford's, and Mr. Villa's work. None of them in my opinion merits anything like the space you have given them. . . . I am also not convinced that you can claim *both* Eliot and Auden as American poets."

Edith wrote back a week later, shamelessly and cheerfully defending her choices: "I, too, agree with what you say about them. But it is very difficult. Because José [Garcia Villa] began to weep at 5:30 on the evening I left, when he came to say goodbye; and although somebody took him out to dinner afterwards, tears rolled down his dark green cheeks, like large pearls, throughout the evening." As to Charles Henri Ford, he was "a curiously interesting poet. And there I am in an awkward position too, because I told him I would put those poems in." And Kenneth Patchen? "He is *literally starving*. I have had a *terrible* letter from his wife about their state. . . . "

She redeemed herself nevertheless: When revisions and proof corrections were alarming Lehmann with their costliness, she suddenly told him that she wanted to make a present of the book to his publishing firm. Her agent David Higham's fee was to be paid, but "I don't want a penny from the book." It was just as well; *The American Genius*, with a dedication to Minnie Astor, was not finally published until February 1951, and was not a great success.

In the spring of 1950 Tchelitchew and Ford went to Italy; in May Edith went to Montegufoni, in the hope of seeing them. Unlike her brothers, who were lifelong and indefatigable travellers, Edith took no pleasure in travel for its own sake. In the years following the war, restrictions of various kinds made travel even more complicated for her. If she wanted to take her jewelry with her, she had to take out an export license, even for a short period. In 1950, her application for a license listed the following:

> 2 large aquamarine rings—one round, one oblong.
> Large square aquamarine pendent surrounded by small jade beads, mounted in brass.
> Large rose-quartz brooch surrounded by jade beads.
> Large jacinth brooch.
> Jade brooch shaped like a lotus flower.
> Very large yellow topaz.
> Pale aquamarine ring (almost white) in shape of two bears.
> Two gold slave bracelets.
> Large cuff-like silver-gilt bracelet.
> Large ring of pale green paste like a peridot.

The journey to Montegufoni, especially when undertaken alone, was always a nightmare for her. She described it to Lehmann shortly after her arrival:

I had a hideous journey ... and left a trail of nervous breakdown and desolation from Victoria to Pisa. At Victoria I lost a permit, which was found with difficulty. Boarding the Blue Train I lost my porter and my luggage (again retrieved with difficulty). . . . At Pisa there was no one to meet me, and my luggage was (again) lost. It is a 2½ hour motor drive, over the mountains, from Pisa to Montegufoni, I can speak no Italian, don't know the way, there was a thick mist, and night was falling. I started off in a taxi, expecting to have to spend the night in the mountains, but was, eventually, rescued.

Osbert and Sacheverell both loved the *castello* itself, for its beauty, its history, and its setting. But it meant very little to Edith, and though she enjoyed the garden — the warmth, the lemon trees, and the fireflies in the evening — she was seldom very happy there. She could not work all the time; she got very bored.

Pavlik arrived for the weekend, with Ford, on May 19. The household was a little apprehensive, necessarily, about how it would work out. Edith was very careful. Parker Tyler has described her demeanour, as recalled by Ford: "[Pavlik's] great old friend, the English poet, herself covered with honours, seems to have arrived at a new, wiser, attitude. She hardly opens her mouth except for the most commonplace exchanges. Pavlik has the floor throughout their waking hours."[5] Ford, "thoroughly bored," was astonished by this new Edith. "Is it superior irony? Perhaps it is her way of being ideally feminine: a sweet, silent, perfect devotion. At last, *she may have guessed*."[6]

Edith had no fight left where the Boyar was concerned, and was taking no risks. She was relieved when there was no trouble — but depressed by what she saw as Pavlik's depression. (He was indeed ill and discontented.) Privately, she still suffered. She confided the most intimate personal and family matters these days to old Evelyn Wiel, foolish and limited though that lady was. Evelyn was outside the gossip ring, her loyalty and devotion were unquestioned, she belonged to the past, and, willy-nilly, she belonged to Edith, who was her sole financial and emotional support. "I owe my life to you and you have the ordering of it," Evelyn wrote to Edith in 1954. In return for this deadweight dependence, she answered Edith's confidences with her outspoken, highly partisan, and always affectionate comments. Her response to the Pavlik situation was tough, bringing all down to the demythologized level of common experience. Four months after the Montegufoni weekend, in October 1950, she wrote to Edith:

What a fool Pavlik is! and what a dog in the manger. He says he is not in love with you, but he expects you to behave as a little lapdog, to be taken up or put down as the mood moves him. Of course he is behaving in such a manner that you will be more and more fed up with him. What does he mean when he says you care about fame. So does everyone, but everyone does not remain natural and charming as you do.

Edith had had an opportunity to talk to Evelyn shortly after she saw Pavlik; for she left Montegufoni again soon after his visit, as she had to rehearse and then perform *Façade* again in England, this time at the Aldeburgh Festival, in June. In July, Evelyn came to London for her summer holiday. Osbert came back to London in July too, and it was now that his Parkinson's disease was finally diagnosed.

Parkinson's is incurable but not a killer; Osbert was fifty-seven. Edith tried hard to be optimistic. But those who saw them in London that summer noticed a change in Osbert—the shaking and the uncertainty. Edith, in contrast, seemed as timeless and resolute as a Henry Moore figure. The Sitwells' old friend Aldous Huxley, who lived now in California, was in Europe that summer, and wrote to Christopher Isherwood on August 11: "I was in England for two weeks. . . . Edith a monument and Osbert suddenly rather old and tired. . . . All very much *Le Temps Retrouvé*."[7]

Edith was writing very little poetry. In October 1950 Duckworth published *Façade* and other poems, written between 1920 and 1935; however exhausting she now found both rehearsals and performances, *Façade* was enjoying a popularity inseparable from Edith's personal success—it was, as John Pearson has said, the "incantatory high mass" of the Sitwell cult. In July 1951 the Oxford University Press published Walton's music and Edith's poems together, with a dedication to Constant Lambert, a close friend of both of them and one of the inner circle of *Façade*'s performing history, who died prematurely that same year. Edith objected strongly to some of the reading directions, and protested to Alan Frank of the Press: " 'Black Mrs. Behemoth' in 'a quiet hard voice'!!! That is not how I wish it to be done. And 'Popular Song' apparently is to be recited 'trippingly'!! (It is to be recited smoothly.)"

For the Duckworth edition of the *Façade* poems, Edith had proposed using her well-worn "Some Notes on My Own Poetry" as an introduction, but was shrewdly headed off by Mervyn Horder of Duckworth: "I believe too much of your 'notes' are taken up with explaining to the groundlings why 'blunt' is a colder word than 'dull'—matters which certainly needed explanation in the 1930s but sound (to me at any rate) a little vieux jeu at this moment in your career." He suggested using Jack Lindsay's essay from *A Celebration* instead, and Edith agreed.

Lindsay, in his own foray into publishing, brought out a short selection of her most recent poems ("The Madwoman in the Park" being the only one previously unpublished—a poem written after reading an essay, "Hanging Goddesses," by Lindsay) as the first in a series of Key Poets booklets to be sold for a shilling. The series was not a commercial success: "Even Edith's booklet hardly sold at all."[8] She compiled another potboiling anthology for Macmillan, *A Book of the Winter*, which Vanguard brought out in the United States the following year; and John Lehmann announced as forthcoming her selection from William Blake. This never saw the light of day, though she did publish an essay, "Whitman and Blake," in the *Proceedings of the American Academy of Arts and Letters* in 1951.

For the lure of America was on her again. The lecture agency had planned an even better and bigger tour for Edith and Osbert starting in the autumn of 1950. As a small fanfare, Little, Brown published her *A Poet's Notebook* in October (this American version included some sections from *A Notebook on William Shakespeare*, thus making the trading relationship between the two books even more complex). American readers, who ten years before had had to be persuaded to read Edith Sitwell, were now ready to take her early work.

Edith, Osbert, and David Horner set off again, aboard the *Queen Elizabeth*. For Osbert, in his shaky state, it was to be a less arduous schedule; Edith was the star of the show. They were going to take in the West Coast this time, and Hollywood: George Cukor and Columbia Pictures were interested in filming *Fanfare for Elizabeth*.

25

Entr'acte: Montages
1950–1952

They stayed once again at the St. Regis. Edith had to decide on a major production of some kind to cap the triumphant *Façade* of the previous year. Undaunted, she elected to give a reading from the part of Lady Macbeth. Nothing pleased her more than to be told she was an actress *manquée*. But here she was overreaching herself. It was not just a reading—it was a performance, with lights, costumes, and makeup. Edith wore a spiky gold crown, barbaric bracelets, and a voluminous gown. Evelyn Waugh, in New York again, sent a macabre verbal caricature of what was going on to Nancy Mitford on November 9: "Poor Osbert is a tottering corpse, Edith is playing Macbeth at the Museum of Modern Art on Nov. 16. Glenway Wescott as Banquo, David Horner in a tartan dinner jacket as Macduff. Lady Ribblesdale as the witches. Cheapest seat £5. I wish I could be there."[1] In fact, Glenway Wescott read Macbeth; the publicity material announced "Dr. Edith Sitwell, assisted by Mr. Glenway Wescott and Miss Gertrude Flynn, in a recital of scenes from Shakespeare's *Macbeth*," to be held at the Museum of Modern Art on November 16 at 9:00 p.m. The tickets cost from three to fifteen dollars for admission, plus twelve dollars as a tax-deductible contribution to the Museum's Program Fund.

The recital was an event of the most unforgettable, unprecedented, and bizarre kind. Only Edith could have got away with it, and not all the critics felt sure that she had; only the panache of the undertaking, and Edith's star quality, saved it from absurdity.

The dress rehearsal was in itself a performance: To it Edith invited her friends, among them Marianne Moore, Tennessee Williams, and Carson McCullers. Edith and Osbert had been to a party given by Tennessee Williams shortly after their arrival, and it was there that Edith had met Carson McCullers, then in her early thirties, for the first time. Afterwards Carson sent Edith copies of her novels, *The Heart Is a Lonely Hunter* and *The Member of the*

Wedding, and Edith responded with respect and admiration. Edith also responded to ill, erratic, alcoholic Carson on another level, recognising as she always could not only a fellow artist but a fellow misfit, and one with less capacity than herself for meeting the world on its own terms. It was this recognition that made her tirelessly sympathetic and patient with her "lame ducks," most of them far less distinguished than Carson McCullers. Carson, in her turn, had a need to hero-worship: Edith became the object of an infatuation. From now on they corresponded at length, "Dear Darling Edith" replying with solicitude to Carson's tales of suffering.

Five days after the *Macbeth* recital, Edith and Osbert set off on what Edith later called "our terrible tour." Osbert was slowed down by the drugs he had to take to keep going; Edith had bronchitis, a poisoned gland, and, in Mexico around Christmas, amoebic dysentery: "I really thought I was dying. However, I didn't die," she wrote to Lehmann in January 1951 from the Fairmont Hotel in San Francisco.

Edith, a star among stars, revelled in Hollywood, which she and Osbert visited for the first time in early 1951:

> As Osbert and I drove the immense distance from the station to the Bel Air Hotel, where we stayed for the first week, moving afterwards to a tall apartment house in Sunset Boulevard, the air of early morning seemed full of glamour. . . .
>
> Great golden stars of dew were falling from the tall mimosa trees, the oleander, the giant tree-ferns. . . . (Although the month was January, the heat was almost tropical.)[2]

Straightaway, they were invited to lunch with George Cukor. Edith, usually so indifferent to her surroundings, never forgot his house, "quite unlike any other house I know," remembering particularly some eighteenth-century chairs with gilded legs, whose backs and seats were "gigantic mother-of-pearl shells." Ethel Barrymore was at the lunch—"a superb statue endowed with life and wit," Edith called her in her autobiography, though at the time Osbert's laryngitis and Edith's second bout of bronchitis were ascribed to the suspicious fact that Miss Barrymore was "breathing heavily." Merle Oberon, "like a dark and lovely swan," was also there that day.

At another party Edith met Mary Pickford, whom she immortalized in her autobiography as "a confectioner's goddess of vanilla-flavoured ice-cream." In her letter of January 17 to Lehmann, she described this encounter as "a Laocoon entanglement that lasted for ¾ of an hour." Miss Pickford "discoursed to me of her role as Little Lord Fauntleroy, and said she always regarded herself as a Spiritual Beacon."

Edith, "coughing my head off" as a result of Ethel Barrymore's heavy breathing, and Osbert gave three poetry readings in Hollywood, one to an audience of over two thousand people, including Dorothy Parker, Harpo Marx, and Aldous Huxley. Edith's early liking for Huxley was undimmed; visiting him later, "I recaptured the fun, the liveliness and the happiness of my lost youth." She included the Lady Macbeth readings in her programme:

> And during my reading of the *Macbeth* sleep-walking scene, I was just announcing that Hell is murky, when a poor gentleman in the audience uttered the most piercing shrieks, and was carried out by four men, foaming at the mouth. As one of the spectators said to me, "You ought to be awfully pleased. It was one of the most flattering things I've ever seen."
>
> I've made records of that scene, the pillow scene from Othello, Cleopatra's death-scene, etc, for the Columbia records. . . . [3]

"I must say," she told Lehmann, "I could not have enjoyed Hollywood more." Her hyperbolic descriptions have a surrealist gaiety — as when she surmises whether the waiters at the hotel were under the influence of marijuana: "They would shriek with laughter suddenly, join in the conversations, and lean on the sofas on which we sat for our meals, putting their heads between ours. . . . "[4] Few maiden Englishwomen, of sheltered background, in poor health, and sixty-three years old, would have the adaptability and the capacity for wholehearted enjoyment that Edith displayed in Hollywood — even if they had the opportunity.

After Hollywood, she and Osbert — David Horner having detached himself from their cavalcade — crossed the continent again, to Florida, where they lectured at the Ringling Museum in Sarasota. Back at the St. Regis Hotel in New York at the beginning of March, Edith found a letter from Maurice Bowra (then the vice-chancellor of Oxford University as well as warden of Wadham College) informing her that in June she was to be given her third and most prestigious honorary doctorate — by the University of Oxford. She replied on March 5: It would be "the proudest and happiest moment of her life."[5]

She and Osbert travelled home to England. Their financial situation was improved by the incoming dollars, and Cukor had told Edith to set to work on a film treatment of *Fanfare for Elizabeth*. But Osbert's condition was the reverse of improved; he was dizzy and giddy, with tremors in the arms, and needed heavy doses of drugs. Edith got bronchitis again, in May.

Her anxiety about her "dear old boy" was discharged in attacks on outsiders: She went to London to open an exhibition "in order to frustrate the knavish tricks of the Griglet [Grigson], who had tried to prevent my being asked"; she shot off a sharp letter to the poet David Lutyens, a friend of Mrs. Vincent Astor, complaining that he had libelled (she meant slandered) her at a luncheon party in New York by saying that her poetry was fascist and anti-Semitic. She cited in her defence an anti-Nazi letter she had had published in the *Times* during the war.

She spent June 18 and 19 in Oxford for the conferring of her degree, along with other honorary graduands who included her old friend Arthur Waley, the Marquess of Salisbury, Field Marshal Lord Alexander of Tunis, and Lester Pearson. She was put up at Wadham College for what were "the most wonderful days of my life," as she wrote to Bowra on the twentieth:

> The day my ten-page book *The Mother* appeared seemed to me then the summit of happiness. But it was the beginning of the journey. And this is the arrival at my destination.
>
> I never did for one moment think, dream, or hope, that this could have happened to me. And I know I owe it entirely to you.[6]

On June 22 Edith gave a "huge luncheon party followed by a tea-party," to celebrate. The name "Dr. Sitwell" was now required, on all correspondence, on pain of sharp reproof, to be embellished with the triple crown of "D. Litt., D. Litt., D. Litt." Delighted as she had been with her first two doctorates, the Oxford one meant more to her. When John Gielgud was given his honorary doctorate from the same noble source two years later, Edith said in her letter of congratulation: "Fools are made doctors by other fools in other universities, but no fool has ever been given an Hon.D.Litt. by Oxford."

The New Yorker had carried a charming French limerick by Roger du Béarn on June 2, a cheerful tribute to her new honour and to the Sitwell phenomenon:

Il y a une soeur et deux frères,
Qui s'appellent Sitwell, pour vous plaire—
Faut les lire quelquefois—
Ils sont drôles tous les trois:
La Docteur, le Sachère, et l'Osbert.

But neither le Sachère nor l'Osbert was present on her great day. She avoided exacerbating the grievances that divided her brothers by what might have been an unfortunate confrontation, and invited neither of them.

Carson McCullers, who felt that in Edith she had found "a spiritual companion and champion,"[7] came to England for three months that summer, not only but largely to see her new friend again. She was looked after by the poet David Gascoyne during her visit: The two of them turned up in the middle of a reading Edith was giving for a summer school at London University, in the Senate House, and Carson interrupted to request Edith to read a poem she had already read before their arrival. Any gathering that included Carson, and even more so her husband, Reeves, was likely to be unorthodox. At a small party at the Sesame to which they came, Reeves McCullers was "imbibing freely" as he listened to his wife and Edith talking; "he suddenly slid to the floor, where he lay for another hour—while the conversation continued uninterrupted, and the distinguished poet revealed not the slightest notice."[8]

In July, after several telegrams, Edith had an enthusiastic letter from George Cukor about her draft for the film of *Fanfare*. He wanted Vivien Leigh for Anne Boleyn, and Laurence Olivier for Henry VIII. Vivien Leigh met Edith, read the draft treatment, and was enthusiastic: "I am simply bowled *over* by your wonderful treatment of the film, and long for us all to be working on it."

In March 1952 Penguin published a volume of her *Selected Poems* in the Penguin Poets series, a healthy index of her position on the poetry scene. And in July there was another of the public appearances that experience was teaching her to view not with increasing equanimity but with increasing apprehension. Her stamina, and her verbal dexterity, were not what they were. "I am doing *Façade* on Monday, to my terror," she told Plomer on May 14; and the July performance was at the Royal Festival Hall, under the auspices of the Society for Twentieth Century Music, of which William Walton—since the year before, Sir William Walton—was president.

Edith's personal success and personal fame during the 1950s and until her death can hardly be overestimated. Her name and her face were familiar to millions of people who had never read a word of her poetry. By being herself, she attracted the sort of notice that public relations organizations would charge a fortune for and still not achieve. Not all her peers viewed her fame with pleasure. Ivy Compton-Burnett said, "Success spoiled her. She got impossible. She's become a mixture of the Blessed Virgin Mary and Queen Elizabeth."[9]

The subtext of this fame shows the price that was paid—not in money. She was, nevertheless, overspending in a way that terrified her (she remembered her mother) when she stopped to think about it. She was living like a rich woman and like a woman of the world, and she was neither. She had no head for business, or for organization of any kind.

In buying her clothes, she veered between the modest and the extravagant. A lady called Agnes Booth, who lived in one of the cottages in Eckington, did alterations for her and made her corsets. Her hats, when they were not specially designed and made, came from Whiteley's, the large and unpretentious department store in Bayswater that she was faithful to from her Pembridge Mansions days. But her parties and her public readings, and her own tastes, called for grand and flamboyant clothes: The red velvet evening coat from Adrienne in South Molton Street, the coral and gold cloak and the black *poult de soie* afternoon and evening gowns from Nina Astier, cost a good many guineas. (Elizabeth Bowen said that she looked like "a high altar on the move.")

When she stayed at the Sesame Club she hired a car from the Daimler carhire firm Raper Bros. of Chelsea—driven by Mr. Raper himself, who came to know her well—not only for her own transport to and from dinners, parties, concerts, and readings, but very often for the transport of particularly fragile or particulary beloved guests as well, to and from her Sesame Club entertainments. The bill from Rapers', after a six-week stay in London in the summer of 1951, ran into three figures.

Then there were the bills for board and lodging, and for her huge parties, from the Sesame Club itself. And her bar bills; and the bills from F. F. Matta, the London wine merchants; and from the Sheffield wine merchants, Hay and Sons, which she ran up—injudiciously and tellingly high—during the months that she spent at Renishaw.

The Sitwells' semifeudal status at Renishaw meant that there were special obligations to be faced there and many calls on their time or money: Edith did not always get to the Annual Flower Show and Gala of the Renishaw Iron Works, but she always sent a cheque. A lady wrote from nearby Rotherham in

1950 regretting that Edith had been unable to come to some local function: "You know we local people admire you all tremendously but I fear we are afraid to show our feelings in the north. . . . Do forgive me for writing at all. I am a very lonely person, and perhaps it is our mutual feeling for animals that makes me love you." Like a poem or a painting, Edith and the idea of Edith served as a magnet for people's feelings, even if they never met her. She had become an icon.

She was in contrast very approachable, and greatly loved, by anyone who served her, starting with the maids and housekeepers who worked for her own family: Barbara Nopper, who looked after her at Renishaw, and Gertrude Stevenson at Weston. To the manageress of Peggy Sage in Bond Street, where she had her hands manicured, she was "Dearest Edith." The Welsh maid who looked after her at the Sesame Club, Hannah Lewis, wrote to her when they were apart, and tickets for Edith's readings were sent round to Hannah in Mr. Raper's car.

Among Edith's papers are grateful letters from many writers to whom she had sent small cheques to tide them over a difficult patch. She ordered coal to be sent to Tambimuttu, then the impecunious editor of *Poetry London*. Added to all this was the permanent charge on her resources of Evelyn Wiel.

Her own greatest benefactor was still and always Bryher, who from her home in Switzerland sent presents of furs, jewelry, clothes, books, cheques: "A little Chinchilla from my mother," a cheque for "a hat or something for one of your autumn parties," another "so that you may go shopping in London." In 1950 she gave Edith £3,000 for a house; but the money went to pay off the Inland Revenue. Bryher's generosity was disinterested and sprang from affection and from reverence for Edith's poetry (and not only Edith's—she helped Sacheverell financially as well).

The Sitwell icon also attracted unsolicited offerings of an embarrassing kind from people she hardly knew: presents of valuable jewelry, for example, from a rich widow, Alice Hunt (she laid siege to Osbert as well), to which Edith put a firm stop: "It is no question of giving way to gossip, it is that nobody of any dignity can allow certain things to be said. It is all too *vulgar* and *déplaisant* for any words."

Edith dined out on lively anecdotes of how she had crushed and annihilated enemies, fools, bores, people who were "impertinent," and lunatics. These anecdotes have passed into legend, along with her delighted and unrestrained laughter. But the legend is only half the story, since she fulfilled to the letter the precept "When thou doest alms, let not thy left hand know what thy right hand doeth." (Much the same relationship existed between her much-juggled bank accounts. She was permanently in overdraft in the 1950s.) Edith was not exaggerating, however, when she spoke of being persecuted by lunatics. The mad and the lonely wrote their souls out to her by every mail.

Lunatics came to her parties and became the subjects of subsequent anecdotes, in the telling of which their lunacy became more catastrophically defined as Edith exercised her poetic license. At the end of July 1952, for example, a young man she had invited to the Sesame Club "went mad at lunch," as she described to Harriet Cohen on the twenty-ninth. "At one moment I thought he was going to commit suicide over the balcony;"[10] he had also "made 'advances' of an unusual character to four ladies—one of them being Alan Searle's wife, Gillen, and another Lady [Kenneth] Clark. The Lindsays, who arrived at the point where the luncheon party became a tea party, later heard from Edith "the full tale, which took about an hour to unfold": additional details being that the young man, who was an ex-monk, had stroked a woman guest's leg at lunch and then tried to remove his clothes. There was also a subplot about another lady who was in hot pursuit of the Australian pianist Gordon Watson, whose playing Edith much admired; any time that Edith could spare from the "mad Trappist" was devoted to bilking the predator of her prey.

After—but not presumably on account of—this particular party, the Sesame was temporarily closed and Edith had to move into a hotel, which she did not enjoy at all. "The guests died like flies of inanition after the token meals," she told William Plomer. She was writing from Montegufoni, where she had fled in September from the uncongenial hotel, with a chill and a sprained ankle. She had to get well; in November she was thinking of having "a thin, *very* dark pine-green dress, with a white velvet coat. . . ."[11]

Being a star and an icon was no substitute for writing. That year, 1952, all she had published was another anthology, *A Book of Flowers*—other men's flowers—for Macmillan, the "Poetry" article for Cassell's *Encyclopaedia of Literature*, and a foreword to Sydney Goodsir Smith's poems, written partly as an act of friendship to the publisher, Peter Russell. King George VI died in February of that year; and Edith sent her anthology to Queen Elizabeth, now the Queen Mother, who had come to the Sitwells' poetry readings during the war, and whose mother-in-law, old Queen Mary, was Osbert's friend. The Queen wrote from Scotland to thank her on September 15:

It is giving me the greatest pleasure, and I took it out with me, and I started to read it, sitting by the river, and it was a day when one felt engulfed by great black clouds of unhappiness and misery, and I found a sort of peace stealing round my heart as I read such lovely poems and heavenly words.

I found a hope in George Herbert's poem, "Who could have thought my shrivel'd heart, could have recovered greennesse. It was gone quite underground" and I thought how small and selfish is sorrow. But it bangs one about until one is senseless, and I can never thank you enough for giving me such a delicious book wherein I found so much beauty and hope, quite suddenly one day by the river.

Edith's heart too needed to recover greennesse. She had published no new poetry. Hollywood lay in wait for her. She still had no formal contract with Columbia, though she was being given £5,000 for her travel and living expenses during her visit, with another $45,000 promised: As she wrote to Geoffrey Gorer from Montegufoni that September, "It really would be nice to have some money just for once."

Columbia Pictures organized a press conference for her in London before she left, at Claridge's. She wore a black Persian lamb coat and—in the *Manchester Guardian*'s words on November 20—"a magnificent piece of millinery—not a hat—of her own designing, with an embroidered band of gold braiding, draped on either side of the head with dark green velvet."

26

Deaths and Entrances
1953-1954

Edith, with Osbert and David Horner, went to Hollywood via New York and Los Angeles. There they saw Wystan Auden, with whom Edith now got on very well; they compared notes about persecutions and played literary games: "We thought out whom one would most hate being locked up with in Hell. . . . Wystan said I should be locked up with Wordsworth; I don't think he was quite right. Because I always think I am not going to like Wordsworth, but when I read him I adore him."[1] (Which was rather her position *in re* the poet she now called Wystan.)

Once Edith was settled in her apartment in Sunset Tower, at 8358 Sunset Boulevard, Osbert went off to Florida and Horner to New York: The two men were leading increasingly separate lives.

Edith was all set to deal with Hollywood on its own terms. Hedda Hopper announced the arrival of the celebrity without doing her homework— as Edith reported to T. S. Eliot on January 22, 1953:

> My principal entrancements here are the columns of the lady gossip-writers, which I read with avidity. . . . Unable to get to me—because I wouldn't see them—one wrote "A *little* old lady" (my italics) "has just come to Hollywood: Edith Sitwell." A man reporter asked me on the telephone: "Is it true you are 78?" I replied: "No. Eighty-two." "But I read last week that you are 78." "Yes, but that was *last* week. . . ." [She was sixty-six.]

She took her revenge by telling everyone that the current epidemic of rabies in Hollywood was "due to the fact that Miss Hopper had pursued the dogs and succeeded in biting them."

Edith liked and trusted Cukor, and he liked and respected her. She had, however, no idea at all about what Columbia expected a film script to be like.

She worked on her own poetry when not struggling with her assignment. By late March she had submitted a lot of material, which in studio terms was unusable. Cukor was tactful and courteous: "There seems to be some confusion." He arranged for Walter Reich, a professional script writer, to prepare a "brief, workmanlike synopsis" in a form that the "powers-that-be" would understand. Another disappointment was that Vivien Leigh had backed out. Cukor was now thinking of trying Audrey Hepburn or Elizabeth Taylor.

The Sitwells were back in England in April 1953, and Reich sent his new treatment for Edith's comments in May. She was appalled. From Renishaw she poured out her humiliation and fury to the Portuguese poet Alberto de Lacerda, with the stricture that he was to tell no one about it except his friend Gordon Watson, *"as I do not want my troubles going all round London and being discussed in potato queues"*:

> The film now opens with what would seem to be a sort of pillow-fight in the "dorm" of the 6th form at St. Winifred's (Anne's awakening): When the atmosphere isn't that of *Young Bess* or *The Tudor Wench*, it is that of *Forever Amber* or *Sweet Nell of Old Drury*. There is a lot of "rough stuff." George Boleyn comes into Anne's room when she is in a bath-towel! Henry is always either rolling drunk on the floor, or roaming about in his night-clothes, or snoring in bed.[2]

Edith went at Reich's script, hacking out the anachronisms and the tastelessness. Then she returned it to George Cukor.

On September 6, just as she was setting out for Montegufoni, Edith was thrown into disarray by reading that week's *Times Literary Supplement*, and tossed off a letter to Lehmann about "a most gross attack on me . . . contained in an article on your old friend Miss or Mrs. Manning. It is really *most* offensive. So is the heading."[3]

The heading was "Displacements by a Newcomer," and the unsigned review was of Olivia Manning's *A Different Face*, set in a long general essay on the Manning opus to date. In the course of this a parallel was drawn between the "gold" imagery in Edith's poetry and in Olivia Manning's story "The Children"; the point being made was that there was a natural process of displacement "continually at work in literature at large as it distils, whether in prose or verse, the poetry of life, by dint of which the purer metal in the end shows up the alloy."

Edith had already written off to the editor of the *TLS*, Alan Pryce-Jones ("really the birds are most dilatory, they don't get up early enough"). She kept Lehmann up-to-date, writing from Montegufoni on September 19 that an "angry" Pryce-Jones had written her "a letter that does him the greatest discredit," and that Arthur Waley had written to protest. Osbert thought the article was by a woman; she herself suspected Honor Tracy: "It is obviously someone who has a personal mania for Miss Manning. Of course I don't know if Miss T knows Miss M." (The article was by William Gerhardie.) "Of course Alan [Pryce-Jones] is furious because I told him his reviewers are in the great tradition, and will go down to posterity as having admired little miseries like J. D. [*sic*] Enright, and having insulted me." And then a true pain, the trigger for this frantic displacement activity, comes through: "In any case, they needn't have bothered, for I am now so *horribly* worried about Osbert, and so desperately miserable that I doubt I shall ever write poetry again. *Only please keep that to yourself—about Osbert I mean.*" "Desperately miserable"—about Osbert's deterioration, about the loss of poetry, about her humiliations over the film script.

This last misery was alleviated: In the same letter she was able to tell Lehmann that she had heard from Cukor that her film was going ahead. Cukor told her that the president of Columbia Pictures had telephoned him at six forty-five on a Sunday morning to say "It is so wonderfully *erotic!*"

So she was off to Hollywood again in November. In the same month Macmillan in London and Vanguard in New York brought out a slim collection of her most recent poetry, *Gardeners and Astronomers*. It included "The Road to Thebes," "A Song of the Dust," three songs dedicated to Roy and Mary Campbell and two for Gordon Watson, written after hearing him play Liszt in May 1952. The imagery is increasingly classical and religious, and there are no new themes. The only noticeable development was that remarked by Cecil Day Lewis, who wrote to her after reading the poems: "How on earth do you keep those long lines going? By rights they ought to fall down and break their backs: it's a sort of levitation—astonishing."

Dylan Thomas was in the United States that autumn too, on the poetry-reading circuit. Edith had described the Thomases' American progress to Jack Lindsay the previous year—at second hand, which meant with free rein given to fantasy: "I hear our dearest Dylan has been painting New York (literally) red, the centre of his activities being the Literary Salon of Mrs. Murray Crane." Dylan and Caitlin had come to blows, and to kicks and punches; blood had flowed. Mrs. Crane "shrieked and fainted"; Dylan was sent home, but "soon reappeared, and demanded money for his taxi."

Caitlin Thomas hated these tours: the women who "hunted singly, in pairs, and more often in packs," and the drink. On this occasion, however, Caitlin was not with him in America—and it was on this trip on November 9, 1953, that Dylan died.

Edith received a cable on the boat from John Malcolm Brinnin saying that Dylan was dead, and Brinnin was on the quay in New York to meet her. Then the horror stories started coming out. Edith retailed them to John Lehmann and Stephen Spender. To Lehmann:

> The only person he loved was Caitlin, but he had, since his first visit to America, got involved with two other women. . . . Something, I think must have happened about money not reaching C. In any case, about ten days before he died, she sent him an appalling telegram. . . . From that moment—egged on by the appalling Oscar Williams—he never stopped drinking. He told people he was at the gate of Hell. Then, one night he fell into a coma from which he never emerged.

Caitlin's arrival on the scene added horror to tragedy. In Edith's account, she "threw herself on the dying Dylan's body," tried to strangle John Brinnin, and "tore the habits off the nursing nuns." The reports, and Edith's imagination, were every bit as uncontrolled as Caitlin Thomas. "*We are going to say he died of diabetes, don't forget!*"[4] Edith warned Stephen Spender. And to Lehmann: "I *cannot* believe my dear Dylan, whom I loved, as well as knowing him to be a really great poet,—is dead. I just feel a dreadful numbness."

Dylan Thomas's death was followed by recriminations, scandals, and accusations. Edith was comforted by Roy Campbell, who wrote to her: "As for you, you always bring out the side that is noblest in all your friends, Dylan and me included. You are the only person of whom Dylan sometimes stood in awe."

Lehmann wanted a poem from her for the *London Magazine*, which he was now editing. She had given several of her new poems recently, including "The Road to Thebes," to the *Atlantic Monthly*. She was working on one, she said, but Dylan's death had exhausted her, and she could not get the poem done because she felt "it would sadden Osbert, whose state is increasingly tragic. . . . His right hand . . . . not badly yet, but . . . " She gave Lehmann the poem, however—"A Young Girl's Song"—for the May 1954 issue.

But in these unhappy circumstances she inevitably overreacted to press reports about a play by Peter Ustinov called *No Sign of the Dove* which had opened in London. The play was about a literary brother and sister called "D'Urt," and the most upsetting part of it all was that the character Edith decided was a skit on herself, Naomi D'Urt, was played by Beatrix Lehmann, the actress sister of John. She wrote off to loyal Arthur Waley, who sent her an equivocating letter from Gordon Square on January 20, 1954:

> About the play there is this to be said: everyone who has seen it is agreed that the sister is not said to be a famous poetess or indeed a poetess at all. . . . I have heard of (but not seen) several critiques that said the model was obviously "a well-known literary ménage." . . . This was generally taken to refer to Connolly and his wife of the moment. . . . Some people thought that the model was Clemence Dane. . . . I personally believe that Beatrix L. had not the faintest idea that it was meant to be you. But I may be wrong.

This kind of diplomatic hedging cut no ice with Edith, who scribbled across the bottom of Waley's letter, presumably for Osbert's eye: "Arthur has been 'got at' by John L. His letter is practically a transcript of John's letter to me. Everyone is going to be lovely and loyal and spare the Lehmanns and prevent us from winning an action if we took one. . . . Of *course* it was meant for us." But their lawyer, Philip Frere, with the expertise of long experience, dissuaded them from action. He had a command of phrase that equalled Edith's own: "Are you wise even to notice these small waves of scurrility breaking at the foot of your pedestal?"

On the day Waley wrote to Edith the *New Statesman* carried a "profile" of her headed "Queen Edith," accompanied by a cartoon by "Vicky." It was a brightly written piece of *Statesman* journalism, no more and rather less critical and malicious than might have been expected. But it would have hurt Edith that the anonymous writer was of the opinion that "not what she writes, but what she is, exerts the real fascination." This reached Edith within a few days, and added to her spleen and depression. She wrote to the paper to protest and so, to her gratification and pleasure, did Tom Driberg and John Pudney—their letters appeared in the issue for January 30. Edith wrote to thank them.

Edith enjoyed her visits to Aldous and Maria Huxley: "It is like being with one's own family, if one likes one's own family," she wrote to Michael Stapleton. "Aldous hasn't changed a bit since he was 23." The Huxleys took her on expeditions—to meet "nice Janet Gaynor" and her husband, to Forest Lawn, the scene of Evelyn Waugh's *The Loved One*, and to visit Edwin Hubble, the great astronomer, who died later in the year. In Hollywood, Edith went to most of the parties she was invited to. She was impressed by her meeting with Katharine Hepburn, whose personality, she said, was "the most outstanding I have ever met." She remarked on Hepburn's "quite extraordinary cleanliness—not only of person, but also, most obviously, of her spiritual life. . . . "[5] But the most publicized of all her Hollywood encounters, on account of its superficially dramatic incongruousness, was that with Marilyn Monroe. It was *Life* magazine that had the idea of bringing them together.

Marilyn Monroe was duly brought to Edith's apartment in Sunset Tower in February 1954. She stayed about half an hour. The film star was wearing a green dress and looked, wrote Edith in her autobiography, "like a daffodil." She touched Edith's heart and her imagination:

> She was very quiet, and had great natural dignity (I cannot imagine anyone who knew her trying to take a liberty with her) and was extremely intelligent. She was also exceedingly sensitive. . . .
>
> In repose her face was at moments strangely, prophetically tragic, like the face of a beautiful ghost—a little Spring-ghost, an innocent fertility-daemon, the vegetation spirit that was Ophelia.[6]

They talked about Rudolph Steiner, whom Marilyn Monroe had been reading recently; and Edith told her funny stories about Helen Rootham's unfortunate Steiner phase, when Edith had been compelled to look on at "what I believe was known as a Nature-Dance (something uniting one, I expect, with Mother Earth) in which ladies of only too certain an age galloped with large bare dusty feet over an uncarpeted floor. . . . I am afraid that Miss Monroe and I could not resist laughing about it."[7]

Edith's daily struggle with Walter Reich over the film script was ceasing to be a laughing matter. In a letter to Driberg on February 4 she had described how Reich "wants to make it naturalistic, as he calls it. One can't contradict him, because if one does he shrieks like a regiment of horses that has been mowed down by cannon." He would "hang head downwards over a sofa shrieking," she told E. M. Forster. By February 18 their collaboration had deteriorated even further, as she described to John Lehmann: "I am beside myself: the whole damned film has got to be done again—because of dear Walter's unconquerable obstinacy. You see, he has a mania for that regal personage Charles Laughton, so dwarfs everything down to his image." Reich's attempts to make the script naturalistic meant, in Edith's opinion, that the atmosphere of the English court became "a cross between that of Le Nid and Mon Repos in Surbiton, and that of a sixth form dormitory at St. Winifreds. Anne Boleyn eats chocs behind a pillar, and pinches Jane Seymour's bottom behind Cardinal Wolsey's back."[8] Edith was out of her element and felt wretched. She wanted to go home. "I have been feeling very unhappy and disorganized—in fact really on the verge of a breakdown," she told Stephen Spender on February 26, explaining why she had written so infrequently. "I have loathed being here."[9]

The very day that she had met Marilyn Monroe she had had another and grimmer experience. She had been driven by the *Life* photographers through Hollywood, through Chinatown, and into the slums of Los Angeles—to Skid Row. Velma LeRoy, her black maid, and a policeman friend went with them. The derelicts and lost souls awoke in Edith pity, horror, and sympathy: These were the outcasts, the unloved; this was the world as in its blackest moments she had seen it when "Gold Coast Customs" had been written, and her wartime poetry. Here was the Sailor's Street, and these homeless men were Lazarus unredeemed and unrisen.

> The people who crawled along the pavements looked as if they were made of either red rags or grey rags. Those made up of red rags coughed all the time. The others merely stared.
>
> There is no contact between one human being and another. If you die of starvation, that is *your* affair. You must not expect me, menaced with the same fate, to care. (Every time I see a poor man, I see the Starved Man on the Cross.)[10]

It was this picture of America that was to stay with her, side by side with that of the other glittering America that was fun and friendship, parties and poetry. At the end of the first week of March 1954 she returned—"thank God!" —to New York, and Osbert; thence to London, where she saw Tennessee Williams's *Camino Real*, liked it, and wrote to tell him so; and on to Montegufoni, to recover in the Tuscan spring. There she worked in rooms on the first floor, reached through a salon decorated by Severini and looking out over what was called the Cardinal's Garden.

A book that had given Edith great pleasure and amusement towards the end of her unhappy months in Hollywood was Kingsley Amis's *Lucky Jim*. There is a reference to her in the novel: Jim Dixon makes "his Edith Sitwell face into the phone" when he is pretending to be a journalist. She wrote Amis a very enthusiastic letter early in February 1954, telling him that she had read his book twice in ten days; she wrote again after she had heard from him, and made plans to meet him at the Sesame Club when both she and he were in London. (Amis was then teaching English at the University College of Swansea, in Wales.) It seemed like the beginning of a pleasant new literary friendship. But her generous and appreciative gesture was made towards one who was part of a movement—the Movement—that excluded her.

The *Spectator* was the newly named Movement's principal platform through its reviewer Anthony Hartley; on January 8, 1954, he had written a review of Edith's *Gardeners and Astronomers*, pointing up all those aspects of her writing that offended against his own idea of poetry, and making a good enough case. Her book, he said,

> illustrates the consequences of letting the imagery rip. The method of her poetry is baroque: images are piled on in decorative heaps that conceal rather than define the form of a poem. . . . One image leads to the next, but the ideas behind them do not follow. Quite the reverse. They are destroyed and made ridiculous. . . . I wish she would get back to the harder rhythms and more economical images of her earlier poems where a modicum of decoration was in place.

But of course one can never "go back." Edith replied to the review, first with a letter making fun of a putative "Little Mr. Tompkins (or whatever his name may be), this week's new great poet," and then with a cable, from Hollywood: "Please have Anthony Harteles [*sic*] stuffed and placed in glass case with moth balls at my expense. Finest specimen in your collection. My reasons will soon be divulged to whole world. Edith Sitwell."

The correspondence proliferated. John Wain, Elizabeth Jennings, and an unknown and facetious person signing himself "Little Mr. Tompkins" had letters in the paper on January 29; on February 4 there was another facetious letter signed "Peridot and Beryl" (imagery of Edith's that Hartley had questioned included "Where the sap like peridots and beryls— /Rises in the budding fig-branches"). Edith wrote again for the issue of February 19, opining that the letter from "Peridot and Beryl" was "obviously written by the same wearisome person who wrote the letter signed 'Little Mr. Tompkins.'" No, it was not, said the editor, in a footnote. Edith's letter continued: "Mr. Hartley and I have at least one thing in common. I gather that he admires the work of Mr. Kingsley Amis. I have not, as yet, read Mr. Amis's poetry, but I have read his most remarkable, most distinguished first novel *Lucky Jim* with enthusiastic admiration." To Kingsley Amis himself she wrote on March 8 that "the whole *Spectator* affair is too extraordinary for words. *Not one* of the persons who has had the impertinence to attack me has even a germ of talent for poetry. They simply can't write."[11]

She cannot have seen the *Spectator* of February 26, in which Kingsley Amis had declared himself. He wrote: "A writer at the outset of his career can rarely hope for such generous praise as that contained in the last paragraph of Dr. Sitwell's letter. At the same time I feel I should point out that I myself am 'Little Mr. Tompkins.'"

The correspondence was finally closed on February 26 by Laura S. Deane, the first wife of Edmund Blunden, who had already supported Edith's stand and who wrote again to defend Edith against those who attacked her for arrogance and illogicality in her response to criticism; her letter begged for a distinction to be made between "creation and behaviour," between "poets and their periphery," and ended with a challenge to "any reader, reviewer, stuffed bird or wandering voice to cite an English-speaking woman poet, dead or living, who can rightfully be placed on a level with Edith Sitwell." No one took up the challenge and the matter rested.

It was like the 1930s all over again: The wheel had turned. The young and not-so-young names associated by critics with the Movement were Kingsley Amis, Donald Davie, D. J. Enright, Elizabeth Jennings, Thom Gunn, Philip Larkin, John Wain, and Robert Conquest.[12]

The Movement was in general anti-Eliot, anti-modernist, anti-symbolist, pro-Leavis. (It never spoke with one voice—but there was a melody discernible in its dawn chorus.) Movement poets were still young in austere postwar Britain. They had profited from the welfare state, and they had done their National

Service. They were not upper-middle-class metropolitans. They were dons and students, and not from Oxbridge. They were, typically, the products of provincial university English departments. They were impatient with Romantic postures, metaphorical lavishness, preciosity, conceits, obscurity, and minority art.

Dylan Thomas's *Collected Poems* came out in 1952. He—even though he was a poor boy from Wales—and Edith Sitwell represented everything they did not want: Did the sort of poetry that they wrote "mean" anything? Movement poets valued precision and demystification, and disliked magic, incantation, and childhood nostalgias. The Movement disliked too the Romantic idea of the poet as a special person; they scorned the idea of walking around—like Dylan Thomas and Edith—wearing Baudelaire's albatross round their necks. The albatross, like Nellie Wallace's feather boa in Edith's old joke, had lost most of its plumage in austerity Britain.

The Movement's poetic style was clipped and conversational. Although Movement poets were forming a new, nonpatrician literary intelligentsia, they worked very hard at being nonintellectual. Here there was an added irony in their threat to Edith. For they were not so much like the Auden generation as they were like the Georgians, against whom her first long-ago crusades had been fought. They assumed the postures of the tough, easygoing, strictly heterosexual, beer-drinking Englishman. Reacting against the large gesture that might be empty, they wrote in disciplined, conventional verse forms. They approved of everything English; foreign modes were seen as affectations. European culture was again pushed into the background. This was partly defensive; the background of most of the Movement poets had not been privileged. They made poetry of what they knew and had, and ridiculed all that seemed to them pseudo, inflated, and unreal. To Edith it seemed, yet again, the advance of the philistine.

It was never so clear-cut as a summary must suggest. Readers of poetry did not stop reading Edith Sitwell overnight. Those who loved her poetry continued to do so, and there were still and always those who came to it for the first time and found what they were looking for: the sensualists, the romantics, the mystics. But the Movement presented a coherent alternative conception of poetry. Although even by the mid-1950s most Movement poets had gone their different ways, a new literary establishment and a new readership had come into being.

Perspectives shifted. In the *Oxford Book of Twentieth Century Verse* compiled by Philip Larkin and published in 1973—nine years after Edith's death—there are four poems by Edith Sitwell: a *Façade* poem, "Sir Beelzebub"; a section from *The Sleeping Beauty*; "Heart and Mind"; and the whole of "The Shadow of Cain"—a selection that shows a catholic recognition of her various modes and qualities. Helen Gardner, the compiler of *The New Oxford Book of English Verse* (1972), put in the same section from *The Sleeping Beauty*, the *Façade* "Polka," and "Still Falls the Rain," giving a similar and not ungenerous recognition of her range. (The major collections of most of the Movement and other contemporary poets, and their significant anthologies, did not fall within her time span, which ended in 1950, and so lessened the competition for space among the moderns.)

The inclusion of Edith Sitwell, in all her phases, in the Oxford Books must reassure her ghost; and the validity of the inclusions is heightened by the fact that only her ghost is there to be reassured. For in her lifetime it was very hard for any critic to make a dispassionate criticism, whether positive or negative, about her poetry. As Charles Osborne wrote in the *London Magazine* in December 1962: "Her fierce sensitivity to criticism is to be regretted if only because it has encouraged extremes of sycophancy in some and enmity in others, and has in recent years not only obscured her real merits but made any serious discussion of them well-nigh impossible."

The Movement did not permanently oust Edith from the canon, and in any case, the wheel keeps turning. Nevertheless, in her last years "the poetry scene" gave her little reassurance about the nature of her achievement; and fearful self-doubt lay like a pain beneath the fame, the distinguished friendships, the public honours, the great set-piece public appearances, the parties, and the laughter.

27
God and Mammon
1954-1955

Edith, disappointed by the way she was being treated by critics in her own country, had promised her obituary article on Dylan Thomas to the *Atlantic Monthly*, where it appeared in February 1954. A new *Collected Poems* of Edith Sitwell was in preparation, but it was to be published only by Vanguard in New York (in December 1954): "It will not be appearing in England," she told William Plomer on July 9.

But suddenly Britain did for her what republican America could never do. The announcement that Dr. Edith Sitwell was now a Dame Commander, Order of the British Empire, was made in the Queen's Birthday Honours List. There was champagne at Renishaw. Letters of congratulation poured in. Edith engaged a secretary. John Sparrow, Warden of All Souls College, Oxford, long one of her "silent correspondents," as he said, was among the hundreds of old friends who wrote to her. "It's great fun being a Dame," she remarked in answer to Cecil Beaton's letter. Alan Searle wrote facetiously that he was letting her into a secret: "Willie [Maugham] is rather peeved that you didn't share and share alike, and nothing I can say will convince him that he really can't be called Dame Willie."

To Plomer she wrote from the Sesame, "I *am* glad to have been made a Dame, because it has slapped down all the miserable little pipsqueaks in the *New Statesman and Nation* and *Spectator*, who have been persecuting me for months." She wrote this on June 18; the *Spectator*, that thorn in her flesh, had responded to her new honour that same day—not, as might be expected, with a sneer or a groan, but with a carillon from Compton Mackenzie:

> Dr. Edith Sitwell is the greatest poet that the women of England have yet produced and the Order of the British Empire was beginning to look rather ridiculous on Parnassus without Dr. Sitwell as a Dame. It was,

indeed, high time that her stature was formally acknowledged. I had a strong suspicion nearly forty years ago that she would in time displace my beloved Christina Rossetti from her supremacy; with the passage of the years a rich maturity has given to Edith Sitwell's genius the glow of a golden harvest. When I shall have the pleasure of addressing her as Dame Edith I shall be addressing, with a prefix hallowed by childhood's fairy dreams, a figure of English history.

Bryher's loving congratulations were accompanied by largesse ("Now we must celebrate this worthily and I wondered how about a tiny new fur coat or cape for the summer?") which was repeated at the end of June, since "you will have extra expenses with the Palace, etc, and you must have everything of the best for such an occasion."

That summer Osbert's walk was very uneven and uncontrolled; he was more and more dependent on the help of others; he grew more reclusive, and gentler, as if resigned to his decline. He and Edith—later they were joined by David Horner—went to Montegufoni in September. Edith told Harold Acton, when he came over from Florence to see them, "I'm not as lame as I seem to be, but I don't want Osbert to feel that I'm bursting with health when he's so shaky."[1]

It was a tranquil interlude. She wrote to Lehmann in October, declining to review for the *London Magazine*, since she was just "on the verge of writing poetry again after ages of nothing happening. (Indeed—but I scarcely dare say this, because it is still in germ—I think I am going to get a new atmosphere.)" But this was a false dawn.

In mid-November 1954, Edith, Osbert, and David Horner set out on what was now their regular winter visit to the United States. Edith had a lecture tour arranged—a new and lively topic, "Hollywood," was now added to her repertoire. Osbert's object was to consult the best doctors in New York and to look for new treatment.

Edith also made a sortie to Hollywood in the new year, but only to exchange courtesies; Columbia had shelved *Fanfare for Elizabeth* inconclusively—but, as it turned out, finally. Any disappointment was counterbalanced by relief at not having to struggle with the script anymore. She had her "wages of sin," as she called the money earned, and bought two more great aquamarines with it.

She had something far more disturbing to worry about. She saw how Osbert in New York suffered when David Horner, healthy and full of energy, left him for long periods while she was away lecturing. Osbert's urbane defences were down. He did not complain, but the mask of sophistication and reserve that he had always worn to conceal his emotional life had worn thin. He was a very sick man, and David's absence with other friends made him unhappy, and Edith saw his unhappiness.

When Osbert's illness had first shown itself, David Horner had been attentive and kind, making light of his symptoms in an affectionate and encouraging way. His attitude never underwent any great change. John Pearson, describing the long relationship between Osbert and David, has said that it was always understood between them that Horner must have some life of his own, and that as Osbert's condition worsened, Horner would need his periods of independence even more, and also that it was a matter for the two people concerned to work out between themselves.[2] Nor is it clear what passed between Osbert and Edith in early December 1954 in New York. But whatever he said and she said, the depth and the nature of Osbert's feeling for Horner were unequivocally brought home to her, just at the time when Horner, it seemed, was abandoning him. She was shocked by the revelation of Osbert's need and filled with anger against Horner; her anger became one with the rage and fear she had felt when Tchelitchew abandoned Allen Tanner. The withdrawal of love was for Edith as for a small child the most dreadful, unforgivable, unforgettable crime.

Bryher, in whom Edith had confided before Christmas, had written on December 14 full of sympathy for Osbert's situation, and tried to draw Edith out of her involvement, back into life and work. Edith had written an introduction to Bryher's novel *The Fourteenth of October*, which had recently come out; and Bryher told Edith how greatly she valued "your love, your sympathy, understanding and above all, your poetry, that magnificence which is really all we have as a shield against the Gorgon"—and she had sent a cheque to Edith's bank, "by way of a Christmas card."

The misery over Horner might all have been justified, from Edith's point of view, if she and Osbert could now have been united against the betrayer; if Horner treated Osbert so badly, Osbert might be better off without him. But Osbert was without resentment. When Horner travelled back to England, and to Renishaw, with them, it was all as if nothing had happened. Edith, for Osbert's and dignity's sake, could have no open quarrel with Horner. All through the 1950s, they remained on civil, familial terms. She suppressed her

violent feelings of distaste and resentment. But she stayed in her cabin for most
of the voyage home, having written to Lehmann before they sailed: "Dear
little Lord Fauntleroy is returning with us, to reinfest the house."

· On August 8, 1955, Edith wrote to John Hayward, "My life in America and
since I got back from America has been *one long hell* . . . and I have been able to
settle down to nothing excepting over-work, and becoming a Catholic (which
I became on Thursday)."[3]

It was partly the need for some authority high enough to contain and
control the turmoil of her feelings about David Horner that drove her to take
the same step as he himself had taken over ten years before. In 1944 Horner had
become a convert to the Roman Catholic Church, and Edith had written to
him on April 2 of that year: "I am certain this is going to bring you great
happiness, and that you were absolutely right and absolutely wise to take the
step.—I have never understood why people are afraid of constructive rules.
Very few people are capable of coming to any great decision, but you have
been." She was sure that such a decision "gives one an immense feeling of calm
and of peace and security, and a great framework on which to build one's day."
(After her own conversion, she said of Horner, to Jack Lindsay and to others,
"If I had not been a Catholic, I would have murdered him.")

But however "absolutely right and absolutely wise" she felt Horner's
decision to be, she had not at that time been very sympathetic to the Catholic
mentality. In an undated wartime letter, Stephen Spender wrote to her:

> Tom [Eliot] has awfully good things to say, but the smugness with which
> he takes shelter in the "Catholic" view of life is always irritating. . . . Nor
> is it true that the Catholic point of view is even as superior an answer to
> the difficulties of being alive as Eliot seems to think. It's all right on paper,
> but in practice Catholics can only get through the day with the help of
> aspirin or whisky. They have acute neuralgia, most of them: and those
> that don't are hypochondriacs.

She might have been disturbed had she reread his words ten years or so later.

Jack Lindsay interpreted her conversion from his Marxist standpoint:
"She still thought rather as Carlyle and Dickens thought. The Fires of God and
the avenging angel, not the activity of organized persons, were what brought
about the destruction and renewal. And so the image of Christ was central in

her concept of revolutionary change. . . ."[4] He thought that while Christ originally appeared in her poetry as "a necessary image of human unity," she came increasingly to need the image "as an external reality, outside as well as inside her poetry." Another friend, John Piper, was less able to understand Edith's need; a staunch Anglican, he saw little of her after her conversion.

Edith had met Father Martin D'Arcy, S.J., with Roy and Mary Campbell, who were both Roman Catholics. In April 1955, when Edith wrote to him announcing her decision, Father D'Arcy was in Notre Dame, Indiana. He replied conveying great pleasure at the news: "I had felt God's love moving in your last volumes of poetry." So had other readers and critics—it had been true since "Gold Coast Customs"—and she had accepted their observations. Writing to Bowra on January 24, 1944, about the essay that later appeared in *A Celebration for Edith Sitwell*, she had said: "Your sentence: 'the earth is more than a garment of God: it is a manifestation of God himself' is wonderful, and it is the truth that lies beneath all my poetry."[5] And the pantheism in her poetry, which Lindsay saw as Marxist, Kenneth Clark in his *Celebration* essay had seen as Christian: "Miss Sitwell is essentially a religious poet; that is to say, she has experienced imaginatively, not merely intellectually, the evil and misery of the world and has overcome that experience by the conviction . . . that all creation is one under the Divine Love." Edith had the religious temperament; but she had not, until now, felt the need for the structure and institution of organized religion.

After exchanging letters with Father D'Arcy, Edith heard Benjamin Britten's setting of her "Still Falls the Rain" at the Wigmore Hall on April 23. "I had no sleep at all on the night of the performance. And I can think of nothing else," she wrote to "My dear Ben." Since Father D'Arcy was in America, he had referred Edith to his colleague Father Philip Caraman, based at Farm Street in London, who was to give her instruction in the Catholic faith. He and Edith met for the first time on April 29. Edith wrote to him that their meeting had given her "a sense of happiness, safety and peace such as I have not had for years. . . . What a fool I was not to have taken this step years ago."[6] She wanted peace of mind above all things. She said once that it was the serenity in the faces of the peasant women praying in the churches in Italy that had drawn her to the Church.

She was off at once to Montegufoni. The *Atlantic Monthly* and Little, Brown had commissioned a large anthology of British and American poetry—

the American one-volume edition finally ran to over a thousand pages—and she was trying to come to grips with it. Father Caraman, to whom she finally dedicated the anthology, wrote to her in Italy on May 1: "Now this may be a bold thing to say—but I am convinced that the Holy Spirit has so worked already in your heart and mind, that there is little left for a priest to do, save take you systematically through the principal articles of Catholic faith." Which was just as well, since her schedule on her return to London in June was packed—"I shall probably be a stretcher case," she warned Bowra, planning a luncheon on June 22 for him, the Clarks, and David Jones, "whom I do not know, but I think he is a really great poet." During June she also had to recite in Cambridge, and rehearse and perform *Façade* at the Festival Hall on the fifteenth. She was also recording *Façade* for Decca—they had paid her an advance of fifty guineas.

None of this, including the award of her fourth honorary degree (from Sheffield University), was conducive to preparation for her new undertaking. But all through May in Italy and June in London she had corresponded regularly with Father Caraman. She confided to him her chief spiritual problem, from Montegufoni, on May 7. She was "under daily temptation to great anger":

> It is because of something terribly cruel which has been done to my dear Osbert, and by his greatest friend. It has made Osbert, who has now even to have his food cut up for him, see himself as a hopeless cripple, dependent on the ordinary kindness that has been denied him. His friend deserted him ... but now he who owes everything in the world to Osbert, is back in this house for his own convenience and intends to live with us again, and it is a great difficulty to me. I have so far shown no anger, but I do feel it. I must, of course, remember my own grave faults.

Father Caraman suggested that they might hope that Osbert's sufferings would bring him too into the Church. Evelyn Waugh, also a convert, but one of twenty-five years' standing, had the same thought. Edith wrote to him in July to tell him she was under instruction, and Waugh replied: "Welcome, welcome. . . . Is it exorbitant to hope that your example and prayers may bring Osbert to the Faith? I have often thought I saw in his writing (tho' not as plain as in yours) that he was near the truth."[7] But neither Osbert nor Sacheverell followed her. "Where are you refuged, my sister, / Among orisons and litanies?" wrote Sacheverell in "Serenade to a Sister":

The telling of the rosary
Is but a counting of the petals,
Is but a rose held in an old and withered hand,
Not hands as yours,
Supple and youthful,
That are the tiger in the tiger-lily.

In July Father Caraman went up to stay at the Jesuit house at Spink-hill, a mile across the valley from Renishaw, to give her instruction. He had already been feeding her with literature: "Mr. Sheed's *Theology and Sanctity* is being a great help to me," she told him. "Saint Thomas Aquinas is a wonder of course from every point of view. I do not find Mgr. Knox's book of great help to me for several reasons. One being that I do not like his style of writing."

But she made no difficulties for her instructor over points of dogma and doctrine. The Church offered her a home and a family, and she gladly embraced its house rules. Her life, though crowded with people, was lonely. The Church, with its confessional relationships, took her and her anxieties on its shoulders more acceptingly and more reassuringly than could have the mother, lover — or analyst — that she had never had. A place on Parnassus cannot be guaranteed; but "in my father's house are many mansions." If Christ did not save, there was nothing but the bones, the dust, the ass's bray, the "heart's dark slum," Skid Row, the eternal Cold. Often, in her own heart as in her poetry, that was all she believed there was. In her commitment to the Starved Man on the Cross she was not only formally aligning herself with the poor and the outcast, and preparing for death, but accepting the hope of life on its own terms — "the blind, all-seeing Power at her great work of death and rebirth," as she wrote in "Bagatelle," one of the *Gardeners and Astronomers* poems.

In her own life, she had no way other than through her poetry (which was drying up) of transcending herself. Most people find a way to flow out of themselves; most know the nonphysical realities that are reached through physical love, or through caring for a child. Edith could not even lose herself in making a garden, a home, a cake. "From pent-up aching rivers, / From that of myself without which I were nothing"[8] — Whitman's litanies express, albeit in too stridently physical a context, something of Edith's frustrations. All rivers, however pent-up, find their way to the sea. The Roman Catholic Church is one great outlet, and it could contain and sustain anything she chose to pour into it. In "How Many Heavens. . ." from *Street Songs* she had written:

"He is the core of the heart of love, and He, beyond labouring seas, our ultimate shore."

"She was an eccentric woman. And she was an eccentric Catholic," said Father Caraman. Evelyn Waugh, a stickler for form, was concerned lest her reception into the Church might be eccentric too. He wrote to Father Caraman on July 19:

> I am an old friend of Edith's and love her. She is liable to make herself a little conspicuous at times. She says she will be received in London. Am I being over-fastidious in thinking Mount St. Mary's much more suitable. What I fear is that the popular papers may take her up as a kind of Garbo–Queen Christina. . . . There are so many malicious people about to make a booby of a Sitwell. It would be tragic if this great occasion in her life were in any way sullied.[9]

The occasion may have been mildly eccentric, but it was unsullied. It took place at noon at Farm Street Church in Mayfair on August 4. She was received by Father Caraman. Waugh was her godfather, wearing a check suit and a straw boater with a red-and-blue ribbon. (Edith's other godparents were the Campbells, but Roy Campbell was ill and they could not come.) Since her conversion was pre–Vatican II and the subsequent reforms, she was obliged to publicly recant all manner of heresies, which she did with aplomb. Evelyn Waugh described the proceedings in the church in his diary:

> A bald shy man introduced himself as the actor Alec Guinness. Presently Edith appeared swathed in black like a sixteenth-century infanta. I was aware of other people kneeling behind but there were no newspaper men or photographers as I had half feared to find. Edith recanted her errors in fine style and received conditional baptism, then was led into the confessional while six of us collected in the sacristy.

The six were himself, Father D'Arcy, Alec Guinness, "an old lame deaf woman with dyed red hair whose name I never learned" (this was Evelyn Wiel), "a little swarthy man who looked like a Jew but claimed to be Portuguese" (Alberto de Lacerda), and "a blond youth who looked American but claimed to be English." They all drove off in Mr. Raper's Daimler to the Sesame Club:

I had heard gruesome stories of this place but Edith had ordered a banquet
—cold consommé, lobster Newburg, steak, strawberry flan and great
quantities of wine. The old woman suddenly said: "Did I hear the word
'whiskey'? " I said: "Do you want one?" "More than anything in the
world." "I'll get you some." But the Portuguese nudged me and said: "It
would be disastrous."[10]

On August 9 Waugh wrote to thank Edith for the luncheon party—"I
thought your circle of friends round the table remarkably typical of the Church
in its variety and goodwill"—and pondered whether, as her godfather, he should
warn her of the "probable shocks" in the "human aspect of Catholicism": "Not
all priests are as clever and kind as Fr. D'Arcy and Fr. Caraman. . . . But I am
sure you know the world well enough to expect Catholic bores and prigs and
crooks and cads. I always think of myself: 'I know I am awful. But how much
more awful I should be without the Faith.' " He ended by saying: "I heard a
rousing sermon on Sunday against the dangers of immodest bathing-dresses,
and thought that you and I were innocent of that offence at least."[11]

Two months later, on October 4, Edith crossed the last rubicon and was
confirmed at Farm Street in front of "a large invited audience, the cream of
Catholic London." Waugh was not there; he repeated in his diary what Lady
Pakenham had told him. The good Archbishop Roberts seemed to take this
sophisticated congregation for "one of his mission schools in Bombay": " 'Now
I want you all to learn this very useful prayer and say it every day if you don't
do so already. Repeat after me—O God—pour down—we beseech thee—thy
grace. . . .' He made them go through it in chorus three times." (One suspects
the archbishop knew precisely what he was doing with "the cream of Catholic
London.") Afterwards, Waugh was told, there was a cocktail party at the
Connaught Hotel, "paid for by the Jesuits." "After Edith left, Father Caraman
announced: 'Before we separate I just want to say that any of you who would
like to ask Dame Edith to a meal, is free to do so.' "[12] There were some things
that even the Roman Catholic Church could not do for Edith.

She had written to Lady Lovat on August 25:

I *am* still feeling bewildered. . . . But when I have finished the anthology
of 1,700 pages I am working at, I shall be able to read works of doctrine
with proper concentration. How wonderful the Theological Texts of St.
Thomas Aquinas, translated by Father Gilbey, are! To read them is like
being put into an oxygen tent when one is dying.

The divine oxygen did not make Edith a *dévote*, nor even a career Catholic. This "eccentric Catholic," once she had espoused Catholicism, made it the background to her life, not the foreground. Perhaps she had hoped for a miracle, and, like a wife after her wedding night, she was disappointed that she was still the same after her reception into the Church—or rather, that even if she had new weapons and new allies, her adversaries, both spiritual and human, were unchanged. She was certainly unhappy in the weeks between her reception into the Church and her confirmation. "You don't know what I've been through,"[13] she told Denys Kilham Roberts on September 14, from Renishaw, leaving him in ignorance.

She never reneged or lost her faith, and she retained her close and confidential relationship with her confessor. But after the first year or so she was an irregular attender at Mass. She became then like a settled married woman who feels no need to keep the fires of courtship blazing. Nor did she proselytize. When Allanah Harper, the following year, was thinking of joining the Church, she wrote at length to Edith about her doubts and spiritual difficulties; she was disappointed by the short shrift Edith gave her.

28
Declines and Falls
1955-1957

The last show that Tchelitchew had in London was at the Hanover Gallery in October 1955. Erica Brausen of the gallery asked Edith to open it; Pavlik, she said, was "so afraid of being forgotten here." Edith was wary too, and asked John Hayward to go with her on the night. Then she and Osbert went off to spend the winter at Montegufoni. Osbert, though he was still writing, now needed help with every physical activity.

Edith slogged away at her giant anthology. Writing to Eliot on November 1 about which of his poems to include, she said: "The book will be what I want it to be until we come to Section III of the modern poetry. . . . Section III not only ends, but also begins, 'not with a bang but a whimper.'"[1] Section II ended with Eliot and Ezra Pound, who sent her one of his characteristic cryptograms about her choice of his poems:

> Yes. nice anthol prob/y best perception of U.S. verse by any brit subject. anyhow not in a lot of bad company

That was written in April 1957; in September Edith was asked to sign a petition from English writers to President Eisenhower appealing for Pound to be released from mental hospital. Edith felt this would be unproductive and would harden American opinion against the fascist-minded Pound, as she explained to Father Caraman:

> Really!! I ask you what the English would say if some Americans started bullying them about Lord Haw-Haw. Can you imagine anything more dangerous for Ezra who is, to my mind, one of the greatest living poets and of whose welfare I therefore am most anxious. Obviously any petition has to come from the Americans.

Not only was her anthology weighing on her; she had also undertaken to write a full life of Queen Elizabeth I for Macmillan, as the natural sequel to *Fanfare for Elizabeth*. The notes and drafts began to pile up. In January 1956 her secretary wrote from England asking whether Edith would consider raising her salary. Edith was already hard pressed for money, and there was little coming in from her writing. Finally the underpaid secretary left Edith's service, and the confusions and disorganisation in Edith's two works in progress mounted unchecked.

It was freezing cold at Montegufoni. One January night in the icy castle, after a day's work, she tottered out of her room and fell down a whole flight of stone stairs. "I picked myself up somehow and crawled upstairs," she told Father Caraman on February 3. "I didn't tell Osbert what actually *had* happened because I knew it would have terrified him, so I lied and told him I had slipped up in a passage."

They came back to London in the spring, and Osbert went to New York to consult doctors. Ted Weeks of *The Atlantic Monthly* was in London and discussed the anthology with Edith, trying to help her and to impose on her his high editorial standards—generally more rigorous in America than in Britain, and Edith, because of her lack of training and natural untidiness, had some difficulty even in reaching English ones. "My life has been a cross between the ancient routine of the treadmill and that led by a poor, worn-out electric hare pursued by particularly ferocious greyhounds,"[2] she wrote at this time.

She had undertaken to review John Malcolm Brinnin's book *Dylan Thomas in America* for the *Sunday Times*, which was, as she told Leonard Russell, who had commissioned the review, "horribly painful and difficult. . . . In the first place, I had to defend (A) Dylan, (B) Caitlin, his wife, and (C) John Brinnin. Nearly all the conduct portrayed in the book seems to me quite indefensible."[3] (Brinnin himself, she had told Stephen Spender at the time of Dylan's death, had behaved "finely.") She did not see Caitlin, "who hates me, so there seems no point"; but she was generous about Caitlin's *Leftover Life to Kill* when it came out in 1957.

Her American experiences followed her to London too: Marilyn Monroe and her husband, Arthur Miller, lunched with her at the Sesame—this time Miller and Edith talking, while the star sat and listened. The party was spoiled by the intrusion of overexcited photographers and journalists. Edith's part in Marilyn Monroe's visit was ludicrously represented: No, Edith wrote to the *Sunday Chronicle*, it was not she who was bringing Miss Monroe to England; she had merely asked her to have luncheon with her *if* she was in England. The juxtaposition of Dame Edith Sitwell and Marilyn Monroe excited the public's imagination. Even Benjamin Britten wrote to her that July, asking whether she could get Miss Monroe to come to the Aldeburgh Festival—where Edith was to give a reading—as a crowd puller, to open the fund-raising bazaar and attend the garden party.

Osbert had been reunited with David Horner in New York. In May 1956 Edith complained to Lehmann from Renishaw, "That man comes here on Thursday—I suppose for the summer and indeed for ever—and I really hate him terribly."

Her dislike of Horner got the better of her. Her conversion had not, in the long run, taken care of her anger. She started making remarks about him of an equivocal kind to her guests at the Sesame Club—shaking hands with him, she said, was "like shaking hands with half-filled sandbags." That summer, she let Osbert know how she felt. Osbert, incapacitated, was torn between the two of them. But his pleasure in David's company was no less, and no less apparent.

Edith was away when Henry Reed gave two broadcasts on her poetry, but the transcript can only have pleased her: "her place in the history of poetry is an assured one," Reed said. And five of her poems—to Eliot's four, and Yeats's and Hardy's six each—appeared in the *Chatto Book of Modern Verse*, edited by C. Day Lewis and John Lehmann, an anthology that has proved more durable than most.

She herself had found a new writer to be enthusiastic about: a young American, James Purdy, sent her from Allentown, Pennsylvania, his book of stories *Don't Call Me by My Right Name*. On October 20 she was writing to tell him that they were "nothing short of masterpieces," and that she was writing to Gollancz about British publication. Purdy sent her another of his books, *63: Dream Palace*, about which she was equally enthusiastic. She advised him to consult her own agent, David Higham; the novel was later published by Gollancz, and praised by Edith in *The Times Literary Supplement*. Purdy was "a *much* greater writer than Faulkner," Edith told Alberto de Lacerda in November.

Purdy's career, like that of many young writers, was greatly furthered by Edith's rather arbitrary championship. She wrote an introduction to his *Color of Darkness* in 1961. He repaid her kindness with the affectionate and reassuring tributes that warmed her sore heart: "The person who should win the

Nobel Prize, my dear Edith, is *you*! So many poets not fit to tie your shoelaces have won it." Edith's need for flattery was a great weakness.

Her life was so filled up with work, emotion, and movement that in spite of her fall it is startling to be reminded, from her own pen, of the realities of her physical limitations. In autumn 1956 the Russians marched into a risen Hungary. Edith, always on the alert to defend the weak against the strong, was as appalled as most Westerners were; but when Stephen Spender invited her to join a group of writers going out to Hungary in support of the rising, she replied from Montegufoni on November 16:

> I shall be seventy on my next birthday, and am now extremely lame. I have arthritis in both knees, acute rheumatism in both feet, and often am only able to walk—and slowly at that—with the aid of a stick. In addition, I get attacks of sciatica in its most acute form. I had it for over a year, and it returns, so that when I travelled back from the Aldeburgh Festival, I . . . had to be carried out of the train, wheeled along the platform in a truck, and carried into my club.[4]

So she would not be much help to anyone, and no good at taking cover if the Russians started firing, as she said.

Even the hazards of everyday life were proving a battlefield for her that autumn. Shortly after she wrote to Spender, she had another bad fall at Montegufoni, as she described to Alberto de Lacerda on November 26. An acquaintance of Osbert's was coming to luncheon:

> I was just advancing to meet him on his arrival when—owing to the fact that the housemaid *will* wax the stone floor—I fell with a crash on my face, and came to to find myself lying in a lake of blood, my dress, three towels, and all the handkerchiefs of everyone present, absolutely swamped in blood, with Miss Andrade [Osbert's secretary] holding ice to my head, and the young butler trying to get brandy down my throat.[5]

But it was not brandy that she needed just then. It is likely that she had already had enough. She was lame, she was aging, and old people do have falls; but Edith's recurrent disasters were largely due to the fact that she was drinking heavily. She never showed it in any obvious way, but alcohol clouded her vision and her judgment; she moved stiffly, and was shakier than she need have been. It had been going on for a long time. But now the sorrow of Osbert's illness, her insoluble conflict over David Horner, her American anthology, her "confounded book" about Elizabeth I, her loneliness at Montegufoni, her doubts and anxieties—drink had become more than a habit; it was a necessity, the only way of getting through the days and nights. She used every subterfuge to keep Osbert from knowing.

Before they left, she heard that T. S. Eliot, long divorced, had made a runaway second marriage to his young secretary. This came as a complete surprise to everyone, including John Hayward, with whom Eliot had been sharing a house for many years. Since neither Eliot nor Hayward was homosexual, there was no betrayal of love—the only arguable betrayal was of trust. Hayward was crippled and confined to a wheelchair; and he was, too, hurt that his friend had taken off without warning. Nevertheless, Edith's reaction was excessive; for her, it was David Horner and the crippled Osbert all over again. She poured out her outrage to Lehmann on January 19:

Oh! What a *beast* Tom is!!! No, no, what you tell me is really too much! You wait! *I'll* take it out of that young woman! I'll frighten her out of her wits before I've done. As for Tom—he will, of course, be punished. He will *never* write anything worth while again. And indeed hasn't for a very long time now. The *Four Quartets* are, to my mind, infinitely inferior to his earlier work—completely bloodless and spiritless.

It makes me quite sick to think of the pain John [Hayward] has endured—that waking up at 5:30 in the morning, or 5:45, to be told that his greatest friend, on whom he depended in his unspeakable physical helplessness and humiliation, had done him this sly, crawling, lethal cruelty.

In that spring of 1957, with all her griefs looming out of proportion, Edith confided her anxieties about Osbert's situation to Georgia and Sacheverell. Her younger brother agreed with her—Osbert was evidently being exploited by David. They all went out to America together at the beginning of March— Sacheverell and Georgia, Osbert and Edith, David Horner and a friend. On board, Sacheverell wrote a bulletin on the state of play to Father Caraman, who was included in the family councils, and who had been with Edith to stay at Weston. An atmosphere of concern, bordering on conspiracy, prevailed. Edith had written to Osbert's doctor: "Something *has* to be done to protect Osbert. He is being made much worse by a situation that is horrible, grotesque and vile. . . . We cannot go on like this. . . . If I were a man I wouldn't have to bother you." All the family now resented the way Horner spent time with other friends while continuing to base his life on Osbert and Edith. They were also afraid of the power and influence that they imagined Horner — whom they referred to among themselves as "Blossom" or "Animal" — exercised over the incapacitated Osbert. "Some people are born with other people's silver spoons in their mouths," Edith said to Evelyn Shrifte, her editor at Vanguard, making it quite clear to whom she was referring. The only unconcerned Sitwell seemed to be Osbert himself, at the eye of the storm. All he wanted was for his family to be as accommodating as he was. Always passive in his relationship with David, all he wanted was not to lose his friendship, and for David to be happy both with him and away from him.

Edith's arduous three-week lecture tour in America was the best thing that could have happened to her — it was a distraction. "I enjoyed Milwaukee," she told Evelyn Wiel, "and the papers said nobody need worry about Mr. Elvis Presley's audiences any more, as I had got him beat at the post." Father D'Arcy had said she could be excused from attending Mass, but "the young people had me out of bed and to church."[6] Back at the St. Regis in New York in mid-April, she wrote to Charles Causley, a poet she admired (she wrote a preface for his third volume, *Union Street*), that "the recitals were a huge success, and I had 'standing audiences' everywhere. (The Americans don't cheer: they get up and stand, to honour one.)"

With many of her American friends she never lost touch; she corresponded with Carson McCullers, Katherine Anne Porter, and Marianne Moore; Betsy Whitney, whose husband became United States Ambassador to the Court of St. James's, she saw in London. This was her last visit to the country where she had been treated so handsomely.

In May Edith gave the 1957 PEN Hermon Ould Memorial Lecture in London, and blasted the Movement as she had blasted the 1930s poets in her Northcliffe Lectures. Antipathy sharpened her sense of humour and restored her vigour. Sitting in Paddington Station with Father Caraman — they were on their way to Weston — she listened to the incomprehensible hooting announcements from the public-address system and said: "I'd like to employ that man to read Robert Conquest's poems."

Once at Weston, the inevitable sad topic was discussed. Edith, after years of nursing a monopoly of resentment against Horner, saw the destructive potential of these conferences and, worst of all, the way it was further dividing her brothers; she was beginning to see Osbert's position in a more realistic light. She wrote to Father Caraman before this visit: "My going [to Weston] is going to make trouble I think here. O. must on *no* account know that anything is being discussed, anywhere." It might lead to her losing Osbert altogether, "and I simply could not bear it."

> He has been a wonderful brother to me. He *did* say something when we were in America that hurt me most terribly but I am getting over it, and am beginning to understand. It's more than platitudinous to say that there are two sides to every question but there is something to be said on both sides. O. has had a terrible lot to put up with . . . but S. is a devoted loving character whom I love dearly.

She was supremely protective in her love for Sacheverell; but Osbert was the only human being about whom she hardly ever said a critical word.

Would that she could have followed Geoffrey Gorer's sound advice: "And dearest Edith, enjoy yourself, rest, forget your quarrelsome family, and *write poetry*." Help was at hand.

There were several young men who formed in London the nucleus of her Sesame court: Alberto de Lacerda, "small, impeccably dressed, his dark eyes luminous with emotion, and poised like a dart-thrower to insert a compliment into the conversation"; Gordon Watson, the Australian pianist, "tall, with an exuberant vitality and a laugh that was loud enough to rattle the carefully socketed windows of Grosvenor Street"; and Michael Stapleton, whom Watson had brought along to a Sesame supper after his Liszt recital at the Overseas League in 1952. It was Gordon Watson and Michael Stapleton who introduced her to Elizabeth Salter, who was to be her secretary and ally for her last seven years.

Elizabeth Salter saw Dame Edith Sitwell for the first time at the Aldeburgh Festival that year. Edith was reading in Aldeburgh Parish Church. Miss Salter sat at the back and looked at her prospective employer, who was wearing dark glasses:

> The most formidable of their kind, they had mirror rims that slanted diabolically towards the temples. They were gold and black beneath a Tudor hat that was studded with gold and framed by two lengths of black chiffon. Her dress was of black satin and worn to the ground; her Chinese coat was gold flecked by green. . . . [7]

How, wondered Elizabeth Salter, could one be "secretary to a legend"?

It worked very well. Miss Salter, in her thirties, was cheerful, resourceful, sensitive, and kind. Being Australian, she was outside the English class and culture hierarchy. She was also a successful crime-writer, which recommended her to Edith at once. Now Edith had someone to whom she could pass the letters from lunatics, pests, and bores, from editors, publishers, and journalists; someone to whom she could despatch the drafts of what was to be *The Queens and the Hive* to be typed; someone who could give commonsense and sincere reassurance, save her from her own caprices, and act as a buffer in the personal confrontations that made her anxious (Miss Salter was surprised that Edith asked her to be present at nearly all the luncheons and parties and during the visits from writer and actor friends). "Because of her age, because of her health, because of so many things, it soon became apparent that my duties were to be wider in scope than those of a secretary," Elizabeth Salter has written. "I miss you as a friend as well as an aide-de-camp," Edith wrote to her from Montegufoni in autumn 1957.[8]

Edith did not keep to her vow of having her *Collected Poems* published in America only. Macmillan brought out her life's work, in much the same form as the Vanguard edition, in July 1957—the agreement was for Edith to take the customary 10 percent of royalties, but Macmillan gave her no advance. Cyril Connolly, now chief reviewer for the *Sunday Times*, headed his piece "Salute to a Major Poet," and ended it with an uncompromising paean: "When we come to compare the collected poems of Dame Edith Sitwell with those of Yeats, or Mr. Eliot or Professor Auden, it will be found that hers have the purest poetical content of them all; the honey may sometimes fail, the comb never."[9] Stephen Spender was equally positive in *Time and Tide*, where Edith now had a friend and ally, the Irish writer Anthony Cronin, in charge of the book pages. A. Alvarez in the *Observer* not surprisingly took a very different view, and wrote of the inflation of her reputation. The Movement poets, in the weeklies, had their sour say too.

A graver disappointment in Edith's eyes was Alan Pryce-Jones in *The Times Literary Supplement*. She had hoped for—and believed she had been led to expect—the long "middle" article to be devoted to her book; but all she got, and two months late at that, was 655 words. (Edith counted them.) The unsigned piece was by the editor himself. "What he wrote was quite nice," wrote Edith to Sir Malcolm Bullock, "but an old lady like myself does not like having her life-work dismissed in 655 words. Perhaps, however, he thought he was spoiling me by giving me five words over the six hundred and fifty."[10] *Interesting* was the rather noncommittal word Pryce-Jones finally used to summarize her achievement: This collection placed her "among the most interesting of modern English poets."[11]

There was little time for anticlimax. In September Edith gave a reading at the Dorchester to raise funds for the restoration of the chapel at Stonor Park, near Henley, where the Blessed Edmund Campion said Mass just before he was captured. This act of piety brought her a new friend, Jeanne Stonor, who was also a close friend of Graham Greene.

September was also her own birthday month; and in September 1957 Dame Edith Sitwell was seventy years old. Vanguard brought out a new, revised edition of *The English Eccentrics*. The British press celebrated their favourite English Eccentric in ritual ways. The *Daily Express* printed a page of photographs and said she ought to sit in the House of Lords; the *Sunday Times* gave a luncheon for her and published a long conversation about her life and works between herself, John Lehmann, William Plomer, Frederick Ashton, and Raymond Mortimer.[12] Her *Collected Poems* were awarded the 1957 William Foyle Poetry Prize of £250, presented at the Dorchester the following March.

Private grief dwarfed professional triumphs and frustrations. During her last visit to America, she had been shocked to hear of the death of Roy Campbell in a car accident. It had been broken to her in a particularly callous way, by a journalist, in the course of a press conference she had given in Boston. "He asked if I knew Roy. I said yes, he is one of my dearest friends, and my godfather. 'Oh, really?' said the oaf. 'Well, he was killed yesterday.' Just like that."[13]

Three months later there was worse news. On August 1, only a few days after the appearance of her *Collected Poems*, a telegram from Rome was delivered to the Sesame Club:

> Dearest Edith this message brings tragic news but also our dearest love last evening at eight Pavlik's great heart beat no more love again dear friend—Choura Charlie.

It was over. The ideal Edith could love the ideal Pavlik, as in their "ten years happy" during the war, but for eternity; without now an answering voice, but without false notes and misunderstandings. Four years later, she wrote:

His power for living was so great, that I cannot believe I shall never see him again.

Thinking of him now, I see him as I saw him shortly after our first meeting. The snow was thick on the ground, and he was leaping in the air and clapping his large painter's hands together, because the snow reminded him of his childhood and earliest youth, before the misery and the grandeur began.

She wrote this not in some loving memoir, but in the catalogue of her Tchelitchew paintings that she was selling at Sotheby's. Edith's love and loyalty were without sentimentality. She had little nostalgia for the middle-distance past, and did not dwell on it either in her thoughts or in her conversation. For her as for Tchelitchew, the only Garden of Eden, irrevocably lost, was that of "childhood and earliest youth, before the misery and the grandeur began."

29

Night Falls
1957-1961

There was one last, loved protégé. In 1957 a book of poems called *The Succession* appeared with a cummerbund blurb by Dame Edith Sitwell. In the *Weekly Dispatch* she wrote under the heading "A Catholic Poet" that its author was, in her opinion, "the most remarkable young poet who has arisen since Dylan Thomas." His name was Quentin Stevenson.

This was the blond young man whom Evelyn Waugh had suspected of being an American on the occasion of Edith's reception into the Roman Catholic Church. He had been an undergraduate at Christ Church, Oxford, when they had first met in 1954. He had wanted to send her his poems, but, as Edith said, "If I read all the poems people send me, I wouldn't have time to write poems of my own." Nevertheless he called on her at Durrant's Hotel, where she was staying while the Sesame was closed for August, and she read his poetry. Quentin assisted the priest at her first communion; but here he felt on the wrong foot from the beginning: Just as Edith was entering Catholicism, he was abandoning it.

In October 1954 he wrote a poem for Edith that she found "beautiful and touching." She discussed and read everything he wrote. Her attitude was lovingly maternal: "Dearest Quentin, I believe strongly in your poetry."

She was temporarily displeased with him when he showed an interest in the Movement poets, and when he chose to write a thesis on the poet Charlotte Mew: "I don't like homespun verse," she wrote to him. "Poetry should never be middle class. It should either be aristo or peasant." Gradually he came to feel that he was in a false position. He felt that he was becoming, as he said, "just a toady." And there were, in his opinion, plenty of those around Edith. He heard so much from her about "traitors"—those to whom she had been kind, and who had let her down. He felt he was bound to become the next traitor. He felt ashamed to be deferring all his own opinions and wishes to hers; yet when he stood out against her, she did not like it. When in early 1957 he decided, against her expressed wish, to go off to Poland for six months, she retaliated with a hailstorm of a letter giving a great many reasons (one would have sufficed) why he should *not* call in at Montegufoni on the way, to see her:

> The cook has quinsy; her two children have bad influenza; the house-maid's baby nephew (they all live in the house) has to go to Florence for an operation (that disrupts everything)—*and* the cook's sister has para-typhoid!!! . . . On top of everything else, it is difficult to get coal, because all the Florence coal is Russian! It is *no* use your going to Florence, alas that it is so; but we are three quarters of an hour's motor drive from Florence, and we have no motor. . . . So, my dear, it won't, alas, be possible for us to see each other until that six months is over.

"But I shall think of you each day, and I always speak of you when I pray," she assured him.

Neither he nor she could live up to the relationship they aspired to. She was too demanding and touchy, but he saw a falsity in his own behaviour. "The more she praised me—which was what I wanted—the more nervous I became." For in his heart he knew perfectly well that he was not as good as she said he was. Finally Joe Ackerley took him by the elbow on the steps of the Sesame Club and said firmly: "You do know—don't you?—she's over-praising you dreadfully." It was a relief to hear it said.

Quentin Stevenson was writing less and less; he wanted now to act, which Edith refused to take seriously. In the matter of honesty, the stand he finally took was a conclusive and rather brutal one. Edith dedicated a poem to him, "The Yellow Girl," which appeared in the *Listener* (of which Joe Ackerley was literary editor) on January 29, 1959. Quentin thought it was not a good poem, so said nothing, and did not even thank her for the dedication. She was very hurt, and wrote to Father Caraman:

> He has not written to thank me. He makes a great mistake from his own point of view by being so appallingly bad-mannered having got exactly what he wanted from me i.e. he has been introduced to *everybody* who could be of use to him. He now never writes to me unless he wants some-thing. . . .

She removed his name from the poem, and rededicated it to Alberto de Lacerda.

Thus Quentin Stevenson joined the ranks of the traitors. He had let her down, as he was doomed to do. The friendship had been pitched too high, and was sustained by too much wishful thinking. It was a meshing of needs and vanities. When Edith wrote about the aging Queen Elizabeth I and the young Earl of Essex in her book *The Queens and the Hive* she had this to say:

> Elizabeth's affection for her young cousin has been, probably, vastly distorted. It was not, the present writer believes, an unpleasant infatuation of an old, vain woman for a young man. The lonely Queen, constantly mourning secretly for her childless state—that state that not only left her alone, but threatened dangers to her kingdom—saw in him, perhaps, the son that she might have had.

At the core of Edith's indignation was a nub of real pain, as once again love had failed. Denton Welch, who died long before his friendship with Edith had time to complete its curve, had had the insight to perceive both her openheartedness and the writing on the wall: "There is beauty in being generous," he had written in his journal, "even if it should lead to difficulties of misunderstanding and withdrawal."[1]

In September 1957, when Edith was praising Quentin Stevenson's book of poems, neither had yet withdrawn. ("He is having awful reviews, poor boy," she confided to her other protégé, James Purdy, around Christmas.) She slogged on with her *Atlantic Book*. Ted Weeks advised her assiduously. He wanted her to cut some of the very early religious poems and, at the other end of the time scale, not to include too many of her personal friends. "What he doesn't seem to realise is," she complained to Father Caraman, "that as I am a poet, naturally all the top English poets *are* friends of mine."

There was still room in her life for new friends—among them Sir Charles and Lady Snow (the novelist Pamela Hansford Johnson). As a girl, Lady Snow had been Dylan Thomas's first love; it was from the Hansford Johnsons' house in Battersea, with his neck forcibly washed for the occasion, that Dylan had issued forth to his very first meeting with Edith. Now, in May 1958, Sir Charles wrote to her, expressing anxiety that a reader of the manuscript of his wife's forthcoming novel, *The Unspeakable Skipton*, had suggested that its central character might be taken for a parody of Edith. Of course this was nonsense, and Edith wittily treated it as such in her reply. "Nonsense apart, it is an ill-wind that blows nobody any good": She had "longed, for ages, to know them both."[3] When she went to dinner with them, she wore the red-and-gold brocade dress she had worn for the first great New York *Façade*: "to give you pleasure," she said.

She made other and more incongruous new aquaintances. Supported by Elizabeth Salter and Quentin Stevenson, she entertained the "beat" poets Gregory Corso and Allen Ginsberg at lunch at the Sesame Club, where her visitors' dress and demeanour caused even more heads to turn than usual. The meeting was precariously successful. Later in the summer she encountered the Beats again at Oxford, when she was performing *Façade* in a programme that included Schoenberg's *Pierrot Lunaire*, sung by Hedli Anderson, Louis MacNeice's second wife. Edith tolerated with remarkable indulgence and dignity the deliberately outrageous conversational gambits of Corso and Ginsberg on this occasion.[3] She tolerated less easily the disastrous dress rehearsal at which the *Façade* screen tilted and fell—or was pushed; and she was furious that *Façade* was given lower billing than a work that she called a "pathological, psychopathic, sadisto-masochistic masterpiece."[4] Elizabeth Salter could always make Edith laugh, afterwards, with her imitation of "Howling Hedli MacNeice" in the hated *Pierrot Lunaire*.

Elizabeth Salter's regime, which brought some order, stability, and a support system into Edith's life, made it possible for Edith to be a poet again. In 1958 she wrote some good poems—new poems, not rearrangements of her ten-year-old litanies and images. She was struck by the sentence "His Blood colours my cheek" when reading about St. Agnes—"Isn't it glorious," she said to Elizabeth—and made it the starting point of a poem which she dedicated to Father D'Arcy; it was published in the Catholic paper *The Month* in May 1958. "The Yellow Girl" (Quentin's ill-fated poem) was in the *Listener*, as was "La Bella Bona Roba." Someone she increasingly consulted now, with the humility born of frailty, was Geoffrey Gorer: He gave critical advice about the punctuation of "La Bella Bona Roba," and questioned the title. He had written to her in January of that year, "You musn't *mustn't* MUSTN'T let the silly little pipsqueaks who review poetry in the papers make the slightest difference to your writing poetry."

She was writing well again, but death was more evident in her poems than ever:

I, an old dying woman, tied
To the winter's hopelessness
And to a wisp of bone
Clothed in the old world's outworn foolishness. . . .

It was not a dreaded death; the poet is "not dismayed":

No more eroded by the seas of the world's passions and greeds, I rise,
As if I never had been ape, to look in the compassionate,
    the all-seeing Eyes.

                                   ("His Blood Colours My Cheek")

Of another poem of this year, "The Death of the Giant," which appeared in the *London Magazine* in November, she wrote to Lehmann: "Incidentally — *only for God's sake don't say so* — were it a novel it might be called a roman à clef. *I* am the giant in question, although for poetic reasons I changed the sex of the giant."

With the autumn came sackfuls of proofs to be corrected for the *Atlantic Book*, which tried her eyesight and her patience to the utmost. Everything began to go wrong again. She was then — as Georgia, in a phrase of great perception, said — "on the point of a nervous gallop"; Edith could scarcely be said to suffer nervous breakdown, with all the term implies of inertia and loss of function. She struck out in all directions. To the *Daily Mirror* on September 9:

In your issue of today you publish the horrible story of George Chobrik, of Hadylane, Chesterfield, who poked a cat out of a tree, and allowed his two Alsatian dogs to tear it to pieces — a process which lasted for *seven minutes.*

    This monster was — fined £3. When will it be possible for a proper punishment to be inflicted for cruelty . . . .

In December she was reproaching Roger Senhouse of Secker and Warburg, who had sent her Edouard Roditi's *Dialogues on Art*, because of its references to Tchelitchew. It was a dreadful mistake, since the book also contained a bravura paragraph about Edith's appearance which would probably seem marvellously funny to someone not concerned, but was not calculated to bring her comfort: Roditi wrote that "her stature, her commanding bearing and her Junoesque proportions gave her the appearance of a hermaphrodite Guards Officer disguised as a Madonna for a religious pageant held in eighteenth-century Portuguese Goa." It was unforgivable, wrote Edith, and she would not forgive it.

A hermaphrodite cat, on the other hand, was forgivable. In Montegufoni as usual for the winter, Edith wrote to Elizabeth in London about her Italian cat, Savonarola, known as the Boy Friend until he produced, and then ate, nine kittens. "So *naughty*!! She has now been accused of transvestism, incest, child-murder and cannibalism. But I won't hear a word against her."[5] Nor would she hear a word against the demanding Evelyn Wiel; but though innocent of all Savonarola's crimes, that raddled old woman was now partly responsible for putting Edith, locked in her nervous gallop, in danger of total rout.

Edith outlined her troubles to Elizabeth:

> For three days I couldn't keep any food down, and got no sleep at all. The nights were an absolute nightmare of retching, and a kind of mental horror. This was simply brought on by the Income Tax badgering me to send them details I have not got here, and by poor darling Evelyn's plaints. *Entre nous*, she has *all* my Mother's money (which should have been one third of my income). . . . [6]

She described in detail all that Evelyn had taken from her, ending up, "She has got all my pictures." These were becoming a weapon in Madame Wiel's hands. Two years earlier, when she was thinking of moving from the rue Saint-Dominique, Evelyn had written to Edith: "I must know what I am to do with all your pictures, books and papers which I have here, I cannot possibly take them with me." In September 1959, after three pictures had been brought back to England, she wrote about what remained:

> About your pictures. I cannot imagine what can be done about them. To be sent would cost a small fortune and there are far too many for a friend to take with their luggage. The only thing I can think of is—that we pretend they belong to me; and as in my will I have left you everything in my flat, they will finally come to you.

This was disingenuous; the problem of transport would be the same whether Evelyn Wiel was alive or dead. The pictures were like hostages in her relation with Edith; they formed a link, and though she was not really likely to sell them without Edith's consent, their presence spelt security of a sort. Edith had already, in 1955, made a gift to Evelyn of her reversionary interest in Helen's estate (about £800). She tried to remind herself that "the old lady in question is in many ways a very heroic person." And it was true that if Evelyn had not hidden the pictures from the Germans during the Occupation, they would not now be there at all.

Edith described her life of the past few years to Father Caraman as "trying to walk a tightrope over an abyss." Elizabeth Salter understood for the first time one aspect of the abyss; she knew now the full reality of Edith's terrors about money. "Her growing debt under pressure from the Inland Revenue became a monster blown up into frightening proportions by the memory of her mother's disgrace."[7]

In her terror of becoming like her mother, Edith had, in the externals of her life, done exactly what she was most afraid of. The mornings, and sometimes afternoons too, spent in bed; the excessive drinking; the extravagant spending on entertaining her friends; the concealed panic about the consequences of that extravagance—this had been her mother's pattern exactly. Perhaps because it was too horrid to contemplate, she did not acknowledge the parallel; it was her father's temperament that she blamed for the "terrible nervous system" she had inherited and for the *"angoisse"* that dogged her.

The *angoisse* was not lessened by the reception by American critics of her *Atlantic Book of British and American Poetry* which had come out in the United States in autumn 1958. The *New York Times* was mildly critical, but made her "ill with rage"; in the *American Review of Literature* Winfield Townley Scott compared it adversely with Auden's *Poets of the English Language*. The American edition was sent to the London *Sunday Dispatch*, which in a notice of very few words complained about the amount of space given to the compiler's brothers.

But before her return to London in spring 1959, Edith had managed to make a triumphant appearance at the British Institute in Florence, reading her own poetry. No lecturer at the Institute, Harold Acton has written, had ever drawn a larger audience. Even the room adjoining the lecture hall was packed, although to little avail, since the microphone refused to function. (Edith seemed to put a jinx on microphones.) "I couldn't hear a word," said a member of the audience, "but it was a pleasure just to see her."[8]

When Edith returned to London, Elizabeth Salter was poised for a rescue operation. It was Edith who made the suggestion that Elizabeth should go to Paris and pick up three of her favourite paintings; it was Elizabeth who persuaded her that these should be converted into cash to settle her debts and ease her mind.

Elizabeth set off for France in early May with a friend, in her old Austin sports car. She arrived at the rue Saint-Dominique and climbed the stairs at number 129, as Edith had so often climbed them long ago. The door to the flat was ajar, and she found her way into the sitting room: "It looked what it was, a room untouched for thirty-five years. The wall-paper was peeling behind the cobwebs in the corners, the chairs hid their scars under cushions that alone had been re-covered." What they were covered with was material from Edith's old dresses, left there like everything else at the outbreak of war. And there was old Evelyn Wiel:

> Lovable, charming, unscrupulously mercenary, she entertained me with the whisky that Edith had sent her. For the time being the purpose of my trip was forgotten, as, clad in Edith's clothes, her arms lined with bracelets that Edith had given her, she regaled me with stories of Edith's visits to Paris with Helen in the years before the war when she herself had been the wife of the Norwegian consul.[9]

Elizabeth came back to London not only with the three paintings that Edith had asked for, but with the realization that the total amount of Edith's possessions, stacked and piled in the dusty apartment, might prove to be more useful to Edith than she had imagined.

While Elizabeth was away in France, Edith was the subject of one of John Freeman's *Face to Face* interviews on television: a famous and never-bettered series in which eminent persons were subjected to rigorous questioning, of a fairly personal nature, about their life and work. It was done with such sympathy and calm that the subjects, disarmed, revealed themselves without knowing it and without resentment. Edith wore for this gentle ordeal a headgear she called her "bird-king's hat," and the Solongoi ermine jacket that she had recently bought from a Regent Street furrier for 271 guineas. Edith was always at her best when allowed to be simply herself; and the interview with Dame Edith Sitwell was generally considered to be one of the two or three most remarkable in the series. She responded well to John Freeman; and "for the first time in her life, ordinary people were given the chance to see her undistorted by press reports and the caricaturist's pen and they liked what they saw."[10]

All the *Face to Face* interviewees were the subjects of portraits by Felix Topolski, which were used to introduce and close the programmes. He was the last of the many artists for whom Edith sat. She did not like the result—she called it an "unspeakable caricature." It is a formidable picture: Topolski painted her in a crown, with hunched shoulders, so that she looks like an ancient crested bird of some exotic species. Four years later Topolski was still trying to explain to her his vision of her, as in a letter written on September 14, 1963: "To me you have the rarest PRESENCE," as of a character in a Japanese Noh play. "This aura of yours (I see now in retrospect) must have been what led me to my painting: fragility, *therefore* style, *therefore* true authority."[11]

That summer Edith shared with W. H. Auden, Robert Lowell, and Edwin Muir the Guinness Poetry Award, which was presented at Londonderry House on Park Lane; in green satin and a black velvet turban, she read aloud "La Bella Bona Roba." In June she read at the Royal Festival Hall: Benjamin Britten had asked her for a poem to celebrate the tercentenary of the composer Purcell. It had been commissioned during her weeks of anxious depression at Montegufoni, and inspiration was lacking. Sending Britten the poem—"Praise We Great Men"—in May, she explained defensively: "I have, in the poem, drawn on past poems of mine, because, obviously, if one can write *at all*, one can only choose the most suitable medium for what one has to say, and cannot put it into other, weaker words."[12]

When Edith was in form, and when she was younger, she could meet hostility head on, accepting it as the price to be paid by a pioneer and a dissident. When she was depressed, and now that she was older, the thought that some people hated her filled her with misery. Anyone with as strong and expressive a personality as hers was bound to provoke dislike as well as admiration; almost no one is liked by all those to whom he is known. But the belief that one is hated is terrifying because it calls up a consent from the self that is indeed hateful, originally sinful, ugly, potentially damaging or murderous. Not all the letters after her *Face to Face* triumph were reassuring. "I had a most horrible anonymous letter yesterday," she wrote to Father Caraman on May 27, "a letter of abuse of my personal appearance, brought down on me by my television appearance. Hatred is about the only fault that was left out of my character and I am terrified of it."[13]

The near-catastrophe of a public reading at the Edinburgh Festival reinforced this terror. She and Elizabeth drove up by car; she wore for the reading, which was chaired by Sir Compton Mackenzie, the great gold "Aztec" collar that had been given to her by Count Fulco Verdura. As so often with Edith, the microphone did not work. People in the audience complained that they could not hear. "Then get a hearing aid," said Edith smartly, stepping out of her regal role. They still could not hear. Backchat and repartee between audience and performer continued. In the end, quiet prevailed. It was a personal triumph of an unorthodox sort, and later there was a crowd of three or four hundred waiting for her outside the stage door to see her and wave her off. But shortly afterwards, in an interview with Robert Muller for the *Daily Mail* of September 10, she lost control and gave way to her fears. "You will be kind to me, won't you?" she begged him. "Because people hate me so very much."[14]

In late October Edith heard from Parker Tyler, who was embarking on his ambitious biography of Tchelitchew. Edith had met Tyler with Pavlik and Ford in New York, and Choura had written asking her to help him as much as she could. Edith wrote to Tyler on November 18:

> The most accurate impression I can give you of our friendship is to say that it was the same kind of friendship as existed between Michael Angelo [*sic*] and Princess Colonna. . . . I dislike discussing my personal life, and never do, and for that reason I never write about my personal friendships — I have had friendships with several great men.
>
> Alas, I *can't* give permission for you to see the letters that passed between Pavlik and me. Not that I would mind. But Pavlik left instructions. . . .

She advised him to see Lincoln Kirstein, Pavlik's executor, who authorized the use of Pavlik's letters.

Tyler came to see Edith the following year — " 'Don't,' she said in her distant bell-like tones, 'hand him [Tchelitchew] over to the wolves' "[15] — and they continued to correspond. In May 1960 she gave him a cursory and rather misleading account of the breach: "You know, probably, that after the hell-upon-earth row

Pavlik made with me (largely because I am a close friend of the Duchess of Windsor—a woman whom I have *never even seen*) he magnanimously forgave me when I was made a Dame, and the correspondence was resumed." And in October 1960 she wrote that she was "a little grieved to realise that some of Pavlik's most deplorably silly friends will figure cheek by jowl with me in the book, and should not have given permission for my letters to appear had I realised this."

Before she wrote her first letter to Parker Tyler in November 1959 Edith had had another violent nocturnal accident, in her room at the Sesame Club. She fell precipitately out of her bed (she said it collapsed—it was supported at one end by a pile of telephone books) and struck her head against a piece of furniture. The next day she was due to give a tea party for a hundred people in honour of David Lutyens, with whom she was once more on good terms. She was in no state to appear; the party was *Hamlet* without the Prince, and Elizabeth Salter acted as host. "I am not telling anyone of the accident but am saying it was influenza," Edith told Father Caraman. Her humour deepened by several tones. To Maurice Cranston she wrote that "the night porter enquired if I had any orders for the morning. I said 'only a coffin.' He asked, 'Black or white?'"

In November she made the arduous two-day journey to Montegufoni as usual, and for the last time. The *Atlantic Book* came out in its two-volume British edition that month from Victor Gollancz, who wrote to her that he was pleased at the way it was selling in the first few weeks. (Gollancz had printed forty-five hundred copies of each volume; seventeen years later, in July 1976, the few hundred left unsold were remaindered.) At Montegufoni, Edith wrote a poem that she dedicated to Elizabeth Salter. Like most of her last poems, it equated love with death and embraced both: "Love me, my ultimate Darkness, kiss me, my infinite Sun!"

Before it appeared, as "Choric Song," in the *Listener* in March 1960, she had had another night fall at Montegufoni. The bedside light went out; ever since her last accident she had hated being left in the dark. She told Father Caraman what had happened:

> Like a fool I tried to find a window to let in some starlight, couldn't, and trying to get back to bed I caught hold of what I thought was my bed but in fact was an extremely flimsy chair which collapsed hurling me on to my back on the stone floor. I lay there in agony from 3 a.m. to about 8 when I was called.[16]

She made a poor recovery. In summer 1961 she spent more than a month in the Claremont Nursing Home in Sheffield. The evening after she went home to Renishaw, she fell again, broke a wrist, and was taken into the Royal Hospital, Sheffield. She returned again to Renishaw—and to a wretched situation.

For years she had been grieving over Osbert's degenerative illness, and railing over David Horner's continual presence. Now the tables were turned. Now David Horner was complaining about Edith's tiresome presence. He was unsympathetic to her secret drinks, to her continual accidents, and to all the frailties of age and weakness that now beset her. He thought something should be done about her. He put Osbert in a very difficult position. He also wrote to Sacheverell and Georgia; but they had no intention of aligning themselves with David Horner against their sister's presence at Renishaw, her own home, and he got a stiff response.

The servants at Renishaw, that house of secrets where nothing remained secret for very long, also saw the danger threatening their Miss Edith. Old Robins was now retired and living in Sheffield, but he heard what was going on, and wrote to her in dramatic terms that showed her he had not lived for half a century with Sitwells without absorbing their style. He had sent her a card for her birthday in September, and was worried because he had not heard from her: "I sent it to Renishaw Hall so perhaps it was kept from you, as I suppose some funny things go on there with some people we know." He asked after Osbert: "Is the creature still with him. I don't mean Miss Andrade. PS. Please destroy this letter. I beg to remain, your Obedient Servant, Robins."[17]

In spite of the conspiratorial atmosphere, the surface relationship between David and Edith was as smooth as ever. But all Edith's friends saw that there was a crisis. Bryher wrote in her matter-of-fact way on September 21, 1960, that she thought Edith ought to have a "personal maid" now: "I should always be glad to help with that financially, you know."[18]

As far as the outside world was concerned, Edith was still going strong. The University of Texas wrote offering her a fee of $750 for a reading at their Poetry Center. In September her *Swinburne: A Selection* was published by Weidenfeld and Nicolson, with a fifty-page introduction on the poet who was among her earliest loves. But she, the eldest of the "deleterious trio," who had conferred with loving concern over Sachie's melancholy and money worries and over Osbert's illness, was now herself the subject of urgent family conferences. Perhaps, in fact, a nursing home would be the answer?

Edith did not think so. Ill and exhausted and frightened, she left Renishaw for the last time in December 1960 and took refuge at the Sesame Club, where she was met by Elizabeth.

But the Sesame was not a permanent refuge. For one thing, it was too noisy: That winter, electric drills and hammering in the house next door, which was being renovated by Longmans, the publishers, drove Edith to distraction. She vented her wrath by writing vivid complaints, and got some satisfaction from her equally vivid contracts with the Noise Abatement Society. "I am delighted to see that your misfortunes haven't dampened your pure and beautiful mischief," Pamela Hansford Johnson wrote to her on January 5, 1961. She spent most of her time in bed, and she wrote one poem, "A Girl's Song in Winter." She called Elizabeth in: "I have written a new poem and I think it's quite good." "She began to read it aloud, but could not go on . . . and the knowledge of what made her write it was heavy in us both," Elizabeth has written.[19] "Oh, soon you will be / Colder, my sweet, than me," sings the snow in Edith's poem. Stephen Spender published it in *Encounter* in January 1962.

Around Christmas, Edith wrote to Choura in her creaking French: "Nos derniers années ont été horriblement triste, pour vous et pour moi. Je pense à vous continuellement, et des jours où nous étions heureuses." Who would have thought, in the past, she asked Choura, after describing Osbert's illness, that "nous serions tous arrivés à ceci?" Evelyn Wiel, unabashed and blind to Edith's plight, wrote to thank Edith for her Christmas present: "My darling . . . you, who keep me alive, what should I do without you. . . . Your electric bed-heater is quite marvellous, it was a perfect godsend. . . . "[20]

It was decided to collect up as many of Edith's assets as possible and sell them at Sotheby's to clear her debts (she had an overdraft of over £5,000). In April 1960 Edith had replied to an enquiring dealer, Jacob Schwartz, that she could not, "under any circumstances," sell her Tchelitchews:

It would be an act of horrible treachery on my part. I was one of his greatest friends. He died, worn out by poverty, and now, I am told, his work fetches huge prices. How disgusting it is to think of collectors who would not buy him when he was alive, snatching at him as soon as he is dead! Don't you agree?

She changed her mind. It was the price of freedom. In early summer 1961 Elizabeth drove up to Renishaw and brought back two trunks of Edith's manuscripts in their folio notebooks, and a load of Tchelitchew paintings and drawings. She paid a second visit to the rue Saint-Dominique. In two sales at

Sotheby's held just before Christmas 1961, the notebooks realised £6,250 and the thirty-nine pictures (Edith kept some back) £10,350. The *Green Venus*—the heavy-bottomed nude in a hammock that had hung in Pembridge Mansions—fetched £900. Pavlik's 1930 portrait of Edith, small-mouthed and dome-skulled, went for £1,200. Sir Kenneth Clark bought three drawings in order to give them back to her; but she was not as pleased as he had hoped she would be, since she had no room to hang them.

By this time Edith was no longer at the Sesame. If she was not keen to end her life in dreary Room 15, the club's administrators were not keen to keep her. She needed more nursing care than a club was equipped to give. Elizabeth found a flat to let up in Hampstead—42 Greenhill. The cheap and rickety old bits and pieces that had furnished 22 Pembridge Mansions were resurrected and sent down from Renishaw, where they had been stored for thirty years. Elizabeth privately thought that Osbert might have been more generous and sent one or two decent pieces for his sister. Money for supplementary furniture, curtains, and carpets were advanced by Sotheby's, who before the sales had gone through were "prepared to back their judgment and stand by their client."[21] Edith was in hospital when the sales took place; when she came out, she went home to Greenhill and to her permanent new nurse, Sister Farquhar.

Edith did not go to Montegufoni again; but Osbert, in his wheelchair, and David Horner spent the winter there as usual. On March 6, 1962, after Osbert had been put to bed, David—a hale sixty-one—had a hideous accident. He was not drunk, he said later, though he had been drinking. In a part of the castle where he had little reason to be, he fell down an ancient flight of thirty-eight stone steps. He had the sensation that he was pushed.[22]

He cracked his skull and broke his right arm and several ribs. He lay all night in his blood at the foot of the stairs, semiconscious from time to time but unable to cry out. Up above, Osbert, who loved him, slept. Miles away in London Edith, who had hated him, lay in her bed at Greenhill. "My mental life is so violent I have no physical life to speak of," she had told Robert Muller of the *Daily Mail*. "If I hadn't been a Catholic, I'd have murdered him," she had often said. Fate, or the ghost that all Sitwells believed haunted Montegufoni, had attempted what in her most fearful fantasies she had imagined being capable of doing herself.

David Horner was found by Luigi early the next morning, and rushed to hospital in a coma. He was not expected to survive. He lived, but his balance and his speech were permanently affected, and his right arm was useless. He had always retained a Peter Pan youthfulness; now, suddenly aged, he would never walk with ease again. He made progress, and a remarkable recovery; but his afflictions at first were only a little less grave than Osbert's.

30

Taken Care Of
1962-1964

At the end of August 1962, Edith's last prose best seller, *The Queens and the Hive*, was published by Macmillan; Little, Brown brought it out in the United States in November. It had given her nothing but trouble. As long ago as November 1957 she had written to Elizabeth Salter, "I am nearly driven *mad* by my book. I've gone dead on it."[1] When Elizabeth Jenkins's *Elizabeth the Great* came out, she was in despair: "The whole of *The Queens and the Hive* will have to be done again." Finally she conceded that she needed help with organizing the vast amount of material and the many drafts of chapters that had piled up over six years. Michael Stapleton offered to take it on, and she gratefully handed over to him the immense pile of typescript. He had no easy task; there were as many as five drafts of a single chapter, and five copies of each of the five drafts. He hived off some of the "subplots" into appendices, and produced a coherent manuscript.

Edith's vision of Elizabeth I had changed little since the brief sketch in *English Women* and the youthful portrait in *Fanfare for Elizabeth*. The woman "who was lonely as the sun in his heaven longed to believe that she could be loved for herself."

> Though the most feminine of women—(the ridiculous female-impersonator's appearance, the fishwifely backslapping jollity and familiarity imputed to her by certain writers in later times, are singularly remote from this being of air and fire)—she yet had a masculine sense of justice, evinced, sometimes, in terrible words. . . . What black and unresolved hatred, resulting, perhaps, from unplumbed depths of suffering, made this otherwise great woman capable of unreasoning, sensual cruelty?

The book is called *The Queens and the Hive* because Elizabeth and Mary Queen of Scots, queen bees, have almost equally important roles to play. Edith's lively interest in violent crime stimulated her to write vividly about Mary, her blood-stained entourage, and her sad end. Edith described Darnley, with zest, in terms that recall one of her own real-life antipathies: "The long and boneless Waxworks King, Lord Darnley, with his white, flaccid, meaningless face . . . with his curling marigold-coloured hair, and his long hands like satin gloves filled with damp sand . . . ."

What had exhausted her in the writing was the sheer narration of the events of a long reign. It is not hard to see where the author is enjoying herself and where she is doing her duty. She responded with pleasure, as always, to the language of the period. For example, a contemporary account has Mary reduced to "owling" by John Knox; Edith makes the most of this and all subsequent fits of "owling." "Cormorant seducers" was a phrase of Elizabeth's aptly exploited by Edith. Some of the best writing is in the appendices: in particular, a short but brilliant account of the costly entertainments deemed necessary on the Queen's progresses, making graphically clear why one of her hosts en route, the Earl of Bedford, begged Lord Burleigh "to provide and help that her Majesty's tarrying" at Woburn "will not be above two nights and a daye."

In short, as a human and social document the book is a success. But the book is not in short; if the author had curtailed her scope to personalities, the evocation of atmosphere at which she excelled, and the key events, it would have been a finer thing. Political and military history did not inspire Edith. She was too old, and insufficiently interested, and too ill organized, to come to grips with that now. But the plums in the pudding, the greatness of her material, and her own name ensured commercial success. The book was reissued in paperback by Penguin four years after it was published, two years after Edith's death.

Fanfare for Elizabeth was reissued, and her last poems published, to coincide with *The Queens and the Hive*. The book of poems, which came out as *The Outcasts* in Britain and, later, as *Music and Ceremonies* in the United States, consisted of the work of her last, fertile phase, which had begun in 1958. Edith had a great deal of pleasant publicity. Cecil Beaton came to Hampstead to take new photographs for a greedy press. "I am very delighted with the photographs in the *Daily Express*," she wrote to him. "It is such a comfort *not* to appear as a cross between a turkey that has been insufficiently fattened up for Christmas and an escapee from Broadmoor."

The Queens and the Hive was dedicated to George Cukor—and it was Cukor who brought about a reconciliation between Edith and Noel Coward. Coward had enjoyed the book, but was afraid to write to Edith about it;

Cukor encouraged him to do so. She responded with a telegram ("Delighted stop friendship never too late...."), they exchanged letters, and finally he came to Greenhill, where she received her visitors from her wheelchair, in a hat and a short fur coat whatever the weather, and bedroom slippers. Coward, who had an eye infection, wore dark glasses. He apologized for his mockery of *Façade* all those years ago. He had been so young, he said; he had not understood. Then they gossiped, making up for forty lost years.

She still had the friendship of all the significant friends from the past—except Eliot's. She never did reconcile herself to his second marriage, and no longer saw him. In November 1960 she wrote about Wyndham Lewis in the *Observer* in an article headed "Hazards of Sitting for My Portrait," and Eliot wrote in Lewis's defence. This alienated her further from him. She had fallen out with Stephen Spender in 1958 for "allowing," as she put it to Father Caraman, "a young gentleman called Levine of whom I had never heard previously"[2] to write critically about her later poetry in *Encounter*; but she always wanted his good opinion, and in 1961 was arranging with his young son Matthew Spender to go and speak at Westminster School.

In October 1960 Edith had a very civil exchange of letters with—of all people—Geoffrey Grigson, about E. W. Tedlock's *Dylan Thomas: The Legend and the Poet*, which had reprinted an essay written by Edith for *The Critic* in 1947. In June 1961 she heard from Sylvia Beach, in whose bookshop in the rue de l'Odéon Edith had so signally failed to extol the genius of Gertrude Stein. Cataloguing the library of Shakespeare & Company, Miss Beach had come across a copy of Sacheverell's *The Hundred and One Harlequins*, inscribed by the author to Edith: "Perhaps you left it when you were so kind as to read for Les Amis de Shakespeare & Company."[3] Time softened the face of the past. She wrote on October 21, 1962, to Cecil Beaton, who remembered the clothes she had worn long ago—the striped dress that was worn with the black tricorne hat, and the bright blue embroidered dress: "Oh, how your letter sent me back to some of the only happy moments of my life! The blue dress you spoke of is now covering a cushion in the Paris flat of Helen Rootham's sister."

Dame Edith Sitwell's seventy-fifth birthday celebration—a concert at the Royal Festival Hall—was masterminded by her nephew Francis, Sacheverell's younger son. He and his elder brother, Reresby, had of course known Edith as children, when she had come to stay at Weston. When Francis was about three, he had been brought one morning into the Oak Room, where Edith slept and worked—a fearful wonder to a very small boy, his eminent aunt propped up in the great bed, its surface piled high with books and papers. Edith said she would like to buy him a present; what would he like? Francis shyly answered that he would like something that went "click." (He was interested in mechanical toys.) "The only thing I can think of that goes 'click,'" said Edith, peering benignly at the child over her spectacles, "is a pair of false teeth."

Francis had gone away to school and then to work for Shell in Kenya; and it was not until his return in 1960, when he was in his twenties, that he came to know Edith well. He visited her at Greenhill once or twice a week, and she came to rely on this cheerful, unhaunted nephew. Finally she appointed him her executor and her principal legatee: Reresby was to inherit Renishaw, and she thought of Francis as a "poor relation" like herself. Francis worked in public relations, and so was well equipped to organize the events of October 9, 1962.

Edith wrote to Noel Coward on September 26 that "the 9th should be a day for all present to remember. Never before, I think, has anyone attended their own Memorial Service."[4] And a week later she reported to John Gielgud that the press were "mad with excitement at the thought of my approaching demise. Kind Sister Farquhar . . . spends much of her time in throwing them downstairs."[5]

As her irony suggested, the occasion was an extraordinary one. The Festival Hall was packed to capacity. All her family were there, and her friends, from Carson McCullers (in appalling health and half-paralysed) and Graham Greene to Mr. Raper and Hannah Lewis. The great and famous were not dragooned into coming. After it was over, Edith had a letter of congratulation from E. M. Forster. Edith replied to him on October 18 that she had not let him know about the concert "because I would hate to bother you."[6] Forster was over eighty, and not strong; but he was to outlive Edith.

One of the best of the many accounts of the evening was by Charles Osborne in the *London Magazine* in December 1962:

A few minutes after eight the lights dimmed, a spot focused on one of the side doors, and into it glided a wheelchair and Dame Edith. She wore red velvet, chunky jewellery, a Plantagenet hat, and her Delphic quasi-smile. In a less vowel-caressing voice than she has used on other occasions she began to read a group of her poems.

Only Elizabeth Salter and Sister Farquhar knew the battle against physical weakness and nerves that had got her there:

To feel the full impact of the moment when she began to read, one would have had to see it against the background of the months that had preceded it; to recall the figure, white-faced and supine, sometimes in tears of fatigue because every movement was an effort, the fragile bone protruding from the flannel nightdress, and the transparent, delicate skin that had remained as vulnerable as it must have been in childhood.[7]

Edith, in a slow and slightly blurred voice, her spectacles pushing up the brim of her golden hat, read from her most recent work: "His Blood Colours My Cheek," "A Girl's Song in Winter," "Choric Song," and the "Prothalamium" she had written for the *Yorkshire Post* to celebrate the wedding of the Duke and Duchess of Kent the year before. (The new Duchess was from a Yorkshire family: Edith had been asked to the wedding, but had been too ill to go.) When she had finished reading, she retired to the Royal Box, where her brothers were waiting for her.

Then Peter Pears sang Benjamin Britten's setting of her "Still Falls the Rain," and finally, Sir William Walton conducted a performance of *Façade*—his music, Edith's poems, first heard in their then strange and now familiar lilting conjunction in the cold drawing room at Carlyle Square half a century before. The readers were Irene Worth and Sebastian Shaw. Charles Osborne wrote of Walton in the *London Magazine*: "One has had . . . occasion to admire him—but never to love him as one did when, at the conclusion of the Edith Sitwell birthday concert, he put down the baton after conducting the most elegant performance of his 1922 *Façade*." After Walton, and the readers, and the instrumentalists had been applauded, the three-thousand-strong audience wheeled round to the Royal Box and cheered Edith to the skies. She could not rise; she waved, and wept.

Acerbic to the last, she found afterwards plenty to criticise. Other than herself, the only readers of *Façade* that she had ever wholly approved of were Constant Lambert and Peter Pears. Sebastian Shaw had been "unspeakably awful," she told Cecil Beaton. And the whole thing, she wrote to Noel Coward, had been "all rather like something macabre out of Proust."[8] This was certainly true of the great supper party afterwards. Edith was exhausted. For once she had drink forced upon her, to get her through it. Bemused and silent, she sat between Sir Kenneth Clark and Sir William Walton, who made conversation over and across her as best they could. "The supper party was sheer terror for me, whatever it was for anybody else," she wrote to Cecil Beaton on October 21. In the days after, she was prostrated.

A few weeks later, on November 19, she was wheeled through the charade of television's *This Is Your Life*, conducted by Eamonn Andrews—"Mr. Andrews' Inquisition," she called it. The subject is meant to be taken by surprise and hustled into the studio to be astonished by his old friends in a "biography" of memories and tributes; given Edith's ill health and temperament, she was fore-warned. Only the news that Velma LeRoy, her black maid at Sunset Tower, was being specially flown over for the programme persuaded her to go through with it. "I could not dream of disappointing her."

Eamonn Andrews's researchers had rustled up a random and rather thin body of witnesses to Edith's life. Marjorie Proops, the popular columnist of the *Daily Mirror*, who had recently done a very successful interview with Edith, headed the list. Edith liked her very much on account of an article she had written about cruelty to animals; and the *Daily Mirror* had been the first paper ever to print one of her poems. Veronica Gilliat, old John Robins, Cecil Beaton, Tom Driberg, Geoffrey Gorer, her brothers and nephews, all appeared and "remembered" stories about Edith in front of the cameras. George Cukor was filmed speaking from Hollywood.

Velma LeRoy recalled on the programme how Edith had come to her thirty-first birthday party, with "a girl friend of mine, my sister, and two policemen." Dame Edith was, she said, "the world's most marvellous woman." It was Velma who, from first to last, justified the rather trivial undertaking for Edith.

Writing to Cecil Beaton thanking him for his contribution, "and for all the *great* friendship he had shown over the years," she asked him to explain to the Queen Mother, whom she was to meet at his house for lunch later in the month, that she could neither stand nor curtsey. On the day, she was driven down from Hampstead to Pelham Place by ambulance—she travelled every-where by ambulance now. Cecil Beaton described her advent in his diary:

> Truman Capote had arrived an hour early and together with Eileen [Hose] we watched from a top window as a huge ambulance drew up to the house, and a pair of stalwart men moved to bring the poet out into the daylight. A pair of very long medieval shoes appeared, then a muffled figure and finally a huge, golden melon of a hat. Edith was wheeled into place and given two strong martinis.[9]

She had finished the martinis before the arrival of the royal guest and enjoyed the party.

With the winter came anticlimax and depression. "Sometimes when I went into her room," wrote Elizabeth, "I felt that the Edith I knew was not there. Her speech would be muzzy, her eyes owlish."[10] When her vitality returned, it was consumed obsessively. Terrified and horrified by cruelty to animals, she wrote letters of protest and pain to individuals and newspapers that Elizabeth sometimes strategically forgot to post. She drank but she could not eat. Her drinking was never discussed—not between Edith and Elizabeth, nor between Edith and her brothers. A friend of Elizabeth's, Lorna Coates, suggested to Edith that she put milk in her brandy. Henceforth she lived, as far as she was allowed, on milk and brandy. Champagne and a morsel of smoked salmon were an acceptable alternative.

One of her more bona fide grievances was against Kenneth Allott, who had written in the introduction to his Penguin *Anthology of Contemporary Verse* that the "astonishing vogue" that Edith's later work had had at the end of the 1940s "is beginning to be forgotten now." Edith got Denys Kilham Roberts to write a letter of protest to Allen Lane of Penguin Books; the days of legal action—as in the not dissimilar *Reynolds News* case—were over. Edith was not represented in the anthology; but that was no one's fault. Allott had asked her for "Still Falls the Rain" and "Anne Boleyn's Song," but she had refused, on the grounds that the two poems did not represent her work fairly. Any omission of Edith Sitwell from contemporary anthologies was very often due to the fact that she rarely agreed to having fewer of her poems in a collection than any other poet represented.

A distraction was essential. In the spring of 1963 Edith, Elizabeth, and Sister Farquhar embarked on a cruise. They were to sail on the *Arcadia* via Colombo as far as Elizabeth's homeland, Australia, change ships, and come back via Miami. Georgia and Sacheverell accompanied them as far as Gibraltar. Edith took a trunkful of books and manuscripts, for she had been sporadically writing her memoirs for the past two years, finally persuaded by Hutchinson, the publishers, and by the need for money, to undertake what she had resisted for so long.

Edith, even when in good health and spirits, had never taken pleasure in travel. On board, her thirty-year-old fountain pen, a present from Osbert, gave up working—a bad omen. At Colombo, where she had hoped to buy a jewel, she was not up to going ashore; Elizabeth illicitly smuggled a selection onto the ship, and Edith chose another aquamarine. At Fremantle, she was mobbed by Australian pressmen. At Sydney, exhausted, she gave a press conference in her hotel, and then they boarded the *Willem Ruys* for the second leg of the voyage.

She did not like the ship, though she was cheered by the news from home that she had been made a Companion of Literature, of which there are never more than ten at one time. At Miami she hemorrhaged during the night. She was dangerously ill. When the ship reached Bermuda she was taken ashore and put in hospital. The diagnosis was uncertain but not reassuring. She was flown home.

Once the crisis was over, Edith seemed none the worse. Back at Greenhill, she was enlivened by discussions with the composer Malcolm Williamson—another Australian—who was using her *The English Eccentrics* as the basis of an opera commissioned by Britten for the Aldeburgh Festival. Robert Helpmann, who was to be the producer, came too; she responded to their vitality. Williamson, unfamiliar with British tribal customs, asked her why titled ladies were sometimes "Lady Mary Smith" and sometimes "Mary, Lady Smith." In the latter case, explained Edith, she is a dowager. "But Tennyson was always known as Alfred, Lord Tennyson," "Ah, but then he *was* a dowager." And her delighted laughter rang out, disturbing Shadow, the Siamese cat, who lay on her bed. Edith was always in bed now. There were four cats altogether at Greenhill: Shadow, and cream-coloured Leo, and two ex-strays, Orion and Belaker.

The day after Christmas, 1963, Elizabeth went again to Paris. Edith had heard that Evelyn Wiel was in hospital with a broken hip. Edith was worried about her condition, but she was also worried that she might be landed with hefty hospital bills. (She still sent Evelyn a monthly allowance, as she had since the war.) Elizabeth saw the old lady, senile now and near the end, and made practical arrangements with the hospital almoner.

Then she went to the now cold and unoccupied flat in the rue Saint-Dominique, for the last time. She was let in by a neighbour. In Edith's old room "a naked bulb threw a yellow light on the piles of dusty books, the bare boards, the crumbling furniture." On impulse, she pulled a heavy nineteenth-century bookcase away from the wall—and there behind it were a dozen more Tchelitchews, drawings and paintings, and a pastel portrait of Edith, spotted with mould: the most beautiful one of all, the delicate early-Renaissance profile with the blue veins at the temple.

Elizabeth looked further, and detected a papered-over recessed cupboard in the wall, which revealed when opened fifty-six of Edith's manuscript notebooks, containing everything she had written during her years in France.

Elizabeth telephoned London and brought the treasure trove home in the car. The manuscripts were sold; the portrait was in time to hang in a major Tchelitchew exhibition at the Museum of Modern Art in New York. When it was returned, it took pride of place in Edith's room, hung where she could best see it from her bed.

In the spring of 1964 Edith made her last move. The flat was proving both noisy and too small for her books and belongings, her four cats, and her numerous visitors. Elizabeth found a Queen Anne cottage to let in Keats' Grove, Hampstead. Edith went with Sister Farquhar to Bournemouth; Michael Stapleton took in the four cats; and by the time Edith's holiday was over the new home was ready, with her books and Tchelitchews in place. She called it Bryher House.

Father Caraman came regularly, and brought her Holy Communion once a month. If he was still her confessor, she was now sometimes his confidante; absorbed in conversation one day, he absently consumed a whole plateful of the cats' biscuits. Marianne Moore, who had herself been ill, came to see her: "They conversed, these women of great talent who were bound by genuine affection, but their conversation reached out and never quite made a connection. The little bird-like woman fluttered away, leaving a trail of disconnected sentences behind her, and Edith closed her eyes and returned to sleep."[11]

Osbert came to see her in early November 1964 before leaving for his customary winter at Montegufoni—without David Horner, this time. He was brought to Hampstead by Frank Magro, who had come as a servant and stayed to be the last nurse, companion, secretary, and friend of the now quite helpless Osbert. Osbert's speech, and his every function, were now hopelessly impaired. As they were leaving, Edith said to Magro, "Look after him for me."

The last irony was that it was Osbert, in the end, who abandoned David Horner. Mentally Osbert was perfectly clear and competent, though more easily influenced than in the past by strong-minded friends—in this case, Christabel Aberconway. Before he left for Montegufoni he had already given instructions to his solicitor to inform David by letter that he was to vacate the London flat they were sharing: The alliance was over. So David Horner, still suffering badly from the results of his fall, was now in the position of all those abandoned friends and lovers to whom, over the years, Edith had given her tigerish support and sympathy. She might not have seen it that way—even if Osbert had let her know of his decision. Events that would seem momentous and greatly to be desired have a way of coming too late, when it no longer matters. Edith was too tired now to take much interest in the final crumbling of the rusty triangle of Osbert, David, and herself.

Her last major outing, with stretcher and ambulance, was to the opening of the opera *The English Eccentrics* in London. But with her physical and emotional frontiers closing in, she found it hard now to leave her room. Elizabeth's role too was narrowed, as Edith's reliance on the comforting nursery skills of Sister Farquhar deepened.

Music and Ceremonies, her final book of poems, came out in America and was highly praised. A last rumble of the guns came from Julian Symons in the *London Magazine* of November 1964. He took Edith Sitwell as the subject of an article in the series "Reputations." Headed, in the manner of Gertrude Stein, "Edith Sitwell have and had and heard," the piece was uncompromising: "It is my object to question the legend . . . ." It was cruelly timed; Edith Sitwell was dying.

For the first time in her life Edith enjoyed being read aloud to: Elizabeth enlisted the help of an actor friend, John Downing. Not only did he read in a way that pleased her, he could make the fine theatrical gestures that filled her, briefly, with life. Returning from the country, he arrived at Bryher House with his arms full of marigolds and scattered the orange flowers all over her grass-green velvet coverlet: "flowers of the sun, those marigolds!" as Edith had written in "The Song of the Beggar-Maid to King Cophetua." She threw up her ringed hands in pleasure, and laughed.

At the beginning of December she was visited by her *Face to Face* interviewer, John Freeman, and his wife. She received them in a peacock-green satin bed jacket; Shadow, the Siamese, stalked over her bed. The newly regained Tchelitchew hung on the opposite wall, and the Freemans, who had seen the exhibition in New York, told her it had been the best thing there. She was in good form: The priest, she said, had been in, hoping to hear her last confession, but "I routed him."

Her autobiography, *Taken Care Of*, was already with the publisher. Graham Nicol of Hutchinson had called once a week to encourage her in the writing of it. It was organization, rather than composition, that was the problem. Finally Elizabeth, with scissors and paste, completed the job. *Taken*

Care Of is a very partial record and, although she put in most of her favourite jokes, it is a bitter one, written as it was in her twilight. When the book was finished, Edith had said to Elizabeth: "It's all over now bar the shouting and the worms," and then wrote out the last paragraph. The book ends:

> But all is more silent now, a shrunken world of no horizons. Yet sometimes I see a giant lion-paw on my window sill, and my three Visitors still come—Her with the one tooth. . . . Her with the one eye, looking into the bleak future. . . . Her with the one ear, still waiting for some message from the Beyond.
>
> These, the three Norns, still visit me. But soon, they will cease to do so.
>
> Then all will be over, bar the shouting and the worms.

Edith Sitwell collapsed during the night of December 8, 1964, and was taken to St. Thomas's Hospital. The family were called. She died, shortly after midday, on December 9.

Twenty years before, she had written to John Lehmann, remembering Helen's death:

> Such humiliating things happen to one's poor body when one is dying,— and one looks so beautiful afterwards,—so beautiful and noble.—Of course one wants the people one cares for to see one—not humiliated, but beautiful and noble, which is what one really is.

ENVOI

There was a funeral Mass at Farm Street Church in London. The burial was in the graveyard at Weedon Lois, near Weston—not in the old churchyard, but in the extension on the other side of the road, an enclosed piece of meadow cut out of farming country. The service was conducted by Father Valentine Elwes and the Anglican vicar of the parish. John Lehmann read the lesson.

The graveyard is sparsely occupied. Edith's tall headstone, centrally placed at the farthest end, stands out against the fields. Sachie and Georgia chose from Henry Moore's studio and had inset in the stone a bronze plaque of a woman's hand and a child's, the child's hand encircling the woman's thumb. Beneath are carved the last lines of Edith's poem "The Wind of Early Spring":

The past and present are as one —
Accordant and discordant, youth and age,
And death and birth. For out of one comes all —
From all comes one.

Notes and References

The vast majority of Sitwell papers—including most of Edith Sitwell's huge correspondence, manuscripts, drafts, personal papers, and working notebooks—are in the Humanities Research Center at the University of Texas in Austin. *Where no source reference for quotations in the text is given in the following notes, the quoted material comes from this generous source.*

All Edith Sitwell's letters to Choura Tchelitchew that are quoted in the text are in the Library of the University of Sussex. All her letters to William Plomer that are quoted in the text are in the Library of the University of Durham. No further references will be given to these two sources.

Bibliographical information is chiefly drawn from Richard Fifoot, *A Bibliography of Edith, Osbert and Sacheverell Sitwell*, 2nd ed. rev. (1971), published by Rupert Hart-Davis in the Soho Bibliographies series, to which I am greatly indebted.

Chapter 1   Little E

Except where indicated, the quotations from Edith Sitwell—other than letters—in this chapter are from her autobiography, *Taken Care Of* (1965).

1 Osbert Sitwell, *Left Hand, Right Hand!* (1945).

2 Ibid.; likewise all further extracts from Florence's diary.

3 Ibid.

4 Sacheverell Sitwell, *Sacred and Profane Love* (1940).

5 O.S., *Left Hand, Right Hand!*

6 Ibid.

7 E.S., "Readers and Writers," *The New Age*, July 1922.

8 O.S., *The Scarlet Tree* (1946).

9 E.S., "Readers and Writers," *The New Age*, August 1922.

10 Ibid.

11 Susan Hill, "A Mutual Scarborough," in *Sacheverell Sitwell: A Symposium*, ed. Derek Parker (1975).

12 S.S., *All Summer in a Day* (1926).

13 O.S., *Left Hand, Right Hand!*

14 S.S., *Splendours and Miseries* (1943).

15 O.S., *The Scarlet Tree.*

16 O.S., *Left Hand, Right Hand!*

17 Ibid.

18 Ibid.

Chapter 2   Splendours and Miseries

Except where indicated, the quotations from E.S.—other than letters—in this chapter are from *Taken Care Of*.

1 E.S., *Selected Letters*, ed. John Lehmann and Derek Parker (1970).
2 O.S., *The Scarlet Tree*.
3 Elizabeth Salter, *The Last Years of a Rebel* (1967).
4 S.S., "Serenade to a Sister."
5 S.S., *All Summer in a Day*.
6 S.S., "Serenade to a Sister."
7 O.S., *Left Hand, Right Hand!*
8 O.S., *The Scarlet Tree*.
9 Ibid.
10 Elizabeth Salter, *The Last Years of a Rebel*.
11 S.S., *Sacred and Profane Love*.
12 O.S., *The Scarlet Tree*.
13 Constance Sitwell, *Bright Morning* (1942).
14 Ibid.
15 E.S., *Selected Letters*.
16 O.S., *Noble Essences* (1950).
17 S.S., *All Summer in a Day*.
18 E.S., Yorkshire *Evening Post*, 1936.
19 O.S., *The Scarlet Tree*.

Chapter 3   To Bayswater, 1914–1918

Except where indicated, the quotations from E.S.—other than letters—in this chapter are from *Taken Care Of*.

1 O.S., *Great Morning* (1948).
2 John Pearson, *Façades* (1978).
3 O.S., *Great Morning*.
4 Peter Quennell, *The Marble Foot* (1976).
5 Donald Davie, "Frost, Eliot, Thomas, Pound," *The New York Times Book Review*, February 19, 1978.
6 T. S. Eliot, introduction to *Literary Essays of Ezra Pound* (1954).
7 Chief sources for the Georgian poets are Robert H. Ross, *The Georgian Revolt* (1965) and Timothy Rogers, *Georgian Poetry 1911–1922: The Critical Heritage* (1977).
8 O.S., *Noble Essences*.
9 *The Life and Letters of Edmund Gosse*, ed. Evan Charteris (1931).
10 Constance Sitwell, *Bounteous Days* (1976).
11 O.S., *Noble Essences*.
12 Peter Quennell, *The Marble Foot*.
13 O.S., *Queen Mary and Others* (1974).
14 Anne Olivier Bell, ed., *The Diary of Virginia Woolf*, vol. 1 (1977).
15 E.S., article in *Sunday Referee*, January 3, 1936.

Chapter 4   Wheels Within Wheels, 1916–1922

E.S.'s letters to Brian Howard, and Howard's account of his contacts with E.S., are from M. J. Lancaster, *Brian Howard: Portrait of a Failure* (1968).

1 O.S., *Great Morning*.
2 Grover Smith, ed., *The Letters of Aldous Huxley* (1969).
3 Nina Hamnett, *Laughing Torso* (1932).
4 Robert Graves, *Goodbye to All That* (1929).

5 John Press, *A Map of Modern English Verse* (1971).

6 O.S., *Laughter in the Next Room* (1949).

7 Robert Gathorne Hardy, *Ottoline at Garsington* (1974).

8 E.S., *Taken Care Of.*

9 *The Letters of Aldous Huxley.*

10 Robert Gathorne Hardy, *Ottoline at Garsington.*

11 Diana Holman Hunt, *Latin Among Lions* (1974).

12 E.S., *Selected Letters.*

13 Olive (Valentine) Glendinning to V.G.

14 December 8, 1920. Arnold Bennett, *Journals*, vol. 1, ed. Newman Flower (1932).

15 Michael Holroyd, *Lytton Strachey* (1968).

16 O.S., *Noble Essences.*

17 *Arnold Bennett's Letters to His Nephew* (1936).

Chapter 5   Façade, 1921–1923

Except where indicated, the quotations from Osbert Sitwell in this chapter are from his *Laughter in the Next Room.*

1 John Pearson, *Façades.*

2 Elizabeth Salter, *The Last Years of a Rebel.*

3 Charles Osborne in *London Magazine*, December 1962.

4 "The Octogenarian" was privately printed.

5 M. J. Lancaster, ed., *Brian Howard: Portrait of a Failure.*

6 Ibid.

7 Harold Acton, *Memoirs of an Aesthete* (1948).

8 Ibid.

9 Peter Quennell, *The Sign of the Fish* (1960).

10 O.S., *Tales My Father Taught Me* (1962).

11 O.S., *Great Morning.*

12 Nigel Nicolson, ed., *The Letters of Virginia Woolf*, vol. 2 (1976).

13 E.S., *Taken Care Of.*

14 John Pearson, *Façades.*

15 *The Letters of Virginia Woolf*, vol. 2.

16 Harold Acton, *Memoirs of an Aesthete.*

17 John Richardson, review of John Pearson's *Façades*, *The New York Review of Books*, April 19, 1979.

18 Noel Coward, *Collected Sketches and Lyrics* (1931).

19 Cole Leslie, *Noel Coward* (1976).

20 C. R. W. Nevinson, *Paint and Prejudice* (1937).

21 E.S., *Taken Care Of.*

22 Constance Sitwell, *Bounteous Days.*

23 Elizabeth Salter, *The Last Years of a Rebel.*

24 To Veronica Gilliat, December 1932, *Selected Letters.*

25 March 27, 1924. Arnold Bennett, *Journals*, vol. 2, ed. Newman Flower (1933).

Chapter 6   Entr'acte: Early Poetry—"Through the dark and hairy wood"

1 Kenneth Clark, "On the Development of Miss Sitwell's Latest Style," *Horizon*, July 1947.

2 L. P. Hartley, "Trends in the Poetry of Edith Sitwell," in *A Celebration for Edith Sitwell*, ed. José Garcia Villa (1948).

3 E.S., "Some Notes on My Own Poetry."
4 Ibid.
5 Ibid.
6 Julian Symons, "Miss Edith Sitwell Have and Had and Heard," *London Magazine*, November 1964.
7 Harold Acton, *Memoirs of an Aesthete*.
8 Kenneth Clark, "On the development of Miss Sitwell's Latest Style."

9 E.S., "Some Notes on My Own Poetry."
10 Jack Lindsay, introduction to E.S., *Façade and Other Poems, 1920–35* (1950).
11 E.S., *Selected Letters*.
12 William Hazlitt, "Character of Cobbett," in *Table Talk* (1821).
13 William Shakespeare, *Measure for Measure*, act 3, sc. 1.

Chapter 7   A Unicorn Among Lions, 1924–1926

1 John Pearson, *Façades*.
2 *A Romantic Friendship: The Letters of Cyril Connolly to Noel Blakiston* (1975).
3 *The Letters of Virginia Woolf*, vol. 3 (1977).
4 University of Iowa Library.
5 Allanah Harper, unpublished memoir.
6 Ibid.
7 *The Diary of Virginia Woolf*, vol. 3 (1980).
8 E.S., *Selected Letters*.
9 Allanah Harper, unpublished memoir.
10 Cecil Beaton, *The Wandering Years* (1961).
11 Ibid.
12 Private collection, the late Sir Cecil Beaton.
13 Elizabeth Salter, *The Last Years*

of a Rebel.
14 Tom Driberg, "Edith Sitwell at Home: A Partial Recall," *Encounter*, May 1966.
15 *The Letters of Virginia Woolf*, vol. 3.
16 Ibid.
17 Berg Collection, New York Public Library.
18 *The Letters of Virginia Woolf*, vol. 3.
19 Westfield College, University of London.
20 Reprinted in Rebecca West, "Two Kinds of Memory," in *The Strange Necessity* (1928).
21 Ibid.
22 E.S., in Sotheby & Co.'s catalogue of sale of her collection of works by Tchelitchew, held on December 31, 1961.

Chapter 8   Gertrude Stein and the Boyar, 1926–1927

1 University of Iowa Library.
2 Alice B. Toklas, *What Is Remembered* (1963).
3 James R. Mellow, *Charmed Circle: Gertrude Stein & Company* (1974).
4 January 16, 1929. E.S., *Selected Letters*.

5 Tom Driberg, "Edith Sitwell at Home: A Partial Recall."
6 *The Letters of Virginia Woolf*, vol. 3.
7 *The Diary of Virginia Woolf*, vol. 3.
8 Harold Acton, *Memoirs of an Aesthete*.
9 Ibid.

10 For information about Tchelitchew's background, I am indebted to Parker Tyler, *The Divine Comedy of Pavel Tchelitchew* (1967).

11 Parker Tyler, op. cit.

12 A. J. P. Taylor, *Beaverbrook* (1972).

13 *The Letters of Virginia Woolf*, vol. 3.

14 E.S., *Selected Letters*.

Chapter 9   Hunnish Practices and Gold Coast Customs, 1927–1929

1 Harry T. Moore, ed., *The Collected Letters of D. H. Lawrence* (1962).

2 For a fuller account of Osbert and *Lady Chatterley's Lover*, see John Pearson, *Façades*.

3 E.S., *Taken Care Of*.

4 Tom Driberg, *Ruling Passions* (1977).

5 O.S., *Laughter in the Next Room*.

6 Tom Driberg, "Edith Sitwell at Home: A Partial Recall."

7 Quoted in Elizabeth Salter, *The Last Years of a Rebel*.

8 York University, Ontario.

9 King's College Library, Cambridge.

10 University of Iowa Library.

11 July 11, 1955. E.S., *Selected Letters*.

Chapter 10   Preoccupations in Prose, 1929–1930

1 All quotations from Allen Tanner are from his letters to E.S., now at York University, Ontario, unless otherwise indicated.

2 Berg Collection, NYPL.

3 Ibid.

4 Elizabeth Salter, *The Last Years of a Rebel*.

5 Berg Collection, NYPL.

6 December 29, 1954. Mark Amory, ed., *The Letters of Evelyn Waugh* (1980).

7 May 24, 1930. Michael Davie, ed., *The Diaries of Evelyn Waugh* (1976).

8 *The Diary of Virginia Woolf*, vol. 3.

9 Berg Collection, NYPL.

10 August 23, 1930. *The Diaries of Evelyn Waugh*.

11 Anthony Powell, Messengers of Day (1978).

12 O.S., *Laughter in the Next Room*.

Chapter 11   French Leave, 1930–1932

1 Quoted in Elizabeth Salter, *The Last Years of a Rebel*.

2 Berg Collection, NYPL.

3 Ibid.

4 An eyewitness account of this debacle is given by Natalie Clifford Barney in *Adam* (1962), an issue subtitled "The Amazon of Letters" and devoted entirely to her.

5 Parker Tyler, *The Divine Comedy of Pavel Tchelitchew*.

6 Quoted in Elizabeth Salter, *The Last Years of a Rebel*.

7 Stella Bowen, *Drawn from Life* (1940).

8 Ibid.

9 Ibid.

10 Private collection, the late Lady Sitwell.

11 Ibid.

12 Cornell University Library.

Chapter 12   Entr'acte: Maiden Voyage

1 Constance Sitwell, *Bounteous Days.*
2 Parker Tyler, *The Divine Comedy of Pavel Tchelitchew.*
3 Ibid.
4 Berg Collection, NYPL.
5 Allanah Harper, unpublished memoir.
6 Privately printed.
7 Elizabeth Salter, *The Last Years of a Rebel.*
8 All quotations from E.S. to John Collier are from the correspondence in the University of Iowa Library.
9 University of Iowa Library.
10 Berg Collection, NYPL.
11 O.S., *Noble Essences.*
12 University of Iowa Library.
13 E.S., *Selected Letters.*
14 John Pearson, *Façades.*
15 Elizabeth Salter, *The Last Years of a Rebel.*

Chapter 13   Good-bye to Bayswater, 1932

1 E.S., *Taken Care Of.*
2 Both letters are from the private collection of Lady Sitwell.
3 Elizabeth Salter, *The Last Years of a Rebel.*
4 Parker Tyler, *The Divine Comedy of Pavel Tchelitchew.*
5 *The Letters of Virginia Woolf,* vol. 5 (1979).
6 Private collection, Diana Sparkes.
7 Ibid.
8 Harold Acton, *Memoirs of an Aesthete.*
9 E.S., *Taken Care Of.*
10 Cecil Beaton, *The Wandering Years.*
11 Private collection, Lady Sitwell.

Chapter 14   Rats in the Woodwork, 1932–1934

1 John Pearson, *Façades.*
2 E.S., *Selected Letters.*
3 For the account of Tchelitchew's friendship with Ford, I am chiefly indebted to Parker Tyler, *The Divine Comedy of Pavel Tchelitchew.*
4 Private collection, Lady Sitwell.
5 E.S., *Collected Letters.*
6 E.S., *Taken Care Of.*
7 Quoted in John Lehmann, *A Nest of Tigers* (1968).

Chapter 15   Brickbats and a Best Seller, 1934–1936

1 Private collection, Lady Sitwell.
2 E.S., *Selected Letters.*
3 Ibid.
4 Ibid.
5 Geoffrey Grigson in *New Verse,* December 1934.
6 *The Letters of Virginia Woolf,* vol. 5.
7 John Lucas, ed., *The 1930s: A Challenge to Orthodoxy* (1978).
8 Hubert Nicholson, "Glimpses of Edith Sitwell," unpublished memoir.
9 Berg Collection, NYPL.

Chapter 16   A Youthful Silenus, 1936–1937

---

1 Constantine FitzGibbon, ed., *Selected Letters of Dylan Thomas* (1967).
2 Constantine FitzGibbon, *The Life of Dylan Thomas* (1965).
3 E.S., *Taken Care Of.*
4 *Selected Letters of Dylan Thomas.*
5 E.S., *Taken Care Of.*
6 *The Life of Dylan Thomas.*
7 Jack Lindsay, *Meetings with Poets* (1968).
8 Private collection, Lady Sitwell.
9 Kenneth Clark, "On the Development of Miss Sitwell's Latest Style," *Horizon*, July 1947.
10 *Selected Letters of Dylan Thomas.*
11 Ibid.
12 Private collection, Lady Sitwell.
13 Ibid.
14 E.S., *Selected Letters.*
15 Harold Acton, *More Memoirs of an Aesthete* (1970).

Chapter 17   Under a Black Sun, 1937–1939

---

1 E.S., *Selected Letters.*
2 King's College Library, Cambridge.
3 February 26, 1939. E.S., *Selected Letters.*
4 For extracts from Victor Gollancz's correspondence with E.S. and for details of her arrangements with Victor Gollancz Ltd., I am indebted to Livia Gollancz and Victor Gollancz Ltd.
5 Private collection, Sir Sacheverell Sitwell.
6 Constantine FitzGibbon, ed., *Selected Letters of Dylan Thomas.*
7 E.S. to John Lehmann, March 29, 1944. *Selected Letters.*
8 Parker Tyler, *The Divine Comedy of Pavel Tchelitchew.*
9 E.S., *Selected Letters.*
10 Ibid.
11 To David Higham, March 8, 1939. E.S., *Selected Letters.*

Chapter 18   War, 1940–1943

---

1 Private collection, Anthony Powell.
2 Private collection, Lady Sitwell.
3 Private collection, Lady Violet Powell.
4 Mugar Memorial Library, Boston University.
5 Mark Amory, ed., *The Letters of Evelyn Waugh.*
6 Private collection, Lady Sitwell.
7 University of Iowa Library.
8 Ibid.
9 Private collection, Lady Violet Powell.
10 Anthony Powell, *Messengers of Day.*
11 J. C. Squire, *Weepings and Wailings* (1935).
12 To Demetrios Capetanakis, July 1, 1943.
13 Private collection, Anthony Powell.
14 Mugar Memorial Library, Boston University.
15 E.S., *Selected Letters.*
16 Parker Tyler, *The Divine Comedy of Pavel Tchelitchew.*
17 Ibid.
18 Mugar Memorial Library, Boston University.
19 E.S., *Selected Letters.*
20 Alice B. Toklas, *What Is Remembered.*
21 Bryher, *The Days of Mars* (1972).
22 Ibid.

23 To Ann Pearn, September 21, 1941. E.S., *Selected Letters*.
24 Ibid.
25 Ibid.
26 Ibid.
27 University of Iowa Library.
28 April 2, 1941. E.S., *Selected Letters*.
29 Ibid.
30 Stephen Spender, *World Within World* (1951).
31 John Lehmann, *A Nest of Tigers*.
32 Bryher, *The Days of Mars*.
33 Ibid.

Chapter 19   Life and Death, 1943–1944

1 Berg Collection, NYPL.
2 Ibid.
3 Ibid.
4 Mugar Memorial Library, Boston University.
5 Ibid.
6 Private collection, Laurence Whistler.
7 Berg Collection, NYPL.
8 Ibid.
9 E.S., *Selected Letters*.
10 *The Letters of Virginia Woolf*, vol. 5.
11 John Lehmann, *I Am My Brother* (1960).
12 E.S., *Selected Letters*.
13 Denton Welch, *Journals* (1952).
14 Ibid. April 20, 1943.
15 Bryher, *The Days of Mars*.
16 University of Iowa Library.

Chapter 20   The Terrible Rain, 1944–1946

1 Bryher, *The Days of Mars*.
2 Donald Sutherland, unpublished memoir.
3 John Lehmann, *I Am My Brother*.
4 Donald Sutherland, unpublished memoir.
5 Mugar Memorial Library, Boston University.
6 Ibid.
7 John Lehmann, *A Nest of Tigers*.
8 Berg Collection, NYPL.
9 Private collection, Lady Sitwell.
10 Berg Collection, NYPL.
11 John Pearson, *Façades*.
12 Mugar Memorial Library, Boston University.
13 Hubert Nicholson, "Glimpses of Edith Sitwell," unpublished memoir.
14 E.S., *Taken Care Of*.
15 Frederick Prokosch, "Edith Sitwell," in *A Celebration for Edith Sitwell*, ed. José Garcia Villa.
16 January 24, 1944. E.S., *Selected Letters*.
17 E.S., "Some Notes on My Own Poetry."
18 Berg Collection, NYPL.
19 Julian Symons, "Miss Edith Sitwell Have and Had and Heard," *London Magazine*, November 1964.
20 John Russell, "Some Notes on Edith Sitwell," in *A Celebration for Edith Sitwell*.
21 Sean Day Lewis, *C. Day Lewis: Anatomy of a Poet* (1979).
22 Berg Collection, NYPL.
23 University of Iowa Library.
24 Anthony Powell, *Messengers of Day*.

Chapter 21   *Postwar Fanfare, 1946–1947*

1 University of Iowa Library.
2 King's College Library, Cambridge.
3 Elizabeth Salter, *The Last Years of a Rebel.*
4 Berg Collection, NYPL.
5 University of Iowa Library.
6 Ibid.
7 E.S., "Some Notes on My Own Poetry," expanded version, in *Collected Poems* (1957).
8 Ibid.

Chapter 22   *Left Turn, 1948*

1 Jack Lindsay, *Meetings with Poets.*
2 Jack Lindsay, "The Latest Poems of Edith Sitwell," in *A Celebration for Edith Sitwell,* ed. José Garcia Villa.
3 Jack Lindsay, *Meetings with Poets.*
4 King's College Library, Cambridge.
5 E.S., *Selected Letters.*
6 Mugar Memorial Library, Boston University.
7 E.S., *Selected Letters.*
8 Parker Tyler, *The Divine Comedy of Pavel Tchelitchew.*
9 *The Times Literary Supplement,* November 20, 1948.
10 Elizabeth Salter, *The Last Years of a Rebel.*
11 Mugar Memorial Library, Boston University.
12 Private collection, Lady Sitwell.
13 Berg Collection, NYPL.
14 Ibid.

Chapter 23   *Pyrrhic Victories, 1948–1949*

1 The account of the reunion is drawn chiefly from Parker Tyler, *The Divine Comedy of Pavel Tchelitchew.*
2 Letter quoted courtesy of Elizabeth Salter.
3 John Pearson, *Façades.*
4 E.S., *Taken Care Of.*
5 C. W. McCann to V.G.
6 Mark Amory, ed., *The Letters of Evelyn Waugh.*
7 To Felix Giovanelli, November 19, 1948. W. K. Rose, ed., *The Letters of Wyndham Lewis* (1963).
8 Harold Acton, *More Memoirs of an Aesthete.*
9 Parker Tyler, *The Divine Comedy of Pavel Tchelitchew.*
10 To Nancy Mitford, November 1948. *The Letters of Evelyn Waugh.*
11 Private collection, Lady Sitwell.
12 Ibid.
13 David Higham, *Literary Gent* (1978).

Chapter 24   *Rows and Reconciliations, 1949–1950*

1 King's College Library, Cambridge.
2 April 12, 1949. E.S., *Selected Letters.*
3 David Wright, "A Poet and His Dragons," *Sunday Telegraph Magazine,* May 6, 1979.
4 E.S., *Taken Care Of.*

5 Parker Tyler, *The Divine Comedy of Pavel Tchelitchew.*

6 Ibid.

7 Grover Smith, ed., *The Letters of Aldous Huxley.*

8 Jack Lindsay, *Meetings with Poets.*

Chapter 25   Entr'acte: Montages, 1950–1952

1 Mark Amory, ed., *The Letters of Evelyn Waugh.*

2 E.S., *Taken Care Of.*

3 Ibid.

4 To John Lehmann, January 17, 1951. E.S., *Selected Letters.*

5 E.S., *Selected Letters.*

6 Ibid.

7 Virginia Spencer Carr, *The Lonely Hunter* (1975).

8 Ibid.

9 Cicely Greig, *Ivy Compton-Burnett: A Memoir* (1972).

10 E.S., *Selected Letters.*

11 Mugar Memorial Library, Boston University.

Chapter 26   Deaths and Entrances, 1953–1954

1 Interview in the *Sunday Times*, September 8, 1957.

2 E.S., *Selected Letters.*

3 University of Iowa Library.

4 Berg Collection, NYPL.

5 E.S., "Hollywood," draft.

6 E.S., *Taken Care Of.*

7 Ibid.

8 To John Lehmann, February 5, 1954. E.S., *Selected Letters.*

9 Berg Collection, NYPL.

10 E.S., *Taken Care Of.*

11 University of Iowa Library.

12 The summary of Movement attitudes is drawn chiefly from Blake Morrison, *The Movement* (1980).

Chapter 27   God and Mammon, 1954–1955

All quotations from E.S. to Fr. Caraman, S.J., are taken from letters in Fr. Caraman's possession.

1 Harold Acton, *More Memoirs of an Aesthete.*

2 John Pearson, *Façades.*

3 King's College Library, Cambridge.

4 Jack Lindsay, *Meetings with Poets.*

5 E.S., *Selected Letters.*

6 July 14, 1955. Mark Amory, ed., *The Letters of Evelyn Waugh.*

7 Walt Whitman, "From Pent-up Aching Rivers," in *Children of Adam.*

8 *The Letters of Evelyn Waugh.*

9 Michael Davie, ed., *The Diaries of Evelyn Waugh.*

10 *The Letters of Evelyn Waugh.*

11 October 9, 1955. *The Diaries of Evelyn Waugh.*

12 University of Iowa Library.

Chapter 28   Declines and Falls, 1955–1957

All quotations from E.S. to Fr. Caraman are from letters in his possession.

1 E.S., *Selected Letters.*
2 To Fr. Caraman, April 14, 1956.
3 April 22, 1956. E.S., *Selected Letters.*
4 Berg Collection, NYPL.
5 E.S., *Selected Letters.*
6 Mugar Memorial Library, Boston University.
7 Elizabeth Salter, *The Last Years of a Rebel.*
8 Ibid.
9 *Sunday Times,* July 28, 1957.
10 September 27, 1957. E.S., *Selected Letters.*
11 *The Times Literary Supplement,* September 20, 1957.
12 *Sunday Times,* September 8, 1957.
13 To Alberto de Lacerda, May 2, 1957. E.S., *Selected Letters.*

Chapter 29   Night Falls, 1957–1961

1 October 31, 1942. Denton Welch, *Journals.*
2 May 31, 1958. E.S., *Selected Letters.*
3 For a fuller account, see Dom Moraes, *My Son's Father* (1968) and Elizabeth Salter, *The Last Years of a Rebel.*
4 To the committee of the Anglo-Austrian Music Society. University of Iowa Library.
5 November 1958. E.S., *Selected Letters.*
6 Ibid.
7 Elizabeth Salter, *The Last Years of a Rebel.*
8 Harold Acton, *More Memoirs of an Aesthete.*
9 Elizabeth Salter, *The Last Years of a Rebel.*
10 Ibid.
11 Berg Collection, NYPL.
12 May 26, 1959. *Selected Letters.*
13 Private collection, Fr. Caraman, S.J.
14 John Pearson, *Façades.*
15 Parker Tyler, *The Divine Comedy of Pavel Tchelitchew.*
16 Private collection, Fr. Caraman, S.J.
17 Quoted by courtesy of Elizabeth Salter.
18 Ibid.
19 Elizabeth Salter, *The Last Years of a Rebel.*
20 Quoted by courtesy of Elizabeth Salter.
21 Elizabeth Salter, *The Last Years of a Rebel.*
22 For a fuller account, see John Pearson, *Façades.*

Chapter 30   Taken Care Of, 1962–1964

The quotations from E.S. to Cecil Beaton are from the private collection of the late Sir Cecil Beaton.

1 E.S., *Collected Letters.*
2 Private collection, Fr. Caraman, S.J.
3 Quoted by courtesy of Elizabeth Salter.
4 E.S., *Selected Letters.*
5 Ibid.
6 King's College Library, Cambridge.
7 Elizabeth Salter, *The Last Years of a Rebel.*
8 October 13, 1962.
9 Cecil Beaton, *The Parting Years* (1978).
10 Elizabeth Salter, *The Last Years of a Rebel,* to which I am chiefly indebted for my account of E.S.'s last months.
11 Ibid.

Index

PICTURE CREDITS

Grateful acknowledgment is made to Sir Sacheverell Sitwell, Reresby Sitwell, and Francis Sitwell for their kind help and for family photographs.

following page 48

Renishaw Hall (BBC Hulton Picture Library); Design for "Wheels" by Severini (Francis Sitwell); Art class in Scarborough (Elizabeth Salter); Edith photographed by Cecil Beaton (Popperfoto); Portrait by Nevinson (Elizabeth Salter); In Carlyle Square by Cecil Beaton (Cecil Beaton photograph, courtesy of Sotheby's Belgravia); Studio portrait (BBC Hulton Picture Library); Group photograph by Cecil Beaton (Cecil Beaton photograph, courtesy of Sotheby's Belgravia); Lewis with portrait of T. S. Eliot (Keystone Press Agency); At Pembridge Mansions, 1928 (Popperfoto); With Tchelitchew and Tanner (Elizabeth Salter); Tchelitchew (Private Collection); At Pembridge Mansions, c. 1930 (Cecil Beaton photograph, courtesy of Sotheby's Belgravia); At Guermantes (Allen Tanner); The Sitwells at Renishaw (Cecil Beaton photograph, courtesy of Sotheby's Belgravia); With Sir Osbert, 1948 (Keystone Press Agency); Sacheverell Sitwell (BBC Hulton Picture Library); Gotham Book Mart (Courtesy of the Gotham Book Mart, New York); As Lady Macbeth (George Platt Lynes photograph); Dame Edith's left hand (Lancelot Law Whyte photograph); Sir Osbert at Renishaw (Hans Wild); Rehearsing for Memorial Concert (Daily Express); Portrait (Mark Gerson).

following page 80

Portrait by Sargent (Collection of the Sitwell Settled Estates); Portrait by Fry (Graves Art Gallery, Sheffield); "The Editor of Wheels" by Guevara (Tate Gallery, London); "Interrupted" portrait by Lewis (Tate Gallery, London); Portrait by Topolski (University of Texas); Portrait by Tchelitchew (Sir Sacheverell Sitwell); "Sibyl" portrait by Tchelitchew (Edward James Foundation).

393

A NOTE ON THE TYPE

↓

The text of this book was set in film in a typeface called Griffo,
a camera version of Bembo, the well-known monotype face. The original
cutting of Bembo was made by Francesco Griffo of Bologna only
a few years after Columbus discovered America. It was named for
Pietro Bembo, the celebrated Renaissance writer and humanist scholar
who was made a cardinal and served as secretary to Pope Leo X.
Sturdy, well balanced, and finely proportioned, Bembo is a face
of rare beauty. It is, at the same time, extremely legible
in all of its sizes.
Composition by Superior Printing, Champaign, Illinois.
Printing and binding by The Haddon Craftsmen, Inc., Scranton, Pennsylvania.
Color reproductions by The Eastern Press, New Haven, Connecticut.
Printing of black-and-white reproductions by The Murray
Printing Company, Westford, Massachusetts.
Design by Betty Anderson.